Evolutionary Economics and Social Complexity Science

Volume 22

The Japanese Association for Evolutionary Economics (JAFEE) always has adhered to its original aim of taking an explicit "integrated" approach. This path has been followed steadfastly since the Association's establishment in 1997 and, as well, since the inauguration of our international journal in 2004. We have deployed an agenda encompassing a contemporary array of subjects including but not limited to: foundations of institutional and evolutionary economics, criticism of mainstream views in the social sciences, knowledge and learning in socio-economic life, development and innovation of technologies, transformation of industrial organizations and economic systems, experimental studies in economics, agent-based modeling of socio-economic systems, evolution of the governance structure of firms and other organizations, comparison of dynamically changing institutions of the world, and policy proposals in the transformational process of economic life. In short, our starting point is an "integrative science" of evolutionary and institutional views. Furthermore, we always endeavor to stay abreast of newly established methods such as agent-based modeling, socio/econo-physics, and network analysis as part of our integrative links.

More fundamentally, "evolution" in social science is interpreted as an essential key word, i.e., an integrative and /or communicative link to understand and re-domain various preceding dichotomies in the sciences: ontological or epistemological, subjective or objective, homogeneous or heterogeneous, natural or artificial, selfish or altruistic, individualistic or collective, rational or irrational, axiomatic or psychological-based, causal nexus or cyclic networked, optimal or adaptive, micro- or macroscopic, deterministic or stochastic, historical or theoretical, mathematical or computational, experimental or empirical, agent-based or socio/econo-physical, institutional or evolutionary, regional or global, and so on. The conventional meanings adhering to various traditional dichotomies may be more or less obsolete, to be replaced with more current ones vis-á-vis contemporary academic trends. Thus we are strongly encouraged to integrate some of the conventional dichotomies.

These attempts are not limited to the field of economic sciences, including management sciences, but also include social science in general. In that way, understanding the social profiles of complex science may then be within our reach. In the meantime, contemporary society appears to be evolving into a newly emerging phase, chiefly characterized by an information and communication technology (ICT) mode of production and a service network system replacing the earlier established factory system with a new one that is suited to actual observations. In the face of these changes we are urgently compelled to explore a set of new properties for a new socio/economic system by implementing new ideas. We thus are keen to look for "integrated principles" common to the above-mentioned dichotomies throughout our serial compilation of publications. We are also encouraged to create a new, broader spectrum for establishing a specific method positively integrated in our own original way.

More information about this series at http://www.springer.com/series/11930

Hideaki Aoyama • Yuji Aruka • Hiroshi Yoshikawa
Editors

Complexity, Heterogeneity, and the Methods of Statistical Physics in Economics

Essays in Memory of Masanao Aoki

Springer

Editors
Hideaki Aoyama
Research Institute of Economy, Trade and Industry
Kyoto University
Kyoto, Japan

Yuji Aruka
Institute of Economic Research
Chuo University
Hachioji-shi, Japan

Hiroshi Yoshikawa
Faculty of Economics
Rissho University
Tokyo, Japan

ISSN 2198-4204 ISSN 2198-4212 (electronic)
Evolutionary Economics and Social Complexity Science
ISBN 978-981-15-4805-5 ISBN 978-981-15-4806-2 (eBook)
https://doi.org/10.1007/978-981-15-4806-2

This Springer imprint is published by the registered company Springer Nature Singapore Pte Ltd.
The registered company address is: 152 Beach Road, #21-01/04 Gateway East, Singapore 189721, Singapore

Foreword: Memories of Masanao Aoki

Masanao and I were colleagues at UCLA for many years. When he decided to branch out from Engineering into Economics, he came to me for suggestions on what to read. I remember that one of my suggestions was Samuelson's *Foundations* but Masanao found it trivial and not at all helpful. From that unpromising beginning, we gradually learned to cooperate more fruitfully. He became a valued colleague.

California's financial crisis in the early 1990s led the University of California to offer early retirement to full professors who met a set of criteria. Masanao and I were two of four in the UCLA economics department who met the criteria. Subsequently, Masanao took a position at the University of Tokyo and I took one at the University of Trento in Italy. In addition to my duties as professor of monetary economics, I began a summer school program in Adaptive Economic Dynamics. Masanao was an invited guest lecturer at our third summer school in July of 2002.

This may have been the last time I saw Masanao and Chieko together. My wife and I invited them to dinner at Castel Toblino, a small medieval castle on a protected lake. As we entered, the hostess told us in Italian that a young Japanese cook was the sous-chef and was learning Italian cooking in the restaurant. It was a balmy evening and we were given a table on a balcony overlooking the lake. At the end of the dinner the Japanese cook came to pay his respects. It was a memorable evening for all of us.

I was sorry to learn of the passing of Masanao but have many good memories of him.

Trento, Italy

Axel Leijonhufvud

Masanao Aoki
(5/14/1931–7/24/2018)

Preface

Professor Masanao Aoki made outstanding contributions to economics. Though his works widely range firstly from the dual and adaptive theory of control and the applications in dynamic programing, the control theory and parameters estimation of large-scaled and decentralized system, the applications of control theory and system theory, the development of a new algorithm for the time series model and its application, and finally to the most exciting stage to construct a new perspective for economic science in line with the Society for Economic Science for Heterogeneous Interacting Agents he co-founded in 2006, we would like to emphasize here that his contribution to macroeconomics based on statistical physics was truly pathbreaking. It provides a well-defined alternative to mainstream micro-founded macroeconomics based on representative economic agents. He was a pioneer. The new approach awaits further investigations.

As Klaus Mainzer, philosopher of science at TU Munich, who is also from the field of physics, suggested, Adolphe Quételet (1796–1874) and Francis Galton (1822–1911) were the most influential figures in promoting the enthusiasm in the law of large numbers and normal distributions as a universal rule in nature and society. Galton, a British medical doctor, was well known as the first person to measure intelligence, emphatically stated from the law of large numbers. It is trivial to see that our traditional way of thinking was much influenced by their opinions as the universal measure at many different spheres of social stages and judgments. At the end of the last century, however, the end of this kind of traditional thought began by the advent of econophysics and other related complexity studies. Due to the last 20 years' studies in these fields, we have witnessed the universality of these studies. To our opinion, this century must be characterized by the era of truly empirical science or data science. Among these new achievements, however, the works of Professor Masanao Aoki must be by far unique. He has greatly contributed to formulate systematically the theoretical foundations for new sciences through the intensive works at his final stage of life. In particular, he has smartly shown us to replace the old approach with the occupancy problem in physics.

In his contributions, we can always learn the usefulness of the classic occupancy problem in physics when we also apply it to social science. There are two kinds in this problem: the Maxwell-Boltzmann and the Bose-Einstein form. The latter is closely related to Professor Aoki, who is mainly interested in the case that agents are exchangeable and their types are not necessarily fixed. This formulation is quite natural for us if we want to deal with any social evolution and innovation, because innovation will almost bring us new unknown agents. There are many of economists who do not know that the theory of increasing return and path dependency by Brian Arthur was driven by the use of Polya urn theory. There are many more economists who do not know that Brian Arthur generalized Polya's original theorem to a finite n balls in cooperation with Ukrainian mathematicians. Much more interestingly, there are extremely fewer economists who do know that Polya's distribution will be potentially transformed to the Maxwell-Boltzmann distribution and the Bose-Einstein distribution.

On the other hand, as long as we are stationed at the two/alternative sector models, even the use of the generalized master equation or the state transition equation system based on new occupancy problem may not explicitly exert the usefulness of the new analytical methods. Until the advent of the systematic works by Professor Aoki, we did not know there could be a new innovative way to analyze the evolution of society. Unfortunately, even now most economists are not familiar with the occupancy problem formulation at all. Economists must find a new way by tracing the new analytical development along new distributions like Ewens distribution while starting from the negative binomial distribution.

All the contributors to this volume respect Professor Aoki's works and try to cultivate the new field in their own ways. We hope that more economists join the march and that they find the papers put together in this volume valuable.

Kyoto, Japan — Hideaki Aoyama
Hachioji-shi, Japan — Yuji Aruka
Tokyo, Japan — Hiroshi Yoshikawa

Contents

Part III Economic Agents and Interactions

Part I
Prof. Aoki's Contribution and Beyond

Chapter 1
Stock Prices and the Real Economy: The Different Meaning of Efficiency

Hiroshi Yoshikawa

Abstract This chapter explores the relationship between stock prices and the real economy. The standard neoclassical approach – so called consumption-based asset pricing model – attempts to explain it based on the assumption of the representative agent. It takes stock prices determined by the intertemporal consumption/saving decisions of the Ramsey consumer. The basic message is that financial market always contributes to efficient resource allocation. The ultimate version is the Arrow/Debreu model of complete capital market. We argue that this neoclassical view is wrong, and that there is in fact a fundamental difference in the meaning of efficiency in financial markets and the real economy. Our approach is based on seminal works of Masanao Aoki (New approaches to macroeconomic modeling: evolutionary stochastic dynamics, multiple equilibria, and externalities as field effects. Cambridge University Press, New York, 1996, Modeling aggregate behavior and fluctuations in economics. Cambridge University Press, Cambridge, 2002), and draws on Aoki and Yoshikawa (Reconstructing macroeconomics: a perspective from statistical physics and combinatorial stochastic processes. Cambridge University Press, Cambridge, 2007).

Keywords Bubbles · Stock price · Efficiency · Real economy

I would like to thank the participants of seminar at Hokkaido University for their helpful comments. Financial supports by Grant-in-Aid for Scientific Research (KAKENHI) 18H03635 and Post-K Exploratory Challenge Macroeconomic Simulations are gratefully acknowledged.

H. Yoshikawa (✉)
Rissho University, Tokyo, Japan

H. Aoyama et al. (eds.), *Complexity, Heterogeneity, and the Methods of Statistical Physics in Economics*, Evolutionary Economics and Social Complexity Science 22,
https://doi.org/10.1007/978-981-15-4806-2_1

1.1 Introduction

This chapter explores the relationship between stock prices and the real economy. The standard neoclassical approach – so called consumption-based asset pricing model – attempts to explain it based on the assumption of representative agent. It takes stock prices determined by the intertemporal consumption/saving decisions of the Ramsey consumer. More generally, asset prices are simultaneously determined by consumers' optimizing behavior. In this framework, financial market and the real economy are nothing but two sides of the same coin. Accordingly, *efficiency*, arguably one of the most important concepts in economics, is identically defined for both financial market and the real economy. The ultimate version is the Arrow/Debreu model of complete capital market.

We argue that this neoclassical view is wrong, and that there is in fact a fundamental difference in the meaning of efficiency in financial markets and the real economy. Our approach is based on seminal works of Masanao Aoki (1996, 2002), and draws on Aoki and Yoshikawa (2007).

1.2 The Neoclassical Theory

The stock prices depend necessarily on the real economy. Their "correct" prices or the fundamental values are the discounted present values of a stream of future dividends/profits. Since business activities, profits in particular, are significantly affected by the state of the real economy, the stock prices are also affected by the real economy. More generally, in the standard neoclassical theory, asset prices are simultaneously determined with all the supplies and demands in general equilibrium. Thus, just like production and consumption, the stock prices depend ultimately on preferences and technologies. The *complete market* model based on the Walrasian general equilibrium theory (Debreu 1959; Arrow 1963) is the symbol of this neoclassical approach. It is well recognized that the Arrow/Debreu complete market does not exist in reality, but it still sets a standard for our understanding of financial market in neoclassical theory. Diamond (1967) is a standard model of stock market in the absence of the Arrow/Debrew complete market. This standard theory translates itself to *efficient market theory* (Fama 1970) in finance. The basic message is that financial market always contributes to efficient resource allocation in the real economy.

Without any doubt, broadly speaking, financial market contributes efficient resource allocation in the real economy. The problem is "not always." In stark contrast to the neoclassical doctrine, economists and the world have long recognized that financial market sometimes falls into turmoil culminating in crisis and seriously disturbs the real economy. For example, Keynes (1936) warned as follows:

> Speculators may do no harm as bubbles on a steady stream of enterprise. But the position is serious when enterprise becomes the bubble on a whirl-pool of speculation. When the

capital development of a country becomes a by-product of the activities of a casino, the job is likely to be ill-done. The measure of success attained by Wall Street, regarded as an institution of which the proper social purpose is to direct new investment into the most profitable channels in terms of future yield, cannot be claimed as one of the outstanding triumphs of *laissez-faire* capitalism — which is not surprising, if I am right in thinking that the best brains of Wall Street have been in fact directed towards a different object. (Keynes 1936, p. 159)

Like Keynes, many believe that the "bubbles" are possible in the market. And whether or not they are "rational," extraordinary changes in the stock prices (either up or down) *by themselves* may do harm to the real economy. By any measure, they are not a mere mirror image of the real economy. In history, depressions were often accompanied by falls in the stock prices. As early as in the nineteenth century, economists were talking about "financial crises." More recently, Minsky (1986) highlighted the importance of the stock prices in the macroeconomy and advanced the "financial accelerator" thesis. It was revived in the 1990s and bore the vast literature. Today, central banks closely monitor asset prices in the conduct of monetary policy.

A crucial problem is whether the stock prices are always equal to their fundamental values. Shiller (1981) in his seminal work performed the ingenious "variance-bound tests" on this issue and drew the following conclusion:

We have seen that measures of stock price volatility over the past century appear to be far too high – five to thirteen times too high – to be attributed to new information about future real dividends if uncertainty about future dividends is measured by the sample standard deviations of real dividends around their long-run exponential growth path. (Shiller 1981, p. 433)

Naturally, Shiller's seminal work spawned the debate over alleged excess volatility of stock price. Rather than accepting that stock prices are too volatile to be consistent with the standard theory, a majority of economists have attempted to reconcile the alleged volatility with efficiency or "rationality" of market.

One way to explain volatility of stock prices is to allow significant changes in the discount rate or the required return on stocks which Shiller (1981) assumes is constant. In fact, in the neoclassical macroeconomic theory, the following relationship between the rate of change in consumption C and the return on capital r must hold in equilibrium:

$$-\left[\frac{u''(C)C}{u'(C)}\right]\left(\frac{\dot{C}}{C}\right)=\frac{1}{\eta(C)}\left(\frac{\dot{C}}{C}\right)=r-\delta. \tag{1.1}$$

Here, the elasticity of intertemporal substitution η is defined as

$$\frac{1}{\eta(C)}=-\frac{u''(C)C}{u'(C)}$$

In general, η depends on the level of consumption C. Equation (1.1) shows that the rate of change in consumption over time is determined by η and the difference between the rate of return on capital r and the consumer's subjective discount rate δ. This Euler equation is derived as the necessary condition of the representative consumer's maximization of the Ramsey utility sum. Thus, according to the neoclassical macroeconomics, the return on stocks must be consistent with the rate of change in consumption over time in such a way that Eq. (1.1) holds.

Now, the results of the tests of Shiller (1981) imply that the volatility of stock prices must come from the volatility of the discount rate or the return on capital r, rather than that of dividends as long as we take it that the neoclassical theory holds true. Since consumption C is not volatile, much *less* volatile than dividends or profits, it, in turn, suggests that given Eq. (1.1), the volatility of stock prices must be explained ultimately by sizable fluctuations of the elasticity of intertemporal substitution η which depends on consumption. Consequently, on the representative agent assumption, researchers focus on the "shape" of the utility function in accounting for the volatility of stock prices (Grossman and Shiller 1981). It is not an easy task, however, to reconcile the theory with the observed data if we make a simple assumption for the elasticity of intertemporal substitution η.

A slightly different assumption favored by theorists in this game is that the utility and, therefore, this elasticity η depend not on the current level of consumption C_t but on its deviation from the "habit" level $\hat{C}_t$, namely, $C_t - \hat{C}_t$. By assumption, the habit $\hat{C}_t$ changes much more slowly than consumption C_t itself so that at each moment in time, $\hat{C}_t$ is almost constant. The trick of this alternative assumption is that although C_t does not fall close to zero, $C_t - \hat{C}_t$ can do so as to make the elasticity of intertemporal substitution η, now redefined as

$$\frac{1}{\eta} = \frac{u''\left(C - \hat{C}\right)\left(C - \hat{C}\right)}{u'\left(C - \hat{C}\right)} > 0, \tag{1.2}$$

quite volatile. Campbell and Cochrane (1999) is a primary example of such an approach. Though ingenious, the assumption is not entirely persuasive. Why does the consumer's utility become minimal when the level of consumption is equal to the habit level even if it is extremely high? In any case, this is the kind of end point we are led to as long as we keep representative agent assumption in accounting for the volatility of stock prices.

Meanwhile, Mehra and Prescott (1985), using representative agent model, presented another problem for asset prices. They considered a simple stochastic Arrow-Debreu model. The model has two assets, one the equity share for which dividends are stochastic and the other the riskless security. Again, on the representative agent assumption, the "shape" of the utility function and the volatility of consumption play the central role for prices of or returns on two assets. For the reasonable values of η, which may be more appropriately called the relative risk aversion in this stochastic model, and the US historical standard deviation of consumption growth, Mehra and Prescott calculated the theoretical values of the returns on two assets. The risk premium, namely the difference between the return on the equity share and the return on the riskless security implied by their model, turns out to be mere 0.4%. On the other hand, the actual risk premium for the US stock (the Standard and Poor 500 Index, 1889–1978) against the short-term security such as the Treasure Bill is 6%. Thus, the standard model with the representative consumer cannot account for such high risk premium that is actually observed. Mehra and Prescott posed this result as a puzzle. Since then, a number of authors have attempted to explain this puzzle.

The "puzzles" we have seen are, of course, conditional on the assumption of the representative-agent. Indeed, Deaton (1992) laughs away the so-called "puzzles" as follows:

> There is something seriously amiss with the model, sufficiently so that it is quite unsafe to make any inference about intertemporal substitution from representative agent models.... The main puzzle is not why these representative agent models do not account for the evidence, but why anyone ever thought that they might, given the absurdity of the aggregation assumptions that they require. While not all of the data can necessarily be reconciled with the microeconomic theory, many of the puzzles evaporate once the representative agent is discarded. (Deaton 1992, p. 67, 70)

We second Deaton's criticism. The standard micro-founded macroeconomics is on the wrong track (Aoki 1996, 2002; Aoki and Yoshikawa 2007; Kirman 1992; Yoshikawa 2016).

Having said that, here, we note that the standard analyses all focus on the *variance* or the *second moment* of asset prices or returns (see Cecchetti et al. 2000, for example, and the literature cited therein). As we will see it shortly, a number of empirical studies actually demonstrate that the variance or standard deviation may *not* be a good measure of *risk*. We must consider probability distributions, not just moments. More fundamentally, we argue that financial markets, stock prices in particular, and the real economy are, in fact, different creatures.

1.3 Volatility of Stock Prices and Returns

We begin with power-law probability distribution. Although economists routinely adopt the normal (including the log-normal) or the Gaussian distribution, it is actually not so generic as they believe. Specifically, power-law plays the central role for understanding financial markets (see Mantegna and Stanley 2000).

Power-law distribution is defined as follows: stochastic variable x is said to obey a power-law distribution when it is characterized by a probability density function $p(x)$ with power-law tails

$$p(x) \propto x^{-(1+\alpha)} \quad (\alpha > 0)\,.$$

Economists, like scientists in other disciplines, have long believed that the normal distribution is the norm, the deviation from which serves only for curiosity of mathematicians. There are several justifications for this belief. The most important one is, of course, the central limit theorem. Random walk model is another (see any textbook on probability such as Feller (1971) for technical details). The central limit theorem allows *any* distribution for x_{is} whose sum is to be investigated as long as the second moment exists. Also, to the extent that random walk model is generic, the normal distribution is the norm. These facts suggest strongly that the normal distribution is very generic; we should expect the normal distribution everywhere in nature.

The central limit theorem appears impeccable. However, a crucial assumption of the theorem is that the probability distribution of x_i has the finite variance. What happens if the variance or the second moment does not exist?

The normal distribution actually belongs to a group of distribution called *stable distribution*. Stable distribution is a specific type of distribution encountered in the sum of *n i.i.d.* random variables with the property that it does not change its functional form for different values of *n*. It is known that the normal distribution is the only stable distribution having all its moments finite. Now, there exists a limit theorem stating that, under certain conditions, the probability density function of a sum of *n i.i.d.* random variables *xi* converges in probability to a stable distribution. Note that the central limit theorem is a special case of this more general limit theorem. When pdf of x_i has a finite variance, it becomes the usual central limit theorem. The limit distribution is the normal distribution. On the other hand, when the variance or the second moment does not exist (namely, it becomes infinite) for the underlying stochastic process, a sum of *n i.i.d.* random variables converges to a distribution with power-law tails which is also a member of the group of stable distribution.

The random walk is another which justifies the normal distribution. It has been regarded as a very generic model with wide applications. However, it is actually restrictive in the sense that the length of a jump of a "ball" is constant. More generally, we can consider a random walk with the following probability distribution of the lengths of a jump of a "ball":

$$\begin{array}{ll} \pm a & \text{with probability } C \\ \pm \lambda a & \text{with probability } C/M \\ \vdots & \qquad\qquad\qquad \vdots \\ \pm \lambda^j a & \text{with probability } C/M^j \\ \vdots & \qquad\qquad\qquad \vdots \\ (a > 0, C > 0, \lambda > 1, M > 1) & \end{array} \tag{1.3}$$

In this generalized random walk model, a ball can fly to any point on one-dimensional lattice with power-law probabilities: A small jump is more likely than a big jump. This is a one-dimensional example of *Lévy flight*. Now, this generalized random walk, or the Lévy flight is much "wilder" than the ordinary random walk model and can lead us to power-law distributions rather than to the normal distribution.[1] In summary, stable distribution is more general than the normal distribution. In this group of probability distribution, we have strong contenders to the normal distribution, namely power-law distributions.

In addition to the kind of limit distribution, we must also take into account the speed of convergence. The problem can be best illustrated by an example. Consider the *truncated* Lévy flight defined by the following distribution:

$$P(x) = \begin{matrix} 0 & \text{for} \quad x > m > 0 \\ cP_L(x) & \text{for} \; -m \leq x \leq m \\ 0 & \text{for} \quad x < -m \end{matrix} \tag{1.4}$$

where $P_L(x)$ is the symmetric Lévy flight explained above. Unlike the Lévy flight in which the length of a jump is unbounded, the truncated Lévy flight has a limit ($m > 0$) on the length of a jump. Since the truncated Lévy flight has a finite variance, the probability distribution of the sum of n random variables from this distribution $P(S_n)$ converges to the normal distribution. The question is how quickly $P(S_n)$ will converge. When n is small, the Lévy flight well approximates $P(S_n)$. Thus, there exists a crossover value of n, n_* such that

$$\begin{aligned} &\text{For } n \ll n^*,\ P(S_n) \sim \text{The Lévy Flight} \\ &\text{For } n \gg n^*,\ P(S_n) \sim \text{The Normal Distribution} \end{aligned}$$

This example illustrates the point that in general the kind of probability distribution we obtain depends on n. See section 8.4 of Mantegna and Stanley (2000) for further details.

In fact, more and more evidences have been gathered to the effect that natural phenomena are characterized by power-law distributions (see, for example, Sornette 2000 and Newman 2005). In economics, empirical size distributions of many variables of interest have been actually known for long to obey power-law distribution. For example, Pareto (1896) found that the distribution of income y was of the following form:

$$N(y > x) \sim x^{-(3/2)} \tag{1.5}$$

where $N(y > x)$ is the number of people having income x or greater than x.

The Pareto distribution is nothing but a particular form of power-law distribution. More recently, electronic trading in financial markets has enabled us to use a rich high-frequency data with the average time delay between two records being as short as a few seconds. By now, a number of empirical analyses based on such data have amply demonstrated that most financial variables such as changes in stock price or

[1]The reader can usefully refer to Figure 4.7 of Sornette (2000, p. 93) to appreciate the point that Lévy flight is much "wilder" than the ordinary random walk.

foreign exchange rates are, in fact, characterized by power-law distributions, *not* by the normal distribution.

What is the significance of these results? The significant difference between the normal and power-law distributions shows up in tails of distribution. Under power-laws, large deviations from the mean have much larger probability (dubbed *fat tails*) than under the normal distribution. Put it another way, given the normal distribution, some of the big earthquakes which actually occurred would not have reasonably occurred, whereas they are quite possible under power-laws. Likewise, under the normal distribution, drops in stock price such as the October 1987 Crash would have insignificant probability, whereas under power-laws, the probability becomes significant. Power-laws have, therefore, important implications for our understanding of financial markets.

Growing evidences dating back to Mandelbrot (1963) now amply demonstrate that changes in asset prices do not obey the normal distribution but power-laws. For our present purpose, it is enough to cite Gabaix et al. (2003) and Gabaix (2008) according to which the probability distribution of changes in stock prices r follows the following power-law with the exponent $\alpha = 3$:

$$P\left(|r| > x\right) \ \propto \ x^{-\alpha}, \quad \alpha = 3 \tag{1.6}$$

Here, r is defined as follows:

$$r_t = \log P_t - \log P_{t-\Delta t} \tag{1.7}$$

Probability density function, $f\ (r)$ corresponding to (1.6) is

$$f(r) \propto x^{-(\alpha+1)} = x^{-4}. \tag{1.8}$$

That is, in terms of density function $f\ (r)$, r obeys the power-law with the exponent $\alpha + 1 = 4$.

That exponent α about 3 is the standard result. The value of the exponent has far reaching implications. First of all, when the exponent of the power-law *density function* is 3, the variance or the second moment does not exist. In general, suppose a random variable X has a power-law *density* $f\ (x)$ in the range $1 \leq x \leq \infty$ with exponent $\mu + 1$. Then, the nth moment of X, M_n exists if and only if

$$\mu + 1 - n > 1 \quad \text{or} \quad \mu > n. \tag{1.9}$$

In other words, the nth moment of the random variable X does not exist for $\mu \leq n$.

Though it appears that the second moment or variance *does* exist for financial returns (see Chapter 9 of Mantegna and Stanley 2000), it is still a matter of dispute. If the variance does not exist, the standard theory of asset prices faces a serious problem because it rests on the basic assumption that the distribution of returns is normal (Gaussian), and that *risk* can be measured by the variance or standard deviation of the rate of return. See Mandelbrot and Hudson (2004) for very readable and forceful criticism of the standard theory of asset prices and finance.

The return on equity obeys the power-law distribution with exponent $\alpha = 3$. What about the rate of change in consumption? Changes in consumption and aggregate income or GDP are similar. Canning et al. (1998) shows that the distribution of the growth rates of GDP, g is exponential.

$$P(g) \sim \exp\left[-\gamma\,|g|\right] \tag{1.10}$$

Stanley et al. (2006) analyzing all US publicly traded manufacturing companies within the years 1975–91 (taken from the Compustat database) drew the conclusion that the distribution of the growth rates of companies is also exponential.

Asset prices and real variables obey different probability distributions. This fact implies that the standard Euler equation (Eq. 1.1) based on representative agent assumption for explaining asset prices is fundamentally flawed.

1.4 Real and Financial Sectors: A Lévy Flight Model

In this section, we explore the fundamental problem: that is, underlying mechanism which generates power-law distributions for returns of financial assets on one hand and exponential distributions for real economic variables such as real GDP or consumption on the other hand.

As we explained it in Sect. 1.3, the random walk leads us to the normal (or Gaussian) distribution. Unlike the standard random walk, *truncated Lévy flight* explained earlier, depending on parameters, can generate a wide class of probability distributions including power-laws and exponential distribution. In what follows, we will consider a particular model of truncated Lévy flight which nests both power-laws and exponential distributions (Aoki and Yoshikawa 2007, Ch. 10). The model we consider is an adapted or modified version of Huang and Solomon (2001).

1.4.1 The Real Economy

We first consider a model of the real economy. The economy consists of N agents or units. For the sake of expositional convenience, we call the variable of interest "consumption." It may be "production," and in that case, the aggregate variable is GDP. N sectors or units may be interpreted either as N types of consumers or as N types of consumption goods. Interpretation of the model can be very flexible.

The aggregate consumption at time t, $C(t)$ is nothing but the sum of the individual consumptions:

$$C(t) = c_1(t) + \cdots \ c_N(t), \tag{1.11}$$

Here, $c_i(t)$ is the ith consumer's consumption. The argument t stands for calendar or real time. We may interpret the period from t to $t + 1$ as one month, one quarter, or one year as the case maybe.

We are interested in the growth rate of the *aggregate* consumption $C(t)$ over $[t, t + 1]$, namely $r(t)$ defined as $(C(t + 1) - C(t)) / C(t)$. Our goal is to derive the probability distribution of r.

The growth of aggregate (or macro) consumption arises from the aggregation of growths of the N individual (or micro) consumptions. We take it that this *micro* growth occurs as a result of a (large) number of *elementary events*. The number of elementary events within a period (namely over $[t, t + 1]$) is τ. One elementary event is that a consumer, consumer i, say, being randomly chosen from the set $\{1, 2, \ldots, N\}$ between t and $t + 1$, changes his/her consumption. We use the term "consumer," but it can be any micro unit such as firm.

A consumer may be chosen either uniformly with probability $1/N$ or with some other probabilities possibly dependent on the size of the initial level of consumption. If consumer i is chosen, $c_i(t)$ grows by a random factor λ:

$$c_i'(t) = \lambda c_i(t) \tag{1.12}$$

Here, $c_i'(t)$ stands for c_i immediately after the elementary growth, *not* time derivative of $c_i(t)$. At this event, no other consumer ($j \neq i$) experiences growth.

For simpler exposition, we assume that

$$\lambda = 1 + g, \quad \text{for } \forall i, t \tag{1.13}$$

where

$$g = \pm\gamma \quad (0 < \gamma < 1). \tag{1.14}$$

Note that this is a particular type of multiplicative process for c_i. As we mention later, the probability distribution of λ does not matter at all.

It is important to keep in mind the difference between t and τ. One is the *calendar time* t and the other is τ, the number of *elementary (micro) events* within a given period of time. We denote the resultant growth rate of aggregate consumption as $r(t; \tau)$. That is, $r(t; \tau)$ is the growth rate of $C(t)$ between t and $t + 1$ when the number of elementary micro events during the period is τ. Although τ can be a random number, for simplicity, we use its expected value and denote it by τ.

Given τ, we can write the rate of growth of aggregate consumption as

$$r(t; \tau) = \frac{C(t+1) - C(t)}{C(t)} = \sum\nolimits_{i,k} g_{i,k} \quad (k = 1, \ldots \tau) \tag{1.15}$$

where

$$g_{i,k} = \frac{\left(c_{i,k+1} - c_{i,k}\right)}{C} = \frac{\pm\gamma c_i\,(t;k)}{C}. \tag{1.16}$$

Here, $g_{i,k}$ indicates the kth elementary growth that has occurred to $c_i(t)$. The total change that defines the growth rate of aggregate consumption $C(t)$ is the sum of these elementary growths that occurred to $c_1, \ldots, c_N$. The total number of the elementary events that have occurred is equal to τ.

In this model, the size of a jump of a micro unit is constant (Eq. 1.13). Thus, the *micro behavior* is described by the ordinary random walk. However, such micro growths occur τ times within a period. As a consequence, the growth of *aggregate* consumption $C(t)$ follows the *truncated Lévy flight* explained in Sect. 1.2 because τ is finite.

We make an important assumption that there is a lower bound constraint to the elementary micro growth process. That is, the level of consumption after an elementary (micro) growth must be above the minimum, $c_{\min}(t)$ defined by

$$c_{\min}(t) = qc_{av}(t), \quad (0 < q < 1) \tag{1.17}$$

where

$$c_{av}(t) = \frac{C(t)}{N} \tag{1.18}$$

Here, q is the fraction of the average consumption that serves as the lower bound to all of c^1s. Thus, we actually obtain $c_i'(t)$ not as (1.12) but as

$$c_i'(t) = \max\left\{\lambda c_i(t), c_{\min}(t)\right\} = \max\left\{(1 \pm \gamma)\, c_i(t), qc_{av}(t)\right\}. \tag{1.19}$$

By scaling c_i by c_{av} (t), we define the fraction $y_i(t)$:

$$y_i(t) = \frac{c_i(t)}{c_{av}(t)} \tag{1.20}$$

By construction, it satisfies the normalization that the average of the fractions is 1. By changing variables into

$$Y_i = \ln\ y_i, \tag{1.21}$$

we observe that the basic dynamics becomes a kind of random walk with varying step sizes, i.e., a *truncated Lévy flight* with a lower reflecting barrier:

$$Y_i'(t) = Y_i(t) + \ln\ \lambda, \tag{1.22}$$

Here again, the prime indicates *the value after one elementary event, not* the *calendar time* derivative.

We can easily derive the master equation. It is shown by Levy and Solomon (1996) that the asymptotic stationary distribution of Y, $P(Y)$ is exponential. Denote the exponent of this exponential distribution α. Then, we can proceed to derive $R(r;\ \tau)$ the cumulative distribution function of r, that is, the probability that the growth rate of aggregate consumption $C(t)$ is less than or equal to r given τ elementary growths. For analytical details, the interested reader is referred to Aoki and Yoshikawa (2007, Ch. 10).

There are many ways how the growth rate of *aggregate* consumption r is realized.[2] The same aggregate growth rate r may be due either to a small number of elementary micro growths with large step size such as $r/2$ and $r/3$ or to a large number of small micro growths each with small step size. This actually makes a difference to the emerging probability distribution of r. We can derive exponential distribution for the aggregate growth rate r, under the condition that the number of elementary events τ does not exceed a critical level $\overline{\tau}$. This upper bound turns out to be defined by

$$\overline{\tau} = \left(\frac{N}{bq}\right)^{\alpha}. \tag{1.23}$$

It depends on N, q, α, and b. Here, b is defined by the following equation:

$$r = bk \times \frac{\gamma}{b} \quad (b = 1, 2, \ldots). \tag{1.24}$$

We assume that there are bk elementary events out of τ with magnitude γ/b each, and that the rest of τ, namely $\tau - bk$ events, makes almost no net contribution to the growth of the aggregate of consumption r. The greater b means the greater number of elementary events each with smaller contribution to make the growth rate r. We can then show that when $\tau < \overline{\tau}$ is satisfied, then the probability distribution of the growth rate r of the aggregate consumption $C(t)$ is exponential.

In summary, to obtain an exponential distribution for the growth rate of aggregate consumption, the number of elementary events within a given calendar time period τ cannot exceed a critical level $\overline{\tau}$ defined by Eq. (1.23). The probability density function of r is then the following exponential distribution:

$$f(r, b) \propto \exp\left[-\frac{b}{\gamma}\log\left(\frac{\overline{\tau}}{\tau}\right)r\right] \tag{1.25}$$

Exponential distribution for the growth rate of *aggregate real* variable is obtained when the number of micro growths within a short period of time τ is sufficiently small.

[2]A positive r and a negative r can be treated in almost identical ways. We focus on positive r.

1.4.2 Financial Market

We next study financial returns using the same model. There are N investors or assets each with financial resources or wealth $w_i(t)$:

$$W(t) = w_1(t) + \cdots + w_N(t). \tag{1.26}$$

As in the real-sector model, one of N stocks is randomly selected for an elementary event, i.e., a micro change. This random selection can be uniform with probability $1/N$ or can be modified to favor great asset values or wealthy investors. There are τ such micro or elementary events within a unit interval of time.

When asset i is selected, it undergoes the change

$$w_i'(t) = (1 + g)\, w_i(t) \tag{1.27}$$

where g is $\pm\gamma$ as in (1.14).

Again, $w_i'(t)$ indicates the value of w_i immediately after the elementary growth in the ith asset or agent's wealth. It is *not* the time derivative of $w_i(t)$.

The rate of return on financial assets or wealth over a calendar period from t to $t + 1$ $r(t)$ is defined, analogously as the rate of growth of the aggregate consumption in (1.15), by

$$r(t) = \frac{W\,(t+1) - W(t)}{W(t)} \tag{1.28}$$

We are interested in the case where probability distribution of r becomes power distribution.

When there are τ elementary events during $[t, t + 1]$, r is denoted by $r(t, \tau)$. By definition, $r(t, \tau)$ is as follows:

$$r\,(t, \tau\,) = \sum\nolimits_{i,k} f_{i,k} \tag{1.29}$$

where

$$f_{i,k} = \frac{\pm\gamma\, w_i\,(t; k)}{W(t)} \tag{1.30}$$

Again, the probability distribution of r depends on parameters τ and γ. Huang and Solomon (2001) demonstrate that depending on parameters, power-law distribution emerges. There are a set of parameters for which power-laws *with the exponent α close to 3* emerge[3] in financial sector model. The boundaries of the region are

[3]Huang and Solomon (2001) demonstrate by their simulations that the exponent α becomes close to 3.

determined by two curves on the $\tau - r$ plane. The interested reader is referred to Aoki and Yoshikawa (2007, Ch. 10)). When τ is larger than a critical value, power-law distribution of the growth rate of the value of financial assets is obtained.

In summary, in a truncated Lévy flight model in which the aggregate growth rate, r is composed of a number of micro or elementary growths within a unit interval of time, the probability distribution of the growth rate of *aggregate* variable r depends crucially on the number of such micro events τ. Specifically, when τ is smaller than a critical value $\overline{\tau}$, the exponential distribution emerges while we obtain power-laws with exponent α close to 3 for $\tau > \overline{\tau}$:

To the extent that the number of micro growths within a period is small in the real economy whereas it is large in financial markets, we must expect that the behavior of the real economy is fundamentally different from that of financial market. That is, we should observe exponential distribution for "real" growth whereas power-laws with the exponent α close to 3 for financial returns.

1.5 Concluding Remarks on Efficiency

Efficiency of financial market has been analyzed in terms of the presence/absence of "bubbles." As seminal analysis of bubbles by Shiller (1981) and subsequent works amply demonstrate, the problem is extremely difficult simply because rationality is the concept which concerns *ex ante* valuation of asset. Eugene Fama states:

> I don't even know what a bubble means. These words have become popular. I don't think they have any meaning. (Cassidy 2010)

This sort of statement actually misses the point and is futile because we know that wild ups and downs of asset prices seriously disturb the macroeconomy whether or not they are rational *ex ante*. Therefore, *ex ante* rationality is irrelevant for the purpose of our minimizing the disturbance of financial market.

The analysis in Sect. 1.3 shows that the real economy and financial market are fundamentally different. The difference lies in the frequency of actions and events or time span of economic agents in the real economy on one hand and financial market on the other hand. This means that *efficiency* in two sectors is actually different. Note that the neoclassical doctrine ranging from Arrow (1963) and Debreu (1959) to Diamond (1967), Fama (1970), Grossman/Shiller (1981), and others all takes it for granted that efficiency of financial market can be ultimately defined on consumers' preferences.

However, whatever the definition, efficiency of financial market cannot be directly related to our preferences in the real economy. If you are to meet your friend at 3 p.m. and your friend appeared 32 seconds past 3, you do not care because 32 seconds normally have no significance for human preference. This is the real economy. Thus, efficiency must be defined in terms of the appropriate time span.

The working of financial market is fundamentally different. A second matters. Thus, short-lived information is irrelevant in the real market, but can be very important, even vital in financial market. Besides, most financial transactions are not anchored to the market participants' real preferences, but are made for the purpose of resale in the market. Scheinkman (2014) presents a model in which stock price can be higher than the present value of a stream of future profits/dividends by option value for resale. Because resale plays the predominant role, financial transactions are bound to be affected by the opinions of others. Keynes's beauty contest analogy vividly describes how financial markets work.

> Professional investment may be likened to those newspaper competitions in which the competitions have to pick out the six prettiest faces from a hundred photographs, the prize being awarded to the competitor whose choice most nearly corresponds to the average preferences of the competitions as a whole: so that each competitor has to pick, not those faces which he himself finds prettiest, but those which he thinks likeliest to catch the fancy of the other competitors, all of whom are looking at the problem from the same point of view. It is not a case of choosing those which, to the best of one's judgment, are really the prettiest, nor even those which average opinion genuinely thinks the prettiest. We have reached the third degree where we devote our intelligences to anticipating what average opinion expects the average opinion to be. And there are some, I believe, who practice the fourth, fifth, and higher degrees. (Keynes 1936)

Thaler (2015, p. 211) believes that Keynes's beauty contest analogy remains an apt description of how financial markets work and, to help understand the gist of this analogy, presents an interesting puzzle game: "Guess a number 0 to 100 with the goal of making your guess as close as possible to two-thirds of the average guess of all those participating in the contest." Try it yourself first and it is a fun to see distribution of FT reader guesses!

Dealers and investors who work for the purpose of resale in financial markets must "rationally" react to short-lived information including the opinions of others if it is irrelevant to consumers and firms in the real economy.

In contrast, when consumer purchases consumables, he/she normally does so for his/her own consumption. Likewise, firm constructs a factory for the purpose of its own production. For them, short-lived information is irrelevant. For example, in the standard theory of investment, Tobin's q is a sufficient statistic for the determination of firm's investment (Tobin 1969; Yoshikawa 1980; Hayashi 1982). However, it is known that empirical performance of q investment function is poor, and that investment reacts systematically to such real variables as firm's sales and profits. Ueda and Yoshikawa (1986) explain why firms rationally ignore temporary fluctuations in the discount rate (stock price), and that as a result, investment responds mainly to real factors. The crucial assumption is that the profit rate contains more permanent movements than does the discount rate. The analysis shows that stock prices are too volatile in terms of firm's decision of investment. Note that this holds true irrespective of whether bubbles are present or not in stock prices, namely whether or not stock price is rationally determined in market.

As we argued above, this perspective, "ex ante" rationality or efficiency in financial market is actually secondary matter because efficiency in the real economy is not directly linked to rationality in financial market. Financial market and the real economy are fundamentally different. Asset prices can be too volatile pertaining to efficiency/welfare in the real economy. We must, therefore, monitor them as a part of macroeconomic policy.

Resale, the fundamental motivation in financial market, makes economic agents' time span short and the frequency of financial transactions high compared to utility arising from consumption in the real economy. Our analysis in Sect. 1.3 demonstrates that the difference in the frequency of transactions or events makes the real economy and financial market fundamentally different. Specifically, financial market is much more unstable than the real economy in the sense that it is characterized by power-law distributions. We must take serious warnings made by Keynes (1936), Minsky (1986), and others. We must also recognize that efficiency in financial market has little relevancy to efficiency in the real economy.

References

Aoki M (1996) New approaches to macroeconomic modeling: evolutionary stochastic dynamics, multiple equilibria, and externalities as field effects. Cambridge University Press, New York

Aoki M (2002) Modeling aggregate behavior and fluctuations in economics. Cambridge University Press, Cambridge

Aoki M, Yoshikawa H (2007) Reconstructing macroeconomics: a perspective from statistical physics and combinatorial stochastic processes. Cambridge University Press, Cambridge

Arrow K (1963) The role securities in the optimal allocation of risk-bearing. Rev Econ Stud 31:91–96

Campbell J, Cochrane J (1999) By force of habit: a consumption-based explanation of aggregate stock market behavior. J Polit Econ 107:205–251

Cassidy J (2010) Rational irrationality: an interview with Eugene Fama. The New Yorker, November, 1

Cecchetti S, Lam P, Mark N (2000) Asset pricing with distorted beliefs: are equity returns too good to be true? Am Econ Rev 90(4):787–805

Deaton A (1992) Understanding consumption. Oxford University Press, Oxford

Debreu G (1959) Theory of value. Wiley, New York

Diamond P (1967) The role of a stock market in a general equilibrium model with technological uncertainty. Am Econ Rev 57(4):759–776

Fama E (1970) Efficient capital markets: a review of theory and empirical work. J Financ

Feller W (1971) An introduction to probability theory and its applications, vol 2. Wiley, New York

Gabaix X (2008) Power laws in economics and finance. NBER working paper series 14299

Gabaix X, Gopikrishnan P, Plerou V, Stanley HE (2003) A theory of power-law distributions in financial market fluctuations. Nature 423:267–270

Grossman S, Shiller R (1981) The determinants of the variability of stock market prices. Am Econ Rev 71:222–227

Hayashi F (1982) Tobin's marginal q and average q: a neoclassical interpretation. Econometrica 50:213–224

Huang Z, Solomon S (2001) Power, Lévy, exponential and Gaussian – like regimes in autocatalytic financial systems. Eur Phys J B 20:601–607

Keynes JM (1936) The general theory of employment, interest, and money. Macmillan, London

Kirman A (1992) Whom or what does the representative individual represent ? J Econ Perspect 6:117–136

Levy M, Solomon S (1996) Dynamical explanation for the emergence of power law in a stock market. Int J Mod Phys C 7:65–72

Mandelbrot (1963) The variation of certain speculative prices. J Bus 36:394–419

Mandelbrot, Hudson RL (2004) The (MIS) behavior of markets. Basic Books, New York
Mantegna R, Stanley HE (2000) An introduction to econophysics: correlations and complexity in finance. Cambridge University Press, Cambridge
Mehra R, Prescott E (1985) The equity premium. J Monet Econ 15:145–161
Minsky H (1986) Stabilizing an unstable economy. Yale University Press, New Haven
Newman M (2005) Power laws, Pareto distributions and Zipf's law. Contemp Phys 46(5):323–351
Pareto V (1896) Cour d'Economie Politique. Lausanne et Paris
Scheinkman J (2014) Speculation, trading, and bubbles. Columbia University Press, New York
Shiller R (1981) Do stock prices move too much to be justified by subsequent changes in dividends? Am Econ Rev 71(3):421–436
Sornette D (2000) Critical phenomena in natural sciences. Springer, Berlin
Stanley HE, Gopikrishnan P, Plerou V (2006) Statistical physics and economic fluctuations. In: Gallegati M et al (eds) The complex dynamics of economic interaction. Springer, New York
Thaler RH (2015) Misbehaving – the making of behavioural economics. W.W. Norton, New York
Tobin J (1969) A general equilibrium approach to monetary theory. J Money Credit Bank 1:15–29
Ueda K, Yoshikawa H (1986) Financial volatility and q theory of investment. Economica 53:11–27
Yoshikawa H (1980) On the q theory of investment. Am Econ Rev 70:739–743
Yoshikawa H (2016) Micro-foundations for macroeconomics: new set-up based on statistical physics. Eur Phys J Spec Topics 225:3337–3344

Chapter 2
The Macroeconomy as a Complex System: Building on Aoki's Statistical Mechanics Approach

C. Di Guilmi, M. Gallegati, and S. Landini

Abstract This chapter provides an overview of the foundations of Aoki's approach for the microfoundation of models with a large number of heterogeneous and interacting agents through the implementation of statistical mechanics. We also provide a short survey of our works that have stemmed from Aoki's intuition.

Keywords Statistical mechanics · Macroeconomics · Master equation

2.1 Introduction

Being among those who had the opportunity to personally meet Masanao Aoki and to read his writings, it is impossible for us to overestimate Masanao's scientific calibre and his outstanding contribution to different fields of economic research.

Between 1996 and 2006, Masanao Aoki advanced a new research stream with a trilogy of books that introduces new approaches in macroeconomics (Aoki 1996) to model and explain aggregate behaviour and fluctuations (Aoki 2002) with the aim of reconstructing this field of research (Aoki and Yoshikawa 2006). Aoki pioneered an original approach to represent the economy as complex systems, introducing in the process a great deal of mathematical tools that were not in the domain of economists.

C. Di Guilmi (✉)
Economics Discipline Group, University of Technology Sydney, Broadway, NSW, Australia

Centre for Applied Macroeconomic Analysis, Australian National University, Canberra, ACT, Australia
e-mail: corrado.diguilmi@uts.edu.au

M. Gallegati
Department of Management, Università Politecnica delle Marche, Ancona, Italy

S. Landini
IRES Piemonte, Turin, Italy

H. Aoyama et al. (eds.), *Complexity, Heterogeneity, and the Methods of Statistical Physics in Economics*, Evolutionary Economics and Social Complexity Science 22,
https://doi.org/10.1007/978-981-15-4806-2_2

The three authors of this article met Masanao at different stages. Mauro Gallegati first estabilished a contact with him and invited him to Ancona in 2004. At that time, Mauro and his research group were trying to find a suitable modelling methodology to account for the modifications in the distribution of micro-financial variables observed during the cycle and identify the causal chain that leads microeconomic idiosyncratic shocks to generate macroeconomic fluctuations. Masanao's approach looked as the most promising methodology to model and explain this phenomenon. Around the same time and independently, Simone Landini was studying Masanao's writings in order to provide a systematic interpretation and some applications in economics for his PhD dissertation (Landini 2005). Subsequently, Corrado Di Guilmi drew inspiration from the meeting with Masanao and from Simone's thesis to further develop this approach in his own PhD dissertation, supervised by Mauro Gallegati (Di Guilmi 2008). Since then, the present authors have worked to foster and popularise the statistical mechanics approach to macroeconomics, with a range of different and prestigious co-authors. In the meantime, Masanao's curiosity led him to move the frontier of research in other areas of economics and finance.

Probably, the most important lesson that we learnt from Aoki concerns the new perspective for interpreting macroeconomic outcomes as originating from microlevel events, as a consequence of the unpredictable and unobservable interacting behaviour of myriads of heterogeneous individuals, coherently with the view of the economy as a complex system. Aoki provided us with the tools to analytically model and understand the apparent chaos of uncoordinated behaviours through the identification of stochastic laws.

The remainder of the chapter is structured as follows. Section 2.2 partially summarises Aoki's reinterpretation of the macroeconomy as a complex system that prepared the field for future advancements. Section 2.3 reviews some results of our research, in particular with reference to the closure of model developed according to Aoki's seminal ideas. Section 2.4 presents few extensions of our basic results that we have developed through the cooperation with other scholars. Section 2.5 concludes.

2.2 Aoki's Intuitions

This section discusses the building blocks of the new approach pioneered by Aoki and the further successive refinements, in particular for the solution of the master equation.

2.2.1 The Building Blocks

The first promising intuition of Aoki may sound like a *theorem*, and it was introduced by highlighting the analogy between the complex systems in natural and social sciences.[1] As a scientist, he was well aware that an analogy can be illustrative in presenting a new idea but then the ontological aspects should also be considered. Therefore, Aoki further developed this analogy founding it on an ontology that hinges in the theories of probability and stochastic processes: *[T]he macroeconomy consists of a large number of heterogeneous interacting agents, [. . .], it is meaningless and impossible to pursue precise behaviour of each unit, because the economic constraints on each will differ, and objectives of the units are constantly changing in an idiosyncratic way [. . .]. [W]e need to recognize that microeconomic behaviour is fundamentally stochastic, and we need to resort to proper statistical methods to study the macroeconomy consisting of a large number of such agents. The starting point of statistical mechanics was the recognition that it was impossible and meaningless to pursue precise motion of an individual molecule in a gas. Macroeconomics must be built on the same premise* (Aoki and Yoshikawa 2006, p. 3).

A second intuition consistently follows as a *corollary* and concerns the relevance of microeconomic fluctuations, i.e., the volatility in single agents' evolution, which are typically downplayed in General Equilibrium Theory since Walras, Arrow, and Debreu. In this tradition, the dynamics of the economic system is essentially deterministic. Its latest incarnation, the Dynamic Stochastic General Equilibrium models (DSGE), introduces compensating random shocks as drawn from a *known* data generating process in such a way that, in the asymptotic limit of the *not-finite time and number of agents*, they become irrelevant or disappear. As a consequence, even the inclusion of heterogeneity does not alter the ,notion of equilibrium as a point in space, where opposite forces balance, evolving along a saddle path. This concept is reminiscent of classical mechanics, whose principles are still validly assumed as appropriated enough to describe the economic world, abstracting from its intrinsic complexity as if physicists could ignore their quantum-leap of about a century ago.[2]

Microeconomic fluctuations enter the picture once interaction is included as *intimately entangled* to heterogeneity. Indeed, heterogeneity and interaction may be understood as opposite faces of the same coin: economies with heterogeneity but without interaction would be like clouds of gases with particles that do not collide, as economies of identical agents where each one behave in isolation, to such an extent that one individual is enough to represent all the others.

Although we cannot model each single individual in the economy, representing their evolution is essential for understanding the aggregate dynamics. Aoki's solution consists in adopting statistical mechanics: the probabilistic description of the system at a scale that is between macro and micro. At this mesolevel, different subsystems of individuals interact through migration from one subsystem to another,

---

[1] We define complex system as a large *ensemble* of heterogeneous interacting agents characterised by specific economic endowments, needs, strategies, and behavioural attitudes.

[2] Classical physics still is a valid basis of knowledge for macroscopic phenomena.

which alter the relative endowments of their subsystems and the configuration of the whole system.

As observing each particle collision is impossible and irrelevant, we do not need to keep track of every individual agent. Consistently with the foundational principles of statistical mechanics (Khinchin 1949), the modeller's aim is to provide a probabilistic description of agents' evolution and how it affects the configuration of the system. Microeconomic fluctuations are included in this representation as transition rates or migration probabilities over the state space. They allow us to approximate all the interactions as *mean-field* interaction. The transition rates are used to model jump Markov processes by means of which we can represent the macroeconomic dynamics: *Time evolution of a large collection of microeconomic units is described in terms of probability densities, and is governed by the master equation* (Aoki 1996, xiii).

The direct and essential *implication* is that Aoki's *new approach leads to a new concept of 'equilibrium'. Specifically, equilibrium is a 'probability distribution' over a set of points, not a single point* (Aoki and Yoshikawa 2006, 3). Accordingly, a situation of an apparent steady-state equilibrium of the system is just a *compatibility* of opposite forces: individuals can continuously be out of equilibrium and move from one group to another, but without altering the macro-configuration as long as their migration flows balance.

If equilibrium is considered as a point in space, then its evolution obeys an ordinary differential equation. In Aoki's approach, equilibrium is a probability distribution, whose dynamics obeys a master equation (ME).

More specifically, Aoki showed how the evolutionary dynamics of the macroeconomy can be described by continuous-time and discrete-space jump Markov processes. As a simplification, if we assume that a given quantity $\mathcal{X}$ (or a set of quantities) characterises the system, then we can consider an associated (possibly multivariate) stochastic process $X(t)$, generating values in the state space Λ, to describe the evolution of the system. As the individual constituents of the system are continuously interacting, regardless whether the interactions alter the configuration of the whole system, $X(t)$ changes states over Λ in continuous time as agents continuously migrate in the *subsystems-within-a-system* structure. For applications in economics, we can consider Λ as a discrete and finite, or at most not-finite and countable, subset of rationals.

The evolution of the system, represented by $X(t)$, is described by the dynamics of the states probability. In particular, we are interested in the probability for the system to visit any given x' at time $t' > t$ starting from x at t. The backward Chapmann-Kolmogorov equations (CKEs), developed within the (jump) Markov processes literature, or the MEs, developed in physics, chemistry and mathematical sociology, provide the necessary inferential tools: *The master equations describe time evolution of probabilities of states of dynamic processes in terms of the probability transition rates and state occupancy probabilities* (Aoki 1996, p. 116). Let us briefly summarise the main steps for the specification of a ME.

2.2.2 The Master-Equation: A Generic Standard Form

Let Δt be the reference unit of time (r.u.t.) that Aoki calls the *basic time increment*. Due to the interacting behaviour of its constituents, the dynamics of the system $X(t)$ on Λ is characterised by conditional probabilities. The changes in the conditional probabilities $P(x', t+\Delta t|x, t) - P(x', t|x, t) = w(x'|x, t)\Delta t + o(\Delta t)$ are such that $w(x'|x, t) = \dot{P}_{x,x'}(t)$, $\sum_{x'} w(x'|x, t) = 0$ and $w(x'|x', t) = -\sum_{x \neq x'} w(x|x', t)$. If $X(t)$ were Markovian then $P(x', t) = \sum_x P(x, t)P(x', t'|x, t)$ is the probability for the system to be in x' at $t' > t$. Being $t' = t + \Delta t$, the conditional probability changes read as $P(x', t') = P(x', t) + \sum_x P(x, t)w(x'|x, t)\Delta t + o(\Delta t)$. As the system's constituents continuously interact within the r.u.t. and continuously change their state, the system may continuously change as well. Therefore, in the limit for $\Delta t \to 0^+$ one finds the backward CKE $\frac{\partial P(x',t)}{\partial t} = \sum_x P(x, t)w(x'|x, t)$, that is the *primitive* form of a ME.

To approach a more convenient form, one should recast the r.h.s. of the CKE as $\sum_x P(x, t)w(x'|x, t) = P(x', t)w(x'|x', t) + \sum_{x \neq x'} P(x, t)w(x'|x, t)$. Therefore, as $w(x'|x', t) = -\sum_{x \neq x'} w(x|x', t)$, the *standard* form ME reads as

$$\frac{\partial P(x', t)}{\partial t} = \sum_{x \neq x'} \left[P(x, t)w(x'|x, t) - P(x', t)w(x|x', t)\right] \tag{2.1}$$

Once an expression for the ME is identified, we need to, first, provide an interpretation for this expression and, second, ascertain whether we can solve it in general or we need some simplifying approximation. If a solution can be identified, the subsequent step will be to use it.

2.2.3 Interpretation of a ME: An Example

As regarding the interpretation, solving (2.1) means finding the probability density function to estimate the probability for the system to be in the state x' at time t. We denote as x' the reference state among others in the set Λ. Within a time interval $[t, t') : t' = t + dt$ of infinitesimal length $dt > 0$, the system may visit all the feasible states with different paths. The first term in the square brackets in (2.1) defines the (probability) *inflow*, i.e., the probability for the system to enter x' from all the other states, and the second term represents the (probability) *outflow*, namely, probability to leave x' toward any other feasible state. Accordingly, we may interpret the ME as dynamic-balance equation describing the instantaneous rate of change of the probability density for the system to be at x', regardless of the amplitude of Λ that, for economic-meaningful purposes, is assumed being discrete-finite.

As general and generic as it is, (2.1) cannot be solved in closed form except in very few cases. But there are at least two ways to use a ME. The first one is *using without solving* it, the second is *solving to use* the ME solution. Before discussing both approaches, let us briefly describe the ME with more details introducing some simplifications.

First, assume the (macro) system Ω is a collection of (meso) subsystems ω each populated by many (micro) agents: the system may be either a real economy or an artificial one that is modelled by means of an *agent-based-model* (ABM) as a data-generating-process (DGP) of macro-quantities. Let $X(\omega, t) \equiv X_\omega(t)$ represent the slots of a transferable quantity $\mathcal{X}$ accumulating in the subsystem ω populated by a number of agents within the system Ω. For example, if we partition households into the employed or unemployed categories, ω may be the set of unemployed consumers; if we divide productive firms in different groups depending on whether they are self-financing or resorting to external finance, ω may represent the not self-financing firms. Accordingly, $X_\omega(t)$ will be the number of unemployed consumers or the aggregate output (profit or else) of the not self-financing firms. In the first case, $X_\omega(t)$ is the *occupation number* of state ω; in the second case, it is the *concentration* of output in the group ω. Assume the state space is $\Lambda = \{x_k : k \in \mathbb{N}\} \subset \mathbb{Q}$. Then, $X_\omega(t) = x_k$ signifies that at time t there were x_k unemployed consumers or that the total output of the not self-financing firms amounts to x_k.

To further simplify without loss of generality, let us focus on the occupation numbers case, usually indicated with $N_\omega(t)$ for each subsystem $\omega \in \Omega$. As an additional simplification, assume that $\Omega = \{\omega, \omega'\}$. This hypothesis allows for a generic scheme known as the *binary-choice* modelling, which contemplates a wide spectrum of macroeconomic phenomena. A number of examples can be found in Aoki and Yoshikawa (2007).

Now assume that the macroeconomy is large enough so that the number of agents does not change significantly over time: i.e., the units conservative constraint $\sum_\omega N_\omega(t) = N$ holds at each t, as if the system was closed although partitionable into subsystems that exchange units. Accordingly, two cases can emerge: *(i) equilibrium*: the system as a whole can be in steady state with a given configuration $\mathbf{N} = (N_\omega, N_{\omega'})$ while its units are migrating with the same intensity from ω to ω' and from ω' to ω; *(ii) out-of-equilibrium*: the macroeconomic configuration $\mathbf{N}(t) = (N_\omega(t), N_{\omega'}(t))$ changes through time due to agents' migration as the observable effect of their interaction. In both cases, the subsystems ω and ω' interact by exchanging units that carry their endowments: this is the *mean-field interaction* that operates at a meso-scale level of description that we can observe. We do not know which units are migrating, nor we can or are interested in knowing them: to us units are *indistinguishable* and *exchangeable* particles, and we are interested in modelling the change of the system configuration. This perspective is consistent with the idea of the economy as a complex system composed of heterogeneous-and-interacting agents, and we can proceed with its analysis from a probabilistic perspective.

As far as the occupation number case is concerned, the state space of $N_\omega(t)$ for each $\omega \in \Omega$ is $\Lambda = \{0, 1, \ldots, N\} \subset \mathbb{N}$, where N represents the total number of agents in the system. As an example, we can express the fact that at time t there are k unemployed workers in the economy as $N_\omega(t) = k$, and therefore $N_{\omega'}(t) = N - k$ is the number of employed workers since $\Omega = \{\omega, \omega'\}$. As workers stochastically change their state from being employed to unemployed and *vice-versa*, it then can happen that the occupation number of subsystem ω increases by some integer value m while that of ω' decreases by the same amount. Hence, $N_\omega(t + \Delta t) = k + m$ means that the number of unemployed workers increased by m units within the time interval $[t, t + \Delta t)$ while the subsystem ω' decreased by m units such that $N_{\omega'}(t + \Delta t) = (N - k) - m$.With fixed N and a binary-choice scheme, we can focus only on $N_\omega(t)$, since $N_{\omega'}(t) = N - N_\omega(t)$.[3] Despite the simplifications that we have introduced, the change $N_\omega(t + \Delta t) - N_\omega(t)$ can assume different values m: if $N_\omega(t) = k$, then $N_\omega(t + \Delta t) \in \{k \pm m : 0 \leq x \pm m \leq N\}$ can happen with some probability for each outcome in Λ.

Assume now that $\Delta t \to dt$ is small to such an extent that within the time interval $[t, t + dt)$ only one unit at time can migrate into ω, i.e., $m = +1$, or out from ω, i.e. $m = -1$. According to this *nearest-neighbourhood* assumption, if $N_\omega(t) = k$ then $N_\omega(t + dt) \in \mathcal{N}(k) = \{k - 1, k, k + 1\}$. Notice that, if $k = 0$ then $\mathcal{N}(0) = \{0, +1\}$ as well as if $k = N$ then $\mathcal{N}(N) = \{N - 1, N\}$ are *boundary conditions* we should consider as far as N is fixed.

Therefore, set $N_\omega(t) = k$ and let (a) $\rho(k, t)dt = r_k(t)dt + o(dt)$ be the probability for the process to move from k *rightward* to $k+1$ due to an inflow (*birth*) into ω from ω', (b) $\lambda(k, t)dt = l_k(t)dt + o(dt)$ be the probability to move *leftward* to $k-1$ due to an outflow (*death*) from ω into ω', and (c) $1-[\rho(k, t)+\lambda(k, t)]dt+o(dt)$ be the probability of no change.[4] The functions $\rho(k, t)$ and $\lambda(k, t)$ define the so-called space-time dependent *transition-rates* and are usually assumed being *regular enough*, meaning twice-differentiable in k and differentiable in t. In the simplest case they can be homogeneous-constant as $\rho(k, t) = r \geq 0$ and $\lambda(k, t) = l \geq 0$. In many applications, they are assumed being constant as $\rho(k, t) = r_k$ and $\lambda(k, t) = l_k$ while depending on the subsystem size k, i.e., on the current state $N_\omega(t) = k$ of the process. Other parameters can be included as $\rho(k, t) = \beta r_k$ and $\lambda(k, t) = \delta l_k$, where $\beta \geq 0$ is named as the *birth-rate* and $\delta \geq 0$ as the *death-rate*. In any case, the functional form of the transition-rates depends on the phenomenology of interactive behaviour of the heterogeneous agents in the system that can be described at the mesolevel in terms of mean-field interaction.

A generic example is provided by Aoki (2002, Sect. 5.1) with different applications. Assume that the probability for a unit to leave ω depends on its size, $l_k = \delta k$, then the probability for a unit to enter ω depends on the size ω', $r_k = \beta(N - k)$.

---

[3] A solution is attainable also when relaxing the constraints on the number of agents and the number of states (Di Guilmi et al. 2017).

[4] Depending on the field of application, an inflow-birth is sometimes defined as a *creation* event while an outflow-death is named a *destruction* event.

Although not-time varying, the functional forms of the transition rates may be more sophisticated; for instance they can include externalities and other aspects depending on the microlevel interacting phenomenology as discussed in Di Guilmi et al. (2017, App. C). For estimating the probability of the process to move state to k at time $t + dt$, three events must be considered: (a) an *inflow* event $\omega' \rightarrow \omega$ that moves the process from $k - 1$ to k and can occur with probability $r_{k-1}dt + o(dt)$, (b) an *outflow* event $\omega' \leftarrow \omega$ that moves the process from $k + 1$ to k and can occur with probability $l_{k+1}dt + o(dt)$, (c) $1 - (r_{k-1} + l_{k+1})dt + o(dt)$, which is the probability for the process *being-and-staying* in state k.[5] Accordingly, the probability for the event $N_\omega(t + dt) = k$ to occur is then $P(k, t + dt) = l_{k+1}dtP(k + 1, t) + r_{k-1}dtP(k - 1, t) + [1 - (r_{k-1} + l_{k+1})dt]P(k, t) + o(dt)$. Therefore, considering $dt \rightarrow 0^+$, the instantaneous rate of change

$$\frac{dP(k,t)}{dt} = l_{k+1}P(k+1,t)+r_{k-1}P(k-1,t)+[1-(r_{k-1}+l_{k+1})]P(k,t) \qquad (2.2)$$

defines the ME as a particular case of the general case (2.1), namely, that of an occupation number process obeying the binary-choice scheme under the nearest-neighbourhood hypothesis and according to the transitory-mechanics of the unit-jump-birth-death processes class. Furthermore, (2.2) represents a set of $N - 1$ equations for $k \in \{1, \ldots, N - 1\} \subset \Lambda$: as far as N is constant the modelling should now be completed by specifying the following boundary conditions

$$\frac{dP(0,t)}{dt} = l_1P(1,t) - r_0P(0,t)\ , \quad \frac{dP(N,t)}{dt} = r_{N-1}P(N-1,t) - l_NP(N,t) \qquad (2.3)$$

If we were able to solve (2.2)–(2.3) in closed form, although this not actually possible in general, we would find the functional form of the density $P(k, t) = W(N_\omega(t) = k, t|N_\omega(t_0), t_0)$ to estimate the probability for $N_\omega(t) = k$ to realise at time t given an initial condition $N_\omega(t_0)$. Accordingly, $1 - P(k, t)$ would estimate the probability for $N_{\omega'}(t) = N - k$ to realise at time t. Therefore, the dynamics of the Ω system configuration over the state space Λ would read as $\widehat{\mathbf{N}}(k, t) = (\widehat{N}_\omega(k, t), \widehat{N}_{\omega'}(k, t))$ where $\widehat{N}_\omega(k, t) = NP(k, t)$ and $\widehat{N}_{\omega'}(k, t) = N[1 - P(k, t)]$ for each $k \in \Lambda$. In order to further the analysis after this point the transition rates should be specified.

Therefore, the specification of a general ME does not solve but posits an *inferential problem*. Differently said, a ME like (2.2)–(2.3) is a *thesis* that follows from some assumption about the transitory mechanics of the system. The *data* of the problem are the state space Λ of the process and the *hypotheses* are the transition rates. Notice that both the thesis and the hypotheses depend on the knowledge about phenomenology of the behaviour at the microlevel. The problem then asks to find

[5]Notice that this scheme is consistent with the so-called birth-death stochastic processes class, among others see Gillespie (1992).

a suitable specification of the transition rates to infer a distribution $P(\bullet, t)$ that satisfies the ME. If a solution is possible then we can probabilistically describe the dynamics of the system.

2.2.4 *Using or Solving the ME*

Assume now a ME like (2.1) for a specific problem with specified transition rates. As mentioned, it cannot be solved in closed form except in very few cases. Let $x' \equiv x_k$ be fixed, as the reference state (i.e., sure), while $x \equiv x_h$ is any other state (i.e., stochastic) in Λ. Accordingly write the transition rates as $w(x'|x,t) \equiv R_t(x_k|x_k)$ and $w(x|x',t) \equiv R_t(x_h|x_k)$. Therefore, $\dot{P}(x_k,t) = 0$ sets the stationary condition and time drops out so we write $P(x) = P^*(x)$, implying that $\sum_{x_k} R(x_k|x_h)P^*(x_h) = \sum_{x_h} R(x_h|x_k)P^*(x_k)$. If the detailed-balance condition $R(x_k|x_{k-1})P^*(x_{k-1}) = R(x_{k-1|x_k})P^*(x_k)$ holds for every pair (x_{k-1}, x_k) then $P^*(x_k) = P^*(x_{k-1})\frac{R(x_k|x_{k-1})}{R(x_{k-1}|x_k)}$. Therefore, if some desirable properties like the Brook's lemma (Brook 1964) hold, one iteratively finds the equilibrium distribution

$$P^*(x_k) = P^*(x_0)\prod_{h=1}^{k-1}\frac{R(x_{h+1}|x_h)}{R(x_h|x_{h+1})} \tag{2.4}$$

and, for Markov processes, the Hammersley-Clifford theorem (Hammersley and Clifford 1971) gives

$$P^*(x_k) = Z^{-1}\exp\left(-U(x_0)\right) \tag{2.5}$$

where Z is a normalizing constant, known as the *partition function*, and U is a Gibbs-potential such that $U(x_k) - U(x_0) = -\sum_{h=1}^{k-1}\log\frac{R(x_{h+1}|x_h)}{R(x_h|x_{h+1})}$: this theorem states that, under some mild conditions, a Markov random field is equivalent to a Gibbs random field. Therefore, given the specified functional forms of the transition rates, the limiting distribution satisfying the ME under the stationary condition can be found for each $x_k \in \Lambda$. The Aoki's trilogy discusses many examples for this kind of solution.

If the detailed-balance condition or the Brook's lemma does not hold then the limiting distribution (2.5) does not hold and other methods need to be applied. Nevertheless, in any case we can *use the ME without solving it* to find the moments' dynamics of the underlying process $X_\omega(t)$, in case of concentration, or $N_\omega(t)$, in case of occupation numbers. To this end, provided that the transition rates are specified, it is possible to identify

$$\frac{d}{dt}\langle X_\omega^p(t)\rangle = \frac{d\mathbb{E}[X_\omega^p(t)]}{dt} = \sum_{y\in\Lambda} y^p\frac{\partial P(y,t)}{dt} \ : \ p > 0 \tag{2.6}$$

where p is the order of the moment: namely, for $p = 1$ one finds the expected trajectory and with $p = 2$ one finds the second moment trajectory such that $\langle X_{\omega}^{2}(t)\rangle - \langle X_{\omega}(t)\rangle^{2}$ is the trajectory of volatility; in the same way, higher order moments may be identified. Notice that, no assumption is needed about the form of the distribution; we just need the functional form of the transition rates that express the mean-field interaction.

Although an *exact* closed form solution cannot generally be found, an *approximated* solution of the ME or with some *approximation* can always be identified. A very restricted set of MEs can be solved in *closed form* and some of them are discussed in Gillespie (1992). A complete development of these methods is far beyond the scope of this article but we can provide a overview of the main features and results.

Aoki (1996, 2002) and Aoki and Yoshikawa (2006) provide a crash course about all the main solution procedures. Aoki himself originally developed a method by means of *lead* and *lag* operators which is similar to the Kramers-Moyal expansion method discussed by Gardiner (1985) and Risken (1989), who give a very rigorous development of the main methods, with (surprisingly) little mention of Kubo et al. (1973). Aoki (1996) provides a short presentation of it together with the van Kampen (1992) method, which is privileged in Di Guilmi et al. (2017). A *bird-fly* summary of all these methods is provided by Landini and Uberti (2008) and the literature cited therein.

The unifying trait is that all these methodologies find a solution composed of two main equations, namely: (a) an ordinary differential equation that drives the drifting trajectory of the expected value of the process underlying the ME, defined by Aoki as the *macroeconomic equation*; (b) a stochastic partial differential equation in the form of a Fokker-Planck equation that drives the dynamics of the distribution of spreading fluctuations about the drift. In this system of coupled equations, the second depends on the first but not the other way around.

Remarkably, Aoki had the illuminating intuition that the ME inferential approach, regardless of the solution method, leads to a system of coupled equations that describe the stochastic dynamics of a systems in terms of its probability distribution and moments. Aoki did not limited his research to the mathematical elegance of the ME approach and solution methods but, in his trilogy, he developed a wide range of applications of interest for economists. Moreover, starting with an initial analogical intuition that the macroeconomy is a complex system, he was able to motivate it by means of a probabilistic ontology that explains two main issues: (a) the macroeconomic dynamics does not comes by axiom but it has an intrinsic emerging nature grounded on the interactive behaviour of its constituents; (b) macroeconomic fluctuations do not occur randomly, but they are the observable outcome of myriads of interactions and transactions of heterogeneous agents that should be described stochastically. Accordingly, he proved that a meaningful rethinking of macroeconomics is possible by means of the statistical mechanics approach, in analogy to what happened to physics when the study of matter moved to the probabilistic ontology of statistical mechanics. History proved that physicists were on that right track, which eventually led them to quantum mechanics.

2.3 Closing the Model

Building on Aoki (2002) and Landini and Uberti (2008), Di Guilmi (2008), Di Guilmi et al. (2008, 2010), and Delli Gatti et al. (2012) propose a further development that allows for a closure of a macroeconomic model and identifies a statistical equilibrium. They use as a workhorse model a simplified version of the framework presented in Delli Gatti et al. (2005, 2007). These seminal papers have implemented in agent-based models the representative agent model by Greenwald and Stiglitz (1993), in which the objective function of the firm is the expected profit function, net of the expected bankruptcy cost. These costs are calculated by weighting the bankruptcy costs (a univariate function of output) by the probability of bankruptcy. The probability of bankruptcy depends on the distribution of the idiosyncratic price shock, which represents the uncertainty on the demand side. As a consequence the accumulation of debt that follows from the investment decision can potentially generate a downturn when debt reaches a critical threshold, according to a narrative firstly developed by Minsky (2008). Delli Gatti et al. (2005, 2007) keep this basic structure but introduce heterogeneity in financial conditions and indirect interaction among firms.

Di Guilmi et al. maintain the agent-based structure but in addition define a classification of firms into two groups depending on whether they have a positive probability of bankruptcy or not. While firms that do not run the risk of default will simply maximise their profit, the other firms will reduce their output to an extent directly proportional to the probability of bankruptcy. As a consequence, aggregate output will depend on the relative density of firms in the two groups, providing a simple but suitable structure on which to implement the probabilistic framework devised by Aoki (2002). In particular, the distribution of the idiosyncratic price shock provides the cumulative distribution function for quantifying the thresholds for firm to transition from one group to another and accordingly define the transition rates. It is worth stressing that these transition rates are endogenous, being dependent on the balance sheets of firms as they evolve due to the initial assumptions of the model and its dynamic evolution through time.

State $\omega = 1$ is the state of firms with a positive probability of bankruptcy and, assuming a constant number of firms (bankrupted firms are immediately replaced), the number of financially sound firms is just a residual.

The transition rate for entry (from state 0 into state 1) is indicated with λ, while the one for exit (from state 1 to state 0) is γ, defined as follows:

$$\begin{aligned} \lambda &= \zeta(1-\eta) \\ \gamma &= \iota\eta \end{aligned} \tag{2.7}$$

Where ζ, ι are the individual probabilities of transition to and from state $\omega = 1$, respectively, and depend on the behavioural rule embedded in the model's assumptions and on the balance sheets of the single units. Using mean-field approximation and identifying a single value for each group, we have one probability for each transition. The symbol η indicated the theoretical probability for a randomly drawn firm to be in state $\omega = 1$.

Further, the expected number of transitions from macrostate N_k[6] to macrostate N_{k+1} is $\lambda(N - N_k)$, while the expected number of transitions from macrostate N_k to macrostate N_{k-1} is γN_k. Within the length of a vanishing reference unit of time $\Delta t \to 0$, the transition rates can be written as follows

$$\begin{aligned} b(N_k) &= P(N^1(t + \Delta t) = N_{k+1}(t') | N^1(t) = N_k(t)) = \lambda(N - N_k) \\ d(N_k) &= P(N^1(t + \Delta t) = N_{k-1}(t') | N^1(t) = N_k(t)) = \gamma N_k \end{aligned} \tag{2.8}$$

where b and d indicate, respectively, "births" (transition to N_{k+1}) and "deaths" (transition to N_{k-1}) of the stochastic process and $t' - t = dt \to 0^+$.

The master equation for this model can be expressed as

$$\begin{aligned} \tfrac{dP(N_k,t)}{dt} &= b(N_{k-1}, t)P(N_{k-1}, t) + d(N_{k+1}, t)P(N_{k+1}, t) + \\ &- \{[(b(N_k, t) + d(N_k, t))P(N_k, t)]\} \end{aligned} \tag{2.9}$$

where N_k is the number of firms in state 1.

Since as shown by Risken (1989), a direct solution of the master equation requires restrictive conditions and hypotheses, Di Guilmi et al. adopt the method introduced by Aoki (2002) and split the control variable N_k into the drift and diffusion components. Accordingly, it is possible to identify the trend and the fluctuations not only of the number of firms in state 1 but also of the aggregate production, since the latter depends on the former. Consistently with the so-called van Kampen anstaz (1992), the share of firms in state 1 is represented as the sum of the trend component m and additive noise normalised by $N^{1/2}$

$$N_k = Nm + \sqrt{N}s \tag{2.10}$$

Di Guilmi et al. (2010) modify the ME and find an asymptotically approximated solution of the master equation is given by the following system of coupled equations:

$$\frac{dm}{dt} = \zeta m - (\zeta + \iota)m^2 \tag{2.11}$$

$$\frac{\partial Q(s)}{\partial t} = [2(\zeta + \iota)m - \zeta] \frac{\partial}{\partial s}(sQ(s)) + \frac{[\zeta m(1 - m) + \iota m^2]}{2} \left(\frac{\partial}{\partial s}\right)^2 Q(s) \tag{2.12}$$

where Q is the master equation (2.9) reformulated as a function of the spread s. In this particular solution algorithm, the drift has a logistic form while the fluctuations

[6]With respect to the occupation number process described above, N_k is a shorthand for $N_1(t) = k$ as the state of reference is $\omega = 1$.

are normally distributed according to

$$\bar{Q}(s) = C \exp\left(-\frac{s^2}{2\sigma^2}\right) \;:\; \sigma^2 = \frac{\zeta\iota}{(\zeta + \iota)^2} \tag{2.13}$$

Among the works that have employed the solution of the ME defined by equations (2.11)–(2.12) it is worth citing (Chiarella and Di Guilmi 2011). They implement this approach to solve a Minskyan ABM inspired by Taylor and O'Connell (1985) and show that analytical approximation closely reproduce the patterns produced by the numerical simulations of the ABM.

2.4 Extensions

Di Guilmi et al. (2017) further develop and generalise the result in (2.11)–(2.12). In particular, the solution is generalised allowing for a more generic functional form that depends on the structure of the ABM. Further extension on the basic solution introduced in Sect. 2.3 have been proposed in subsequent works.

2.4.1 Learning

In a context of asymmetric information, agents are necessarily heterogeneous because of their different informative sets. As a consequence, they interact with each other in order to achieve the most possible complete information inferring from others' behaviours. While statistical physics provides the tools for analysing systems of heterogeneous interacting agents, an important caveat is that in social sciences we deal with social atoms (Buchanan 2007), who, due to interaction, learn from their environment rather than passively adapt to its changes. In order to consider this factor, Landini et al. (2014) use the ME to model the evolutionary dynamics of agents' behaviours. To this aim, they introduce in economics the Combinatorial (Chemical) ME (Prigogine and Nicolis 1977; Gardiner 1985).

Firms adapt their choices among a set of simple behavioural rules through interaction and learning. In particular, the rules determine the target output as dependent on the net worth of a firm and the market price. The distribution of firms over the possible rules is modelled through a Combinatorial ME. The choice of this particular tool is due to the fact that the learning process is iterative and subject to the limited information available to agents. As a consequence, the choice of strategy that is ex-ante the most profitable can be ex-post suboptimal once all the other agents have revealed their strategy on the market (re-configurative learning). More in detail, the chapter uses two MEs: a standard ME for the financial heterogeneity (different net worth) and the Combinatorial ME for learning. The solution of first ME quantifies the distribution of firms according to their net worth; the solution of the Combinatorial ME provides the distribution of firms over the set of rules. A bi-dimensional state space is therefore identified.

The nonlinear patterns displayed by the numerical simulations is generated by the transitions of agents across this bi-dimensional state-space and are captured by the solution of the MEs, which is composed by a drift and a spread component as detailed in the previous section.

2.4.2 Network

Di Guilmi et al. (2012) are the first to apply the ME approach to a network model. More precisely, the ME is employed to derive an analytical solution for an agent-based network model composed of heterogeneous firms and banks.

Besides the novelty of the application, the chapter proposes two relevant methodological innovations. First, the analytical solution is attained by means of a system of two MEs, one nested into the other. The first ME provides the dynamics of the number of firms that cannot internally finance their production and thus resort to the credit market, becoming nodes of the network. The solution of this ME feeds into the second ME which models the evolving structure of the network, focusing on the degree distribution. The second relevant contribution comes from the fact that the network degree can take any value between 1 and the total number of firms demanding for credit, which is a time-varying quantity. The ME for the network is therefore able to deal with a state-space which has a dimension larger than 2, as in the models presented above, and is open-ended.

Also in this instalment, the ME replicates to a large extent the outcomes of the numerical solution of the ABM, in particular generating a power-law distribution of the degree that mimics the one observed in the simulations.

2.4.3 A Possible Bridge with the DSGE and the Stock-Flow Consistent Approaches

On the other side of the spectrum from the contribution presented in Sect. 2.4.1, Catalano and Di Guilmi (2016) tested the statistical physics approach in a context of perfect rationality. They adapt the model by Russo et al. (2007) in which firms and households have a simple set of binary choices and interact in the goods and in the labour market. A system of MEs is set up in order to study the evolving distribution of agents for each strategy in the two markets. The solutions of the MEs define a dynamical system which is coupled with the aggregate equations for output, price, demand and wealth, which in turn depend on choices of agents. The system is studied under two different scenarios: one in which agents behave heuristically, as in standard ABMs, and one in which a central planner maximises the future streams of firms' profits and agents aggregate utility using as a control variable the share of agents choosing a particular strategy. The analysis provides two main insights. The first is that the economy can reach full employment and an efficient allocation only in the full rationality scenario. Accordingly, this scenario defines a benchmark for to quantifying the efficiency loss due to the suboptimal behaviour of agents in the heuristics setting. The second relevant result is that market imbalances generate frequent and mild crises in the heuristic setting. Introducing full-rationality only in a subset of choices causes what Aoki and Yoshikawa (2006) define as *uncertainty trap*: increasing uncertainty locks the macroeconomy out from the optimal equilibrium.

Di Guilmi and Carvalho (2017) provide an application of the ME to an agent-based stock-flow model. Stock-flow consistent models achieve a comprehensive representation of the economy that accounts for all flows of income between different sectors in the economy as well as their accumulation into financial and tangible assets (Godley and Lavoie 2007). This type of models has been traditionally developed as aggregative but more recently they have integrated with agent-based modelling (for a survey see Di Guilmi 2017). Di Guilmi and Carvalho (2017) make a step towards the bottom-up construction of dynamical disequilibrium systems which include microlevel variables and can therefore shed new light on the transmission of shock from the micro- to the macrolevel. They present a stock-flow consistent model that is microfounded on the firm side while keeping the household sector as an aggregate. The ME solution replicates closely the dynamics generated by the numerical simulations of the ABM and provides a number of insights into the causal relationship that are the root of the result, opening the "black-box" of the simulations that is so much a concern for mainstream economists.

2.5 Conclusion

This chapter provides a (necessarily brief) overview of the seminal contributions of Masanao Aoki to the implementation of statistical mechanics in macroeconomics for the aggregation of models with a large number of heterogeneous and interacting agents. The works by the present authors that have stemmed from Aoki's intuition are referenced, highlighting the main results and developments. In particular, we have shown that the statistical mechanics approach is able to provide a closed form solution in which the microlevel quantities are explicitly linked to the macro-dynamics.

More recent contributions together with different coauthors have demonstrated the reliability and flexibility of this approach to be employed in a number of different macroeconomic models, ranging from those with a standard microfoundation with intertemporal optimisation to the stock-flow consistent models of Keynesian inspiration.

The necessity of a reformulation of macroeconomics in the wake of the Great Recession has created the conditions for a shift of paradigm that is testified by the interests of students and young scholars in the approach initiated by Aoki. We are confident that, despite its technical complexity and the idiosyncrasy with respect to the mainstream, Aoki's work can represent a credible and promising alternative for a development of a scientifically sounder macroeconomic modelling. Fundamentally, we need to recognise the macroeconomy as a complex system and consequently adopt proper methodologies.

Acknowledgments We thank the editors of this book in honour of Masanao Aoki for inviting us to contribute.

The opinions expressed in this article are our own and do not involve the responsibility of our institutions. We declare no conflict of interest.

References

Aoki M (1996) New approaches to macroeconomic modeling. Cambridge University Press, Cambridge

Aoki M (2002) Modeling aggregate behaviour and fluctuations in economics. Cambridge University Press, Cambridge

Aoki M, Yoshikawa H (2006) Reconstructing macroeconomics. Cambridge University Press, Cambridge

Aoki M, Yoshikawa H (2007) Non-self-averaging in macroeconomic models: a criticism of modern micro-founded macroeconomics. Discussion papers 07057, Research Institute of Economy, Trade and Industry (RIETI). http://ideas.repec.org/p/eti/dpaper/07057.html

Brook D (1964) On the distinction between the conditional probability and the joint probability approaches in the specification of nearest-neighbour systems. Biometrica 51:481–483

Buchanan M (2007) The social atom: why the rich get richer, cheaters get caught, and your neighbor usually looks like you. Bloomsbury, New York

Catalano M, Di Guilmi C (2016) Uncertainty, rationality and complexity in a multi-sectoral dynamic model: the Dynamic Stochastic Generalized Aggregation approach. Tech. rep., mimeo

Chiarella C, Di Guilmi C (2011) The financial instability hypothesis: a stochastic microfoundation framework. J Econ Dyn Control 35(8):1151–1171

Delli Gatti D, Di Guilmi C, Gaffeo E, Giulioni G, Gallegati M, Palestrini A (2005) A new approach to business fluctuations: heterogeneous interacting agents, scaling laws and financial fragility. J Econ Behav Organ 56(4):489–512

Delli Gatti D, Di Guilmi C, Gallegati M, Giulioni G (2007) Financial fragility, industrial dynamics, and business fluctuations in an agent-based model. Macroecon Dyn 11(S1):62–79

Delli Gatti D, Di Guilmi C, Gallegati M, Landini S (2012) Reconstructing aggregate dynamics in heterogeneous agents models. A Markovian approach. Revue de l'OFCE 124(5):117–146

Di Guilmi C (2008) The generation of business fluctuations: financial fragility and mean-field interaction. Peter Lang Publishing Group, Frankfurt am Main

Di Guilmi C (2017) The agent-based approach to Post Keynesian macro-modeling. J Econ Surv 31(5):1183–1203. https://doi.org/10.1111/joes.12244

Di Guilmi C, Carvalho L (2017) The dynamics of leverage in a demand-driven model with heterogeneous firms. J Econ Behav Organ 140(Supplement C):70–90. https://doi.org/10.1016/j.jebo.2017.04.016

Di Guilmi C, Gallegati M, Landini S (2008) Economic dynamics with financial fragility and mean-field interaction: a model. Physica A Stat Mech Appl 387(15):3852–3861. https://doi.org/10.1016/j.physa.2008.01.0
Di Guilmi C, Gallegati M, Landini S (2010) Financial fragility, mean-field interaction and macroeconomic dynamics: a stochastic model. In: Salvadori N (ed) Institutional and social dynamics of growth and distribution. Edward Elgar, UK, pp 323–351
Di Guilmi C, Gallegati M, Landini S, Stiglitz JE (2012) Dynamic aggregation of heterogeneous interacting agents and network: an analytical solution for agent based models. Tech. rep., mimeo
Di Guilmi C, Landini S, Gallegati M (2017) Interactive macroeconomics. Stochastic aggregate dynamics with heterogeneous and interacting agents. Cambridge University Press, Cambridge
Gardiner CW (1985) Handbook of stochastic methods. Springer, New York
Gillespie D (1992) Markov processes. An introduction for physical scientists. Academic Press, San Diego
Godley W, Lavoie M (2007) Monetary economics: an integrated approach to credit, money, income, production and wealth. Palgrave Macmillan, London
Greenwald B, Stiglitz JE (1993) Financial markets imperfections and business cycles. Q J Econ 108(1):77–114
Hammersley JM, Clifford P (1971) Markov field on finite graphs and lattices, unpublished
Khinchin A (1949) Mathematical foundations of statistical mechanics. Dover Publications, New York
Kubo R, Matsuo K, Kitahara K (1973) Fluctuations and relaxation in macrovariables. J Stat Phys 9:51–93
Landini S (2005) Modellizzazione stocastica di grandezze economiche con un approccio econofisico. Ph.D. thesis, University Bicocca, Milan
Landini S, Uberti M (2008) A statistical mechanic view of macro-dynamics in economics. Comput Econ 32(1):121–146
Landini S, Gallegati M, Stiglitz JE, Li X, Di Guilmi C (2014) Learning and macroeconomic dynamics. In: Dieci R, He XZ, Hommes C (eds) Nonlinear economic dynamics and financial modelling. Springer, Berlin/Heidelberg, pp 109–134
Minsky HP (2008) Securitization, Economics Policy Note Archive 08-2. Levy Economics Institute
Prigogine I, Nicolis G (1977) Self-Organization in non-equilibrium systems: from dissipative structures to order through fluctuations. J. Wiley & Sons, New York
Risken H (1989) Fokker-Planck equation. Method of solutions and applications. Springer, Berlin
Russo A, Catalano M, Gaffeo E, Gallegati M, Napoletano M (2007) Industrial dynamics, fiscal policy and R&D: evidence from a computational experiment. J Econ Behav Organ 64(3–4):426–447
Taylor L, O'Connell SA (1985) A Minsky crisis. Q J Econ 100(5):871–85
van Kampen NG (1992) Stochastic processes in physics and chemistry. North-Holland, Amsterdam

Chapter 3
On the Analytical Methods Considered Essential by Prof. Masanao Aoki in His Japanese Textbook

Yuji Aruka

Abstract Professor Masanao Aoki was a great scholar who sincerely challenged to exit from the secular world fettered by the representative method of economic modeling. He resolutely focused on a stochastic dynamic system, i.e., cluster dynamics with a *finite* number of heterogenous agents of different types, which could change the methodological regime from the pure homogeneous agents to the actual world. The desired model may be described by partition vectors with multiple state. Aoki's model has renovated the traditional restrictive views. In this article, by referring to the sole textbook of Prof. Aoki written in Japanese, we will discuss his insightful analytical methods, which Prof. Aoki considered essential for economic modeling.

This article refers to the first and the last textbook single-authored by Professor Masanao Aoki in 2003 titled: *Introduction to Stochastic Dynamic Approach of Heterogeneous Agents* in Japanese (Aoki, Ishitsuteki e-jennto no Kakuritsudougaku nyumon (Introduction to stochastic dynamic approach of heterogeneous interacting agents). Kyoritisu Publishing Co. Ltd., Tokyo, 187pp, 2003). Textbook in general usually surpasses monographs in view of transmission of the author's general mind of way of thinking. We briefly/partially introduce the content of his textbook and reveal his essential messages of the new approach for the reconstruction of macroeconomics.

Keywords Different types · Multiple states · Partition vectors · Stochastic/cluster dynamics · Heterogeneous interaction

---

Y. Aruka (✉)
Institute of Economic Research, Chuo University, Hachiōji-shi, Tokyo, Japan
e-mail: aruka@chuo-u.ac.jp

H. Aoyama et al. (eds.), *Complexity, Heterogeneity, and the Methods of Statistical Physics in Economics*, Evolutionary Economics and Social Complexity Science 22,
https://doi.org/10.1007/978-981-15-4806-2_3

3.1 Ontological Background

3.1.1 Events with Multiplicity

There are over-flooded news of macroeconomic problems in the mass media, which are connected with some pushy abduction based on the stereotyped knowledge of the standard economics: Interest cut brings either a rise of investment or decreasing unemployment. Can we believe such a news? We have the simple answer "No." Because we have a very smart historical database given by a piece of the Wolfram Demonstration Project titled: "Macroeconomic Effects of Interest Rate Cuts" (Cawley and Meinberg 2011).[1] This simulator gives us a remarkable insight on a macroscopic phenomenon which may coexist with some multiple states. For example, the interest rate cut may make either upward or downward the currency exchange rate or decrease from history to history, and fluctuating from elapsed time to time due to some autocorrelation. We should know that here could be often generated a multiplicity of the results around a certain action like the interest rate cut.

It may be a best way to use the simulator of Cawley and Meinberg (2011) to understand the multiplicity of the subsequential states due to a policy change. It is very interesting to know the profile of this demonstration. The data base categorized three distinguished periods as follows:

Period I The period before 1979 when interest rates were rising and inflation gradually became a major problem

Period II The Volcker period in the 1980s, in which interest rates reversed their long-term trend

Period III The Greenspan-Bernanke period from 1987 to the present(2011).

If we take an example of Period I in this demonstration, we will reproduce the next figures of the historical charts like Figs. 3.1 and 3.2. By inspection from the data base, we will discover many similar events. The idea of ABM (Agent Based Modeling) will also suffice us to methodologically renovate our traditional idealistic modeling structures to permit such a multiplicity emerging in the model.

3.1.2 The Fifth Stage of Aoki's Life Work

Professor Aoki has worked with a wide coverage of topics from the 1st to the fifth stage summarized in Aruka et al. (2015). His textbook dealt with here belongs to the fifth stage, where "[t]he new method is featured by Statistical Physics and Combinatorial Stochastic Processes. Equilibria is not treated as a fixed points. The

[1] "Major Fed rate cuts can have wide and varying effects on major macroeconomic variables. This Demonstration shows the change in selected time series following reductions in the Fed Funds rate of 0.5 or more, after a period of rising or level interest rates."

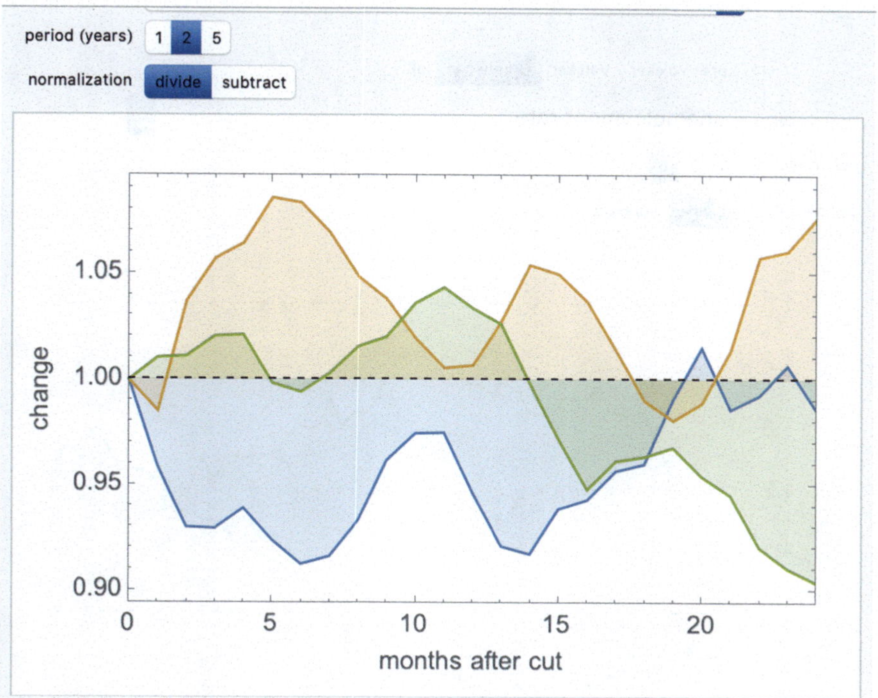

Fig. 3.1 The effects on exchange rate

system may be subject to non-self averaging and mutant could emerge internally. These studies can rightly establish a set of theoretical foundations to socio-econophysics." The books at this stage include:

Aoki 1996 *New approaches to macroeconomic modeling: evolutionary stochastic dynamics, multiple equilibria, and externalities as field effects*

Aoki 2002 *Modeling aggregate behavior and fluctuations in economics: stochastic views of interacting agents*

Aoki 2003 *Introduction to Stochastic Dynamic Approach of Heterogeneous Agents*

Aoki and Yoshikawa 2006 *Reconstructing macroeconomics: a perspective from statistical physics and combinatorial stochastic processes*

That is to say, Aoki (1996, 2002, 2003) and Aoki and Yoshikawa (2006) had a keen awareness of this multiplicity problem.

Agents involved in the economic system are divided into several subsets (clusters), and the size of the agents changes over time with the probability of entry, exit, and change in agent type. And new subsets emerge as new types of agents enter. Here all sizes and numbers are defined finitely in the discrete system.

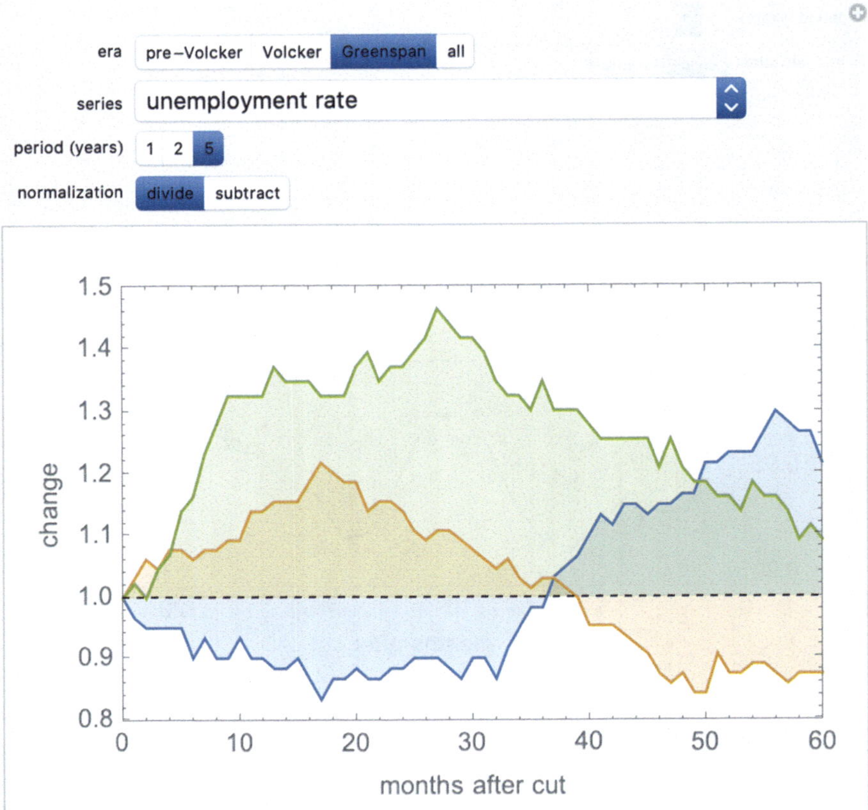

Fig. 3.2 The effects on unemployment

In fact, there are as usual various heterogeneous types of people and companies, that is, agents (subjects) interact in society. In other words, agents can be allowed to immigrate in and/or emigrate to other clusters. The type is not necessarily fixed. A new type of agent, who is currently *unknown*, will emerge in the future. Even a given fixed group can also be, to same extent, transformed by the replacement of agents through entry or exit differently according to purpose. Such a group/crowd is forming a common subset/cluster where any component of the group is characterized by exchangeability, or the same kinds. The association of clusters will generate **a cluster dynamics** consisting of several heterogeneous interacting groups. This idea is traditionally inheriting from **the master equation**, or synergetics.[2] In the following, it is noted that we do not know all the types any time. This point of view will suggest us a new prediction based on empirical stochastic distributions. This is just the innovative standpoint in Aoki's textbook.

[2]See Weidlich (2000) for the details of synegetics.

At some point, there are n agents in the system. Now, in the case that n are classified into K_n types, it needs us to know what type of agent can arrive in the next short span δ by a conditional probability rate. Thus the textbook of Aoki (2003) has consistently demonstrated how to deal with a model to allow **unknown types** selection in stochastic cluster dynamics around the environment of **exchangeability**. Thus, in the finite discrete domain, we can arrange two stochastic analytical frames, i.e., the analytical frame based on the circumstance of exchangeable agents, firstly for the known type, and secondly for the unknown types. In physics, so far, these kinds of formulation have been regarded as **the classic occupancy problem**. According to Aoki, we regard the first frame as the Maxwell-Boltzmann form and the second as the Bose-Einstein form.[3] In the context of this text book, in the following, we mainly focus on the above two streams chronically. First of all, we start to overview how Aoki argue **the standard master equation** to derive **multiple equilibria**.

3.1.3 The Basic Profile of Aoki's Japanese Textbook in Aoki (2003)

The textbook Aoki (2003) is a relatively small concise book of 187 total pages, which has been published just after the books of Aoki (2002) came out. The contents of both books naturally are overlapping.[4] Needless to say, the textbook in general has a relaxed expression familiar to readers rather than a professional styles of arguments. His textbook also follows this custom. But the presentations in this textbook are not necessarily oriented for general readers. Because his super skill of analytical calculation has been frankly exerted almost everywhere in the book. Those who are interested in analytical procedure must be useful to learn many classical analytical and computational procedures without using the computer. The readers may be astonished by the excellence of his analytical power. In this chapter, we will only pick up a few subjects from the book chapters which Prof. Aoki highlighted to characterize his essential method.

In the following, we introduce the contents of the book:

Chapter 1 Introduction
Chapter 2 Master equations
Chapter 3 Transition rates and the stationary distribution
Chapter 4 Partition vectors
Chapter 5 Generating functions

---

[3]See Aoki (1996, 13) as for the relationship of both distributions. This relationship will be discussed late in Sect. 3.2.

[4]In Aoki and Yoshikawa (2006) written after his textbook, "non-self-averaging" has been newly focused. This is also one of the most important key ideas at the fifth stage. See Aruka and Akiyama (2009) as an application of this idea.

3.2 The Standard Master Equation in the Case That Types Are Known and the Derivation of Stationary Multiple Equilibira

We define a Markov chain X_t on the state space S which dynamically describes a flux of probabilities. In a state j at time t, we can imagine a probability $P_j(t) = \Pr(X_t = j)$. We suppose that there are a number of independent agents, each of whom is in one of finite microeconomic states, and its each state evolves according to the master equation

$$\frac{dP_j(t)}{dt} = \sum_{k \neq j} [P_k(t) w_{kj} - w_{jk} P_j(t)] \; j \in S. \tag{3.1}$$

where w_{kj} denotes the transition rates from state j to state k, or the in-flow rates, and w_{jk} the rates from k to j, the out-flow rates.

In the textbook, the fundamental formulas of the master equation are provided in Chap. 2. Here we argue some examples in the alternatives model provided in Chap. 8.

[5] A1. Identical equations of matrices and determinants, A2. Stochastic generating functions, A3. Characteristic curves and auxiliary equations, A4. Differential equations to be fulfilled by generating functions, A5. Examples on the difference between the deterministic system and the stochastic system, A6. The calculation method of Viarengo's order statistics, A7. The Laplace transform, A8. Cauchy's formula, A9. Error functions, A10. The Dirichlet distribution and gamma function, A11. The density function of Z_K, A12. The partition of $[n]$, A13. The two-parametric model, A14. The entry rate with two parameters, A15. The partition vector and the expectation calculation on $E(a_j)$, A16. The growth process of Poisson groups, A17. The growth process for a model of two-typed agents, A18. Distribution functions: Bernoulli, Binomial, Multi-nomial, Lognormal, Beta, Random alms (Residual allocation model), GEM, Size-biased replacement, A19. Gibbs distribution, A20. The minimum sojourn time.

3.2.1 A Gibbs Distribution in Terms of the Master Equation

The system of two states: Then the economy is composed by

$$S = \{a, b\}.$$

Given the nonnegative transition rates $w_{ab}, w_{ba} \geq 0$, the master equation system is constituted by the next two ordinary differential equations:

$$\frac{dP_a(t)}{dt} = P_b(t)w_{ba} - P_a w_{ab}, \tag{3.2}$$

$$\frac{dP_b(t)}{dt} = P_a(t)w_{ab} - P_b w_{ba}. \tag{3.3}$$

Here

$$P_a(t) + P_b(t) = 1.$$

In this case, given an initial condition $P_a(0)$, and $w_{ab} + w_{ba} > 0$, it follows:

$$\pi_a = \lim_{t\to\infty} P_a(t) = \frac{w_{ba}}{w_{ba} + w_{ab}}. \tag{3.4}$$

In general, the master equation may be

$$\frac{\partial P(s,t)}{\partial t} = \sum_{s \neq s'} P(s,t)w(s' \mid s,t) - \sum_{s \neq s'} P(s',t)w(s \mid s',t).$$

In the stationary state or in equilibrium, the probability in-flows and out-flows balance at every state:

$$\pi_j \sum_{k \in S} w_{jk} = \sum_{k \in S} \pi_k w_{kj} \ \forall j \in S, \tag{3.5}$$

$$\pi_j \geq 0, \sum_{j \in S} \pi_j = 1. \tag{3.6}$$

If there exist a j, and a π_j, we call the distribution

$$\{\pi_j, j \in S\}$$

"an equilibrium distribution."

If the probability flows balance for every pair of states, it then holds **the detailed balance condition**:

$$\pi_j w_{jk} = \pi_k w_{kj}.$$

Given an **irreducible** Markov chain, for any state s_j, we can find a finite sequence

$$\{s_1, s_2, \cdots, s_j\}$$

starting from some initial state s_0. If the detailed balance condition holds, it follows *a Gibbs distribution*

$$\pi_j = \pi(s_0) \prod_{i=0}^{j-1} \frac{w_{i+1,i}}{w_{i,i+1}}.$$

Here

$$\pi(s) = K \exp[-U(s)]$$

with

$$U(s_j) - U(s_0) = \sum \ln \frac{w_{i+1,i}}{w_{i,i+1}}$$

implies $U(s)$ to be *a potential.*

The probability distribution is *independent of paths* from s_0 to s_j due to the property of Markov chain process. See Aoki (1996, 118).

3.2.2 Multiplicity of the Microeconomic Configurations

For clarity, now we adopt a more elegant formulation cited from These descriptions are cited from Aoki (1996, 139–141), instead of employing a direct expression in Chapter 8 of the textbook Aoki (2003, 98–101). The total number of states is set N. The $n(t)$ indicates the state variable. We have ${}_N C_n$ ways to realize **the same** $\frac{n}{N}$. In other words, the equilibrium distribution gives the idea of multiplicity of the microconfiguration that produces the same macro value. By use of $\frac{n}{N}$, we employ a variable x such that

$$\frac{x+1}{2} = \frac{n}{N}. \tag{3.7}$$

x measures the fraction from the median. It follows

$$dx = \frac{2}{N}. \tag{3.8}$$

The base e Shannon entropy, by use of the above variable x, is given by

$$H(x) = -\frac{1+x}{2} \ln \frac{1+x}{2} - \frac{1-x}{2} \ln \frac{1-x}{2}. \tag{3.9}$$

It also is verified

$$\frac{dH}{dx} = \frac{1}{2} \ln \frac{1-x}{1+x}. \tag{3.10}$$

The approximation formula thus gives

$$_N C_n = \exp\left[NH\left(\frac{x+1}{2}\right)\right] + O(\frac{1}{N}). \tag{3.11}$$

3.2.3 *The Microeconomic Birth-and-Death Process in a Discrete Form*

Now suppose that the number of microeconomic agents in this subclass is reduced by one(a death), and the number of agents increases by one (a birth). It then follows the master equation in the discrete case:

$$P_{t+1}(n) = W_{n-1,n} P_t(n-1) + W_{n+1,n} P_t(n+1) + W_{n,n} P_t(n), \tag{3.12}$$

where $W_{n,n-1}$ is the probability of transition rate from state n to $n-1$, and where $W_{n,n+1}$ denotes the probability of transition from n to $n-1$.

Let the time step to be small enough.

$$W_{n,n} = 1 - W_{n,n+1} + W_{n,n-1}. \tag{3.13}$$

expresses the probability that the number of agents may remain the same, normally as assumed to be positive.

The detailed balance condition

$$\Pi(n) W_{n,n+1} = \Pi(n+1) W_{n+1,n} \tag{3.14}$$

gives the equilibrium probability Π's. The equilibrium probability distribution will form a *Gibbs distribution*.

The solution of the above difference equation gives

$$\Pi(n) = \Pi(0) \prod_{k=1}^{n} \frac{W_{k-1,k}}{W_{k,k-1}}. \tag{3.15}$$

In the simplest case, a death shows $W_{n-1,n}$, while a birth $W_{n,n+1}$. Thus, for some constants μ, λ, it holds

$$W_{n,n-1} = \mu n$$
$$W_{n,n+1} = \lambda(N - n).$$

In the following, we set for convenience

$$\mu = \lambda.$$

Let $u_i(x)$ to be a *perceived random benefit*

over some unspecified planning horizon of adopting alternative i when fraction x of agents are using it (Aoki 1996, 138).

Given the two choices 1 and 2, we define the **benefit difference** between two states[6] :

$$\triangle G = \pi_1(x) - \pi_2(x). \tag{3.16}$$

$$\eta_1(x) = \Pr(\pi_1(x) \geq \pi_2(x)). \tag{3.17}$$

Taking some **nonlinear effects** into account, we assume

$$W_{n,n-1} = N\left(1 - \frac{n}{N}\right)\eta_1 \frac{n}{N}, \tag{3.18}$$

$$W_{n,n+1} = N\left(\frac{n}{N}\right)\eta_2 \frac{n}{N}. \tag{3.19}$$

[6]In a continuous case, we may make

$$\eta_1(x) = \frac{\exp[\beta \triangle \pi(x)]}{\exp[\beta \triangle \pi(x)] + \exp[-\beta \triangle \pi(x)]}.$$

Here β expresses a degree of uncertainty over the concerned system.

The **potential** is given

$$-\beta NU\left(\frac{n}{N}\right) - \ln Z = \ln \Pi(0) + \ln_N C_n + \sum^{n} \ln \frac{\eta_1(k/N)}{\eta_2(k/N)}.$$

Here

$$Z = \sum_n \exp[-\beta NU\left(\frac{n}{N}\right)] < \infty \tag{3.20}$$

is the **partition function**.

We set

$$\ln \frac{\eta_1(k/N)}{\eta_2(k/N)} = 2\beta\Delta G\left(\frac{k}{N}\right).$$

According to Aoki (1996, 141), we can interpret β with

> **the degree of uncertainty** in the economic environment surrounding agents, or the general level of economic activity.

Then **the equilibrium probability** can be expressed by

$$\Pi(n) = \frac{\exp[-\beta NU\left(\frac{n}{N}\right)]}{Z} \tag{3.21}$$

Neglecting the items $O(1/N)$, it follows:

$$U\left(\frac{n}{N}\right) = -\frac{2}{N}\sum_{k=1}^{n} \Delta G\left(\frac{k}{N}\right) - \frac{1}{\beta}H\left(\frac{n}{N}\right). \tag{3.22}$$

Hence,[7]

$$U(x) \approx -\int \Delta G(y)\mathrm{d}y - \frac{1}{\beta}H(x) \tag{3.23}$$

$$= -G(x) - \frac{1}{\beta}H(x). \tag{3.24}$$

Taking the relations obtained in the above preliminaries into consideration,

$$\frac{\mathrm{d}U(x)}{\mathrm{d}x} \approx -\Delta G(x) - \frac{1}{2\beta}\ln\frac{1-x}{1+x}. \tag{3.25}$$

[7]If $\Delta G = 0$, it holds the simple birth-and -death process.

In the equilibrium in which the potential never be changed, it holds

$$2\beta \triangle G(x) = \ln \frac{1+x}{1-x}. \tag{3.26}$$

This is just a *Gibbs distribution* derived from the discrete time formulation. This approach rather demonstrates a *qualitative* prediction in social interaction of heterogeneous agents by use of the concept of **equilibrium distribution** or an ensemble mean.

3.2.4 Choice Under Uncertainty and the Multiple Local Equilibria: Cluster Dynamics

Finally, we close this section to take an example employed in Chapter 2 of the textbook Aoki (2003, 17–20). When all the members in this system succeed to maximize their utilities, the system can reach the level of $u(a)$. If some of the members failed to maximize utility, the level of the system could go down to $u(b)$. In other words, the system may be constituted by the two groups, one of which is successful for optimization, the other of which failed optimization. We may construct the average utility by

$$pu_1 + (1-p)u_2,$$

where p is the ratio of the failure subgroup (Fig. 3.3).

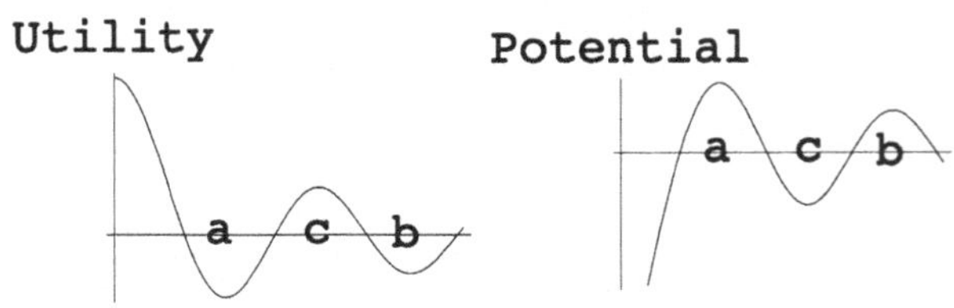

Fig. 3.3 Utility and potential

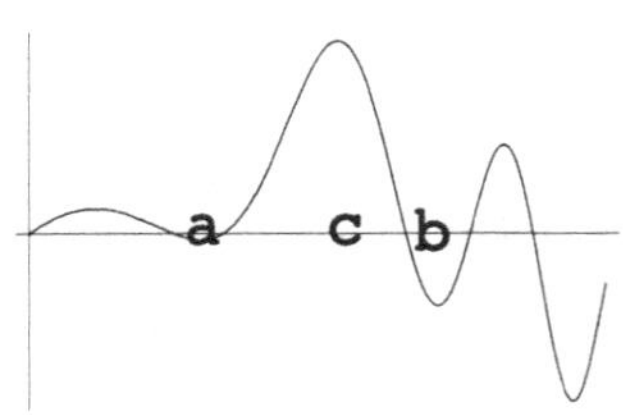

Fig. 3.4 Critical states in terms of potential

The state point a and b are the equilibrium points. Between them we imagine a Markov process by employing the transition rates[8]

$$w_{ab} = \mathrm{e}^{-\beta(V+v)}$$
$$w_{ba} = \mathrm{e}^{-\beta V}, \ \beta > 0.$$

On the side of potential, we assume

$$v = V_b - V_a > 0.$$

It then follows from the equation (3.4) that

$$\pi_a = \frac{w_{ba}}{w_{ba} + w_{ab}} = \frac{1}{\mathrm{e}^{\eta v + 1}} \tag{3.27}$$

$$\pi_b = 1 - \pi_a = \frac{\mathrm{e}^{\beta v}}{\mathrm{e}^{\beta v + 1} + 1}. \tag{3.28}$$

If v is taken small enough,

$$\pi_a \approx \pi_b \to \frac{1}{2}.$$

This system then has equally **two local equilibria**. Either of them can equally occur.

First passage times of unstable dynamics Measured in the levels of potential, the figure suggests an unstable situation of the macroeconomic states. There are three critical points arranged as

$$\phi_a \geq \phi_b \geq \phi_c.$$

Here ϕ is a macroeconomic state. We take ϕ_a the initial state and ϕ_c the final state. The final state may be interpreted an absorbing state (Fig. 3.4).

van Kampen (1992) and Aoki (1996, Sect. 5.11) showed that a **passage time** τ_{ca} from c to a is given by

$$\tau_{ca} \propto \mathrm{e}^{\beta N V(v)}.$$

> **the critical values** of the potential are the critical points of the equilibrium probability distribution $[P_i(n)]$ and are the same as **the critical points** of the macroeconomic dynamics. (Aoki 1996, 142)

[8] As β changes, the number of equilibrium changes.

3.3 Preliminaries for the Stochastic Cluster Dynamics in the Case That Types Are Unknown

3.3.1 The Elementary Polya Process

Now we turn to illustrate an elementary **Polya Urn Process**, which was just introduced into Economics by Brian Arhtur, **Snata Fe Institute** and also generalized by him and others,[9] which has been applicable to illustrate *a path-dependent process* as well as to confirm an evolutionary end point like industrial locational by spin-off, and a dual autocatalytic chemical reaction, and the like.[10] According to Arthur, **Polya Urn Process**, which was formulated by Polya and Eggenberger (1923), can be illustrated as follows:

> Think of an urn of infinite capacity to which are added balls of two possible colors - red and white, say. Starting with one red and one white ball in the urn, add a ball each time, indefinitely, according to the rule: Choose a ball in the urn at random and replace it: if it is red, add a red; if it is white, add a white. Obviously, this process has increments that are path-dependent - at any time the probability that the next ball added is red exactly equals the proportion. We might then ask: does the proportion of red (or white) balls wander indefinitely between zero and one, or does a strong law operate, so that the proportion settles down to a limit, causing a structure to emerge?

Arthur called a limit **proportion** in such a path dependent stochastic process an asymptotic **structure**. As long as the classical proposition of two balls is considered, we shall be faced with a limit of proportion, i.e., a simple structure, as Polya proved in Polya (1931). In the classical Polya example, we have a restriction such that the probability of adding a ball of type j exactly equals the proportion of type j. In the following, we will see a generalization of Polya urn process of n different balls (types) which Arthur challenged in cooperation with Ukranian mathematicians, and furthermore a more generalization to **the Ewens distribution** in Ewens (1990).

The original Polya urn model Suppose k kinds of balls $\alpha_1, \alpha_2, \ldots, \alpha_k$ in an urn. Here we introduce the stochastic variables $X_1, X_2, \ldots, X_k$ to regard X_k as the ball colored k. These balls may be distinguished by color, weight, and so on. Take out a ball, check the color of the ball, and add the same colored ball to the urn. Repeat the same procedure n times to take n_j balls. It is then generated $n = n_1 + \cdots + n_k$ in total. Hence there are $\alpha_j + n$ balls in the urn. Thus the probability to take the ball colored j is $\frac{\alpha_j + n_j}{\alpha + n}$. Here it is noted that the emergence of colors is irrelevant to the order of color emergence. This circumstance is relevant to the idea of exchangeability to be illustrated soon later. At this stage, $X_1, X_2, \ldots, X_n$ are the stochastic variable

[9] Yuri M. Ermoliev and Yuri M. Kaniovski, the Glushkov Institute of Cybernetics, Kiev, Ukraina, originally have proved some generalized theorems.

[10] See Chaps. 3, 7 and 10 in Arthur (1994).

of exchangeability. In this view, we regard the state vector of the Polya distribution function as follows:

$$n = (n_1, n_2, \ldots, n_k).$$

Denote the set of color i by S_i. Thus, we can represent the probability to take the ball colored j in the following manner:

$$Pr(X_{n+1} \in S_j | n_1, N_2, \ldots, N_k) = \frac{\alpha_j + n_j}{\alpha + n}. \tag{3.29}$$

Here $\alpha = \sum_{i=1}^{k} \alpha_i$. As for a state vector n and $n' \neq n$, it holds the detailed balance condition:

$$\pi(n)p(n'|n) = \pi(n')p(n|n'). \tag{3.30}$$

Hence, we obtain the detailed balance condition in this case:

A derivation of the Polya distribution function We specify n' as a state where an agent of type j transitions to the agent of type k as follows:

$$n' = n - e_j + e_k.$$

Here e_j is the unit vector where only j-th component is 1 excepting all the others 0. In order to confirm the detailed balance condition on this transition, we can refer to the next probabilities as follows: The probability that an agent of type j leaves by one:

$$P(n - e_j|n) = \frac{n_j}{n}$$

The probability that an agent of type k enter by one:

$$P(n + e_k|n) = \frac{\alpha_k + n_k}{\alpha + n}$$

The probability that an agent of type j transitions type k, also an agent of type k enters:

$$P(n - e_j + e_k|n - e_j) = \frac{\alpha_k + n_k}{\alpha + n - 1}. \tag{3.31}$$

Thus, assuming the stationary distribution to be the form of

$$\pi(n) = \pi_1(n_1)\pi_2(n_2)\cdots\pi_k(n_k), \tag{3.32}$$

it follows the next relationship:

$$\pi(n)=\frac{P(n|n')}{P(n'|n)}\pi(n')=\frac{n_k+1}{n_j}\frac{\alpha_j+n_j-1}{\alpha_k+n_k}\pi(n'). \tag{3.33}$$

Hence we can assure for $l=1,\ldots,k$:

$$\pi_l(n_l)=c\frac{\alpha_l+n_l-1}{n_l}\pi_l(n_l-1) \tag{3.34}$$

Here c is some constant.[11] By the successive iteration,[12] we found that $\pi_l(n_l)$ would be proportional to $\frac{\alpha_i^{[n_i]}}{n_i!}$., i.e.,

$$\pi(n)=\Pi_{l=1}^k\pi_l(n_l)\propto\Pi_{i=1}^k\frac{\alpha_i^{[n_i]}}{n_i!}. \tag{3.35}$$

Under the condition $\sum_n^k\pi(n)=1$, it holds:

$$\pi(n)=\frac{n!}{\alpha^{[n]}}\Pi_{i=1}^k\frac{\alpha_i^{[n_i]}}{n!}=\frac{n!}{n_1!\cdots n_k!}\frac{\Pi_{i=1}^n\alpha_i^{[n_i]}}{\alpha^{[n_i]}} \tag{3.36}$$

We then call this expression **the Polya distribution function**.

From the Polya distribution to the Dirichlet distribution It is quite useful in practice to know the approximation. Let the population of agents to be composed by agent type j whose ratio is allocated by p_j for $\sum_{j=1}^k p_j=1$ for $p_j\geq 0$ which is defined on:

$$\Delta=\left\{p_i\geq 0, i=1,\ldots,k,\sum_{j=1}^k p_j=1\right\}.$$

11

$$\frac{\pi_j(n_j)}{\pi_j(n_j-1)}\frac{n_j}{\alpha_j+n_j-1}=\frac{\pi_k(n_k+1)}{\pi_k(n_k)}\frac{n_{k+1}}{\alpha_k+n_k}=c.$$

12 It is noted that

$$\alpha_l^{[n_l]}=\alpha_l(\alpha_l+1)\cdots(\alpha_l+n_l-1).$$

This is called the ascending factorial. Hence it then holds:

$$\frac{1}{n_l!}\alpha_l(\alpha_l+1)\cdots(\alpha_l+n_l-1)=\frac{\alpha_l^{[n_l]}}{n_l!}.$$

Given the types of agent that there are n heterogenous agents, this ratio is then will be represented by **the multinomial distribution** for a partition vector $n = (n_1, \ldots, n_k)$:

$$\Pr(n) = \frac{n!}{n_1! \cdots n_k!} p_1^{n_1} \cdots p_k^{n_k}.$$

With $K \geq 2$ the probability distribution δ_K with a simple structure is defined on the simplex δ_K by the density

$$\frac{\Gamma(\sum_{i=1}^K a_i)}{\Pi_{i=1}^K \Gamma(a_i)} \Pi_{i=1}^K p_i^{a_i - 1}$$

where $1 \geq p_i \geq 0, i = 1, 2, \ldots, K-1$, and p_k is substituted out by $1 - p_1 - p_2 - \cdots p_{K-1}$, so that the density is defined for $K - 1$ variables, $p_1, p_2, \ldots, p_{K-1}$. This is called the **Dirichlet distribution** Aoki (2002, 230)

In the case that the expression of $1 - p_1 - p_2 - \cdots p_{K-1}$ is unchanged for any replacement of indices $1, 2, \ldots, k$, i.e., types are *exchangeable*, it then holds the *symmetric* Dirichlet distribution $\vartheta(p, \alpha)$ for some parameter $\alpha \geq 0$.

$$\Phi(p_1, p_2, \ldots, p_k) = \frac{\Gamma(k\alpha)}{\Gamma(\alpha)^k} (p_1, \ldots, p_k)^{\alpha - 1}. \tag{3.37}$$

In short, according to Aoki, it follows:

Chen (1978) introduced a distribution that a mixure of multinomial distribution where the mixture is a symmetric (exchangeable) Dirichlet distribution and has shown that his Dirichlet-multinomial distribution reduces to the Bose-Einstein and maxwell-Bolzmann distributions. Aoki (1996, 13)

In the later section when we deal with the majority voting paradox, we will employ an approximation of the Polya distribution by the Dirichlet continuous distribution if n is a large number.

Among excellent evolutionary models of evolutionary economics, I have learned the Polya urn distribution from Brian Arthur (Arthur 1994), and also learned the Master equation from Wolfgang Weidlich (Weidlich 2000). These studies have decisively been influential to renovate my way of thinking about the emergence of events in general until I meet the works of Professor Masanao Aoki. In retrospect, the latter works have been different in the standpoint to observe the events, although either works are dealing with the same kinds of nonlinear phenomena. In particular, in the finite discrete domain, Aoki mainly focused on the economic motions of heterogeneous agents whose activities can be categorized by *type selection*, but those can be *exchangeable*. The latter characteristics may be in line with *Bose-Einstein* form of **the classic occupancy problem**, contrary to the distinguishable *Maxwell-Boltzmann* form.

Definition 1 Two vectors x and y are called exchangeable if the empirical distribution of the two vectors are the same.

3.3.2 A Flat Prior for Our Stochastic Dynamics

We are interested in studying the evolution allowing the advent of new types, under which circumstances Bayesian approach is invalid. Also in Bayesian approach, if we have no prior information available, a commonly used non-information prior distribution has a uniform distribution as Non-informative, NI it then is called **a flat prior distribution**. Alternatively, we must look for **a specific prior** for our own purpose.

de Finetti representation Aoki (2002, 220–1) Suppose each of the exchangeable sequences whose frequency vector is the same to be equally probable. It then holds

$$\Pr(X_1, X_2, \dots, X_n \mid n) = \frac{n_1! n_2! \cdots n_K!}{n!}$$

where $n = n_1 + n_2 + \cdots + n_K$. The observed frequency counts n_j are called **sufficient statistics.**[13]

We have **the de Finetti representation theorem** for exchangeable sequences: if an infinite sequence of k-valued random variables $X_1, X_2, \dots$ is exchangeable, then the infinite limiting frequency

$$Z := \lim_{N \to \infty} \left(\frac{n_1}{N}, \frac{n_2}{N}, \cdots, \frac{n_K}{N} \right),$$

and if $\mu(A) = \Pr(Z \in A)$ denotes the distribution of this limiting frequency, then,

$$\Pr(X_1 = e_1, X_2 = e_2, \dots, X_N = e_N)$$
$$= \int_{\Delta_K} p_1^{n_1} p_2^{n_2} \cdots p_K^{n_K} \, d\mu(p_1, p_2, \dots, p_{K-1}).$$

Johnson sufficientness postulate Here we show the derivation of a flat prior for our stochastic dynamics. By virtue of **Johnson sufficientness postulate**, it uniquely determines $d\mu$[14] as a flat prior as follows:

$$\Pr(X_{N+1} = c_i | X_1, X_2, \dots, X_N) = \Pr(X_{N+1} = c_i | n) = f(n_i, n), \tag{3.38}$$

if $\Pr(X_1 = c_1, \dots., X_N = c_N) > 0$ for all c's.

---

[13]These probabilities conditional on the frequency counts depend only on n. They also are independent of the choice of the exchangeable probability P.

[14]

$$d\mu(p_1, p_2, \dots, p_K) = d(p_1, p_2, \dots, p_{K-1})$$

3.3.3 The Partition Vector and the Transition Rates

The multinomial distribution will not be applied to the case that the types of agents in the economic system are *unknown*. In such a circumstance, it does not hold the Bayesian learning may be valid. Instead of using **the state vector**, we rather use **the partition vector** $a = (a_1, a_2, \ldots, a_n)$ where its component a_j is the number of boxes in which there are j balls. That is to say, we study the so-called occupancy problem in the case of n indistinguishable balls. In Aoki (2003), it is mentioned several application examples to explain the partition vector: $a_{50} = 3$ means 3 different rules which 50 traders currently use when traders are dealing with financial commodities. If we take an example of insect collecting, $a_4 = 5$ means 5 subsets in which group there are 4 insects of the same kind each. The subset of these groups may be called the cluster of size i.

It is trivial that

$$a_j = 0 \text{ for } j = 1, \ldots, n-1; a_n = 1,$$

if all the agents use the same rule.

$$a_1 = n, a_j = 0 \text{ for } j = 2, \ldots, n,$$

if each agent follows each independent rule.

If we assume that agents are not distinguishable even in different categories, that is, exchangeable in the technical terminology of the probability literature then the total number of possible configurations is given by

$$W(N) = \Pi_j \frac{(N_j + g_j - 1)!}{N_j!(g_j - 1)!},$$

where g_j is the number of possible microeconomic states that an agent can assume.[15] Aoki (1996, 13).

Type i belongs to a subset of size i. This subset is called the cluster. Here,

$$a_i = \#\{n_j = i, j = 1, \ldots, k\}, i = 1, \ldots, n.$$

If we introduce the following function

$$\chi_j(i) = \begin{cases} 1, & n_j = i \\ 0, & n_j \neq i \end{cases}$$

$$a_i = \sum_{j=1}^{K} \chi_j(i).$$

[15] Recall that the number of ways n identical balls can be placed in g boxes is given by $(n + g - 1)!/n!(g - 1)!$.

In this context, by the use of transition rate among the clusters, we can derive the stationary equilibrium state distribution. Suppose to be n discrete number of clusters categorized by the finite types among where each agent freely moves. If one quits from the cluster size of j, the size of its cluster a_j will be reduced $a_j - 1$, correspondingly while a_{j-1} will be $a_{j-1} + 1$. If we define

$$u_j = e_j - e_{j-1},$$ [16]

it then holds the conditional transition rate:

$$P(a - u|a) = \frac{ja_j}{n}. \tag{3.39}$$

Conversely, if an agent joins in the crowds of size j, a crowd of size $j + 1$ increases while the crowds of size j will be reduced by one. The transition rate of this event, which means that an agent leaves from the crowd of size j and joins in a crowd of size $i - 1$, will be described as follows:

$$\Pr(a - u_j + u_i|a - u_j).$$

3.3.4 *From Negative Binomial Distribution to Ewens Distribution*

Now we are ready to derive the equilibrium distribution as an **Ewens distribution**.

3.3.4.1 Example 1

We firstly assume the transition rates in the next three different manners:

$w(a, a + e_1) = \nu\lambda$: Agents enter in the system but do not belong to any existing boxes. New agents then form e_1, a subset of size 1.
$w(a, a + u_{j+1} = \lambda j a_j)$: An agent joins by one in the crowd of size j.
$w(a, a - u_{j+1} = \mu j a_j)$: An agent exits by one from the crowd of size j.

It hen holds the detailed balance condition:

$$\pi(a)w(a, a + u_{j+1} = \pi(a + u_{j+1})w(a + u_{j+1}, a). \tag{3.40}$$

[16] e_j is a unit vector where the j-th component is 1 while all the components except for j are zero.

Thus the equilibrium distribution of this case will be solved as follows:

$$\pi(a) = \left(1 - \frac{\lambda}{\mu}\right) \Pi_{j=1}^{\infty} \frac{\beta_j^{[a_j]}}{a_j!}.^{17} \tag{3.41}$$

Here it is defined:

$$\beta_j = \frac{\nu}{j} \left(\frac{\lambda}{\mu}\right)^j,$$

$$\beta_j^{[a_j]} = \beta_j(\beta_j + 1) \cdots (\beta_j + a_j).$$

3.3.4.2 Example 2

Similarly in the above argument, suppose the transition rate of entry to be

$$w(n, n + e_j) = \frac{h_i + n_i}{h + n}.$$

Here $h = \sum_{i=1}^{K} h_i$, $n = \sum_i^K n_i$. It then holds the recursive relationship from the detailed balance condition for $j = 1, \ldots, K, n_j \geq 0$.

$$\pi_j(n_j) = (\frac{c_j}{d_j}) \frac{n_j - 1 + h_j}{n_j} \pi_j(n_j - 1) \tag{3.42}$$

We then confirm the next **negative binomial expression**[18] :

$$\pi_j(n_j) = c_j \binom{-h_j}{n_j} \left(-\frac{c_j}{d_j}\right)^{n_j} \tag{3.43}$$

---

[17] By taking into account the next formula,

$$\frac{1}{(1-x)^{\nu}} = \Pi_{j=1}^{\infty} \exp \frac{\nu x^j}{j},$$

it is easily verified $\sum_a \pi(a) = 1$.

[18] The negative binomial expression will be described as follows:

$$\begin{aligned} \binom{-n}{k} &= \frac{(-n)(-n-1) \cdots (-n-k-1)}{k!} \\ &= \frac{(n)(n+1) \cdots (n+k-1)}{k!} (-1)^k \\ &= \binom{n+k-1}{k} \end{aligned}$$

Thus the stationary distribution of this system will be given:

$$\pi(n) = \binom{-\sum_j h_j}{\sum_j n_j}^{-1} \Pi_{j=1}^{K} \binom{-h_j}{n_j} \tag{3.44}$$

For simplicity, let c_j/d_j to be all common to g for all j. It then holds

$$\pi(n) = \frac{n!}{h^{[n]}} \Pi_{j=1}^{k} \frac{h_j^{[n_j]}}{n_j!}. \tag{3.45}$$

3.4 Majority Rule for Voting and the Tree Structure

In social choice theory, it is quite well known the Possibility Theorem proven by Arrow (1951), when one must choose an alternative from a given multiple alternatives. That is to say, the transitivity rule socially generated by the voting aggregation will cause a social contradiction, i.e., a possibility that only one agent may fulfill any social outcome of socially formed ordering by the majority voting. This is a logically inferred deduction. In the context of Prof. Aoki, however, this possibility may be neglected if the number of alternatives is large.[19] Incidentally, this part has not been found either in Aoki (1996) or Aoki (2002) in his books of the fifth stage. So, we then deserve referring to this example.

3.4.1 A Stochastic Assessment on the Majority Voting Rule

According to Aoki (2003, 78–79), it is shown that there may be few emergence of Arrow's contradiction by applying the Polya urn theory. Let K be 3 in the following. By the Polya theory, we attach color respectively each ordering of the alternative A, B, C. Suppose to allocate six different colors to the next ordering:

$$A \succ B \succ C, A \succ C \succ B, B \succ A \succ C, A \succ C \succ A, C \succ A \succ B, C \succ A \succ B.$$

Suppose also n to be:

$$n = n_1 + n_2 + \cdots + n_6 \text{ for } i = 1, 2, \ldots, 6$$

[19]The stream of a probablistic view on Arrow's theorem was initiated by Williamson and Sargent (1967). As for Sen's theorem in view of a probablistic theory, see Li and Saari (2008). Also see Aruka (2015) on an assessment of the standard choice theory in view of imperfect identification.

Thus it follows the partition vector on the concerned distribution that

$$P(n) = \frac{n!}{n_1!n_2!\cdots n_6!} \frac{a^{[\sigma,n_1]}\cdots a^{[\sigma,n_6]}}{6a^{[\sigma,n_6]}}. \tag{3.46}$$

Here $a^{[\sigma,n]}$ is the ascending factorial:

$$a^{[\sigma,n]} = a(a+\sigma)(a+2\sigma)\cdots(a+(n-1)\sigma).$$

The expression (3.46) means in the Polya urn that there exist a balls in the urn at the beginning, and after identifying the color of taken balls, σ balls of the same colored in return added in the urn. It is then denoted q by a/σ.

While applying the **Stirling formula** for large factorials to q,[20] it holds:

$$a^{[\sigma,n]} = a(a+\sigma)(a+2\sigma)\cdots(a+(n-1)\sigma) \tag{3.47}$$

$$= \sigma^n q(1+q)(2+q)\cdots(n_{i-1}+q) \tag{3.48}$$

$$\simeq \sigma^n \frac{\Gamma(n_i+q)}{\Gamma(q)}. \tag{3.49}$$

Hence

$$P(n) \sim \sigma^n \frac{\Gamma(6q)}{\Gamma(q)^6} \Pi_{i=1}^6 p_i^{q-1}$$

Here

$$p_i = \frac{n_i}{n} \geq 0, \sum_{i=1}^{6} p_i = 1.$$

Aoki (2003, 86–87) has shown that the alternative A will be assessed as the majority among the alternatives if the above density function is integrable on the domain that

$$p_1 + p_2 + p_3 \geq \frac{1}{2} \text{ and } p_1 + p_2 + p_5 \geq \frac{1}{2}. \tag{3.50}$$

these conditions naturally imply that

$$A \succ C \text{ and } A \succ B$$

both hold, then always confirm A as the majority. This situation will naturally remove the Arrow paradox.

[20] $\Gamma(n_i+q) \simeq \sqrt{2\pi} e^{-n_i} n_i^{n_i+q-(1/2)}$.

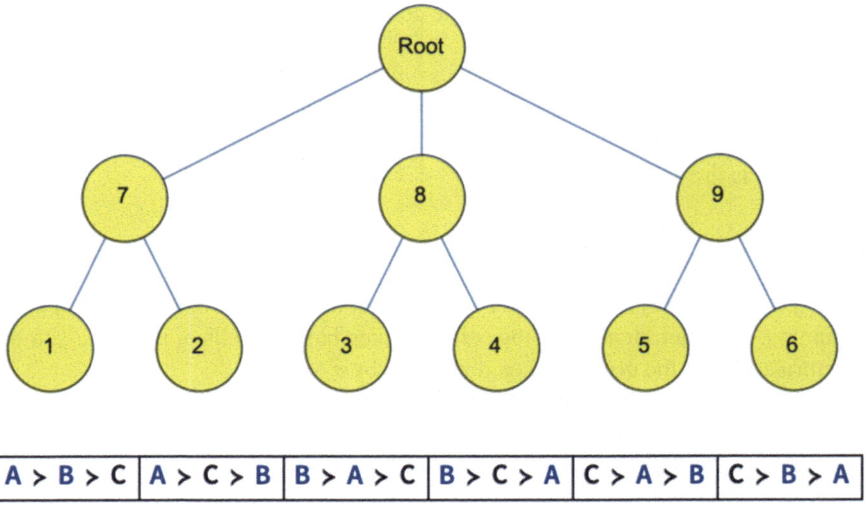

Fig. 3.5 Majority rule and the ultrametrics

3.4.2 A Tree Dynamics

On the contrary, it is interestingly to see an ultimate attainment through the transitions among the leaves of alternative orderings, when starting from an initial conditions (3.50). We firstly construct a tree dynamics by applying the ultrametrics to the tree structure represented by Fig. 3.5 to obtain the next master equation system on the transition dynamics among the alternatives. In the case of our tree structure, it is seen that

$$d(1,2) = d(2,1) = d(3,4) = d(4,3) = d(5,6) = d(6,5) = \epsilon_1 = 1$$

As for the other pairs of (i, j),

$$d(i, j) = d(j, i) = \epsilon_2 = 2.$$

Hence, we can formulate the transition state equation system on this transition dynamics:

$$\begin{aligned}
p_1'(t) &= \epsilon_1 (p_2(t) - p_1(t)) + \epsilon_2 (-4p_1(t) + p_3(t) + p_4(t) + p_5(t) + p_6(t)) \\
p_2'(t) &= \epsilon_1 (p_1(t) - p_2(t)) + \epsilon_2 (-4p_2(t) + p_3(t) + p_4(t) + p_5(t) + p_6(t)) \\
p_3'(t) &= \epsilon_1 (p_4(t) - p_3(t)) + \epsilon_2 (p_1(t) + p_2(t) - 4p_3(t) + p_5(t) + p_6(t)) \quad (3.51) \\
p_4'(t) &= \epsilon_1 (p_3(t) - p_4(t)) + \epsilon_2 (p_1(t) + p_2(t) - 4p_4(t) + p_5(t) + p_6(t))
\end{aligned}$$

$$P_5'(t) = \epsilon_1 \left(p_6(t) - p_5(t)\right) + \epsilon_2 \left(p_1(t) + p_2(t) + p_3(t) + p_4(t) - 4p_5(t)\right)$$
$$p_6'(t) = \epsilon_1 \left(p_5(t) - p_6(t)\right) + \epsilon_2 \left(p_1(t) + p_2(t) + p_3(t) + p_4(t) - 4p_6(t)\right)$$

We then look for the initial values to satisfy the conditions (3.50). We may then allocate the initial values such that

$$p_1(0) = 0.2,\ p_2(0) = 0.2,\ p_3(0) = 0.2,\ p_4(0) = 0.1,\ p_5(0) = 0.2,\ p_6(0) = 0.2.$$

It then holds that

$$\begin{aligned}
p_1(t) &= 0.166667e^{-6t\epsilon_2-2t(\epsilon_1+2\epsilon_2)}\left(0.2e^{2t(\epsilon_1+2\epsilon_2)} + 1.e^{6t\epsilon_2+2t(\epsilon_1+2\epsilon_2)}\right),\\
p_2(t) &= 0.166667e^{-6t\epsilon_2-2t(\epsilon_1+2\epsilon_2)}\left(0.2e^{2t(\epsilon_1+2\epsilon_2)} + 1.e^{6t\epsilon_2+2t(\epsilon_1+2\epsilon_2)}\right),\\
p_3(t) &= 0.166667e^{-6t\epsilon_2-2t(\epsilon_1+2\epsilon_2)}\left(0.3e^{6t\epsilon_2} - 0.1e^{2t(\epsilon_1+2\epsilon_2)} + 1.e^{6t\epsilon_2+2t(\epsilon_1+2\epsilon_2)}\right),\\
p_4(t) &= 0.166667e^{-6t\epsilon_2-2t(\epsilon_1+2\epsilon_2)}\left(-0.3e^{6t\epsilon_2} - 0.1e^{2t(\epsilon_1+2\epsilon_2)} + 1.e^{6t\epsilon_2+2t(\epsilon_1+2\epsilon_2)}\right),\\
p_5(t) &= 0.166667e^{-6t\epsilon_2-2t(\epsilon_1+2\epsilon_2)}\left(0.3e^{6t\epsilon_2} - 0.1e^{2t(\epsilon_1+2\epsilon_2)} + 1.e^{6t\epsilon_2+2t(\epsilon_1+2\epsilon_2)}\right),\\
p_6(t) &= 0.166667e^{-6t\epsilon_2-2t(\epsilon_1+2\epsilon_2)}\left(-0.3e^{6t\epsilon_2} - 0.1e^{2t(\epsilon_1+2\epsilon_2)} + 1.e^{6t\epsilon_2+2t(\epsilon_1+2\epsilon_2)}\right).
\end{aligned} \tag{3.52}$$

Now we may examine how our transition system will eventually evolve into the final situation, according to each initial condition. We focus on the first condition of $p_1(0) = 0.2$, $p_2(0) = 0.2$, $p_3(0) = 0.2$ to how the ratio will be changed by transition among the nodes.

$$p_1 + p_2 + p_3 \to 0.51 \text{ as } t \to \infty.$$

It is interesting to know that $A \succ C$ will still be guaranteed as the majority. As for on the second condition of $p_1(0) = 0.2$, $p_2(0) = 0.2$, $p_r50) = 0.2$, it also then holds:

$$p_1 + p_2 + p_5 \to 0.51 \text{ as } t \to \infty.$$

This suggests that $A \succ B$ will still be guaranteed as the majorityness. In summing up, the majority of A will be eventually guaranteed even through transition among the nodes if we start the initial ratio of $p_1(0) = 0.2$, $p_2(0) = 0.2$, $p_3(0) = 0.2$, $p_4(0) = 0.1$, $p_5(0) = 0.2$, $p_6(0) = 0.1$. Finally, it is noted that Figs. 3.6 and 3.7 are formally same shaped because the particular solutions are the same forms.

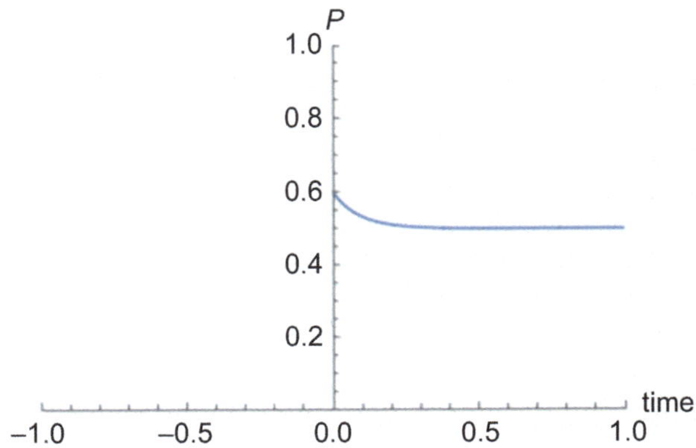

Fig. 3.6 Trajectory of $p_1(t) + p_2(t) + p_3(t)$ given the initial condition $p_1(0) = 0.2, p_2(0) = 0.2, p_3(0) = 0.2, p_4(0) = 0.1, p_5(0) = 0.2, p_6(0) = 0.1$

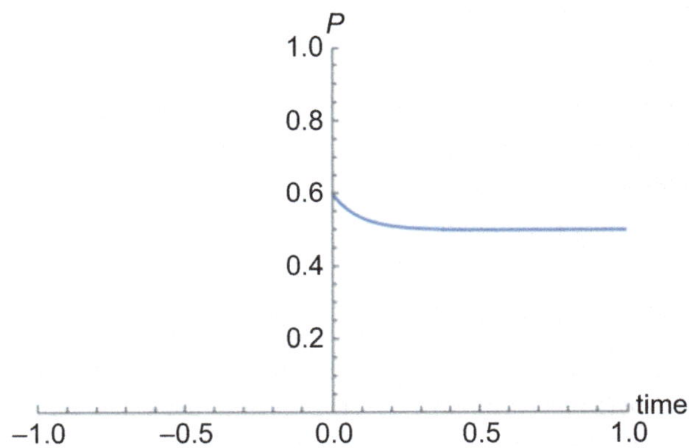

Fig. 3.7 Trajectory of $p_1(t) + p_2(t) + p_5(t)$ given the initial condition $p_1(0) = 0.2, p_2(0) = 0.2, p_3(0) = 0.2, p_4(0) = 0.1, p_5(0) = 0.2, p_6(0) = 0.1$

References

Aoki M (1996) New approaches to macroeconomic modeling: evolutionary stochastic dynamics, multiple equilibria, and externalities as field effects. Cambridge University Press, New York, 288pp

Aoki M (2002) Modeling aggregate behavior and fluctuations in economics: stochastic views of interacting agents. Cambridge University Press, New York, 263pp

Aoki M (2003) Ishitsuteki e-jennto no Kakuritsudougaku nyumon (Introduction to stochastic dynamic approach of heterogeneous interacting agents). Kyoritisu Publishing Co. Ltd., Tokyo, 187pp

Aoki M, Yoshikawa H (2006) Reconstructing macroeconomics: a perspective from statistical physics and combinatorial stochastic processes. Cambridge University Press, New York, 333pp

Arrow KJ (1951) Alternative approaches to the theory of choice in risk-taking situations. Econometrica 19(4):404–437

Arthur WB (1994) Increasing returns and path dependence in the economy. University of Michigan Press, Ann Arbor. Japanese edition

Aruka Y (2015) Hodgson's bibliometric report and the reconstruction plan of economics. Evol Inst Econ Rev 15(1):189–202

Aruka Y, Akiyama E (2009) Non-self-averaging of a two-person game with only positive spillover: a new formulation of Avatamsaka's dilemma. J Econ Interac Coord 4(2):135–161

Aruka Y, Gallegati M, Yoshikawa H (2015) Preface: special issue in honor of Masanao Aoki. J Econ Interac Coord 10(1):1–4

Cawley J, Meinberg F (2011) Macroeconomic effects of interest rate cuts. Wolfram Demonstrations Project. http://demonstrations.wolfram.com/MacroeconomicEffectsOfInterestRateCuts/

Chen W-C (1978) On Zipf's law. Ph.D. dissertation, University of Michigan, Ann Arbor

Ewens WJ (1990) Population genetics theory – the past and the future. In: Lessard S (ed) Mathematical and statistical development of evolutionary theory. Kluwer Academic Publishers, London, pp 81–104

Li L, Saari DG (2008) Sen's theorem: geometric proof, new interpretations. Soc Choice Welf 31(3):383–413

Polya G (1931) Sur quelques points de la théorie des probabilités. Annales de l'Institut Henri Poancaré 1:117–161

Polya G, Eggenberger F (1923) Uëber die statistik verketteter vorgange. Zeitschrift für Angewandte Mathematik und Mechanik 3:279–289

van Kampen NG (1992) Stochastic process in physics and chemistry. North Holland, Amsterdam. Revised edition

Weidlich W (2000) Sociodynamics. Harwood Academic Publisher, London. English edition

Williamson OE, Sargent TJ (1967) Social choice: a probabilistic approach. Econ J 77(308):797–813

Chapter 4
Masanao Aoki's Solution to the Finite Size Effect of Behavioral Finance Models

Thomas Lux

Abstract This chapter provides an appraisal of Aoki's solution to the finite size effect that plagues many agent-based models in behavioral finance. Combining an asset pricing model with an elementary process for the choice of strategies his model predicts that under relatively mild conditions, markets will be dominated by a small number of clusters of agents choosing identical strategies.

Keywords Agent-based models · Jump Markov models · Strategy choice

JEL codes: D4, D7, G0

4.1 Introduction: Memoirs and Dedication

In 1993, Masanao Aoki gave an invited plenary talk at the annual meeting of the Society for Economic Dynamics and Control that appeared in print in 1994 in the society's house journal under the title "New Macroeconomic Modelling Approaches: Hierarchical Dynamics and Mean-Field Approximation" (Aoki 1994). This article signaled an important change in the research agenda of the then 63-year old scholar: Masanao who at this time had been looking back on a very successful career that had established him as one of the leading specialists on the application of optimal control theory, dynamic system theory, and state-space models in economics, at retirement age embarked on a complete new agenda. While others at this age might have a tendency to nourish exotic interests and fiddle around with methods and theories outside their primary field of expertise, Masanao rather initiated a new field of research once more and became one of its main authorities. His endeavor for new directions was of the greatest earnestness and his contributions were as profound and technically ambitious as all the work he had contributed

T. Lux (✉)
Department of Economics, University of Kiel, Kiel, Germany
e-mail: lux@economics.uni-kiel.de

H. Aoyama et al. (eds.), *Complexity, Heterogeneity, and the Methods of Statistical Physics in Economics*, Evolutionary Economics and Social Complexity Science 22,
https://doi.org/10.1007/978-981-15-4806-2_4

before. Over the following 25 years, he indeed contributed an enormous body of research, part of which is well summarized in his three books (Aoki 1996, 2002; Aoki and Yoshikawa 2006) that all became landmarks of the emerging literature on economic models with interacting heterogeneous agents. While the need to move beyond the representative agent was perceived very widely, Masanao's unique position in this nascent community was due to his eagerness to develop analytical tools to understand such models and confront them with data. Such analytical tools were largely missing or unknown at that time.

For me, reading his programmatic 1994 article was a revelation. Already before stumbling over this extraordinary piece, I had developed some interest in the possibility of describing the behavior of ensembles of agents via mean-field approximations and related tools from statistical physics. There had been another very original pioneer of applications of such approaches to the social sciences: The work of Wolfgang Weidlich, professor of theoretical physics at the University of Stuttgart, had already stirred interest in such seemingly esoteric modeling concepts in certain circles, mainly in Germany (most notably through the book Haag and Weidlich 1983). However, to me as a young post-doc this appeared very peripheric to what was pursued within the orthodox mainstream of our field, and less than promising career-wise. It was exciting then to see a person as prominent as Masanao Aoki making the point that such methods would be what we needed to tackle models with heterogeneity and interaction, and asking for an open minded adaptation of what other fields had to offer in this respect. Together with Alan Kirman's famous ant model (Kirman 1993), published at the same time, this convinced me that there was a new and promising research area that was worth to pursue, and it seemed actually more exciting to start to new shores than to work within the sheltered bay of some older, time-honored "orthodox" approach. Many must have felt it this way as the almost explosive growth of the community around the Annual Workshop of Economics with Heterogenous Interacting Agents (WEHIA) shows.

In terms of material economic problems, Masanao's interests were quite broad. As a short glance at his voluminous output shows, most of his work was devoted to problems in macroeconomics and economic growth. However, he also showed vivid interests in other areas such as asset pricing which had perhaps been the most prominent showcase for agent-based modelling in at least the first decade after the launch of the WEHIA community.

Around 2000, the community stumbled across the following problem: If one takes a model with an ensemble of interacting agents, who might follow different strategies, change between strategies, and even be subject to certain social factors of influence (i.e., some form of herding or imitation of others) then increasing the number of agents in the market leads to some law of large numbers. If the agents were treated as independent decision makers (despite their potential tendency to initiate others, they would still decide themselves whether they wanted to imitate the observed trading strategies of others or not) then all "interesting dynamics" that one obtains with a smaller set of agents will inevitably be lost once one allows the number of agents to increase beyond some threshold.

This is cumbersome since it is well-known that asset markets all share some important "stylized facts" that are extremely robust and even in their quantitative appearance appear to be practically constant across time[1] and between countries. These are the "cubic law" of decay of the tail of the probability distribution of returns (Lux 1996; Gopikrishnan et al. 1998) and the similarly universal decay rates of the autocorrelation of absolute or squared returns that quantify the well-known feature of volatility clustering.

The consequence is that if heterogenous agent models converge to a central limit law with Gaussian statistics, they are apparently unable to reproduce the "universal" stylized facts in a robust way. While in reality markets of very different depth (say the US stock market compared to that of a small country like Slovenia) show hardly any remarkable statistical differences, a model implemented with a significantly larger or smaller number of traders would show distinctly different behavior. Economists have first not been aware of this problem, and the problem of such cumbersome "finite-size effects" has been first pointed out to me by the eminent physicist Dietrich Stauffer. Indeed, in our subsequent collaboration we found such effects when simulating various agent-based models with much higher numbers of agents than commonly used (e.g., Egenter et al. 1999).[2]

For certain models, a possible remedy consisted in the appropriate formalization of interpersonal influences (e.g., Alfarano et al. 2008). Masanao became also interested in this problem and pursued his own avenue towards a solution that has been published in his paper (Aoki 2002). Basically, his point is that under relatively general conditions, dynamic processes for the choice of strategies by an ensemble of agents will favor the emergence of a small set of strategies that dominates the market, independently of the nature of agents operating in the market, and even if this number is continuously increasing. Hence, even a large number of agents will self-organize into a few (two or three) major clusters with uniform behavior, and finite-size effects would be absent from such a framework.

Since Masanao's original paper makes relatively heavy use of the mathematics of random partitions, I will here provide a more didactical introduction to his model that might help to spure additional research along this important line of argumentation.

---

[1]"Universal" as the natural scientist would say.

[2]At these times, a supercomputer was needed to simulate even relatively simple models with, say, 10^6 agents. Due to Dietrich's affiliation with the German nuclear research center in Jülich we were allowed to use their supercomputer for this purpose.

4.2 Aoki's Open Model of an Asset Market with Many Investors

The model basically consists of two building blocks: the dynamics of agents choosing one out of multitude of k available strategies, and the asset price formation part, that takes the current configuration (i.e., distribution of agents across strategies) as input.

The strategy choice has three elements: market entry, market exit, and change from one strategy to another. All these components are formalized via transition rates which means we consider a continuous-time model of jump Markov processes in which at any point in time any one of the three component processes might lead to a change in the configuration of agents.

Given the current configuration $n = n_1 + n_2 + \ldots + n_k$ of the number of agents pursuing the different k strategies and $\mathbf{n}$ the vector $(n_1, \ldots, n_k)'$, market entry is formalized by the transition rates:

$$w(\mathbf{n}, \mathbf{n} + e_l) = c_l(n_l + h_l) \tag{4.1}$$

with e_l the vector $e_l = (0, \ldots, 1, \ldots 0)$ with unity appearing in the l-th position. The first term $c_l n_l$ formalizes the attractivity of large groups, i.e., new agents would be more likely to choose more popular strategies. $c_l h_l$, in contrast, stands for the entry of agents independent of the current configuration.

Market exit is described simply by a propensity of current market participants to leave, possibly dependent on their strategy:

$$w(\mathbf{n}, \mathbf{n} - e_j) = d_j n_j. \tag{4.2}$$

Finally, switching between strategies depends on the same forces plus a pairwise propensity of changes from some strategy j to l symbolized by a parameter λ_{jl}:

$$w(\mathbf{n}, \mathbf{n} - e_j + e_l) = \lambda_{jl} d_j n_j c_l(n_l + h_l). \tag{4.3}$$

In his paper, Masanao moves on from this set-up to the mathematical theory of large partitions and shows that under certain conditions, the above process will generically lead to the dominance of two strategies even if k is large, and if n is ever-increasing.

To provide some more intuition, let us consider a special case of the above dynamic process. In particular, we assume complete symmetry, i.e., we let all parameters $c_l, h_l, d_l, \lambda_{jl}$ be the same for all j, l and we restrict the number of strategies to $k = 3$.

Since the transition rates of a jump Markov process are the expected flows within a unit time period, we can simply use them to collect all the flows in a differential equation for the expected change of the mean value of the number of agents using strategy j, n_j. For example, for the strategy 1 we obtain[3] :

$$\begin{aligned}\frac{dn_1}{dt} &= c(n_1+h) - dn_1 \\ &\quad + \lambda dn_2 c(n_1+h) + \lambda dn_3 c(n_1+h) \\ &\quad - \lambda dn_1 c(n_2+h) - \lambda dn_1 c(n_3+h) \\ &= (c-d)n_1 + ch + \lambda dch(n_2+n_3-2n_1). \end{aligned} \tag{4.4}$$

Similar equations in n_2 and n_3 are easily obtained.

To keep track of the total number of market participants, we have to consider the change in time of $n = n_1 + n_2 + n_3$:

$$\begin{aligned}\frac{dn}{dt} &= \frac{dn_1}{dt} + \frac{dn_2}{dt} + \frac{dn_3}{dt} \\ &= (c-d)n + 3ch. \end{aligned} \tag{4.5}$$

This simple equation results because all the expressions for the changes of strategies of agents cancel out as they leave the overall number of agents unchanged. What remains is only aggregate market entry and exit.

The last equation already allows some conclusion on the limiting behavior of the market. Setting $\frac{dn}{dt} = 0$ we obtain:

$$\frac{dn}{dt} = 0 \Longleftrightarrow n^* = \frac{3ch}{d-c}. \tag{4.6}$$

If $d > c$, the population of market participants converges to the statistical limit n^*, if $c \geq d$, unbounded growth of the number of agents (in expectation) would result.

What about market fractions? Since the fraction of type 1 agents, x_1, is defined as $x_1 = \frac{n_1}{n}$, we can derive it expected time evolution as follows:

$$\begin{aligned}\frac{dx_1}{dt} = \frac{d}{dt}\left(\frac{n_1}{n}\right) &= \frac{1}{n}\left(\frac{dn_1}{dt}\right) - \frac{n_1}{n^2}\frac{dn}{dt} \\ &= (c-d)\frac{n_1}{n} + \frac{ch}{n} + \lambda dch\frac{n_2+n_3-2n_1}{n} - (c-d)\frac{n_1}{n} - 3ch\frac{n_1}{n^2} \\ &= \frac{ch}{n}\left(1 - 3\frac{n_1}{n}\right) + \lambda dch\frac{n_2+n_3-2n_1}{n} \\ &= \frac{ch}{n}(1-3x_1) + \lambda dch(x_2+x_3-2x_1). \end{aligned} \tag{4.7}$$

[3] We neglect the expectation operator in the following for better readibility.

For $d > c$, we can compute the dynamics around the equilibrium

$$\left.\frac{dx_1}{dt}\right|_{n=n^*} = (d-c)\left(\frac{1}{3} - x_1\right) + \lambda dch(x_2 + x_3 - 2x_1) \tag{4.8}$$

Together with the pertinent equations for x_2 and x_3 we obtain the expected fractions in statistical equilibrium as $x_1{}^* = x_2{}^* = x_3{}^* = \frac{1}{3}$ because of the assumed symmetry of all transition rates.

For $c > d$, n diverges which, however, implies that the first term on the right hand side of eq. (4.7) vanishes asymptotically. Retaining only the second term reveals again the long-term fractions $x_1{}^* = x_2{}^* = x_3{}^*$. Of course, following the derivations above, we could also compute the equilibrium fractions for any set of nonsymmetric parameter values.

However, the values of the average fractions are not too informative. As the time evolution in Fig. 4.1 demonstrates for a numerical example with $k = 3$ strategies, the dynamics of this jump Markov process does not converge to some close neighborhood of the expected average fractions. The fractions of the three strategies rather all show wide variations across the unit interval. Most of the time we find a clear dominance of one alternative. Apparently, large deviations from the

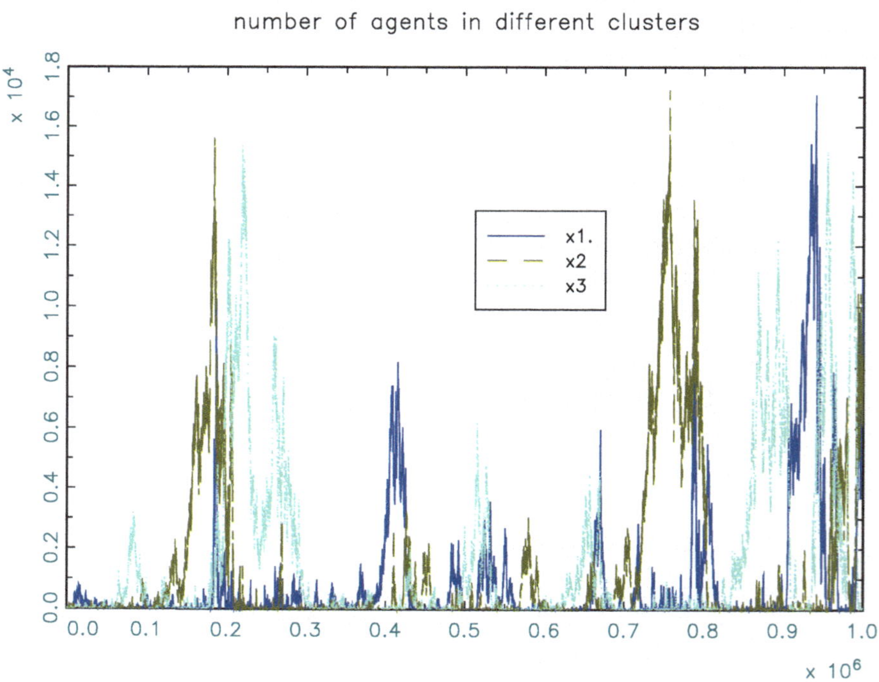

Fig. 4.1 Illustration of the change over time of group occupation numbers in a model with $k = 3$ strategies. The other parameters are $c = 0.1$, $d = 0.1$, $\lambda = 0.005$ and $h = 0.1$

Table 4.1 Largest and average fractions

	y_1	$y_1 + y_2$	x_1	x_2	x_3
$\theta = 0.3$					
theor	0.84	0.97	0.27	0.31	0.42
simul.	0.88	0.99			
$\theta = 0.4$					
theor	0.79	0.95	0.36	0.26	0.37
simul.	0.85	0.99			
$\theta = 0.5$					
theor	0.76	0.92	0.35	0.34	0.31
simul.	0.84	0.98			

Note: The table shows the average fractions of different strategies and the average of the largest fraction y_1 or the two largest fractions $(y_1 + y_2)$ over exact discrete-event simulations with a time horizon of $T = 10^6$. Results are compared with the theoretical predictions of Aoki (2002). The remaining parameters are: $c = 0.1$, $d = 0.1$ and $\lambda = 0.005$

expectations are more important than the expected values of the group occupation numbers. Masanao derived approximate expressions of the size of the largest and the two largest clusters in his 2002 paper that only depend on the composite parameter $\theta = hk$, i.e., the product of the available number of strategies and the autonomous entry rate.

Table 4.1 shows a comparison of the analytical predictions with numerical results obtained for different values of θ and simulations using the exact discrete-event simulation of the dynamic system (using the so-called Gillespie method, cf. Gillespie 1977). The time horizon is $T = 10^6$ in all cases. The results indeed show that while over time the fractions are close to their expected values $x_1^* = x_2^* = x_3^* = \frac{1}{3}$, at most single time periods, one strategy accounts for 80% or more of all agents, and the two most popular strategies are chosen by almost 100% of the population of agents. As shown in Aoki (2002), these patterns still persist largely if a larger pool of strategies is available. Hence, the market dynamics can be described to a high degree of accuracy if one considers only the two dominating strategies at any point in time. Most importantly, the dominance of a small number of strategies also holds independently of the size of the population and, thus, the statistical characteristics of an asset price process coupled with this population dynamics would be independent of the size n of the population of traders.[4] Hence, any "interesting dynamics" would not be a finite-size effect vanishing with larger population.

To illustrate this, I choose the same asset pricing framework as in Aoki (2002) with only a slight change of the model setup. Aoki follows Day and Huang (1990) who assume that the asset price is determined by an auctioneer or market maker

[4]Note that for $c \geq d$, the population size n is not stationary anyway.

who adjusts prices upward or downward depending on current excess demand:

$$\frac{dp}{dt} = \beta ED_t \tag{4.9}$$

with p the asset price, β the price adjustment speed, and ED excess demand. Day and Huang assume that there are two groups of investors, fundamentalists and chartists, and Aoki (2002) determines their time-varying fractions by the above jump Markov process. Here we add as a third alternative inactive traders following a buy-and-hold strategy to allow to link the model with the previous illustration of this framework with $k = 3$ strategies.

Overall excess demand is then given by:

$$ED_t = ax_{1,t}\,(p_{f,t} - p_t)h(p_t) + bx_{2,t}\,(p_t - p_{f,t}) + \epsilon_t \tag{4.10}$$

with $p_{f,t}$ the fundamental value at time t, $x_{1,t}$ and $x_{2,t}$ the current fractions of agents pursuing strategy 1 (fundamentalism) and 2 (chartism). Strategy 3 does not appear explicitly as it does not generate excess demand. $h(p_t)$ is a nonlinear weight function as in Day and Huang (1990):

$$h(p_t) = ((p_t - m_1)(m_2 - p_t))^{-\frac{1}{2}} \tag{4.11}$$

that makes fundamentalists' excess demand more elastic when high levels of overvaluation or undervaluation are reached and, in this way, avoids explosive instability of the price process. Finally, $\epsilon_t \sim N(0, \sigma^2)$ is a small noise trading or microstructural component that enters in addition to the well-known speculative strategies.

Figure 4.2 shows a simulation of this price formation process using the simulations of occupation numbers displayed in Fig. 4.1. For better visibility of the resulting patterns, the figure only shows a time window of 20,000 periods. The lower panel exhibits the fractions of strategies 1 and 2 (in contrast to the raw occupation numbers shown in Fig. 4.1) while the upper panel exhibits the price process. As it can be observed, periods with a dominance of chartists lead to the outbreak of positive or negative bubbles which end in a crash when the majority swings back to the fundamentalist strategy. There might also be periods in which none of both strategies have many followers (e.g., shortly before period 1600) and the majority of the market participants belongs to group 3 and stays inactive. Note that in this case, the previous undervaluation at about t = 15,000 is corrected much more slowly than after a turn from dominating chartism to dominating fundamentalism. Note also that indeed the visual appearance of the price process suggests stationary increments although the population undergoes large changes of its overall number as can be seen in Fig. 4.1. The properties of the price process are, thus, independent of the size of the market in terms of its number of market participants.

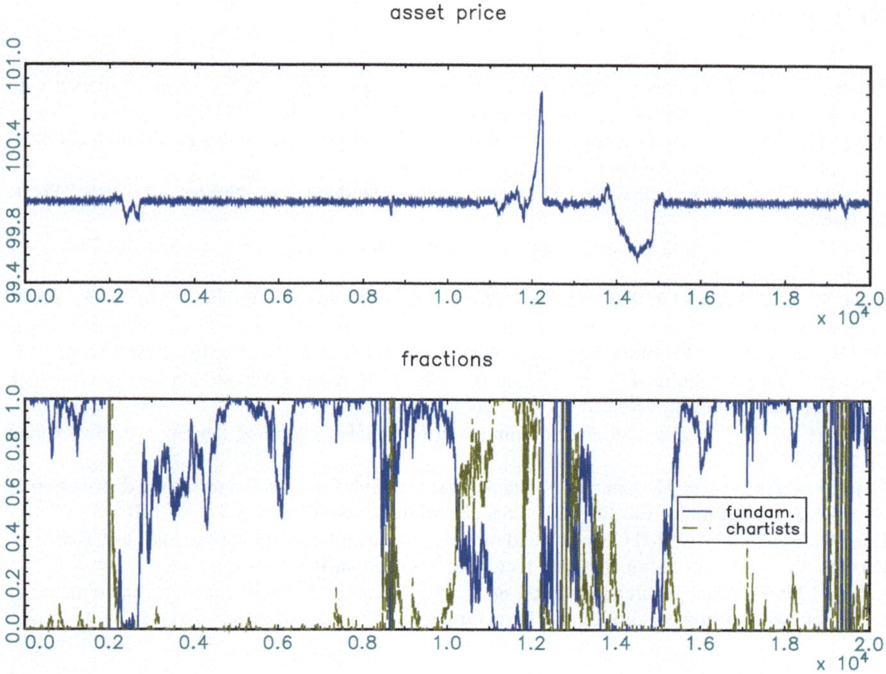

Fig. 4.2 Illustration of the asset pricing model of Day and Huang combined with the group dynamics of Fig. 4.1. The parameters of the asset pricing model are: $p_f = 100$, $m_2 = 100$, $m_1 = -100$, $\beta = 0.05$, $a = 750$, $b = 0.2$

4.3 Conclusion

Like so many of the topics that Masanao Aoki has touched in his long and extremely productive career, his short foray into behavioral asset pricing has shed a completely new light on a puzzling feature of previous models. The very different size of markets that all share the same stylized facts seems to preclude that their origin lies "merely" in finite-size phenomena that would eventually vanish with increasing number of market participants. Hence, there must be some form of self-selection of agents into a small number of groups with relatively uniform behavior. Masanao Aoki has clarified the basic mathematical structures that would lead to dominance of a few groups only, despite a potentially large number of alternative strategies. These insights still deserve to be integrated into the current generation of behavioral asset pricing market.

References

Alfarano S, Lux T, Wagner F (2008) Time variation of higher moments in a financial market with heterogeneous agents: an analytical approach. J Econ Dyn Control 32(1):101–136

Aoki M (1994) New macroeconomic modeling approaches: hierarchical dynamics and mean-field approximation. J Econ Dyn Control 18(3–4):865–877

Aoki M (1996) New approaches to macroeconomic modeling. Cambridge University Press, Cambridge

Aoki M (2002) Modeling aggregate behavior and fluctuations in economics. Cambridge University Press, Cambridge

Aoki M, Yoshikawa H (2006) Reconstructing macroeconomics. Cambridge University Press, Cambridge

Day R, Huang W (1990) Bulls, bears, and market sheep. J Econ Behav Organ 14:299–329

Egenter E, Lux T, Stauffer D (1999) Finite-size effects in Monte Carlo simulations of two stock market models. Phys A Stat Mech Appl 268(1):250–256

Gillespie DT (1977) Exact stochastic simulation of coupled chemical reactions. J Phys Chem 81(25):2340–2361

Gopikrishnan P, Meyer M, Amaral LN, Stanley HE (1998) Inverse cubic law for the distribution of stock price variations. Eur Phys J B-Condens Matter Complex Syst 3 2, 139–140.

Haag G, Weidlich W (1983) Concepts and models of a quantitative sociology. Springer, Berlin

Kirman A (1993) Ants, rationality, and recruitment. Q J Econ 108:137–156

Lux T (1996) The stable Paretian hypothesis and the frequency of large returns: an examination of major German stocks. Appl Financ Econ 6(6):463–475

Part II
Wealth, Income, Firms

Chapter 5
Continuum and Thermodynamic Limits for a Wealth-Distribution Model

Bertram Düring, Nicos Georgiou, Sara Merino-Aceituno, and Enrico Scalas

Abstract We discuss a simple random exchange model for the distribution of wealth. There are N agents, each one endowed with a fraction of the total wealth; indebtedness is not possible, so wealth fractions are positive random variables. At each step, two agents are randomly selected, their wealths are first merged and then randomly split into two parts. We start from a discrete state space, discrete time version of this model and, under suitable scaling, we present its functional convergence to a continuous space, discrete time model. Then, we discuss how a continuous time version of the one-point marginal Markov chain functionally converges to a kinetic equation of Boltzmann type. Solutions to this equation are presented and they coincide with the appropriate limits of the invariant measure for the marginal Markov chain. In this way, in this simple case, we complete Boltzmann's programme of deriving kinetic equations from random dynamics.

Keywords Wealth distribution · Stochastic processes · Markov chains · Kinetic equations

Mathematics Subject Classification (2000) 60J05, 35Q91, 35Q20, 60J10, 60J20, 82B31, 82B40

B. Düring · N. Georgiou · E. Scalas (✉)
Department of Mathematics, University of Sussex, Brighton, UK
e-mail: bd80@sussex.ac.uk; n.georgiou@sussex.ac.uk; e.scalas@sussex.ac.uk

S. Merino-Aceituno
Faculty of Mathematics, University of Vienna, Vienna, Austria

Department of Mathematics, University of Sussex, Brighton, UK
e-mail: sara.merino@univie.ac.at

H. Aoyama et al. (eds.), *Complexity, Heterogeneity, and the Methods of Statistical Physics in Economics*, Evolutionary Economics and Social Complexity Science 22,
https://doi.org/10.1007/978-981-15-4806-2_5

5.1 Introduction

In their 2007 book, *Reconstructing Macroeconomics* (Aoki and Yoshikawa 2007), Aoki and Yoshikawa presented a new approach to macroeconomics modelling based on (directly quoting from their book) *(1) continuous-time Markov chains to model stochastic dynamics interactions among agents and (2) combinations of stochastic processes and non-classical combinatorial analysis, called combinatorial stochastic processes*. They go on mentioning that, in case (1), the master equation describes how states of the models evolve stochastically in time and, in case (2), combinatorial stochastic processes are applied to describe the random formation of clusters of agents as well as the distribution of cluster sizes.

Indeed, it turns out that the two approaches are so strictly related that it is not necessary to distinguish between them. This point was already implicitly made in Chapter 10 of Garibaldi and Scalas (2010). Moreover, not surprisingly, they are also related to kinetic equations of Boltzmann type used in statistical physics (Pareschi and Toscani 2014).

It is the purpose of this chapter to explore the latter connection, whereas in this introduction we will focus on the connection between combinatorial stochastic processes, diffusions, and related master equations. As it will become clearer in the following, the connection is given by functional limit theorems of properly scaled processes (Billingsley 1999; Ethier and Kurtz 2005; Jacod and Shiryaev 2003).

In order to illustrate the connection, let us consider a simple specific model, the so-called Ehrenfest-Brillouin model with unary moves (Garibaldi and Scalas 2010; Garibaldi et al. 2007). This was used in Garibaldi et al. (2007) as a model for taxation and redistribution, but it was introduced in Costantini and Garibaldi (1997, 1998) as a foundation for statistical physics based on an idea of Brillouin (Brillouin 1927) and Carnap's continuum of inductive methods (Zabell 1997).

Let us start with discrete combinatorial processes and consider n objects falling into $g > 1$ categories. The objects and the classes can be interpreted in different ways, depending on the system under scrutiny. For instance, if one is interested in industrial dynamics, geographical regions could be seen as classes and the objects could represent firms active in those regions (for this interpretation, see Bottazzi et al. 2007). For the purpose of this chapter, it is useful to interpret the objects as *tokens* or *coins* and the categories as *individuals* or *economic agents*. A state of this system is completely specified by the so-called individual description where one specifies for each object to which class it belongs. If one is not interested in this detail or this information is not easily accessible, another way of describing the state is using occupation numbers of classes; this is the so-called *statistical* or *frequency description*, where the random vector $\mathbf{Y} = \mathbf{n} = (n_1, \ldots, n_g)$ represents the number of objects in class 1 and so on, up to the number of objects in class g. Let S_g^n denote the state space of $\mathbf{Y}$. Consider the following homogeneous Markovian stochastic dynamics on the occupation states. First, an object is randomly selected, then this object is moved into a new class according to a Pólya allocation probability. This leads to the following transition probability

$$\mathbb{P}(\mathbf{Y}_{t+1} = \mathbf{n}_i^k | \mathbf{Y}_t = \mathbf{n}) = \frac{n_i}{n} \frac{\alpha_k + n_k - \delta_{k,i}}{\alpha + n - 1}, \tag{5.1}$$

where $\mathbf{n}_i^k$ is an occupation vector with one object less in class i and one more in class k, $\boldsymbol{\alpha} = (\alpha_1, \ldots, \alpha_g)$ is a vector of parameters, $\alpha = \sum_i \alpha_i$, and $\delta_{k,n}$ is the usual Kronecker delta. The parameter α_i is proportional to the *prior* probability of occupying class i if it is empty. For the sake of simplicity, in this introduction, let us assume that $\alpha_i > 0$ for every i. Given an initial state or an initial distribution on the state space S_g^n, whose cardinality is

$$\left| S_g^n \right| = \binom{n+g-1}{n}, \tag{5.2}$$

equation (5.1) represents the transition probability of an irreducible and aperiodic Markov chain. It is possible to use detailed balance to get the invariant distribution. This is given by a multivariate Pólya distribution

$$\mathbb{P}(\mathbf{Y} = \mathbf{n}) = \pi(\mathbf{n}) = \frac{n!}{\alpha^{(n)}} \prod_{i=1}^{g} \frac{\alpha_i^{(n_i)}}{n_i!}, \tag{5.3}$$

where $x^{(n)} = x(x+1)\cdots(x+n-1)$ is the Pochhammer symbol for the ascending factorial. Consider now the situation in which all the classes are characterised by the same weight θ; all categories being on a par, one can consider the first one and focus on the random variable Y_1 or even omit the class label. From (5.3), using the aggregation property of the multivariate Pólya distribution, one gets a bivariate Pólya distribution a.k.a. beta-binomial distribution

$$\mathbb{P}(Y = k) = \pi(k) = \frac{n!}{k!(n-k)!} \frac{\theta^{(k)}[(g-1)\theta]^{(n-k)}}{(g\theta)^{(n)}}. \tag{5.4}$$

This result can also be obtained starting from the marginal random dynamics for Y_1. This is a birth-death Markov chain with the following transition probabilities

$$\mathbb{P}(Y_{t+1} = k+1 | Y_t = k) = w(k, k+1) = \frac{n-k}{n} \frac{\theta + k}{g\theta + n - 1},$$

$$\mathbb{P}(Y_{t+1} = k-1 | Y_t = k) = w(k, k-1) = \frac{k}{n} \frac{(g-1)\theta + n - k}{g\theta + n - 1},$$

$$\mathbb{P}(Y_{t+1} = k | Y_t = k) = w(k, k) = 1 - w(k, k+1) - w(k, k-1),$$

for $k = 1, \ldots, n-1$. For $k = 0$, one has $w(0, -1) = 0$ and, for $k = n$, one correspondingly has $w(n, n+1) = 0$. The invariant measure of this Markov chain coincides with (5.4). The continuous limit of the beta-binomial distribution can be derived by simultaneously setting $n \to \infty$ and $k \to \infty$ while, at the same time, keeping $u = k/n$ constant; this leads to a beta-distributed random variable U. With the parameters of equation (5.4), the limiting probability density of U is

$$f_U(u) = \frac{u^{\theta-1}(1-u)^{(g-1)\theta-1}}{B(\theta, (g-1)\theta)}, \tag{5.5}$$

in the interval [0, 1] and 0 elsewhere, where $B(\theta, (g-1)\theta)$ is the beta function of argument θ and $(g-1)\theta$. In order to illustrate that the two approaches presented by Aoki and Yoshikawa do coincide, we will now derive this result in an alternative and instructive way, based on the functional convergence of birth and death Markov chains to diffusions. Here, the discussion remains at the heuristic level, whereas in the following we will use the full power of the theory of functional convergence of stochastic processes. Define $\psi_k = w(k, k+1)$ and $\varphi_k = w(k, k-1)$ so that $w(k.k) = 1 - \psi_k - \varphi_k$. If the $t-1$ step transition probability is known, then assuming that $Y_{t-1} = k$, one gets for the t step transition probability

$$w_t(j,k) = w_{t-1}(j, k-1)\psi_{k-1} + w_{t-1}(j,k)(1-\psi_k-\varphi_k) + w_{t-1}(j, k+1)\varphi_{k+1}. \tag{5.6}$$

To fix ideas, suppose that $Y_{t-1} = k$ represents the position of a diffusing particle on a lattice with lattice spacing Δu and that the time interval between jumps to nearest neighbour positions is Δt. Then (5.6) can be re-written as

$$\begin{aligned} p(u, t|u_0, 0)\Delta u &= p(u-\Delta u, t-\Delta t|u_0, 0)\Delta u \psi(u-\Delta u) + \\ p(u, t-\Delta t|u_0, 0)\Delta u(1-\psi(u)-\varphi(u)) &+ p(u+\Delta u, t-\Delta t|u_0, 0)\Delta u \varphi(u+\Delta u), \end{aligned} \tag{5.7}$$

where the probability density $p(u, t|u_0, 0)$ is such that $w_t(u_0, u) = p(u, t|u_0, 0)$ Δu. The lattice spacing can be simplified leading to

$$\begin{aligned} p(u, t|u_0, 0) &= p(u-\Delta u, t-\Delta t|u_0, 0)\psi(u-\Delta u) + \\ p(u, t-\Delta t|u_0, 0)(1-\psi(u)-\varphi(u)) &+ p(u+\Delta u, t-\Delta t|u_0, 0)\varphi(u+\Delta u). \end{aligned} \tag{5.8}$$

If one lets $\Delta u \to 0$ and $\Delta t \to 0$, one can see that equation (5.8) converges to a *Fokker-Planck equation* given by

$$\frac{\partial}{\partial t} p(u, t|u_0, 0) = -\frac{\partial}{\partial u}[\mu(u) p(u, t|u_0, 0)] + \frac{1}{2}\frac{\partial^2}{\partial u^2}[\sigma^2(u) p(u, t|u_0, 0)], \tag{5.9}$$

where the diffusive limit has been taken keeping the ratio $(\Delta u)^2/\Delta t$ constant and the drift and diffusion coefficients are, respectively, given by

$$\mu(u) = \lim_{\Delta u, \Delta t \to 0} [\psi(u) - \varphi(u)] \frac{\Delta u}{\Delta t} = \theta(1 - gu), \tag{5.10}$$

and

$$\sigma^2(u) = \lim_{\Delta u, \Delta t \to 0} [\psi(u) + \varphi(u) - (\psi(u) - \varphi(u))^2] \frac{(\Delta u)^2}{\Delta t} = 2u(1 - u). \tag{5.11}$$

Equation (5.9) corresponds to the following Itô diffusion (stochastic differential equation)

$$dU_t = \theta(1 - gU_t)\, dt + \sqrt{2U_t(1 - U_t)}\, dW_t, \tag{5.12}$$

where U_t is the limiting stochastic process and W_t is standard Brownian motion. It turns out that equation (5.5) is indeed the invariant distribution for the diffusion given by (5.12).

As mentioned above, in this chapter, we will explore another connection, the one between combinatorial stochastic processes and kinetic equations of Boltzmann type. We will introduce a simple discrete model for wealth dynamics. This is the same we have already discussed in Düring et al. (2017), and we will study the convergence of the discrete space, discrete time Markov chain to a continuous space, discrete time Markov chain under appropriate scaling. Then, using the Poissonisation trick (Pollard 1984), we will change time and consider a continuous time version of our continuous space Markov chain. In an other appropriate scaling limit, this will lead to kinetic equations of Boltzmann type as studied, e.g. in Bassetti and Toscani (2010). In this chapter, we present the main results and their meaning, but not the detailed proofs of propositions, lemmata, and theorems which will be published elsewhere (Düring et al. in preparation).

5.2 Markovian Models for Wealth Exchange, Under Fixed Wealth and Fixed Number of Agents

We describe the various models we are using. The rigorous proofs of all the results can be found in Düring et al. (2017) and Düring et al. (in preparation). We consider N agents (initially N is fixed) and wealth W_N (initially fixed to be n).

The *discrete space, discrete time (DS-DT)* model is a Markov Chain on the integers partitions of n that have size N. In other words, the state space is comprised of all non-negative integer vectors $\mathbf{x}^{n,N} = (x_1, \dots x_N) \in \mathbb{Z}_+^N$ so that $\sum_{i=1}^N x_i = n$. The x_i's represent the wealth of the i-th individual and the superscripts are there to remind us of the total wealth and number of agents. We denote the state space by

$S_{N-1}^{(n)} = n\Delta_{N-1} \cap \mathbb{Z}^N$, where

$$\Delta_{N-1} = \left\{ \mathbf{x} = (x_1, \ldots, x_N) : x_i \geq 0 \text{ for all } i = 1, \ldots, N \text{ and } \sum_{i=1}^{N} x_i = 1 \right\}, \tag{5.13}$$

is the N-dimensional unit simplex.

At every discrete time step, we choose an ordered pair of indices from 1 to N uniformly at random (say (i, j)) and add the individual wealths $x_i + x_j$ of the agents. After that, the first chosen agent i receives a uniform portion of the total wealth between 0 and $\max\{x_i + x_j - 1, 0\}$ and the rest goes to the second agent j. Let $\mathbf{X}_t^{n,N}$ denote the wealth distribution at time t. The transition probabilities for this chain are given by

$$\mathbb{P}\{\mathbf{X}_{t+1}^{n,N} = \mathbf{x}' | \mathbf{X}_t^{n,N} = \mathbf{x}\}$$

$$= \sum_{(i,j):i\neq j} \left\{ \frac{1}{N} \frac{1}{N-1} \left(\frac{\mathbb{1}\{x_i + x_j \geq 1, x_j' \geq 1\}}{x_i + x_j} + \mathbb{1}\{x_i + x_j = 0\} \right) \delta_{x_i + x_j, x_i' + x_j'} \prod_{k \neq i,j} \delta_{x_k, x_k'} \right\}. \tag{5.14}$$

Note that we have seemingly introduced a slight asymmetry; the agent picked first runs the risk of ending up with zero fortune. The dynamics are overall not asymmetric, however, since we select i before j with the same probability as selecting j before i. In fact, this particular concession simplifies the calculations to obtain that

Proposition 1 (Düring et al. (2017), Proposition 7.2) *The invariant distribution of this Markov chain* $\mathbf{X}_t^{n,N}$ *is the uniform distribution on* $n\Delta_{N-1} \cap \mathbb{Z}^N$.

This is a direct consequence of the fact that the stochastic matrix defined by (5.14) is the doubly stochastic matrix of an irreducible, aperiodic chain which has a unique invariant distribution. Since all doubly stochastic matrices have the uniform distribution as invariant, and the chain is irreducible and aperiodic, the result follows.

After studying the discrete chain, it would be more realistic to allow the total wealth n to increase, but in general that would only alter the state space. However, there is a way to converge to a *continuous space, discrete time (CS-DT) model*, if we alter the discrete model slightly. In particular, instead of looking at the distribution of wealth, we look at the distribution of the **proportion** of wealth, namely, the process $\mathbf{Y}^{n,N} = n^{-1}\mathbf{X}^{n,N}$ which is a rescaling of the original discrete process by the total wealth. The state space for the $\mathbf{Y}^{n,N}$ process is the meshed simplex

$$\Delta_{N-1}(n) = \left\{ (q_1, \ldots, q_N) : 0 \leq q_i \leq 1, \sum_{i=1}^{N} q_i = 1, nq_i \in \mathbb{N}_0 \right\} \subset \Delta_{N-1}. \tag{5.15}$$

Then, it was shown in Düring et al. (2017), that as $n \to \infty$ one has weak convergence of one-dimensional marginals:

Proposition 2 (Düring et al. (2017), Proposition 7.3) *Assume the weak convergence* $\mu_0^{n,N} \Longrightarrow \mu_0^{\infty,N}$ *as* $n \to \infty$*. Then for each fixed* $t \in \mathbb{N}$*, the sequence* $\{\mathbf{Y}_t^{n,N}\}_{n\in\mathbb{N}}$*, when* $\mathbf{Y}_0^{n,N} \sim \mu_0^{n,N}$ *converges in distribution to a random variable* $\mathbf{X}_t^{\infty,N}$*, i.e.,*

$$\mathbf{Y}_t^{n,N} \Longrightarrow \mathbf{X}_t^{\infty,N} \quad \textit{as } n \to \infty.$$

Process $\{\mathbf{X}_t^{\infty,N}\}_{t\in\mathbb{N}}$ can be uniquely identified as a Markov chain on Δ_{N-1} so that $\mathbf{X}_0^{\infty,N} \sim \mu_0^{\infty,N}$. It is a continuous space, discrete time Markov chain on Δ_{N-1}. At each discrete time step t, an ordered pair of agents, say (i, j), is selected uniformly at random, with total proportion of wealth $x_i + x_j$. Then an independent uniform random variable $u_{t,(i,j)} \sim \mathrm{Unif}[0, 1]$ is drawn and the new proportion of wealth for agent i is $u_{t,(i,j)}(x_i + x_j)$ while for agent j it is $(1 - u_{t,(i,j)})(x_i + x_j)$. Note that the x_i are exchangeable random variables; while the description above needs ordered pairs of agents, it has no bearing on the distribution of the eventual wealth, as both $u_{t,(i,j)}$ and $1 - u_{t,(i,j)}$ are uniformly distributed on $[0, 1]$.

In our work (Düring et al. in preparation) we take things a step further, and we prove a process-level convergence. For that, we first need a way to construct a process $\mathbf{Y}^{n,N}$. For any $n \in \mathbb{N}$, the process $\mathbf{Y}^{n,N}$ is defined on $\Delta_{N-1}(n)$ given by (5.15), and we emphasise that for every n, $\Delta_{N-1}(n) \subset \Delta_{N-1}$, given by (5.13). $\Delta_{N-1}(n)$ is treated as the meshed simplex Δ_{N-1}; the mesh size is n^{-1} which is precisely the reciprocal of the total wealth $W_n = n$.

Let $\mathscr{P}^n$ denote the law of the process $\mathbf{Y}^{n,N} = (\mathbf{Y}_0^{n,N}, \mathbf{Y}_1^{n,N}, \ldots, \mathbf{Y}_k^{n,N}, \ldots) \in (\Delta_{N-1}(n))^{\mathbb{N}_0} \subset (\Delta_{N-1})^{\mathbb{N}_0}$. The measure for $k+1$-th dimensional marginal $(\mathbf{Y}_0^{n,N}, \mathbf{Y}_1^{n,N}, \ldots, \mathbf{Y}_k^{n,N})$ is denoted by

$$\mathscr{P}_k^n\{\cdot\} = \mathscr{P}^n\{(\mathbf{Y}_0^{n,N}, \mathbf{Y}_1^{n,N}, \ldots, \mathbf{Y}_k^{n,N}) \in \cdot\}. \tag{5.16}$$

Similarly, denote by $\mathscr{P}^\infty$ and $\mathscr{P}_k^\infty$ the corresponding quantities for $\mathbf{X}^{\infty,N}$. The laws of $\mathbf{Y}_0^{n,N}, \mathbf{X}_0^{\infty,N}$ are denoted by $\mu_0^{n,N} = \mathscr{P}_0^{(n)}$ and $\mu_0^{(\infty)} = \mathscr{P}_0^{(\infty)}$, respectively.

Starting from an initial distribution $\mu_0^{(n)}$ we construct the process $\mathbf{Y}^{(n)}$ using an i.i.d. sequence of uniform random variables

$$U_{i,j}^{(n)}(k) \sim \mathrm{Unif}[0, 1], \qquad 1 \le i, j \le N, i \neq j, k \in \mathbb{N}_0, n \in \mathbb{N}. \tag{5.17}$$

These random variables from (5.17) suffice to construct the whole process. k is the time index, and (i, j) the ordered pair of agents that are selected. We assume – and use without a particular mention – that the random variables (5.17) are independent of the initial distribution $\mu_0^{(n)}$.

For any $x \in \mathbb{R}_+$ we define

$$[x]_n = \frac{a}{n}, \qquad \text{so that } \frac{a}{n} \le x < \frac{a+1}{n}, \qquad a \in \mathbb{N}_0,$$

and use this symbol for notational convenience when we define the evolution of the process directly on $\Delta_{N-1}(n)$.

Let $\mathbf{Y}_k^{n,N} = (y_1(k), \dots y_N(k)) \in \Delta_{N-1}(n)$ be the vector of discrete wealths, normalised so that the total wealth is 1. Then, if indices i, j were chosen to interact at time step k, the total wealth at time $k+1$ becomes

$$\begin{aligned}\mathbf{Y}_{k+1}^{n,N} &= (y_1(k), \dots, \underbrace{[U_{i,j}^{(n)}(k)(y_i(k) + y_j(k))]_n}_{y_i(k+1)}, \dots, \underbrace{y_i(k) + y_j(k) - y_i(k+1)}_{y_j(k+1)}, \dots, y_N(k)) \\ &= g_{i,j}(\mathbf{y}_k, U_{i,j}^{(n)}(k)).\end{aligned}$$

Check to see that the coordinate $[U_{i,j}^{(n)}(k)(y_i(k) + y_j(k))]_n$ is uniformly distributed on the set $\{0, n^{-1}, \dots, (y_i(k) + y_j(k) - n^{-1}) \vee 0\}$, and therefore, this procedure gives the same process as described in Düring et al. (2017). Function $g_{i,j}$ is measurable and depends on the value of the current state and the new uniform random variable, and the last display acts as the definition of $g_{i,j}$.

We prove the following theorem, which guarantees process-level convergence.

Theorem 1 (Düring et al. (in preparation)) *Assume the weak convergence of initial distributions*

$$\mu_0^{n,N} \Longrightarrow \mu_0^{\infty,N}, \qquad as\ n \to \infty. \tag{5.18}$$

Furthermore, assume the weak convergence (as $n \to \infty$) of the i.i.d. sequence

$$\{U_{i,j}^{(n)}(k)\}_{i,j,k} \Longrightarrow \{U_{i,j}^{(\infty)}(k)\}_{i,j,k}, \tag{5.19}$$

so that the limiting sequence $\{U_{i,j}^{(\infty)}(k)\}_{i,j,k}$ is a sequence of i.i.d. uniform $[0, 1]$ random variables that are also independent from $\mu_0^{\infty,N}$. Then

$$\mathscr{P}^n \Longrightarrow \mathscr{P}^\infty, \qquad as\ n \to \infty.$$

Remark 1 (Almost sure convergence for finite sample paths) Assume that the initial distributions satisfy $\mathbf{Y}_0^{n,N} \to \mathbf{X}_0^{\infty,N}$ a.e. as $n \to \infty$ and that we use common uniforms for each time step k, i.e.

$$U_{i,j}(k) \equiv U_{i,j}^{(n)}(k) = U_{i,j}^{(m)}(k) = U_{i,j}^{(\infty)}(k), \qquad \text{for all } n, m \in \mathbb{N},$$

while maintaining the independence across the time index. Then for any fixed $k \in \mathbb{N}$

$$(\mathbf{Y}_0^{n,N}, \dots, \mathbf{Y}_k^{n,N}) \xrightarrow{a.s.} (\mathbf{X}_0^{\infty,N}, \dots, \mathbf{X}_k^{\infty,N}),$$

provided the same indices (i, j) are selected at each step. This is because of the compact state space for these processes. For any fixed n, the construction using now the common (in n) uniform random variables $U_{i,j}^{(n)}(\ell)$ creates an error of at most $2/n$ per step in the supremum norm of the state space, so the total error is $2k/n$, which vanishes as $n \to \infty$.

The proof of Theorem 1 goes by proving that for any bounded continuous function f

$$\mathbb{E}_{\mathscr{P}_k^n}(f(\mathbf{Y}_0^{n,N}, \mathbf{Y}_1^{n,N}, \dots, \mathbf{Y}_k^{n,N})) \to \mathbb{E}_{\mathscr{P}^\infty}(f(\mathbf{X}_0^{\infty,N}, \mathbf{X}_1^{\infty,N}, \dots, \mathbf{X}_k^{\infty,N}))$$

for an arbitrary k. In order to show that, we show how we can find a measurable function g so that

$$\mathbf{Y}_k^{n,N} = g_{i,j}(U_{i,j}^{(n)}(k), \mathbf{Y}_{k-1}^{n,N}).$$

Then, from the Markov property, we conclude that there exists a bounded measurable function G so that $\mathbf{Y}_k^{n,N} = G(\{U_{i,j}^{(n)}(\ell)\}_{i,j,0\le\ell\le k-1})$ in distribution and prove the limit using the uniform variables instead which we know they weakly converge by assumption.

Continuous space but discrete time Markov chains are more technical than their discrete counterparts, so in order to study invariant distributions one usually needs more. For the CS-DT model described here, an invariant distribution was obtained in

Proposition 3 (Bertoin (2006), Corollary 2.1) *If* $\mathbf{X}_t^{\infty,N} \sim \mathrm{Unif}[\Delta_{N-1}]$ *then* $\mathbf{X}_{t+1}^{\infty,N} \sim \mathrm{Unif}[\Delta_{N-1}]$, *and in particular the uniform distribution on the simplex is time invariant.*

The technical difficulty arises when one wishes to verify that this is the unique invariant distribution and it is also the *equilibrium* distribution. The first objective is to replace the notion of irreducibility for discrete space chains with an appropriate one for continuous space. This is done by means of the notion of ϕ-irreducibility.

Definition 1 (Phi-irreducibility) Let $(S, \mathscr{B}(S), \phi)$ be a measured Polish space. A discrete time Markov chain $\mathbf{X}$ on S is ϕ-irreducible if and only if for any Borel set A the following implication holds:

$$\phi(A) > 0 \Longrightarrow L(u, A) > 0, \qquad \text{for all } u \in S.$$

We used the notation

$$L(u, A) = P_u\{X_t \in A \text{ for some } t \geq 1\} = P\{X_t \in A \text{ for some } n |\, X_0 = u\}.$$

This replaces the notion of irreducibility for discrete Markov chains and it implies that the chain is visiting any set of positive measure with positive probability; in other words, the image of the chain is dense in the state space. To obtain uniqueness of the invariant distribution and convergence to equilibrium, one then needs to show that there exists a Foster-Lyapunov function for the chain. This is defined as

Definition 2 (Foster-Lyapunov function) For a *petite* set C we can find a function $V \geq 0$ and a $\rho > 0$ so that for all $x \in S$

$$\int P(x, dy)V(y) \leq V(x) - 1 + \rho \mathbb{1}_C(x), \tag{5.20}$$

The existence of the Foster-Lyapunov function implies convergence of the kernel P of ϕ-irreducible, aperiodic chain to a unique equilibrium measure π,

$$\sup_{A \in \mathscr{B}(S)} \left| P^t(x, A) - \pi(A) \right| \to 0, \text{ as } t \to \infty, \tag{5.21}$$

(see Meyn and Tweedie 1993) for all x for which $V(x) < \infty$. If we define τ_C to be the number of steps it takes the chain to return to the set C, the existence of a Foster-Lyapunov function (and therefore convergence to a unique equilibrium) is equivalent to τ_C having finite expectation, i.e.

$$\sup_{x \in C} \mathbf{E}_x(\tau_C) < M_C,$$

which is in turn is implied when τ_C has geometric tails. This is true for $\mathbf{X}^{\infty,N}$ as it is defined on a compact set. The final result is encapsulated in the following proposition.

Proposition 4 (Düring et al. (2017), Proposition 7.5) *Let $t \in \mathbb{N}$. The discrete chain $\mathbf{X} = \{\mathbf{X}_t^{\infty,N}\}_{t \in \mathbb{N}}$ is ϕ-irreducible, where $\phi \equiv \lambda_{N-1}$ is the Lebesgue measure on the simplex, and in particular, the uniform distribution obtained in Proposition* 3 *is the unique invariant distribution and is the equilibrium distribution.*

If we combine all the results together, we observe that the order in which we take limits in the following diagram (Fig. 5.1) is immaterial and the diagram is commutative.

Finally, we can introduce continuous time in the continuous space CS-DT model. In order to switch to a continuous time Markov chain, where jump times coincide with those of a rate 1 Poisson process, one can use what is called a "Poissonisation trick." It is standard to argue that the long-time behaviour of the discrete time process is the same as that of the Poissonised one when N is fixed, irrespective of the rate of the Poisson process. The finite time distribution of the proportions of wealth for the CS-CT Poissonised process, which we momentarily denote by $\mathbf{X}_t^{\text{Pois}}$, can also be rigorously obtained by standard conditioning on the number of Poisson

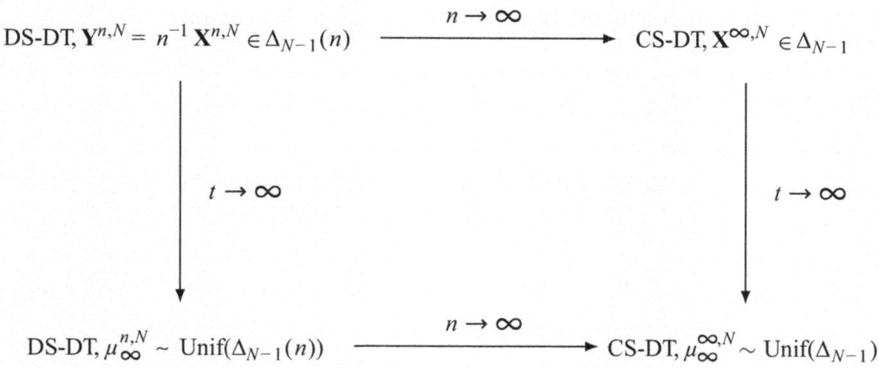

Fig. 5.1 Commutative diagram demonstrating the various limiting measures, depending on the order limits are taken, when the total wealth remains constant. Measures $\mu_\infty^{n,N}$ and $\mu_\infty^{\infty,N}$ denote the invariant distributions for the two Markov chains, respectively. Horizontal arrows in the diagram denote weak convergence, but the top one can be upgraded to almost sure convergence if we are concerned with finite sample paths

events up to time t, using the following

$$\mathbb{P}\{\mathbf{X}_t^{\mathrm{Pois}} \in A\} = \sum_{\ell=0}^{\infty} \mathbf{P}\{\mathbf{X}_\ell^{\infty,N} \in A\} P\{N_t = \ell\} = \sum_{\ell=0}^{\infty} \mathbf{P}\{\mathbf{X}_\ell^{\infty,N} \in A\} e^{-t/N} \frac{t^\ell}{\ell!\, N^\ell}. \tag{5.22}$$

Herein, N_t denotes the background Poisson process with rate $1/N$ and A is any Borel subset of the simplex.

We conclude this section with the argument that the limiting distribution is still uniform on the simplex in this Poissonised chain. We only present the upper bound of the approximation and leave the lower bound to the interested reader in Düring et al. (in preparation).

Proposition 5 *Let* $\mathbf{X}_t^{\mathrm{Pois}} = \mathbf{X}_{N_t}^{\infty,N}$ *denote the Poissonised version of* $\mathbf{X}_\ell^{\infty,N}$. *Then*

$$\mathbf{X}_t^{\mathrm{Pois}} \Longrightarrow \mathrm{Unif}(\Delta_{N-1}), \; \textit{as } t \to \infty. \tag{5.23}$$

Proof Let U_N denote the uniform random variable on the simplex Δ_{N-1}. Pick an f bounded continuous function with $\|f\| \le M_f$, an $\varepsilon > 0$ and find an $L = L(f, \varepsilon)$ so that for all $\ell > L$

$$|\mathbb{E}(f(\mathbf{X}_\ell^{\infty,N})) - \mathbb{E}(f(U_N))| < \varepsilon,$$

with $U_N \sim \mathrm{Unif}(\Delta_{N-1})$. Furthermore, without loss of generality, assume that in taking the limit $t \to \infty$ in the calculation below already satisfies $t/N > 1$ and

$t^{1/4} \gg L$. Then, start with the law of total expectation, and compute

$$\begin{aligned}
\overline{\lim_{t\to\infty}}\, \mathbb{E}(f(\mathbf{X}_t^{\mathrm{Pois}})) &= \overline{\lim_{t\to\infty}} \sum_{\ell=0}^{\infty} \mathbb{E}(\mathbf{X}_\ell^{\infty,N})\, e^{-t/N} \frac{t^\ell}{\ell!\, N^\ell} \\
&\le \overline{\lim_{t\to\infty}} \sum_{\ell=0}^{L} \mathbb{E}(\mathbf{X}_\ell^{\infty,N})\, e^{-t/N} \frac{t^\ell}{\ell!\, N^\ell} + \overline{\lim_{t\to\infty}} \sum_{\ell=L+1}^{\infty} \mathbb{E}(\mathbf{X}_\ell^{\infty,N})\, e^{-t/N} \frac{t^\ell}{\ell!\, N^\ell} \\
&\le \overline{\lim_{t\to\infty}}\, M_f(L+1)\, e^{-t/N} \left(\frac{t}{N}\right)^L + \overline{\lim_{t\to\infty}} \sum_{\ell=L+1}^{\infty} (\mathbb{E}(f(U_N)) + \varepsilon)\, e^{-t/N} \frac{t^\ell}{\ell!\, N^\ell} \\
&\le 0 + \overline{\lim_{t\to\infty}}\, (\mathbb{E}(f(U_N)) + \varepsilon) \sum_{\ell=L+1}^{\infty} e^{-t/N} \frac{t^\ell}{\ell!\, N^\ell} \\
&\le \mathbb{E}(f(U_N)) + \varepsilon.
\end{aligned}$$

The upper bound follows by letting $\varepsilon \to 0$. □

5.3 Kinetic Equations as Thermodynamic Limit of the Markov Chain with Continuous State Space

5.3.1 The CS-DT Model and the Kinetic Equation

In this section we describe the Poissonised model. As above, we denote the total wealth in a system of N agents by $W_N \in \mathbb{R}_+$, which we allow to be zero and that can depend on N. The state of the process at time t is a vector of non-negative real numbers

$$\mathbf{X}_t^N = (X_t^{1,N}, \ldots, X_t^{N,N})$$

with state space

$$\Delta_{W_N} := \left\{(x_1, \ldots, x_N) : x_i \ge 0 \text{ for all } 1 \le i \le N \text{ and } \sum_{i=1}^N x_i = W_N\right\}.$$

Then, as decribed previously, the dynamics on Δ_{W_N} are given by binary interactions where an ordered pair of two agents (i, j) is chosen uniformly at random. The interactions are assumed to happen at constant rate $1/N$, at the events of a background Poisson process. After the interaction, the wealth of the pair $(X^{i,N}, X^{j,N})$ is changed to $((X^{i,N})', (X^{j,N})')$ given by

$$\begin{aligned}
(X^{i,N})' &= r(X^{i,N} + X^{j,N}), \\
(X^{j,N})' &= (1-r)(X^{i,N} + X^{j,N}),
\end{aligned}$$

where r is a random variable with uniform law on $[0, 1]$ that is drawn at time t, independently of the past of the process. These interactions preserve the number of agents and the total wealth

$$W_N := \sum_{i=1}^{N} X^{i,N}, \tag{5.24}$$

and, therefore, the dynamics take place on Δ_{W_N}. We will consider two cases:

(i) Absolute wealth: $X^{i,N}$ represents the wealth of agent i and W_N represents the total wealth of the system;
(ii) Relative wealth: in this case $X^{i,N}$ represents the proportion of wealth of agent i and $W_N = 1$ for all N.

We are now interested in studying the case in which the number of agents grows large, i.e. $N \to \infty$. The first thing to observe is that agents are *exchangeable* by virtue of the nonpreferential dynamics. For the asymptotic analysis, we will focus our study on the empirical distribution

$$\mu_t^N(x) = \frac{1}{N} \sum_{i=1}^{N} \delta_{X_t^{i,N}}(x). \tag{5.25}$$

The empirical distribution μ_t^N is a random probability measure on $\mathbb{R}_+$ that depends on the realisation of the Markov chain $\mathbf{X}_t^N$ defined above. For any interval $[a, b] \subset \mathbb{R}_+$,

$$\begin{aligned}\mu_t^N([a, b]) &= \frac{1}{N} \sum_{i=1}^{N} \delta_{X_t^{i,N}}[a, b] = \frac{1}{N} \sum_{i=1}^{N} \mathbb{1}\{a \leq X_t^{i,N} \leq b\} \\ &= \frac{\text{card}\{i : \text{agent } i\text{'s wealth } \in [a, b]\}}{N}.\end{aligned}$$

The total wealth in the system at time t (5.24) can be expressed in terms of the empirical distribution as

$$W_N = N \int_{\mathbb{R}_+} x \, \mu_t^N(dx). \tag{5.26}$$

Particularly, if $W_N/N \to m$ as $N \to \infty$, then we have that

$$\lim_{N \to \infty} \int_{\mathbb{R}_+} x \, \mu_0^N(dx) = m. \tag{5.27}$$

If $\mu_0^N \Longrightarrow \mu_0$ weakly for some probability measure μ_0 and $m = 0$, Eq. (5.27) would imply that $\mu_0^N(x) \Longrightarrow \delta_0(x)$, as the measure has no support in the negative reals.

For a fixed t, the empirical measure μ_t^N is an element of the space of probability measures $\mathscr{M}_1$ on $\mathbb{R}_+$ and it only changes whenever an interaction event occurs. It is a function of the Markov chain $\mathbf{X}_t^N$, and it is itself a Markov chain.

In order to describe its infinitesimal generator $\mathscr{G}$, we define the measure $\mu^{(x,y,r),N}$ after an interaction between an agent of wealth x (chosen first) and one of wealth y (chosen second) to be

$$\mu^{(x,y,r),N} = \mu^N - \frac{1}{N}\delta_x - \frac{1}{N}\delta_y + \frac{1}{N}\delta_{r(x+y)} + \frac{1}{N}\delta_{(1-r)(x+y)}.$$

This expresses the fact that in an interaction the Markov chain makes a jump where we 'lose' two agents with wealth x and y and 'gain' two agents with wealth $r(x+y)$ and $(1-r)(x+y)$.

Finally, we define the pair-measure $\mu^{(2,N)}$ on rectangles that generate the Borel σ-algebra $\mathscr{B}(\mathbb{R}\times\mathbb{R})$ to be

$$\mu^{(2,N)}(A \times B) = \mu^N(A)\mu^N(B) - \frac{1}{N}\mu^N(A \cap B), \qquad A, B \in \mathscr{B}(\mathbb{R}). \tag{5.28}$$

This is a natural choice of the pair measure, as it is a simplified version of the joint empirical measure for a pair of variables. Note that it is not a probability measure, but this does not matter, as we will only use it as $N \to \infty$. The reason for considering this measure is to take into account that agents do not self-interact, otherwise, we would consider directly the product measure of sets $\mu^N(A)\mu^N(B)$. However, in the mean-field limit leading to the kinetic equation, we will obtain the product measure as the limit, since the diagonal terms appearing in (5.28) are of order $1/N$ and vanish as $N \to \infty$.

The generator for the evolution of μ_t^N, considering an interaction rate of $1/N$, is given by

$$\mathscr{G}F(\mu^N) = \int_0^1 \int_{\mathbb{R}_+} \int_{\mathbb{R}_+} \{F(\mu^{(x,y,r),N}) - F(\mu^N)\}\mathbb{1}_{\{x+y\le W_N\}} N\mu^{(2,N)}(dx, dy)\, dr. \tag{5.29}$$

In the equation above, function F belongs to $C_b(\mathscr{M}_1)$, i.e. bounded measurable functions on the space of probability measures $\mathscr{M}_1$. We impose the term $\mathbb{1}_{\{x+y\le W_N\}}$ in the generator to ensure that the two masses created after the jump fulfil $r(x+y) \le W_N$ and $(1-r)(x+y) \le W_N$.

Given the generator (5.29), we have that the process M_t^F, defined by

$$M_t^F = F(\mu_t^N) - F(\mu_0^N) - \int_0^t \mathscr{G}F(\mu_s^N)\, ds, \tag{5.30}$$

is a martingale (Kipnis and Landim 1999) for any $F \in C_b(\mathcal{M}_1)$. The martingale represents the *fluctuations* of the Markov chain around its expected value. In the mean-field limit, we will show that the martingale vanishes as $N \to \infty$. This means that the random measure μ_t^N converges to its expected value, i.e. in the limit it becomes a deterministic measure (this is a generalisation of the law of large numbers).

In particular, for any function $g \in C_b(\mathbb{R}_+)$ (measurable bounded functions in $\mathbb{R}_+$), we define $F_g \in C_b(\mathcal{M}_1)$ by

$$F_g(\mu) = \langle g, \mu \rangle := \int g(x)\mu(dx).$$

Expression (5.30) can now be rewritten as

$$M_t^{g,N} = \langle g, \mu_t^N \rangle - \langle g, \mu_0^N \rangle - \int_0^t \langle g, Q^{(N)}(\mu_s^N) \rangle \, ds, \tag{5.31}$$

where we are denoting $\mathcal{G}(\langle g, \mu^N \rangle)$ by

$$\begin{aligned}\mathcal{G}(\langle g, \mu^N \rangle) &= \int_0^1 \int_{\mathbb{R}_+} \int_{\mathbb{R}_+} \Big(g(r(x+y)) + g((1-r)(x+y)) - g(x) - g(y) \Big) \mathbb{1}_{\{x+y \le W_N\}} \mu^{(2,N)}(dx, dy) dr \\ &= \langle g, Q^{(N)}(\mu^N) \rangle.\end{aligned} \tag{5.32}$$

Indeed, the last line allows us to define $Q^{(N)}(\mu)$ implicitly via its brackets with bounded continuous functions g.

We will see in Theorem 2 below that μ_t^N converges in probability as $N \to \infty$ to a measure μ which is solution of the following kinetic equation in weak form:

$$\mu_t = \mu_0 + \int_0^t Q(\mu_s) \, ds, \tag{5.33}$$

where the operator Q is defined as follows: for any $g \in C_b(\mathbb{R}_+)$

$$\langle g, Q(\mu) \rangle = \int_{[0,1]} \int_{\mathbb{R}_+} \int_{\mathbb{R}_+} (g(r(x+y)) + g((1-r)(x+y)) - g(x) - g(y)) \, \mathbb{1}_{\{x+y \le w_0\}} \mu(dx)\mu(dy) \, dr, \tag{5.34}$$

with $w_0 = \lim_{N\to\infty} W_N$. We say that $(\mu_t)_{t\ge 0}$ is a solution of (5.33) if it satisfies (5.33) for all functions f which are bounded and measurable. As for the Smoluchowski equation (Norris 1999, Proposition 2.2), one can show the following existence result:

Proposition 6 (Existence and uniqueness of solutions) *Suppose that* $\mu_0 \in \mathcal{M}_1(\mathbb{R}_+)$. *The kinetic equation* (5.33) *has a unique solution* $(\mu_t)_{t\ge 0}$ *with initial data* μ_0.

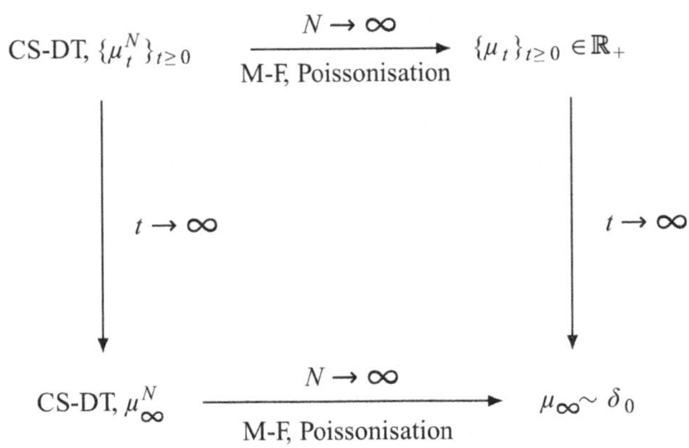

Fig. 5.2 Commutative diagram demonstrating the various limiting measures, depending on the order limits are taken, when the total wealth remains constant. There are two parameters that scale; the number of agents N and the time t. Time is discrete for the left down-arrow, but continuous in the right down-arrow. There is an intermediate step missing from the diagram in which discrete time events are changed with time events arising from a Poisson process of rate $1/N$ which simultaneously scales with N. That is called the Poissonisation step, and when the mean-field limits (M-F) are taken, the rate of the poisson process also scales with N

We will also investigate the limit $t \to \infty$ and obtain different families of limiting invariant measures, in the process verifying the following commutative diagram of Fig. 5.2 in the simple case of fixed wealth $W_N = c$ for all N.

In Fig. 5.2, the left down-arrow was obtained in Düring et al. (2017). The lower horizontal arrow is given in the present article in Proposition 8, and the remaining arrows are discussed in following sections. Everything is proven in Düring et al. (in preparation).

5.3.2 *The Mean-Field Limit*

The following theorem shows how the kinetic equation (5.33) is obtained as the limit in probability of (5.31) as $N \to \infty$. We introduce the symbol $D(K, S)$ that denotes the space of càdlàg (right continuous with left limit) functions from K to S, called the Skorokhod space. For any fixed N, the sequence $\{\mu_t^N\}_{t\geq 0}$ is an element of $D([0, \infty); \mathscr{M}_1(\mathbb{R}_+))$. The mean-field limit result is the following:

Theorem 2 (Mean-field limit) *Suppose that W_N is a non-decreasing sequence converging to $w_0 \in (0, \infty]$ as $N \to \infty$. Suppose that for a given measure μ_0 one has that*

$$\langle x, \mu_0^N \rangle \leq \langle x, \mu_0 \rangle < \infty, \tag{5.35}$$

and that as $N \to \infty$

$$\mu_0^N \Longrightarrow \mu_0 \qquad \text{weakly, as } N \to \infty. \tag{5.36}$$

Then the sequence of random measures $(\mu_t^N)_{t\geq 0}$ *converges as* $N \to \infty$ *in probability in* $D([0,\infty); \mathscr{M}_1(\mathbb{R}_+))$. *The limit* $(\mu_t)_{t\geq 0}$ *is continuous in* t *and it satisfies the kinetic equation* (5.33). *In particular, for all* $g \in C_b(\mathbb{R}_+)$ *the following limits hold in probability, for any time* t

(A) $\lim_{N\to\infty} \sup_{s\leq t} \langle g, \mu_s^N - \mu_s \rangle \overset{\mathbb{P}}{=} 0,$

(B) $\lim_{N\to\infty} \sup_{0\leq s\leq t} |M_s^{g,N}| \overset{\mathbb{P}}{=} 0,$

(C) $\lim_{N\to\infty} \int_0^t \langle g, Q^{(N)}(\mu_s^N)\rangle\, ds \overset{\mathbb{P}}{=} \int_0^t \langle g, Q(\mu_s)\rangle\, ds.$

As a consequence, equation (5.33) *is obtained as the limit in probability of* (5.31) *as* $N \to \infty$.

A similar mean-field limit result and proof can be found, for example, in Merino Aceituno (2016).

Some remarks based on Theorem 2 follow. From equation (5.26) we have that $N\langle x, \mu_0^N\rangle = W_N$. If we now assume that $\lim_{N\to\infty} N^{-1} W_N = m \in (0,\infty)$ then we see that W_N grows linearly in N and condition (5.35) implies

$$m \leq \langle x, \mu_0 \rangle.$$

Now if W_N grows superlinearly, i.e. $\lim_{N\to\infty} N^{-1} W_N = \infty$, then condition (5.35) in Theorem 2 is violated and the theorem does not necessarily hold.

Finally, if either $\lim_{N\to\infty} W_N = w_0$ for some absolute constant w_0 or $W_N \to \infty$ as $N \to \infty$, but $\lim_{N\to\infty} N^{-1} W_N = 0$, we can actually study the asymptotic behaviour ($N \to \infty$) of the measures μ_t^N and show that the limiting measure is a δ mass as $N \to \infty$. This is discussed in the next subsection.

5.3.3 Closing the Diagram of Fig. 5.2

In this section we discuss the case where W_N grows sublinearly and show that under Theorem 2, δ_0 is the only possible candidate for invariant equilibrium measure. Proposition 7 asserts that under the assumptions of Theorem 2 and Proposition 8 argues that the assumptions of Theorem 2 hold when the total wealth $w_0 = 1$ and we start from a uniform density on the simplex. Together, these propositions verify the commutativity of the diagram in Fig. 5.2.

Proposition 7 (Sub-linear growth for W_N) *Suppose the same assumptions on the initial data as in Theorem 2. If it holds that*

$$\langle x, \mu_0^N \rangle = \frac{W_N}{N} \to 0, \quad \text{as } N \to \infty,$$

(which is in particular true if $w_0 < \infty$), then, we have that $\lim_{N\to\infty} \mu_t^N \stackrel{\mathbb{P}}{=} \delta_0$ in probability for all times t.

Proof If $\langle x, \mu_0^N \rangle \to 0$ as $N \to \infty$, by positivity of the support of the measures and conditions (5.35) and (5.36), it follows that

$$\langle x, \mu_0 \rangle = 0.$$

On the other hand, μ_0 is a probability measure, so the above implies that $\mu_0(x) = \delta_0(x)$. Then it follows that $\mu_t(x) = \delta_0(x)$ since we already argued that the delta distribution is an invariant solution of (5.33). □

Proposition 8 (Mean field limit of the empirical wealth under equilibrium measures) *Suppose $\mu_0^{\infty,N} \sim$ Unif$[\Delta_{N-1}]$ (therefore we assume the total wealth is fixed and equal to 1) for each $N \in \mathbb{N}$ and consider the empirical measure on $\mathbb{R}_+$*

$$\mu_0^N = \frac{1}{N} \sum_{i=1}^{N} \delta_{X_0^{i,N}}, \quad (X_0^{1,N}, \ldots, X_0^{N,N}) \sim \mu_0^{\infty,N}.$$

Then as $N \to \infty$,

$$\mu_0^N \Longrightarrow \delta_0.$$

In particular the assumptions of Theorem 2 hold and, since $w_0 = 1$, Proposition 7 is in effect.

Proof *(Proof of Proposition 8)* This proof does not need the technicalities associated with martingales, as the initial distributions of the process are invariant, and every time an interaction event occurs their distribution remains unchanged. The theorem can be proven in a direct way, without even the Poissonisation trick.

Consider a continuous function g on $[0, 1]$ and assume that $\|g\|_\infty \leq B$. Let $\epsilon > 0$ and select a $\delta > 0$ so that $\delta < \epsilon/2 \wedge B$. Furthermore, assume that N is large enough so that for a fixed β, $0 < \beta < 1$ we have that

$$\sup_{x \in [0, N^{-\beta}]} |g(0) - g(x))| < \delta.$$

In order to prove the result we just need to show that $\langle g, \mu_0^N \rangle \to g(0)$ as $N \to \infty$. We will show that this happens $\mathbb{P}$- a.s., when $\mathbb{P} = \otimes_{N=2}^{\infty} \mu_0^{\infty,N}$ the product measure on the space $\otimes_{N=2}^{\infty} \Delta_{N-1}$.

We have that $\langle g, \mu_0^N \rangle = N^{-1} \sum_{i=1}^N g(X^{i,N_0})$, so for the $\mathbb{P}-$ a.s. convergence we estimate

$$
\begin{aligned}
\mathbb{P}\Big\{\Big|\frac{1}{N}\sum_{i=1}^N g(X_i) - g(0)\Big| > \epsilon\Big\} &= \mathbb{P}\Big\{\Big|\sum_{i=1}^N (g(X_i) - g(0))\Big| > N\epsilon\Big\} \\
&\le \mathbb{P}\Big\{\sum_{i=1}^N |g(X_i) - g(0)| > N\epsilon\Big\} \\
&\le e^{-\epsilon N}\mathbb{E}\Big(\exp\Big\{\sum_{i=1}^N |g(X_i) - g(0)|\Big\}\Big) \\
&= e^{-\epsilon N}\mathbb{E}\Big(\exp\Big\{\sum_{i=1}^N |g(X_i) - g(0)|\Big\} \\
&\qquad \sum_{I \subseteq [N]} \mathbb{1}\{X_i \ge N^{-\beta}, i \in I\}\mathbb{1}\{X_i < N^{-\beta}, i \notin I\}\Big) \\
&= e^{-\epsilon N}\mathbb{E}\Big(\sum_{I \subseteq [N]} e^{\sum_{i\in I} |g(X_i) - g(0)|}\mathbb{1}\{X_i \ge N^{-\beta}, i \in I\} \\
&\qquad e^{\sum_{i\notin I} |g(X_i) - g(0)|}\mathbb{1}\{X_i < N^{-\beta}, i \notin I\}\Big) \\
&\le e^{-\epsilon N}\mathbb{E}\Big(\sum_{I \subseteq [N]} e^{2B|I|}\mathbb{1}\{X_i \ge N^{-\beta}, i \in I\}e^{(N-|I|)\delta}\mathbb{1}\{X_i < N^{-\beta}, i \notin I\}\Big) \\
&\le e^{-\epsilon N}\sum_{k=0}^N \binom{N}{k} e^{2Bk+(N-k)\delta}\mathbb{E}(\mathbb{1}\{X_i \ge N^{-\beta} \text{ for } k \text{ indices}\}).
\end{aligned}
$$

The last line has the simplified sum index because of exchangeability of the coordinates, and it is an upper bound, because we dropped the second indicator function. Before proceeding with the calculation, we just bound the last expectation when k is not zero. Note that if $k > [N^{1-\beta}]$, the indicator inside is identically zero, otherwise the total wealth cannot be one. We also restrict the index of summation to $[N^{1-\beta}]$ as the indicator vanishes otherwise.

$$
\begin{aligned}
\mathbb{P}\Big\{\Big|\frac{1}{N}\sum_{i=1}^N g(X_i) - g(0)\Big| > \varepsilon\Big\} &\le e^{(\delta-\epsilon)N} \sum_{k=0}^{[N^{1-\beta}]} \binom{N}{k} e^{(2B-\delta)k} \\
&\le e^{-\epsilon N/2} N^{1-\beta} \binom{N}{[N^{1-\beta}]} e^{(2B-\delta)N^{1-\beta}}. \qquad (5.37)
\end{aligned}
$$

The last line follows because eventually δ will vanish and the exponent $(2B-\delta)$ will be eventually positive. Therefore, the maximum term in the sum is the last one, when $k=[N^{1-\beta}]$ as combinations are also increasing until around $N/2$. Finally, one can use Stirling's formula to see that asymptotically there exists a constant c so that

$$\binom{N}{[N^{1-\beta}]} \sim e^{cN^{1-\beta}}.$$

Therefore, the upper bound in equation (5.37) is summable over N. A final application of the Borel-Cantelli lemma completes the proof. □

Remark 2 If $w_0=\infty$, and assuming that $\mu_t(dx)=f(x)dx$ (absolutely continuous), one can show that the exponential distributions

$$\tilde{f}(x)=\frac{e^{-x/m}}{m}, \tag{5.38}$$

are equilibria for the kinetic equation for some $m>0$ depending on the initial data. Moreover, if f_t is differentiable in $\mathbb{R}_+$, these are the unique equilibria as it is expected from the behaviour of the Markov chain.

5.4 Remembering Masanao Aoki

Only one of us (E.S.) had the privilege of meeting Masanao Aoki. Aoki came to Genoa, Italy, for the 4th Workshop on Economics with Heterogenous Interacting Agents (WEHIA) which was held on 4–5 June 1999. During this conference, Aoki had several discussions with Domenico Costantini and Ubaldo Garibaldi, in the presence of E.S., where it emerged that the techniques developed by Costantini and Garibaldi for statistical physics (Costantini and Garibaldi 1997, 1998) were strictly related to the work on economics presented by Aoki in his book (Aoki 1998). As in the next decade, E.S. started a collaboration with Garibaldi on finitary models in econophysics, it became natural to write a book highlighting this approach (Garibaldi and Scalas 2010). The stimulus to write that book came during the Econophysics Colloquium in November 2006 in Tokyo, out of a discussion with Thomas Lux and Taisei Kaizoji, who encouraged E.S. to pursue the enterprise of writing a textbook on the approach to economics developed by Masanao Aoki. Even if rather indirect, Masanao Aoki had a deep influence on the work and even the career of E.S. who matured the idea of moving from physics to mathematics and, namely, to probability in the years between 1999 and 2010.

References

Aoki M (1998) New approaches to macroeconomic modeling: evolutionary stochastic dynamics. Multiple equilibria, and externalities as field effects. Cambridge University Press, Cambridge

Aoki M, Yoshikawa H (2007) Reconstructing macroeconomics. Cambridge University Press, Cambridge

Bassetti F, Toscani G (2010) Explicit equilibria in a kinetic model of gambling. Phys Rev E 81:066115

Bertoin J (2006) Random fragmentation and coagulation processes. Cambridge University Press, Cambridge

Billingsley P (1999) Convergence of probability measures. Wiley, New York

Bottazzi G, Dosi G, Fagiolo G, Secchi A (2007) Modeling industrial evolution in geographical space. J Econ Geogr 7:651–672

Brillouin L (1927) Comparaison des différentes statistiques appliqueés aux problèmes de quanta. Ann Phys Paris 7:315–331

Costantini D, Garibaldi U (1997) A probabilistic foundation of elementary particle statistics. Part I. Stud Hist Philos Mod Phys 28:483–506

Costantini D, Garibaldi U (1998) A probabilistic foundation of elementary particle statistics. Part II. Stud Hist Philos Mod Phys 29:37–59

Düring B, Georgiou N, Scalas E (2017) A stylised model for wealth distribution. In: Akura Y, Kirman A (eds) Economic foundations of social complexity science. Springer, Singapore, pp 95–117

Düring B, Georgiou N, Merino-Aceituno S, Scalas E, Continuum and thermodynamic limits for a simple random-exchange model. arXiv:2003.00930 [math.PR]

Ethier SN, Kurtz TG (2005) Markov processes, characterization and convergence. Wiley, New York

Garibaldi U, Scalas E (2010) Finitary probabilistic methods in econophysics. Cambridge University Press, Cambridge

Garibaldi U, Scalas E, Viarengo P (2007) Statistical equilibrium in simple exchange games II. The redistribution game. Eur Phys J B Condensed Matter Complex Syst 60:241–246

Jacod J, Shiryaev AN (2003) Limit theorems for stochastic processes. Springer, New York

Kipnis C, Landim C (1999) Scaling limits of interacting particle systems. Springer, New York

Merino Aceituno S (2016) Isotropic wave turbulence with simplified kernels: existence, uniqueness, and mean-field limit for a class of instantaneous coagulation-fragmentation processes. J Math Phys 57:121501

Meyn SP, Tweedie RL (1993) Markov chains and stochastic stability. Springer, London

Norris JR (1999) Smoluchowski's coagulation equation: uniqueness, nonuniqueness and a hydrodynamic limit for the stochastic coalescent. Ann Appl Probab 9:78–109

Pareschi L, Toscani G (2014) Interacting multiagent systems: kinetic equations and Monte Carlo methods. Oxford University Press, Oxford

Pollard D (1984) Chapter V in the book by Pollard D, Convergence of stochastic processes. Springer, New York, 1984 contains a historical note on Poissonization

Zabell S (1997) The continuum of inductive methods revisited. In: Earman J, Norton JD (eds) The cosmos of science: essays of exploration. University of Pittsburgh Press, Pittsburgh

Chapter 6
Distribution and Fluctuation of Personal Income, Entropy, and Equal a Priori Probabilities: Evidence from Japan

Wataru Souma

Abstract Following Fujiwara et al.'s (Physica A 321(3):598–604, 2003) joint paper with the late professor Masanao Aoki of UCLA, we review the functions proposed to explain personal income distribution, changes in distribution of Japanese personal income, the fluctuation of personal income of high taxpayers in Japan, the entropy, and Kullback-Leibler divergence as a measure of inequality and the principle of equal a priori weighting as a definition of equality.

Keywords Personal income · Beta type distribution · Entropy · Equality · Equal a priori probabilities

6.1 Introduction

The study of income distribution and inequality has a distinguished pedigree and remains an interest among scholars of natural science and social welfare. Vilfredo Pareto (1897) pioneered the field using data from several countries across different years and proposed the Pareto distribution functions. Many subsequent scholars – summarized in Kleiber and Kotz (2003) – suggested functions to explain personal income distribution. Attention to the subject hit a crescendo when the Lehman Shock revealed the incredible disparity between income in the financial sector and high- and middle-income earners in other sectors. Thereafter, Piketty and Goldhammer (2014) documented this serious inequality, largely in Europe and in the United States (US), using long-term income data.

Personal income distribution generally is disclosed as the data by income class, making it difficult to trace the variation of income at the individual level. The exception is Japan from 1947 to 2005. Fujiwara et al. (2003), in a noteworthy paper with the late professor Masanao Aoki of UCLA, investigated the fluctuation

---

W. Souma (✉)
College of Science and Technology, Nihon University, Funabashi, Chiba, Japan

H. Aoyama et al. (eds.), *Complexity, Heterogeneity, and the Methods of Statistical Physics in Economics*, Evolutionary Economics and Social Complexity Science 22,
https://doi.org/10.1007/978-981-15-4806-2_6

of personal income of high taxpayers from 1987 to 2000. They clarified for the normal economy that the power-law distribution, the detailed balance, and Gibrat's law hold simultaneously in the high-income range. During the bubble economy, all three break simultaneously in the high-income range.

The distribution and fluctuation of personal income are interesting subjects in the viewpoint of natural science. On the other hand, measuring inequality is a significant subject in social welfare. Defining inequality requires answering two questions, i.e.: What is equality? What statistical or other divergence from parity constitutes inequality? To answer the former question, Lorenz (1905) introduced the Lorentz curve to visualize the changing inequality, and Gini (1912) (see also Ceriani and Verme 2012) introduced the Gini index to quantify it. Drawing from information theory, Theil (1967) introduced entropy to quantify inequality. The customary definition of income equality is "every individual has the same income"; however, Roemer (1998) introduced the concept of equality of opportunity.

The present study proceeds as follows. Section 6.2 reviews several distribution functions that explain personal income distribution. Section 6.3 explains the distribution and fluctuation of personal income in Japan. Section 6.4 analyzes the deviation from inequality through the viewpoint of entropy and the principle of equal a priori weighting as a definition of equality. Section 6.5 concludes the study.

6.2 Distribution Functions of Personal Income

Pareto's (1897) table of income distribution in Great Britain and Ireland from 1893 to 1894 (Pareto 1897, p. 305, Schedule D) suggests that personal income distribution decreases monotonically with the increase in income and has a fat-tailed distribution. Aoyama et al. (2017, p. 84, Fig. 3.9) depict a double-logarithmic plot of data in Pareto's table and confirm that personal income follows a power-law distribution, now called Pareto's law. Pareto introduced the probability density function for a type I Pareto distribution given by

$$f_{\mathrm{P1}}(x, ; b, \mu) = \frac{\mu b^{\mu}}{x^{\mu+1}} , \tag{6.1}$$

for $x \geq b > 0$. Here, b is the Pareto scale and $\mu > 0$ is the Pareto index. After investigating income distributions in other countries across years, Pareto concluded that his index takes the value $\mu = 1.0 \sim 2.0$.

Coincident with Pareto, March (1898) investigated and displayed data for wage distributions in France, Germany, and the US (March 1898, p. 196, Table 1). We can guess from the table that the wedge distributes in the narrow range with a peak and follows skew distributions with fat tail in the high wedge range. To explain this,

March introduced the probability density function, so called the gamma distribution, given by

$$f_{\mathrm{GA}}(x;\beta,\mu)=\frac{x^{\mu-1}}{\beta^{\mu}\Gamma(\mu))}\exp\left[-\frac{x}{\beta}\right], \tag{6.2}$$

for $x>0$, $\beta>0$, and $\mu>0$. Here, $\Gamma(\mu)$ is the gamma function defined by

$$\Gamma(\mu)=\int_0^{\infty}due^{-u}u^{\mu-1}. \tag{6.3}$$

Equation (6.2) is a type III Pareto distribution. Amoroso (1925) investigated Prussian income distribution in 1912 and generalized Eq. (6.2) to a generalized gamma distribution function:

$$f_{\mathrm{GG}}(x;a,\beta,\mu)=\frac{ax^{a\mu-1}}{\beta^{a\mu}\Gamma(\mu)}\exp\left[-\left(\frac{x}{\beta}\right)^{a}\right], \tag{6.4}$$

for $x\geq 0$, $a>0$, $\beta>0$, and $\mu>0$.

After Pareto, numerous studies dispute the power-law distribution of personal income. Shirras (1935) investigated the Indian income and super tax (income tax) data across years and concluded that "There is indeed no Pareto law. It is time that it should be entirely discarded in studies on the distribution of income." However, Macgregor (1936) and Johnson (1937) supported the power-law distribution of personal income.

The log-normal distribution was introduced to explain personal income distribution, which was first suggested by Galton (1879) and mathematically formulated by McAlister (1879). The probability density function of the log-normal distribution is given by

$$f_{\mathrm{LN}}(x;\langle x\rangle,\sigma)=\frac{1}{\sqrt{2\pi}\sigma x}\exp\left[-\frac{(\ln x-\langle x\rangle)^2}{2\sigma^2}\right], \tag{6.5}$$

where $\langle x\rangle$ is the averaged value of $\ln x$ and σ^2 is the variance. The mathematical formulation was re-discovered by Kapteyn (1903). Motivated by his discovery, Gibrat (1931) introduced "the law of proportional effect" to explain income distribution.

Burr (1942) and Singh and Maddala (1976) introduced the Burr XII or Singh-Maddala distribution of which the probability density function is given by

$$f_{\mathrm{SM}}(x;a,b,\nu)=\frac{a\nu x^{a-1}}{b^{a}}\left[1+\left(\frac{x}{b}\right)^{a}\right]^{-(1+\nu)}, \tag{6.6}$$

for $0<x<\infty$ and zero otherwise with a, b, and ν positive.

Burr (1942) and Dagum (1977) introduced the Burr III or Dagum distribution, the probability density function of which is given by

$$f_{\mathrm{BR3}}(x; a, b, \mu) = \frac{a\mu x^{a\mu-1}}{b^{a\mu}} \left[1 + \left(\frac{x}{b}\right)^a\right]^{-(\mu+1)} , \tag{6.7}$$

for $0 < x < \infty$ and zero otherwise with a, b, and μ positive.

McDonald (1984) introduced the generalized beta distribution of second kind (GB2) of which the probability density function is given by

$$f_{\mathrm{GB2}}(x; a, b, \mu, \nu) = \frac{a x^{a\mu-1}}{b^{a\mu} B(\mu, \nu)} \left[1 + \left(\frac{x}{b}\right)^a\right]^{-(\mu+\nu)} , \tag{6.8}$$

for $0 < x < \infty$ and zero otherwise with a, b, μ, and ν positive. Here, $B(\mu, \nu)$ is the beta function defined by

$$B(\mu, \nu) = \int_0^1 du u^{\mu-1}(1-u)^{\nu-1} = \frac{\Gamma(\mu)\Gamma(\nu)}{\Gamma(\mu+\nu)} = B(\nu, \mu) . \tag{6.9}$$

McDonald and Xu (1995) introduced the generalized beta distribution (GB) of which the probability density function is given by

$$f_{\mathrm{GB}}(x; a, b, c, \mu, \nu) = \frac{|a| x^{a\mu-1}}{b^{a\mu} B(\mu, \nu)} \left[1 - (1-c)\left(\frac{x}{b}\right)^a\right]^{\nu-1} \left[1 + c\left(\frac{x}{b}\right)^a\right]^{-(\mu+\nu)} , \tag{6.10}$$

for $0 < x^a < b^a/(1-c)$ and zero otherwise with $0 \le c \le 1$, and b, μ, and ν positive.

Drăgulescu and Yakovenko (2001) introduced the exponential distribution, the probability density function of which is given by

$$f_{\mathrm{Exp}}(x; \lambda) = \frac{1}{\lambda} \exp\left[-\frac{x}{\lambda}\right] , \tag{6.11}$$

for $0 \le x < \infty$ with λ positive. Probability density functions from Eqs. (6.1) to (6.11) consist the beta-type distribution tree shown in Aoyama et al. (2017, p. 61, Fig. 3.1).

Yakovenko and Rosser Jr (2009) introduced the Boltzmann-Gibbs distribution, the probability density function of which is given by

$$f_{\mathrm{BG}}(x; T) = Ce^{-x/T} , \tag{6.12}$$

where C is a normalization constant. Here, T equals to the average amount of money per earners, i.e., $T = M/N$, where M is the total money and N is the number of income earners. Yakovenko and Rosser Jr (2009) called T the "money temperature."

The surge of research on income distributions that followed is listed in Kleiber and Kotz (2003, pp. 278–279; Table B.2) and Aoyama et al. (2017). New distribution functions continue to emerge, stimulated by the impossibility of obtaining complete income data for each individual. Nonetheless, scholars commonly agree that the distribution of high-income ranges follow the power-law.

6.3 Distribution of and Fluctuation in Japanese Personal Income

Japan generates three categories of personal income data (Table 6.1): employment income, self-declared income, and high-income taxpayer data. Employment income is disclosed as the data by income class. We obtained post-1951 data from the website of the National Tax Agency of Japan (NTAJ), a survey used to create basic Private Salary Statistics based on the Statistics Law. Private Salary Actual Statistics clarifies annual salaries at private establishments by salary class, establishment size, and other criteria. It forms a basic document for tax administration. Its characteristics are a wide survey of establishments with 1 to more than 5,000 employees; clear delineations by salary class, gender, age, and length of service; and a breakdown of salaries by size of the paying entity.

Self-declared income data are disclosed as the data by income class. We obtain post-1951 data (available on paper from 1887 to the present) from the NTAJ website. Japanese workers must file an individual tax return if they earn at least ¥20 million

Table 6.1 Number of persons and classes contained in Japanese data for employment income, self-declared income, and income taxes 1987–2000

	Employment income		Self-declared income		High income tax	
Fiscal year	# individuals	# classes	# individuals	# classes	# individuals	# classes
1987	42,652,250	14	7,707,308	14	110, 817	None
1988	43,686,503	14	7,797,019	14	111, 765	None
1989	45,057,032	14	7,965,871	18	141, 211	None
1990	46,549,065	14	8,547,375	18	172, 183	None
1991	48,146,547	14	8,562,552	18	175, 723	None
1992	49,090,672	14	8,577,661	18	125, 066	None
1993	49,869,037	14	8,428,477	18	128, 666	None
1994	50,157,991	14	8,223,171	18	95, 683	None
1995	51,598,961	14	8,020,634	18	95, 358	None
1996	52,009,683	14	8,239,858	18	99, 284	None
1997	52,521,112	14	8,271,709	18	93, 394	None
1998	52,682,839	14	6,224,254	18	84, 571	None
1999	52,649,968	14	7,400,607	18	75, 272	None
2000	52,691,963	14	7,273,506	18	79, 999	None

from two salary sources. Workers who earn below ¥20 million from only one source of salary need not file a tax return, as employers adjust tax deducted from monthly salary at year end and that becomes final tax paid. We extracted samples from 524 tax offices nationwide by income earner category and total income class and estimated total population from data in the sample.

High-income taxpayers are those who filed an income tax exceeding ¥10 million. Based on the high-taxpayer notice system, the data were disclosed from 1947 to 2005 and provided by Tokyo Shoko Research. The system was initially intended to prevent tax evasion by publicizing the name, address, and tax paid of high-income earners. The system was abused and was abolished in 2006.

6.3.1 Distribution

Following Aoyama et al. (2000) and Souma (2001, 2002), we review the distribution of Japanese personal income. Figure 6.1 shows the double logarithmic plot of rank-size distributions of personal income from 1987 to 2000. White circles correspond to unified data for employment and self-declared income. We represent the rth person's income as I_r for these unified data and income tax as T_r. To combine income and high-income tax data, we moved the latter horizontally, i.e.,

$$I_r = aT_r \ . \tag{6.13}$$

For example, in 1999 the income of the 40,623th person is ¥50 million ($I_{40,623} =$ ¥50 million). That person's income tax is ¥15.13 million ($T_{40,623} = 15.13$). Therefore,

$$I_r = 3.3 \times T_r \ . \tag{6.14}$$

We multiply a by all income tax data to obtain the overall income distribution. Although values of a depend on the year, differences are small. Small dots in Fig. 6.1 correspond to the high-income distribution translated by Eq. (6.13).

Figure 6.1 shows that the wide range of high-income follows the power-law distribution except during 1989–1992. We investigate changes in equity and land prices to isolate 1989 to 2002. The solid line in Fig. 6.2 depicts the daily change in closing value of TOPIX normalized by its closing value on March 31, 2000. The dashed line with black circles depicts changes in the monthly land price index normalized by its value on March 31, 2000. Figure 6.2 shows that TOPIX increased rapidly from around 1985 to the end of 1990 and began suddenly to decline in early 1991. Figure 6.2 also shows that the land price index rose rapidly from around 1986 to 1992 and fell gradually after 1992. The period December 1986 to February 1991 is the Heisei Bubble. Therefore, we conjecture that the stylized fact, i.e., *the high-income range always follows the power-law distribution*, is broken around of the top of the bubble economy. Fujiwara et al. (2003) demonstrate that this stylized fact

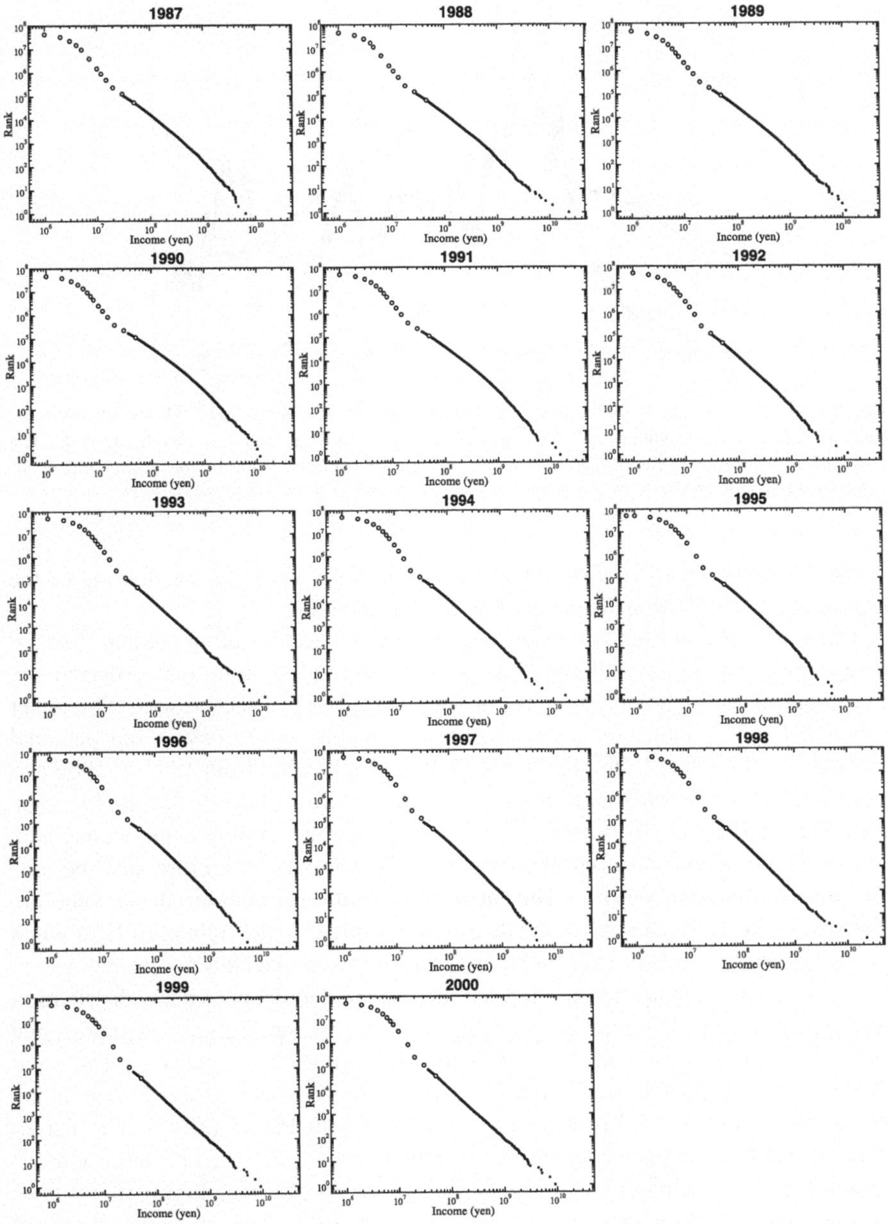

Fig. 6.1 Changes in personal income distribution from 1987 to 2000. These figures are double logarithmic plots of personal income and rank. (See also Aoyama et al. 2017)

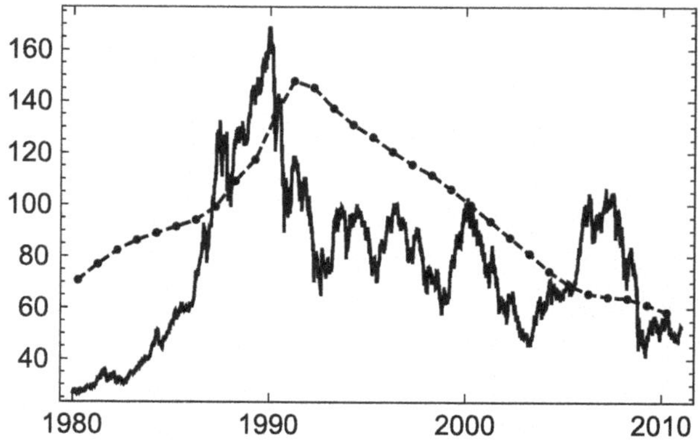

Fig. 6.2 Changes in the TOPIX and the land price index from 1980 to 2012. The solid shows the daily change of closing value of TOPIX normalized by its closing value on March 31, 2000. The dashed line with black circles shows changes in the monthly land price index normalized by its value on March 31, 2000

is wrong. However, to confirm this observation more precisely, we investigate the high-income distribution during another bubble economy.

Changes in Japan's tax system altered the criterion for declaring income changed many times. Therefore, although data are not recorded by a uniform criterion, we can obtain data for income tax and income from 1887 to the present. The upper panel in Fig. 6.3 depicts changes in personal income tax (crosses) and personal income (open circles) from 1887 to 2003. Personal income from 1951 to 1986 and from 2001 to 2003 consists of employment income data and self-declared income data. Personal income from 1987 to 2000 consists of the employment income data, self-declared income data, and high-income taxpayer data. Therefore, distributions are same as those in Fig. 6.2. The far left distribution represents the income tax distribution in 1897. Thereafter, the distributions moved to the right until 1991 when the Heisei bubble ended. After 1991, the distributions moved left.

Although the data are not highly accurate, we applied the power-law distribution (the type I Pareto distribution given by Eq. (6.1)) to the high-tax income range and investigated every year from 1887 to 2003 using Pareto index μ. The solid line with filled circles in the lower panel of Fig. 6.3 shows the Pareto index fluctuates around $\mu = 2.0$, a finding consistent with Pareto (1897). The Pareto index quantifies inequality distribution of high-income range, i.e., large (small) values for μ correspond to an equal (unequal) distribution. Figure 6.3 shows that inequality declined gradually during the 1945–1968 economic expansion, and observation coincides with Piketty's (2014) for France (Piketty and Goldhammer 2014). Inequality increased during the oil shock and land boom from 1968 to 1973 and the Heisei Bubble from 1985 to 1991.

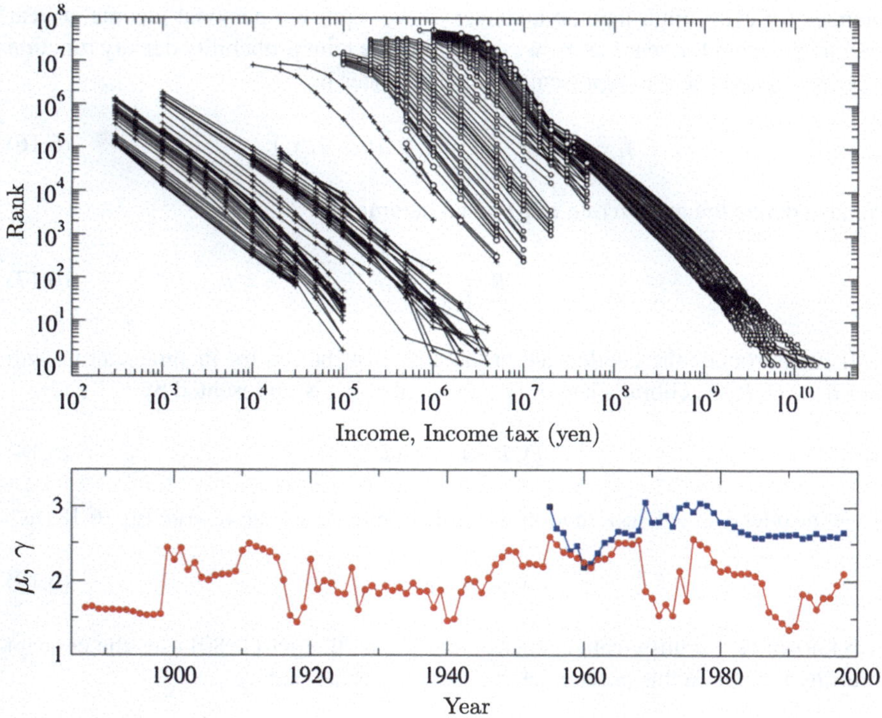

Fig. 6.3 The upper panel depicts changes of rank-size distribution in personal income tax (crosses) and personal income (open circles). The lower panel depicts changes in Pareto index μ and Gibrat's Index γ. (See also Souma 2001, 2002)

We also applied the log-normal distribution given by Eq. (6.5) to the mid- and low-income range and investigated Gibrat's index defined by

$$\gamma = \frac{1}{\sqrt{2\sigma^2}} \,. \tag{6.15}$$

Large (small) values for γ correspond to equal (unequal) distribution. The solid line with filled squares in the lower panel in Fig. 6.3 shows that γ is stable after around 1985 in contrast to changes in the Pareto index μ. Mid- and low-income Japanese were unaffected by the Heisei Bubble.

6.3.2 Fluctuation

Following Fujiwara et al. (2003), we review fluctuations in Japanese personal income. Data for high-income taxpayers capture individuals, so we can trace yearly changes for every high-income taxpayer. If we represent personal income at year $t-1$ as x_{t-1} and for year t as x_t, we can define the joint probability density function $f(x_t, x_{t-1})$ and use it to represent detailed balances by

$$f_{t,t-1}(x_t, x_{t-1}) = f_{t,t-1}(x_{t-1}, x_t) \ . \tag{6.16}$$

We also define the growth rate of personal income by

$$R = \frac{x_t}{x_{t-1}} \ . \tag{6.17}$$

If we introduce the conditional probability distribution for income x at growth rate R as $Q(R|x)$, Gibrat's law of proportional effect is represented by

$$Q(R|x) = Q(R) \ . \tag{6.18}$$

If we introduce $a_t > 0$ as a random variable at time t, we can rewrite Eq. (6.18) as

$$x_t = a_{t-1} x_{t-1} \ , \tag{6.19}$$

also known as a multiplicative stochastic process. Badger (1980) uses the concept of utility to explain this process. Here, utility U_t is defined by

$$U_t = \frac{\Delta x_t}{x_{t-1}} = a_{t-1} \ , \tag{6.20}$$

where $\Delta x_t = x_t - x_{t-1}$ means an increase or decrease in annual income for consecutive years. Thus, Eq. (6.20) is equivalent to Eq. (6.19), except that a_t is shifted to $a_t + 1$.

Fujiwara et al. (2003) clarified for the normal economy that the power-law distribution, the detailed balance, and Gibrat's law hold simultaneously in the high-income range. During the bubble economy, all three break simultaneously in the high-income range.

6.4 Equality and Inequality

We turn now to equality and inequality of personal income. We noted earlier the two questions that must be answered when discussing equality and inequality. Section 6.4.1 considers the first question, i.e., how far from equality, and Sect. 6.4.2 the second, i.e., what is equality.

6.4.1 Entropy and Kullback-Leibler Divergence as a Measure of Inequality

Lorenz (1905) introduced the Lorentz curve to visualize changes in inequality. Gini (1912) (see also Ceriani and Verme 2012) introduced the Gini index to quantify inequality. Theil (1967) introduced entropy to quantify inequality from an information-theoretical perspective. Following Theil, we consider a society with total income M and total population N. We assume people have positive or zero income, making the income of the ith individual $x_i \geq 0$ $(i = 1, 2, \ldots, N)$. We then obtain

$$\sum_{i=1}^{N} x_i = M \,. \tag{6.21}$$

We define the normalized income vector $\boldsymbol{p} = (p_1, \ldots, p_N)$ in which normalized income of the ith individual is defined by

$$p_i = \frac{x_i}{M} \geq 0 \,, \tag{6.22}$$

and the normalized income vector satisfies

$$\sum_{i=1}^{N} p_i = 1 \,. \tag{6.23}$$

Thus, we can treat p_i as the probability event x_i occurs and use p_i to define entropy $H(\boldsymbol{p})$:

$$H(\boldsymbol{p}) = -\sum_{i=1}^{N} p_i \log(p_i) \,. \tag{6.24}$$

In a completely equal world, every person has identical income and $\boldsymbol{p} = (1/N, \ldots, 1/N)$. Therefore, Eq. (6.24) becomes

$$H(\boldsymbol{p}) = \log N \,. \tag{6.25}$$

This is the maximum value of the entropy. On the other hand, in a completely unequal world, one person earns all income and others none. That is, $\boldsymbol{p} = (0, \ldots, 0, 1, 0, \ldots, 0)$. Eq. (6.24) becomes

$$H(\boldsymbol{p}) = 0 \,. \tag{6.26}$$

This is the minimum value of the entropy.

Now, we consider the substitution of $\log N$ minus $H(\boldsymbol{p})$:

$$\log N - H(\boldsymbol{p}) = \sum_{i=1}^{N} p_i \log (Np_i) = \sum_{i=1}^{N} p_i \log \left(\frac{p_i}{1/N} \right) . \tag{6.27}$$

If we denote the normalized equal vector as $\boldsymbol{q} = (1/N, \ldots, 1/N)$, Eq. (6.27) becomes

$$D_{\mathrm{KL}}(\boldsymbol{p}||\boldsymbol{q}) = \sum_{i=1}^{N} p_i \log \left(\frac{p_i}{q_i} \right) , \tag{6.28}$$

which is the same as the Kullback-Leibler divergence (also called relative entropy) (Kullback and Leibler 1951). Here, $D_{\mathrm{KL}}(\boldsymbol{p}||\boldsymbol{q})$ varies between 0 (complete equality) and $\log N$ (complete inequality).

Although Theil (1967) mainly uses Eq. (6.28) to discuss inequality of income distribution, in the Appendix, he proposes

$$D_{\mathrm{KL}}(\boldsymbol{q}||\boldsymbol{p}) = \sum_{i=1}^{N} q_i \log \left(\frac{q_i}{p_i} \right) . \tag{6.29}$$

Equation (6.29) is more suitable than Eq. (6.28) to measure inequality of income distribution.

6.4.2 Equal a Priori Probabilities as a Definition of Equality

Following Kubo (1952), we suppose a society has total money M and N people and consider the number of ways to distribute M across N. The distribution pattern is given by

$$W_N(M) = \frac{(M + N - 1)!}{(N - 1)!M!} . \tag{6.30}$$

When some person has money x, the number of possible distributions is given by

$$W_{N-1}(M - x) . \tag{6.31}$$

The total for each case of $x = 0, 1, \ldots, M$ is

$$\sum_{x=0}^{M} W_{N-1}(M - x) = W_N(M) . \tag{6.32}$$

If we suppose equal a priori probabilities, the probability someone has money x is given by

$$p(x) = \frac{W_{N-1}(M-x)}{W_N(M)} \ . \tag{6.33}$$

When $N \gg 1$ and $x \ll M$, Eq. (6.33) becomes

$$p(x) = \frac{N}{M+N}\left(\frac{M}{M+N}\right)^x \ . \tag{6.34}$$

If we define average money n by $T = M/N$, Eq. (6.34) becomes

$$p(x) = \frac{1}{1+T}\left(\frac{T}{1+T}\right)^x \ . \tag{6.35}$$

By introducing $\beta = \log\{(1+T)/T\}$, we rewrite the probability to

$$p(x) = C' e^{-\beta x} \ , \tag{6.36}$$

where C' is the normalization constant. Equation (6.36) is the Boltzmann-Gibbs distribution that appeared in Eq. (6.12). Thus, if we assume equal a priori probabilities as a definition of equality, Kullback-Leibler divergence with equal distribution given by Boltzmann-Gibbs represents the degree of inequality.

6.5 Summary

This study has reviewed selected topics concerning personal income distribution based on Fujiwara et al. (2003), a joint paper with the late professor Masanao Aoki of UCLA. We revisited the distribution functions of personal income, the distribution and fluctuation of Japanese personal income, entropy and Kullback-Leibler divergence as measures of inequality, and the principle of equal a priori weighting as a definition of equality. We did not review stochastic modes of personal income distribution; however, for example, Nirei and Souma (2007) successfully did so for Japan and the US. Although the study of personal income distribution and inequality is not mainstream in economics today, its continued study is necessary to realize an equal world.

Reminiscence

I first met Masanao in 2000 at the inaugural Nikkei Econophysics Conference. He always encouraged me. I last saw him in 2012 at the salon of the Graduate School of Economics, Faculty of Economics, University of Tokyo. At that time, he introduced me to Kadanoff (2000) and said that concepts in this book will be important in future economics.

Acknowledgments This chapter derives from discussions during the Symposium on Inequality, Entropy, and Econo-physics organized by Professors Venkat Venkatasubramanian (Columbia University), Ravi Kanbur (Cornell University), and Sitabhra Sinha (Institute for Mathematical Sciences, India). I am deeply grateful to them and the participants of the symposium.

References

Amoroso L (1925) Ricerche intorno alla curva dei redditi. Annali di Matematica Pura ed Applicata 2(1):123–159

Aoyama H, Souma W, Nagahara Y, Okazaki MP, Takayasu H, Takayasu M (2000) Pareto's law for income of individuals and debt of bankrupt companies. Fractals 8(3):293–300

Aoyama H, Fujiwara Y, Ikeda Y, Iyetomi H, Souma W, Yoshikawa H (2017) Macro-econophysics: new studies on economic networks and synchronization. Cambridge University Press, Cambridge

Badger WW (1980) An entropy-utility model for the size distribution of income. In: J. B. West (Ed) Mathematical models as a tool for the social science. Gordon and Breach, New York, pp 87–120

Burr IW (1942) Cumulative frequency functions. Ann Math Stat 13(2):215–232

Ceriani L, Verme P (2012) The origins of the gini index: extracts from variabilità e mutabilità (1912) by Corrado Gini. J Econ Inequal 10(3):421–443

Dagum C (1977) New model of personal income-distribution-specification and estimation. Economie Appliquée 30(3):413–437

Drăgulescu A, Yakovenko VM (2001) Evidence for the exponential distribution of income in the USA. Eur Phys J B 20(4):585–589

Fujiwara Y, Souma W, Aoyama H, Kaizoji T, Aoki M (2003) Growth and fluctuations of personal income. Physica A 321(3):598–604

Galton F (1879) The geometric mean, in vital and social statistics. Proc Roy Soc Lond 29(196–199):365–367

Gibrat R (1931) Les Inégalités Économiques. Librairie du Recueil Sirey, Paris

Gini C (1912) Variabilità e mutabilità. Reprinted in Memorie di metodologica statistica (Ed. Pizetti E, Salvemini, T). Libreria Eredi Virgilio Veschi, Rome

Johnson NO (1937) The Pareto law. Rev Econ Stat 19(1):20–26

Kadanoff LP (2000) Statistical physics: statics, dynamics and renormalization. World Scientific Publishing Company, River Edge

Kapteyn JC (1903) Skew frequency curves in biology and statistics. P. Noordhoff, Groningen

Kleiber C, Kotz S (2003) Statistical size distributions in economics and actuarial sciences. John Wiley and Sons, Inc., Hoboken

Kubo R (1952) Statistical mechanics (written in Japanese). Kyoritsu Shuppan, Tokyo

Kullback S, Leibler RA (1951) On information and sufficiency. Ann Math Stat 22(1):79–86

Lorenz MO (1905) Methods of measuring the concentration of wealth. Publ Am Stat Assoc 9(70):209–219
Macgregor DH (1936) Pareto's law. Econ J 46(181):80–87
March L (1898) Quelques exemples de distribution des salaires. Journal de la société française de statistique 39:193–206
McAlister D (1879) The law of the geometric mean. Proc R Soc Lond 29(196–199):367–376
McDonald JB (1984) Some generalized functions for the size distribution of income. Econometrica 52:647–663
McDonald JB, Xu YJ (1995) A generalization of the beta distribution with applications. J Econ 66(1):133–152
Nirei M, Souma W (2007) A two factor model of income distribution dynamics. Rev Income and Wealth 53(3):440–459
Pareto V (1897) Cours d'économie politique: professé a l'université de lausanne – tone second. LAUSANNE F. ROUGE
Piketty T, Goldhammer A (2014) Capital in the twenty-first century. Harvard University Press, Cambridge, MA
Roemer JE (1998) Equality of opportunity. Harvard University Press, Cambridge, MA
Shirras GF (1935) The Pareto law and the distribution of income. Econ J 45(180):663–681
Singh SK, Maddala GS (1976) A function for size distribution of incomes. Econometrica 44(5):963–970
Souma W (2001) Universal structure of the personal income distribution. Fractals 9(4):463–470
Souma W (2002) Physics of personal income. In: Empirical science of financial fluctuations. Springer, Tokyo, pp 343–352
Theil H (1967) Economics and information theory. Studies in mathematical and managerial economics. North-Holland, Amsterdam
Yakovenko VM, Rosser JB Jr (2009) Colloquium: statistical mechanics of money, wealth, and income. Rev Modern Phys 81(4):1703

Chapter 7
Firms Growth, Distribution, and Non-Self-Averaging Revisited

Yoshi Fujiwara

Abstract During my last conversation with Masanao Aoki, he told me that the concept of non-self-averaging in statistical physics, frequently appearing in economic and financial systems, has important consequences to policy implication. Zipf's law in firms-size distribution is one of such examples. Recent Malevergne, Saichev, and Sornette (MSS) model, simple but realistic, gives a framework of stochastic process including firms' entry, exit, and growth based on Gibrat's law of proportionate effect and shows that the Zipf's law is a robust consequence. By using the MSS model, I would like to discuss about the breakdown of Gibrat's law and the deviation from Zipf's law, often observed for the regime of small and medium firms. For the purpose of discussion, I recapitulate the derivation of exact solution for the MSS model with some correction and additional information on the distribution for the age of existing firms. I argue that the breakdown of Gibrat's law is related to the underlying network of firms, most notably production network, in which firms are mutually correlated among each other leading to the larger volatility in the growth for smaller firms that depend as suppliers on larger customers.

Keywords Gibrat's law of proportionate effect · Zipf's law · Firm size · Firm growth · Non-self-averaging

7.1 Introduction

Masanao Aoki had been, and is still, inspiring me with a lot of ideas and methods he brought into the study of macroeconomic phenomena. I first met him at the 3rd Tohwa University International Conference on Statistical Physics held at Fukuoka City of Japan in November 1999. He was one of the invited speakers of the conference and gave a talk to the audience, mostly physicists, about his work on

Y. Fujiwara (✉)
University of Hyogo, Kobe, Japan

H. Aoyama et al. (eds.), *Complexity, Heterogeneity, and the Methods of Statistical Physics in Economics*, Evolutionary Economics and Social Complexity Science 22,
https://doi.org/10.1007/978-981-15-4806-2_7

how to study macroeconomic systems that comprise interacting and heterogeneous agents. Having a background in physics, I was really interested in his unique approach, which employs statistical physics and random combinatorics including population genetics in biology.

As a postdoc trying to expand my career from physics to social science, I was so fascinated by his book Aoki (1996) (translated later by me and my colleagues, although he was Japanese!) and began to communicate with him since then. I recall that whenever we had a conversation, he always used to say "although I am not a mainstream economist, ..." Later, I knew that he had a background in physics at University of Tokyo, then worked at UCLA on optimization of stochastic systems and state-space modeling including his famous work, equivalent to but independent of Granger's work on what is known Granger causality today.

At the early stage of conversation with him, I was studying distribution and fluctuation of personal income with my colleagues. By employing surprisingly exhaustive data of high-income people in Japan, we found that it is possible to perform a precise measurement not only on the distribution of personal income with several orders of magnitudes but also on the fluctuation or growth of individual income for a huge number of people. With Hideaki Aoyama and Wataru Souma, we discovered very interesting empirical facts about *Pareto-Zipf's law* or power-law in distribution, *Gibrat's law of proportionate effect* in growth, and *detailed balance condition* in stochastic dynamics; in particular, mathematical relationship between the facts. We were quite excited with our finding, but were a bit nervous being all physicists, so went to two economists, Masanao Aoki and Taisei Kaizoji, and finally published a paper (Fujiwara et al. 2003).

After a while, Masanao invited me to give a talk on this work at an international conference in Tokyo. I still remember that during my talk and Q&A, he was so encouraging and defended the paper against unfriendly questions by some audience. At the banquet, he introduced to me his friend sitting on an electric wheelchair, who proposed a collaboration with him and his colleagues on firm-size distribution and growth in Italy, Ancona, where I later extended the work to the dynamics of firm-size, not personal income, at much larger and further extent (Fujiwara 2004). See Aoyama et al. (2010, 2017) for the outcome done with my colleagues.

I had been talking and discussing with Masanao at many occasions including conferences and workshops where a mainstream economist seldom goes (see Fig. 7.1, for example). He always had new ideas and mathematical equations with his mind and hands, whenever I met him. I don't know why, but he usually looked enjoying conversation with me, although I always made silly questions to him. He even put my name in acknowledgments of his working papers, quite often.

At the late stage of conversation with him, who had a health problem, he had interest in the concept of *non-self-averaging* used in the study of random systems in statistical physics and its relevance to macroeconomics (Aoki and Yoshikawa 2012). See Appendix 1 for the concept and relevance to the present manuscript. During the conversation, I arbitrarily asked him, "What about power-laws found in economics? They are all examples of non-self-averaging, if so, it should have a considerable

Fig. 7.1 Masanao Aoki (circled) in the participants of the Second Nikkei Econophysics Symposium, Tokyo, November 12–14, 2002. The author is the second person from the right in the front row

consequence to macroeconomics." I remember that he began to contemplate it without replying to me and left the place. After a while, he passed away.

While I have been finding the empirical laws for the dynamics of firms growth and failures, as stated above, it is really a pity that I did not have a chance to talk with Masanao about how to model the dynamics in the framework of stochastic method, like what is written in the pioneering book Aoki (1996) and also more recent one Aoki and Yoshikawa (2007) (see a review in Fujiwara 2008).

In this manuscript, I would like to revisit a recent model by Malevergne et al. (2013), which includes essential mechanisms of entry, exit, and growth of firms, while being exactly solvable, in order to argue about how one can understand the breakdown of Zipf's and Gibrat's laws for the regime of smaller firm-size. In addition, I would like to derive from the model the distribution for age of the existing firms and to have a look at a recent dataset which includes more than a million firms in Japan. In Sect. 7.2, I shall revisit the model and see how it can be solved analytically in order to clarify how the firm-size distribution in the regime of small firms depends on the parameters in the model. Such dependence is closely related to the breakdown of Zipf and Gibrat's laws, which are shown by employing our empirical studies in Sect. 7.3. I will argue about this point as well as the distribution for firms' age. Finally, I conclude this manuscript.

7.2 Malevergne-Saichev-Sornette's Stochastic Model

Malevergne et al. (2013) recently presented a simple but realistic stochastic process of firms' birth and death with Gibrat's law of proportionate effect, namely, firm's growth-rate is, in average, independent of its size (see Sutton (1997) for a readable review of the Gibrat's law). Denoting by $P(s)$ the probability to observe that a firm's size is greater than s, one observes the so-called Zipf's law, i.e.,

$$P(s) \sim s^{-m} \tag{7.1}$$

for several orders of magnitude at least in the regime of large firms, where m is very close to 1 (see Axtell 2001; Aoyama et al. 2010, for instance). The main result of their approach is that the Zipf's law is a consequence from a balance between the effective growth rate of existing firms (effective in the sense that a hazard-rate, constant for all firms, is taken into account) and the growth rate of investments in entrant firms.[1]

Another aspect of their model is that one can analyze deviation from $m = 1$ under a variety of circumstances resulting transient imbalances between the effective growth rate of existing firms and the growth rate of investments in entrant firms. This aspect provides a framework in which one can discuss about possible origins of such deviation.

Technically speaking, the model can be solved analytically for transient time as well as asymptotic behavior and for all the regime of firm-size including the regime of small and medium firms. Such a solvable and realistic model gives a framework in which one can argue about possible breakdown of Gibrat's law and deviation from Zipf's law especially for small-sized firms. I would like to recapitulate the Malevergne-Saichev-Sornette (MSS) model with a derivation of their solution with corrections in order to write about such breakdown.

7.2.1 Assumptions of MSS Model and Zipf's Law

The model assumes the following entry, exit, and growth of firms.

1. Stochastic flow of firm entry:
   Entry of new firms follows a Poisson process with Poisson rate being possibly time-varying $\nu(t)$ at time t. It is assumed that

   $$\nu(t) = \nu_0 \, e^{dt} \,, \tag{7.2}$$

   where $\nu_0 > 0$ and d are constants.
2. Size of new entrant firms:
   The initial size of new firms, entrant at time t, is given by

   $$s_0(t) = s_0 \, e^{c_0 t} \,, \tag{7.3}$$

[1] Its relevance to previous literature including (Simon 1955, 1960; Steindl 1965; Ijiri and Simon 1977; Gabaix 1999; Bottazzi and Secchi 2003, 2006; Luttmer 2007, 2011; Rossi-Hansberg and Wright 2007a,b) is also discussed in the paper.

where $s_0 > 0$ is given by independent and identically distributed random draws from a given random variable $\tilde{s}_0$. In a degenerate case, $\tilde{s}_0 = \delta(s - s_0)$ for a constant s_0.
As a consequence from the assumptions 1 and 2, the average capital investment in the creation of new entrant firms, $dI(t)$, is given by $dI(t) = \nu(t) \cdot \mathrm{E}\left[\tilde{s}_0\right] e^{c_0 t} dt = \nu_0 \cdot \mathrm{E}\left[\tilde{s}_0\right] e^{(d+c_0)t} dt$. Note that $d + c_0$ is the *growth rate of investments in entrant firms.*

3. Gibrat's law:
After the birth, each firm change its size according to a Ito's stochastic differential equation[2] given by

$$ds(t) = s(t)\,(\mu\, dt + \sigma\, dW(t)) \,, \tag{7.4}$$

where μ and $\sigma > 0$ are constants, and $W(t)$ is a standard Wiener process. μ represents *ex ante* growth rate or rate of return. σ is the volatility of the stochastic process. (7.4) dictates the Gibrat's law at all firm levels, namely, that firm's growth-rate is, in average, independent of its size.
4. Exit due to a threshold of minimum size:
If a firm's size shrinks below a threshold $s_{\min}(t)$ at time t, the firm will exit or dies forever. It is assumed that

$$s_{\min}(t) = s_1\, e^{c_1 t} \,, \tag{7.5}$$

where $s_1 > 0$ and c_1 are constants. It is assumed that $c_1 > c_0$ for the obvious reason that a new entry firm should not be below the minimum threshold.
5. Exit due to a constant hazard rate:
There is a random exit of firms with a constant hazard rate $h > 0$, which is independent of the firm and age of the firm. It is assumed that $h \geq \max\{0, -d\}$ (see Malevergne et al. 2013).
Under the assumptions 3 and 5, during an interval of dt, a firm can either exit with probability $h \cdot dt$ (size shrinks by a factor of -1) or grow at an average rate equal to $\mu \cdot dt$ (conditional on survival). The average growth rate of an existing firm for dt is given by $h \cdot dt \times (-1) + (1 - h \cdot dt) \times \mu \sim (m - h)dt$. Therefore, $\mu - h$ represents the *average growth rate of an existing firm.*

The main result for the stochastic process under the assumptions 1–5 is the average distribution of firm's sizes follows a power law with the index m in (7.1) given by

$$m = \frac{1}{2}\left[1 - \frac{\mu - c_0}{\sigma^2/2} + \sqrt{\left(1 - \frac{\mu - c_0}{\sigma^2/2}\right)^2 + 4 \cdot \frac{d + h}{\sigma^2/2}}\,\right] \tag{7.6}$$

[2]See Gardiner (2009) for a readable textbook for stochastic differential equation and Fokker-Planck equation used later.

asymptotically for large size s after a sufficiently long time (given in the Proposition 1 in Malevergne et al. (2013)) under the assumption that the moment, $\mathrm{E}\left[(\tilde{s}_0)^m\right]$, is finite (in the assumption 2). As a corollary, it follows that Zipf's law, $m = 1$, follows if and only if

$$\mu - h = d + c_0 \,, \tag{7.7}$$

that is, when the balance holds between the effective growth rate of existing firms (see the remark in the assumption 5) and the growth rate of investments in entrant firms (see the assumption 2).

Discussed to some extent in Malevergne et al. (2013) are how the index, m, depends on the essential parameters introduced in the model, i.e., μ, σ, d, h, c_0, and how one can consider a variety of circumstances. It is shown the fact that the condition $m = 1$ is quite robust and also how one can understand possible deviations from it.

7.2.2 Fokker-Planck Equation and Solution

The paper Malevergne et al. (2013) employs a Fokker-Planck (FP) equation corresponding to the stochastic differential equation (SDE) (7.4) and solves it under the initial and boundary conditions corresponding to the assumptions on entry and exit. I shall recapitulate the proof hopefully in a compact manner but with some corrections.

First, due to the nature of multiplicative process or Gibrat's law in (7.4), it would be reasonable to perform a change of variable as $x(t) := \ln s(t)$. Because the assumption 4 for the exit due to the presence of minimum size, one would change the variable as

$$x(t) = \ln \frac{s(t)}{s_{\min}(t)} \tag{7.8}$$

so that the term in logarithm is dimensionless. Then the boundary condition for the exit in this assumption can be written as $x = 0$, irrespective of the possibly moving position of the boundary, $s_{\min}(t)$.

Using the Ito's formula (Gardiner 2009, Chap. 4.3) for a change of random variable, one has

$$dx(t) = \left(\mu - \frac{\sigma^2}{2} - \frac{\dot{s}_{\min}(t)}{s_{\min}(t)}\right) dt + \sigma \, dW(t) \tag{7.9}$$

$$= \left(\mu - \frac{\sigma^2}{2} - c_1\right) dt + \sigma \, dW(t) \,, \tag{7.10}$$

where (7.5) was used.

One can then use the FP equation which corresponds to the SDE. Appendix 2 gives a general formula for the FP equation. By looking at (7.23) and (7.24), one has

$$\frac{\partial \phi(x,t|y,u)}{\partial t} + v \frac{\partial \phi(x,t|y,u)}{\partial x} = D \frac{\partial^2 \phi(x,t|y,u)}{\partial x^2} , \tag{7.11}$$

where

$$v := \mu - \frac{\sigma^2}{2} - c_1 , \tag{7.12}$$

$$D := \frac{\sigma^2}{2} , \tag{7.13}$$

and y is the initial value at time u. As explained in Appendix 2 (7.31), v is a "drift," and D is the "diffusion" coefficient in the diffusion process. v can be positive and negative depending on the parameters.

Now suppose that a firm had an entry at a given time u according to the Poisson process (assumption 1) with a given size $s_0(u) = s_0 \cdot \exp(c_0 u)$ (s_0 drawn from $\tilde{s}_0$, assumption 2), which is equivalent to

$$x_0(u) := \ln \frac{s_0(u)}{s_{\min}(u)} = \ln(s_0/s_1) + (c_0 - c_1)\, u . \tag{7.14}$$

Then the initial and boundary conditions for the FP equation are respectively

$$\phi(x, t = u|x_0(u), u) = \delta(x - x_0(u)) , \tag{7.15}$$

$$\phi(x = 0, t|x_0(u), u) = 0 , \qquad \text{for all } t > u . \tag{7.16}$$

Appendix 2 gives the exact solution for (7.11) which satisfies (7.15) and (7.16).

Under the condition that s_0 is given, the probability density function for s, denoted by $f(s, t|u, \tilde{s}_0 = s_0)$, is given by

$$f(s, t|u, \tilde{s}_0 = s_0) = \frac{1}{s} \cdot \phi(x = \ln(s/s_{\min}(t)), t|x_0(u), u) \tag{7.17}$$

under the change of variable (7.8).

Finally, under the assumption 1 for the entry process and the assumption 5 for constant hazard rate for all existing firms, the number density function for all the firms, denoted by $g(s, t|\tilde{s}_0 = s_0)$, can be calculated by

$$g(s, t|\tilde{s}_0 = s_0) = \int_{t_0}^{t} du\; \nu(u)\, e^{-h(t-u)}\, f(s, t|u, \tilde{s}_0 = s_0) , \tag{7.18}$$

because $\nu(u)$ is the new firms born at time u. Here t_0 is the starting time of the entire stochastic process. Taking the average for $\tilde{s}_0$, one obtains the average distribution.

Appendix 3 gives the explicit form of the solution with a seemingly minor correction to the paper Malevergne et al. (2013). See (7.45) in the appendix and the correction. By taking the limit for large t and s and averaging for $\tilde{s}_0$, one obtains the main result of Malevergne et al. (2013), that is, the probability density function for s is asymptotically proportional to $s^{-(1+m)}$, where $m = (-\alpha + \beta)/2$, equivalent to (7.6), the main result.

It should be emphasized that the solution gives not only the asymptotic behavior $t \to \infty$ in time, but also the transient behavior. Also, it provides the entire picture of distribution over all firm-size level, in particular, how Zipf's law breakdown for small and medium firms.

The resulting distributions for firm-size are given in Figs. 7.2 and 7.3 for the cases of positive and negative drifts, respectively. The parameters are: $\mu = 0.05, c_0 = c_1 = 0, s_0 = 20, s_1 = 1, \nu_0 = 1000, d = 0, h = 0.05, \theta_0 = 100$. For Fig. 7.2, $\sigma = 0.2$ so that the drift $v = 0.03 > 0$; for Fig. 7.3, $\sigma = 0.4$ so that the drift $v = -0.03 < 0$. The number density $g(s, t|\tilde{s}_0 = s_0)$ is drawn at time $t = 200$ in each plot. Both cases correspond to $m = 1$ as shown in Figs. 7.2a and 7.3a.

Note that as depicted in Fig. 7.2b, if the volatility σ is small, the distribution decays towards the minimum threshold s_1. On the other hand, Fig. 7.3b shows that the distribution grows towards s_1, if σ is small.

7.2.3 *Distribution for Age of Existing Firms*

Because one has the exact solution for the distribution, it is possible to calculate, for example, the number of firms as a function of time, and also the total sum of firms' sizes, in other words the entire size of the economy. See Malevergne et al. (2013, Sect. 3, Appendix 2) and discussion therein.

Let me pay attention to another aspect. Look at the firms surviving at the present time, what is the distribution for how long each firm has survived. In Appendix 2, it is shown that one can calculate such a distribution by using the so-called backward FP equation. Note that it is different from the survival probability that a firm does not hit the minimum threshold with exit but is still alive from its birth or entry time u to the present time t. Instead, one considers the situation in which firms are born continuously in time following the Poisson process in the assumption 1. Then one asks what is the probability that a surviving firm with a certain size s at the present time t was born at time u or earlier, that is, the probability that the age $t - u$ is greater than a certain value. See Fig. 7.9 in Appendix 2.

Let me now turn to an empirical data in Japan in the next section.

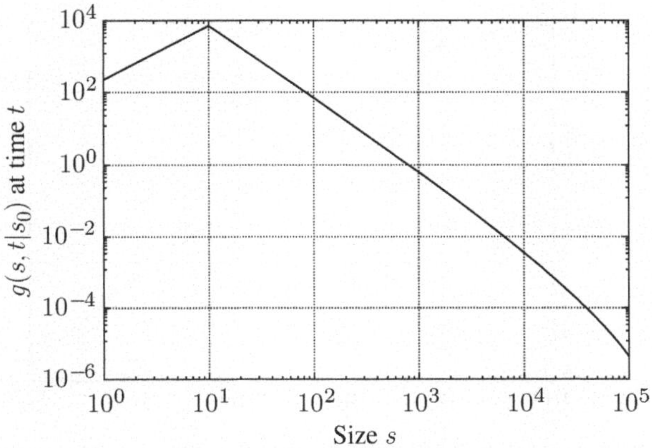

(a) All firm-size level in log-log plot.

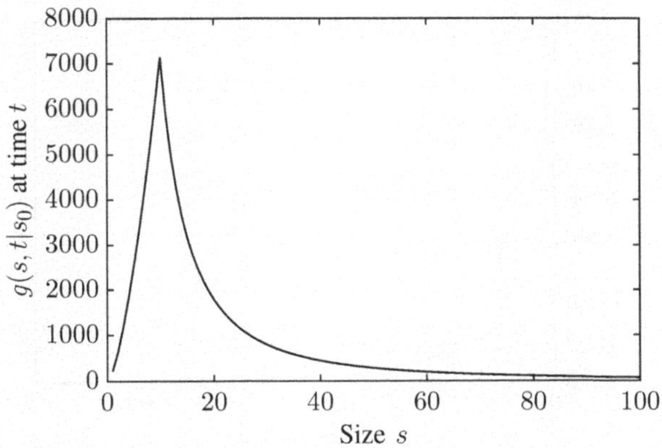

(b) Small firm-size in linear plot.

Fig. 7.2 Exact solution for the number density $g(s, t|\bar{s}_0 = s_0)$ given in (7.45) for the case of *positive* drift (7.12). (**a**) All firm-size. The tail distribution obeys the Zipf's law $m = 1$ (as seen from the slope close to -2). (**b**) Small firm-size. Note that the peak corresponds to s_0, the entry size, and the number decays towards s_1, the minimum size. See the main text for the parameters

7.3 Empirical Analysis of Gibrat and Zipf's Laws and Age Distribution

7.3.1 Breakdown of Gibrat and Zipf's Laws

The Zipf's law is dominated by "a few giants" comprising a considerable fraction of the total size the economy. However, equally important are "many dwarfs," small and medium firms, the number of which is much larger than that the number of giants. Moreover, because the total sum of firm-size between s_0 and s_1 is

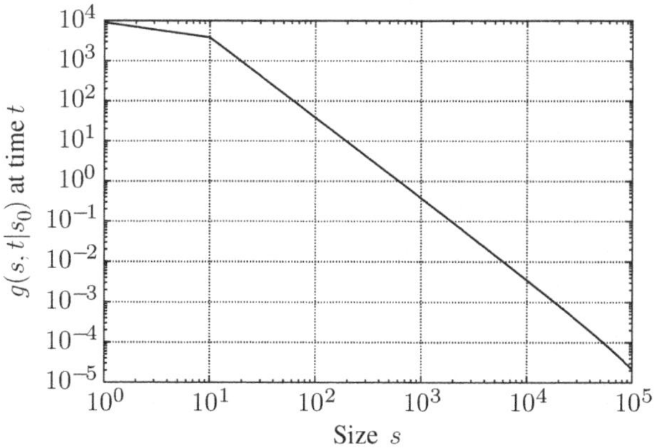

(a) All firm-size level in log-log plot.

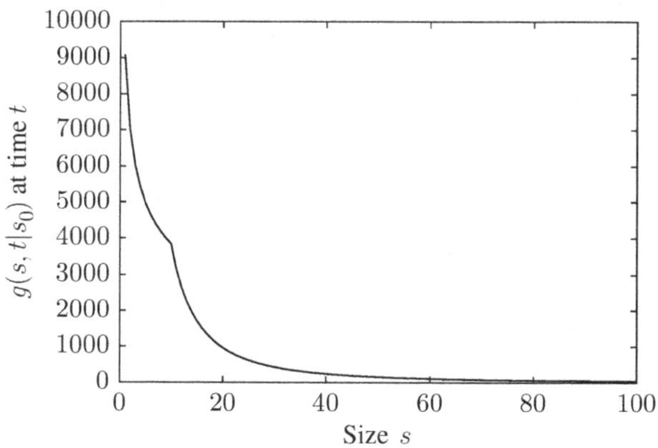

(b) Small firm-size in linear plot.

Fig. 7.3 The same as Fig. 7.2 but for the case of *negative* drift. (**a**) All firm-size. Note that the tail distribution obeys the Zipf's law, i.e., m is close to 1.0. (**b**) Small firm-size. Note that the distribution grows towards s_1, the minimum size, due to the drift. See the main text for the parameters

proportional to $\ln(s_1/s_0)$ due to the very nature of $m = 1$, one can easily see[3] that the total sum of sales, for example, below 10^4 dollars (dwarfs), and that from it to 10^8 dollars (giants), are essentially the same.

Figure 7.4 shows the cumulative distribution for firm-size (number of employees) in the whole range where data are available based on the Establishment and Enterprise Census (Ministry of Internal Affairs and Communications, Japan) in the fiscal year of 2001, and also on an exhaustive list of the listed firms. A deviation

[3]Denote by $p(s)$ the probability density function for size s, whose integral is the cumulative probability (7.1). Then $\int_{s0}^{s1} s \cdot p(s)ds \propto \ln(s_1/s_0)$, when $p(s) \propto s^{-2}$, or Zipf's law.

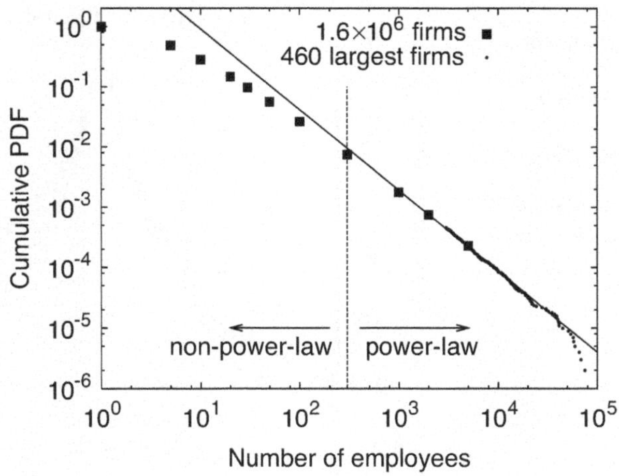

Fig. 7.4 Cumulative distribution for firm-size measured by number of employees in the entire regime (Japan, year 2001). (Taken from Fig. 3.16 in Aoyama et al. (2010) with permission from Cambridge University Press)

from the Zipf's law can be observed in the smaller region, with a qualitative change occurring round about the a few hundred employees, coinciding to the small and medium enterprise defined by the government.

One can examine the growth-rate by using a few variables such as total-assets, debt, and sales. We can expect the character of fluctuation in the non-power-law region and its transition to the power-law, to differ from that considered for large firms. Figure 7.5 is the results of the distribution for growth-rate of individual firm, which is defined by $\log_{10}(s(t)/s(t-1))$ where $s(t-1)$ and $s(t)$ are the sizes in successive years (years 2000/2001, in this case). In each plot, different lines correspond to different size levels for $s(t-1)$. If Gibrat's law holds, the lines should collapse to a single distribution. To quantify the validity of the law, one can check how the standard deviation of the distribution for the grow-rate depends on the size level. Figure 7.5 is the typical result, which clearly shows that Gibrat's law holds for the large firms,[4] but does not for the small firms. Note that the breakdown of Gibrat's law occurs around the same level of firm-size where is the deviation from Zipf's law (Fig. 7.6).

[4]In the passing, it would be worth mentioning that one can observe that the distribution of growth-rate has a tent-shaped or Laplace-like functional form, being different from what can be expected from Gaussian distribution as assumed in (7.4). See Bottazzi and Secchi (2003, 2006) and Arata (2014) for further and interesting discussions.

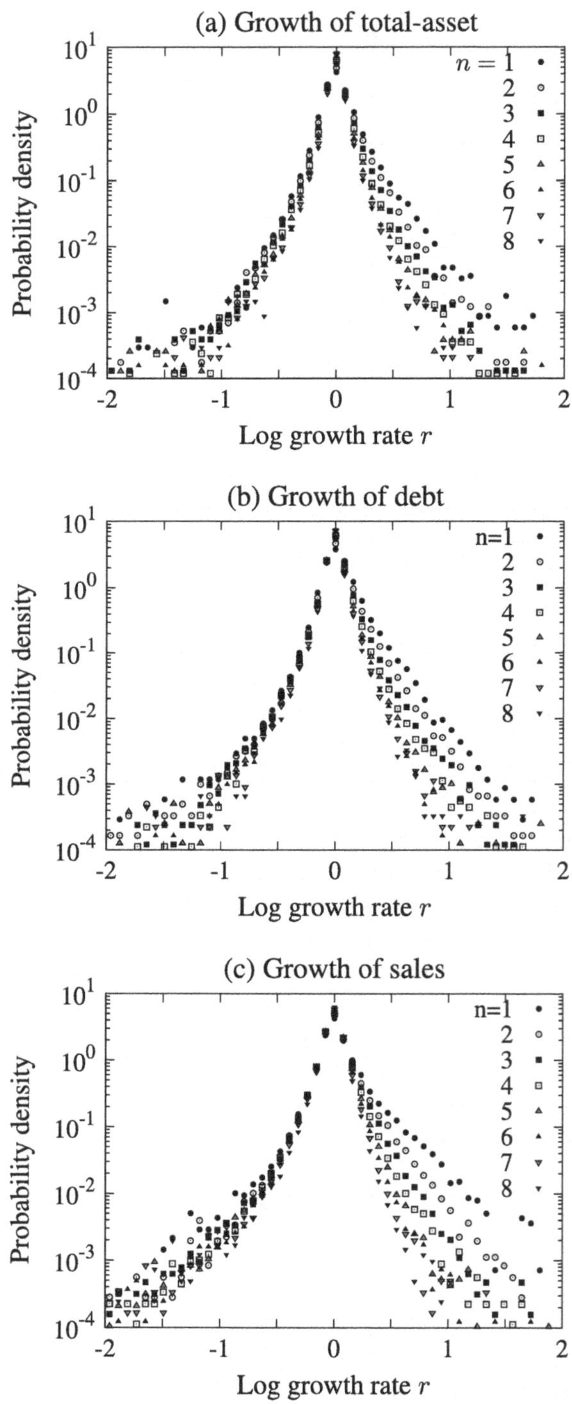

Fig. 7.5 Probability distribution for growth-rates of small and medium firms: (**a**) total assets (**b**) debt (**c**) sales (Japan, year 2000–2001). (Taken from Fig. 3.17 in Aoyama et al. (2010) with permission from Cambridge University Press)

Fig. 7.6 Relation between firm-size and standard deviation of growth-rate for small and medium firms: (**a**) total assets (**b**) debt (**c**) sales (Japan, year 2000–2001). (Taken from Fig. 3.18 in Aoyama et al. (2010) with permission from Cambridge University Press)

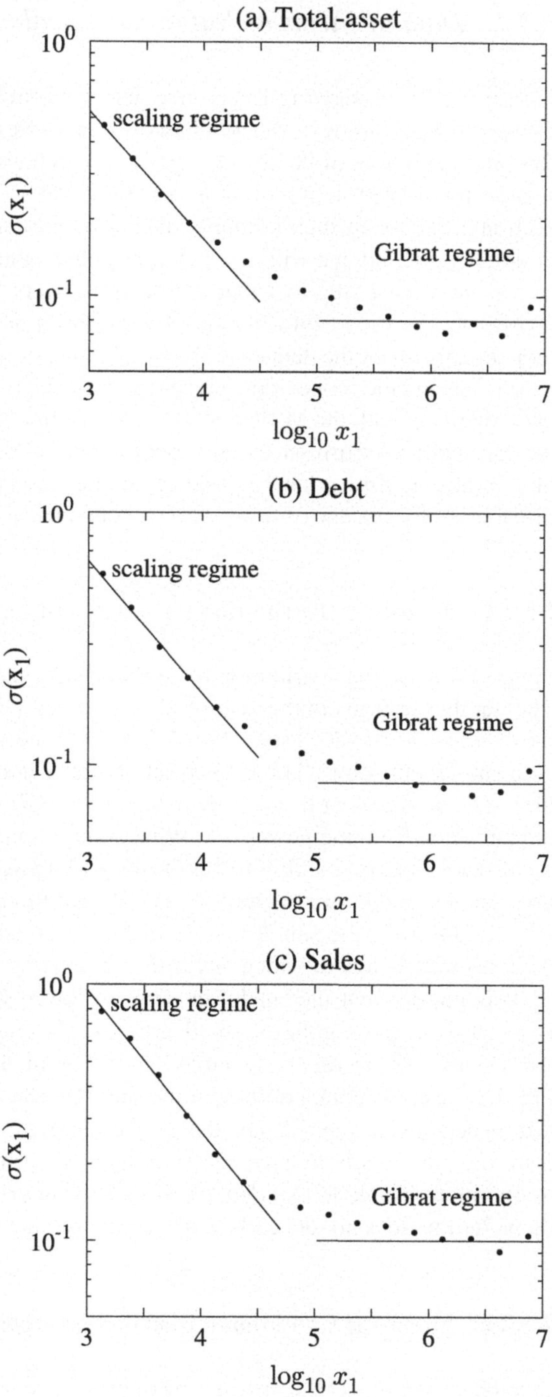

7.3.2 *Data of Firms at Nationwide Scale*

For a purpose of studying large-scale data for firm-size as well as age of existing firms, let me employ a dataset based on a survey conducted by Tokyo Shoko Research, Inc., one of the leading credit research agencies in Tokyo, which covers a large fraction of active firms at a nationwide scale in Japan with more than a million firms. As attributes of individual firm, one can examine sales, profit, number of employees, and age with respect to establishment in months. What is important for our purpose is the fact that the dataset covers "active" firms, for which they investigate the credit information. See Fujiwara and Aoyama (2010, Sect. 2) for more details about the dataset.

It is beyond the scope of the present manuscript to perform the empirical analysis in comparison with the MSS model, but let me briefly show the empirical results on the distribution for firm-size in this section. Then I shall discuss how the breakdown of Gibrat and Zipf's laws is related to the observed properties, as well as the distribution for the age of firms with its dependence on firm-size.

7.3.2.1 Firm-Size Distribution for Small and Large Firms

Figure 7.7 gives the distribution for sales of individual firm at the nationwide scale. The number of firms in the year of 2016 exceeds 1.3 million, covering presumably most active firms. As usual, Fig. 7.7a shows the cumulative distribution that is compatible with Zipf's law for several orders of magnitude. In the regime of small firm-size, on the other hand, as depicted in Fig. 7.7b in a rank-size plot, one can see the deviation from the power-law. What is important is the observation that there is a non-vanishing probability to find firms with extremely small firms. Because the horizontal scale of size is close to 10^0–10^1 (in thousand Yen, approximately 10 to 100 USD/Euros), the smallest scale in the observation corresponds to presumably the threshold, below of which any firm can survive.

This implies that the "drift" in terms of the MSS model explained in Sect. 7.2 is negative in the regime of small firm-size. If one supposes that (7.12) is valid, the volatility σ is relatively larger than that in the regime of large firms. See Fig. 7.3b. This is compatible with the fact that the volatility depends on the firm-size as depicted in Fig. 7.5, i.e., that one has larger volatility for smaller firms. Small firms are quite likely to have relatively large volatility so that they can reach to the minimum threshold to exit (bankruptcy), but can grow by luck to the regime where the volatility does not depend on size anymore, that is, the regime of Gibrat's law.

7.3.2.2 Firm-Age Conditional Distribution Depending on Firm-Size

Finally, let me look at the distribution of firms' age, because the availability of age in the dataset. One can observe that some firms have age, longer than 100 years, but the typical age is decades, 50 years or shorter. It would be an interesting question to ask

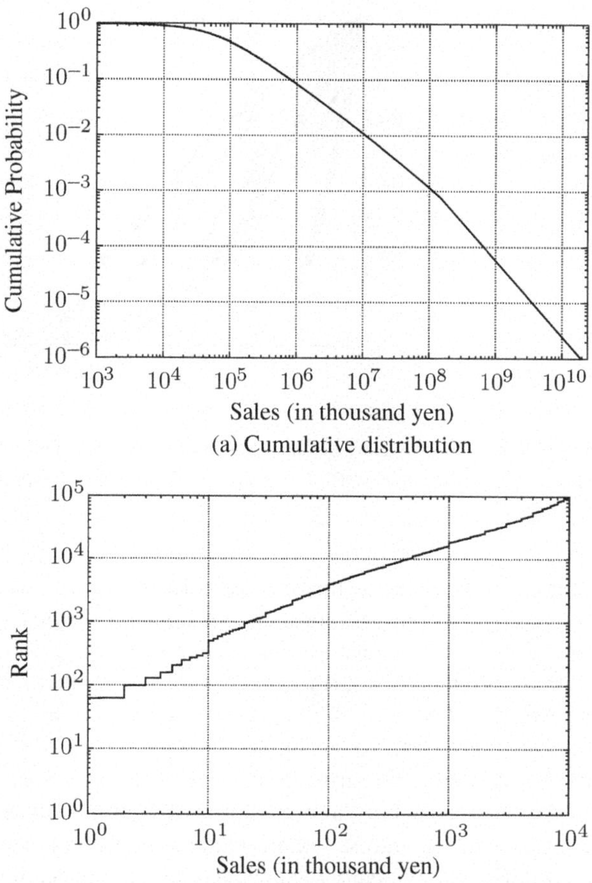

(a) Cumulative distribution

(b) Focus on the regime of small firms in a size-rank plot.

Fig. 7.7 Distribution for sales of individual firms at nationwide scale (sales in thousand Yen, approximately in 10 USD/Euros). The number of firms is 1,330,856. (**a**) Cumulative distribution in a log-log plot. The tail has the slope being close to Zipf's law. (**b**) Focus on small firms in a size-rank plot. The rank is the order of increasing sales. Note the presence of non-vanishing probability to find extremely small firms

if the age depends on the firm-size. One can naively expect that the large the firm is, the longer its age is. Actually, one can see that this is true in Fig. 7.8. Here, the firm-size is divided into different classes according to the sales as $[10^{2+(n-1)}, 10^{2+n})$, denoted by size class n in the figure. One can compare with the prediction of MSS model, at least qualitatively, given in Fig. 7.9b, but the quantitative analysis is beyond the scope of this manuscript.

7.4 Summary and Final Remark

During the last conversation with the late Masanao Aoki, I learned that heavy-tailed distributions, such as Zipf's law, frequently observed in the macroeconomic system are all examples of *non-self-averaging* quantities. Consider firm-size, individual

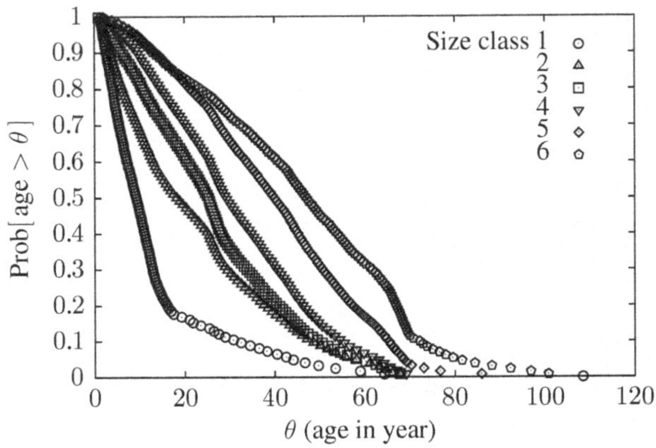

Fig. 7.8 Cumulative distribution for age of existing firms. Different points correspond to different class of firm-size with respect to sales. Size class n corresponds to $[10^{2+(n-1)}, 10^{2+n})$ ($n = 1, 2, \ldots, 7$)

output for example, as random variables $x_1, x_2, \ldots, x_n$. The fact that the total sum $X_n = \sum_{i=1}^{n} x_i$ has the property of non-self-averaging, that is, the coefficient of variation $\mathrm{CV}(X_n)$ does not vanish for sufficiently large n implies that individual outputs produced by firms are related among them in a heterogeneous manner, presumably because of the *network effect* of production network or supplier-customer network, for example. In such a case, the fluctuations matter and are closely related to the structure of underlying economic network.

In this viewpoint, the breakdown of Gibrat's law and resulting deviation from Zipf's law is a manifestation of interaction of small firms with large firms. Actually, small firms are typically connected with large firms in the production network (see Fujiwara and Aoyama (2010) and references therein and in Aoyama et al. (2017), for example). The stochastic process for the firms' growth in the regime of small firms is different from the Gibrat's law for large firms, because those small firms depend as suppliers on those large firms as customers. The large firms enjoy the law of proportionate effect (7.4) implying that they can invest relatively freely at will. The smaller firms have the volatility σ being larger for smaller size (and possibly μ is smaller for smaller firms) so that the drift (7.12) is negative to yield the deviation from Zipf's law in the regime of small firms.

I would like to dedicate this manuscript to Masanao Aoki. I wish I could have had a chance to talk with him, like what I did at places in the past, who always had great passion and curiosity in him. *RIP*.

Acknowledgments I would like to thank the late Masanao Aoki for his continuous encouragement, insightful conversation, and helpful guidance, all of which led a jobless postdoc in physics to come across with ideas, methods, projects, and, most importantly, people including economists, Yuji Aruka, Mauro Gallegati, and Hiroshi Yoshikawa. I am grateful to my master student, Masaya Nakamura, for discussion and showing me the simulation results in his master thesis. This work was supported in part by MEXT as Exploratory Challenges on Post-K computer (Studies of Multilevel Spatiotemporal Simulation of Socioeconomic Phenomena), and Grant-in-Aid for Scientific Research (KAKENHI) by JSPS Grant Numbers 17H02041.

Appendix 1: Property of Non-Self-Averaging

Definition of non-self-averaging property can be stated as follows. Consider a random variable which depends on the size of a system under consideration. A typical example is the sum of n random variables, $x_1, x_2, \ldots, x_n$, i.e.,

$$X_n = \sum_{i=1}^{n} x_i \; . \tag{7.19}$$

For example, n is the number of elements or agents comprising the system; and X_n is a macroscopic variable.

The so-called coefficient of variation (CV) of X_n is defined by

$$\mathrm{CV}(X_n) := \frac{\sigma(X_n)}{\mu(X_n)} \, , \tag{7.20}$$

where $\mu(X_n)$ and $\sigma(X_n)$ are, respectively, the mean and the standard deviation of X_n. $\mathrm{CV}(X_n)$ represents the degree of uncertainty in the random variable X_n. If $\mathrm{CV}(X_n)$ approaches to zero when n becomes large, X_n is called *self-averaging*. Otherwise, it is called *non-self-averaging*. A self-averaging random variable can be well quantified by its mean when the system size becomes large. A non-self-averaging random variable cannot be represented by its mean and leads to a misleading picture; its fluctuation matters.

Quoting the book Kadanoff (2000, Chap. 5.6), examples can be given as follows:

> In statistical physics we distinguish between two kinds of statistical behavior produced by events with many steps and parts. The simpler kind of behavior is described by the phrase *self-averaging*. A self-averaging behavior is one in which the effects of the individual events add up to produce an almost deterministic outcome. An example of this is the pressure on a macroscopic surface. This pressure is produced by huge numbers of individual collisions, which produce a momentum transfer per unit time which seems essentially without fluctuations. The larger the number of collisions, the less is the uncertainty in the pressure.
>
> In contrast, multiplicative random processes all have a second behavior called *non-self-averaging*. When different markets or different securities are described by any kind of multiplicative random process, as we have described in this section, then the different securities can have huge and (mostly) unpredictable price swings. The larger the value of M, the more the uncertainty in price. There are other examples of measurements which do not self-average. For example, the electrical resistance of a disordered quantum system at low temperature is determined in awful detail by the position of each atom. Change one atomic position and you might change the resistance by a factor of two. Here too, the large number of individual units does not guarantee a certainly defined output. (pp.85–86)

where a multiplicative random process is considered to describe securities prices, as an illustrative example, namely, S_M at time $t = t_0 + M\,\Delta t$ is given by

$$S_{M+1} = S_M\, e^{\xi_M}\,, \tag{7.21}$$

where ξ_M is (logarithmic) return or growth rate in the price at time M. After M steps, one has

$$S_M = S_0 \exp\left[\sum_{i=1}^{M} \xi_i\right]. \tag{7.22}$$

Because of the multiplicative property, S_M is subject to large fluctuations when M is sufficiently large. Indeed, one can show that CV for S_M does not converge to zero when M goes to infinity. See Kadanoff (2000, Chap. 5.6) and also Sornette (2006, Chap. 16) for other examples.

Note that the Gibrat's law of proportionate effect is a multiplicative process. S_M in (7.21) is the firm-size at time M, and ξ_M is its growth rate at that time. The heavy-tailed distribution, or a power-law in this case, corresponds to the non-self-averaging property of the random variable of firm-size. The conversation with Masanao and his paper with Hiroshi Yoshikawa Aoki and Yoshikawa (2012) reminded me of this fact that statistical behavior produced by events with many *steps* of time in a multiplicative process can lead to non-self-averaging property as one frequently encounter with heavy-tailed distributions in economics.[5]

Moreover, there are other cases in which statistical behavior produced by events with many *parts* in "space" can lead to non-self-averaging property. Consider random variables, $x_1, x_2, \ldots, x_n$ being mutually independent for any pair of them. Obviously, the sum X_n is self-averaging, because $\mathrm{CV}(X_n)$ is proportional to $1/\sqrt{n}$ when n is sufficiently large. However, if those random variables are correlated even if the system is large, X_n can be non-self-averaging. A typical example is total output (GDP) as the sum of individual outputs produced by firms, which are connected with each other on a production network, for example. In such a case, the fluctuations matter and are closely related to the structure of underlying economic networks. See Aoyama et al. (2017) for a variety of such examples in large economic networks. At the time of conversation with Masanao, I was trying to communicate with him about this point, but failed to convey my idea concretely without any specific data and models.

[5]See Sornette (2006, Chap. 14) for other mechanisms for power laws.

Appendix 2: Fokker-Planck Equation

Suppose in general that one has a stochastic differential equation, SDE for short (in Ito's sense; see Gardiner (2009, Chap. 4)):

$$dx(t) = a[x(t), t]\, dt + b[x(t), t]\, dW(t) , \tag{7.23}$$

where $W(t)$ is the standard Wiener process, and $a[x, t], b[x, t]$ are arbitrary functions of x and t, it is useful to consider the probability that one finds the random variable or "particle" $x(t)$ at a given location x provided that at the initial time $u < t$, the particle is at the position $x(u) = y$. Denote the probability by $p(x, t|y, u)$, one has the so-called Fokker-Planck (FP) equation corresponding to the SDE, (7.23):

$$\frac{\partial p(x, t|y, u)}{\partial t} = -\frac{\partial}{\partial x} [a(x, t)\, p(x, t|y, u)] + \frac{1}{2}\frac{\partial^2}{\partial x^2} [b(x, t)\, p(x, t|y, u)] . \tag{7.24}$$

The initial condition is given by

$$p(x, t = u|y, u) = \delta(x - y) , \tag{7.25}$$

where $\delta(\cdot)$ is the delta function. See Gardiner (2009, Chap. 4) for example.

Note that the FP equation can be rewritten as a conservation of probability:

$$\frac{\partial p(x, t|y, u)}{\partial t} + \frac{\partial J(x, t|y, u)}{\partial x} = 0 , \tag{7.26}$$

where

$$J(x, t|y, u) := a(x, t)\, p(x, t|y, u) - \frac{1}{2}\frac{\partial}{\partial x} [b(x, t)\, p(x, t|y, u)] \tag{7.27}$$

represents the "flow of probability."

In addition to the initial condition, one often has boundary conditions. Consider an "absorbing barrier" at $x = 0$, for example. This means that once the particle $x(t) \geq 0$ reaches the boundary $x = 0$ for the first time, it will die or be removed from the system. The boundary condition can be expressed as

$$p(x = 0, t|y, u) = 0 \qquad \text{for all } t > u . \tag{7.28}$$

In this case, the *survival probability* that the particle does not hit the boundary and is still surviving at time t given the initial condition (7.27) can be calculated by

$$\mathrm{S}(t|y, u) = \int_0^\infty p(x, t|y, u)\, dx , \tag{7.29}$$

because the right-hand side is the total probability that the particle is still alive. Because of the conservation of probability, one can also write the survival probability as:

$$\mathrm{S}(t|y,u) = 1 - \int_u^t J(0,t|y,u)\,dt\ , \tag{7.30}$$

because the second term on the right-hand side is the total outflow of probability integrated from $t = u$ to the present time. See Gardiner (2009, Chap. 5) for more general discussion.

Now let me consider a simple case that all the coefficients of FP equation are constants, that is

$$\frac{\partial p(x,t|y,u)}{\partial t} + v\,\frac{\partial p(x,t|y,u)}{\partial x} = D\,\frac{\partial^2 p(x,t|y,u)}{\partial x^2}\ , \tag{7.31}$$

where $D > 0$, v are constants. The solution satisfying the initial condition (7.25) is

$$p(x,t|y,u) = \frac{1}{\sqrt{4\pi D\theta}}\,e^{-\frac{x-y-v\theta}{4D\theta}}\ , \tag{7.32}$$

where θ is the elapsed time from the initial time defined by

$$\theta := t - u\ . \tag{7.33}$$

The solution has diffusion with a drift in terms of physics. The average is moving with the drift velocity equal to v. The standard deviation is equal to $\sqrt{2D\theta}$. D is called diffusion coefficient of the process.

It is an exercise to find the solution for the positive region $x(t) \geq 0$ which satisfies the boundary condition (7.28) in addition to the initial one (7.25). The solution is given by

$$p(x,t|y,u) = \frac{1}{\sqrt{4\pi D\theta}}\left[e^{-\frac{(x-y-v\theta)^2}{4D\theta}} - e^{-\frac{vy}{D}}\,e^{-\frac{(x+y-v\theta)^2}{4D\theta}}\right] \tag{7.34}$$

$$= \frac{1}{\sqrt{4\pi D\theta}}\left[e^{-\frac{(x-y-v\theta)^2}{4D\theta}} - e^{\frac{vx}{D}}\,e^{-\frac{(x+y+v\theta)^2}{4D\theta}}\right]\ , \tag{7.35}$$

which can be obtained by the so-called image method (see Redner (2011, Chap. 3; see also errata). One can easily verify that (7.34) satisfies (7.25) and (7.28).

Survival probability in this case can be calculated explicitly by using either (7.29) or (7.30) to obtain that

$$\mathrm{S}(t|y,u) = \frac{1}{2}\left[1 + \mathrm{erf}\left(\frac{y+v\theta}{\sqrt{4D\theta}}\right) - e^{-\frac{vy}{D}}\left(1 - \mathrm{erf}\left(\frac{y-v\theta}{\sqrt{4D\theta}}\right)\right)\right]\ . \tag{7.36}$$

Here erf(·) is the error function defined by

$$\mathrm{erf}(x) := \frac{2}{\sqrt{\pi}} \int_0^x e^{-t^2} dt \,, \tag{7.37}$$

which satisfies that $\mathrm{erf}(-x) = -\mathrm{erf}(x)$; $\mathrm{erf}(0) = 0$; $\mathrm{erf}(\infty) = 1$ (see Abramowitz and Stegun 1965). Note that the survival probability $S(t|y, u)$ is the probability to find the particle still alive at time t *given* the initial position y in the past at time $u < t$.

On the other hand, one may want to consider a situation in which particles are born continuously in time, for example, following a Poisson process.[6] Then one can ask what is the probability that a particle still alive with a given position x at present time t was born at $u = t - \theta$ or earlier, in other words, that such a particle has its "age" being greater than θ.

For such a purpose, it is convenient to use *backward* FP equation:

$$\frac{\partial p(x,t|y,u)}{\partial u} = -a(x,t)\frac{\partial p(x,t|y,u)}{\partial y} - \frac{1}{2}b(x,t)\frac{\partial^2 p(x,t|y,u)}{\partial y^2} \,. \tag{7.38}$$

Note that the left-hand side is the derivative with respect to u. The initial condition is given by

$$p(x,t|y,u=t) = \delta(x-y) \,, \tag{7.39}$$

for all t. Derivation of (7.38) from (7.23) is given in Gardiner (2009, Chap. 3) for example.

In the case above, where all the coefficients of FP equation are constants, (7.38) reads

$$\frac{\partial p(x,t|y,u)}{\partial u} + v\,\frac{\partial p(x,t|y,u)}{\partial y} = -D\,\frac{\partial^2 p(x,t|y,u)}{\partial y^2} \,. \tag{7.40}$$

The diffusion coefficient is "negative" meaning that the particles "diffuse" from the past to the present time to converge to the condition (7.39). The boundary condition in this case is given by

$$p(x,t|y=0,u) = 0 \qquad \text{for all } u < t \,. \tag{7.41}$$

By changing the variable from u to θ that runs backward in time, one can see that the backward FP equation and the initial and boundary conditions are precisely the same as those for the forward ones except that the drift should be read as $v \to -v$.

[6] I assume a homogeneous Poisson process, i.e., that the Poisson rate is constant in time, for simplicity.

Denote by $\mathrm{S}(\theta|x,t)$ that a particle still alive with a given position x at present time t has age larger than θ. Then it immediately follows that

$$\mathrm{S}(\theta|x,t) = \frac{1}{2}\left[1 + \mathrm{erf}\left(\frac{x - v\theta}{\sqrt{4D\theta}}\right) - e^{+\frac{vy}{D}}\left(1 - \mathrm{erf}\left(\frac{x + v\theta}{\sqrt{4D\theta}}\right)\right)\right], \tag{7.42}$$

See Fig. 7.9 for the behavior of and difference between the survival probabilities in (7.36) and (7.42). In the context of firms' stochastic process of entry, exit, and growth, this is precisely the distribution of existing firm's age given its present size

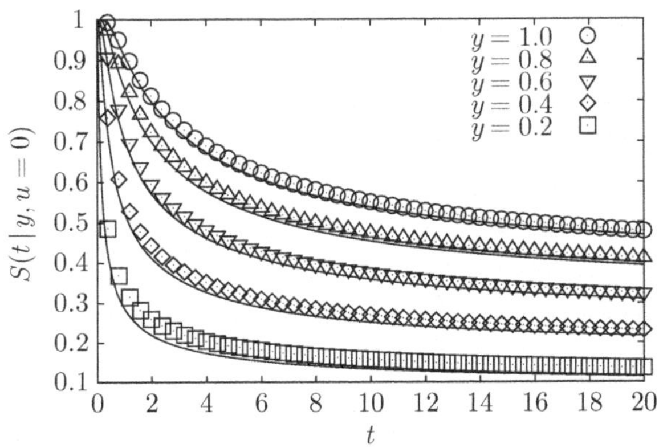

(a) Points and lines are respectively simulation results (10^5 particles) and (36), for different initial positions and with $\mathrm{v} = 0.1$, $\mathrm{D} = 0.2$.

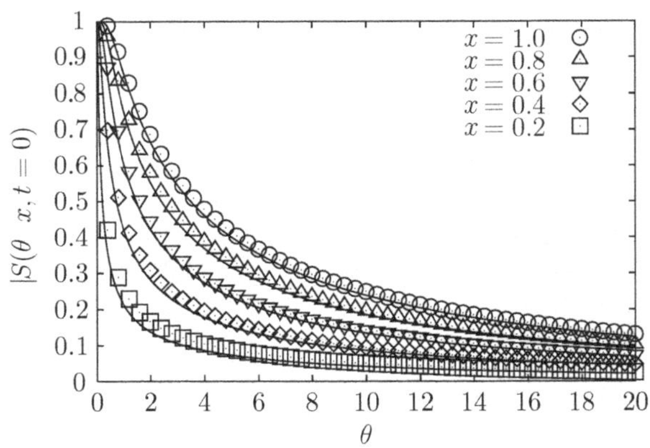

(b) Points and lines are respectively simulation results (10^5 particles) and (42), for different present positions and with $\mathrm{v} = 0.1$, $\mathrm{D} = 0.2$.

Fig. 7.9 Survival probabilities. (**a**) $\mathrm{S}(t|y,u)$ for finding a particle still alive at time t given the initial position y at time $u = 0$, given by (7.36). (**b**) $\mathrm{S}(\theta|x,t)$ for finding that a particle still alive with a given position x at present time t has age larger than θ, given by (7.42) (under the assumption of a homogeneous Poisson process for the entry of firms, i.e., $d = 0$ in (7.2)).

Appendix 3: Exact Solution

Here the explicit form of the solution for the MSS model is shown with a minor correction in the original paper Malevergne et al. (2013).

The solution of the FP equation (7.11) with (7.12), (7.13) for the initial and boundary conditions (7.15), (7.16) under the assumption for the initial size (7.14) with s_0 fixed is given by (7.35). By introducing $\theta := t - u$, one can rewrite (7.18) as

$$g(s, t|\tilde{s}_0 = s_0) = \frac{1}{s}\nu(t) \int_0^{\theta_0} d\theta\; e^{-(d+h)\theta}\, \phi(x = \ln(s/s_{\min}(t)), t|x_0(t-\theta), t-\theta)\,, \tag{7.43}$$

where $\theta_0 := t - t_0$, and (7.2) was used. Here and hereafter in this appendix, it is understood that $x = \ln(s/s_{\min}(t))$ (see (7.8)).

Noting that $x_0(t-\theta) = x_0(t) - (c_0 - c_1)\theta$, (7.43) can be explicitly written as

$$g(s, t|\tilde{s}_0 = s_0) = \frac{1}{s} \cdot \frac{\nu(t)}{\sqrt{4\pi D}} \times$$
$$\int_0^{\theta_0} \frac{d\theta}{\sqrt{\theta}} e^{-(d+h)\theta} \left[e^{-\frac{(x - x_0(t) - (v - (c_0 - c_1))\theta)^2}{4D\theta}} - e^{vx/D}\, e^{-\frac{(x + x_0(t) + (v - (c_0 - c_1))\theta)^2}{4D\theta}} \right]. \tag{7.44}$$

Changing the variable $\sqrt{\theta} =: \xi$, one has

$$g(s, t|\tilde{s}_0 = s_0) = \frac{1}{s} \cdot \frac{\nu(t)}{\sqrt{\pi D}} \left[e^{\frac{v - (c_0 - c_1)}{2D}(x - x_0(t))} \int_0^{\sqrt{\theta_0}} d\xi\; e^{-A^2\xi^2 - B_-^2/\xi^2} \right.$$
$$\left. - e^{vx/D}\, e^{-\frac{v - (c_0 - c_1)}{2D}(x + x_0(t))} \int_0^{\sqrt{\theta_0}} d\xi\; e^{-A^2\xi^2 - B_+^2/\xi^2} \right], \tag{7.45}$$

where

$$A := (1/\sqrt{4D})\sqrt{(v - (c_0 - c_1))^2 + 4D(d+h)}\,, \tag{7.46}$$

$$B_\pm := (1/\sqrt{4D})|x \pm x_0(t)|\,. \tag{7.47}$$

The integrals in (7.45) can be expressed with error functions (7.37) (see Abramowitz and Stegun 1965, see Eq.(7.4.33)). After some calculation and using the definitions (7.12) and (7.13) to recover the original parameter, one arrives at the final form:

$$
\begin{aligned}
& g(s,t|\tilde{s}_0 = s_0) = \frac{1}{s}\cdot\frac{\nu(t)}{\sigma^2/2}\cdot\frac{1}{2\beta}\times \\
& \left[e^{\frac{1}{2}(\alpha x_- - \beta|x_-|)}\mathrm{erfc}\left(\frac{|x_-| - \beta\tau_0}{2\sqrt{\tau_0}}\right) - e^{\frac{1}{2}(\alpha x_- + \beta|x_-|)}\mathrm{erfc}\left(\frac{|x_-| + \beta\tau_0}{2\sqrt{\tau_0}}\right)\right. \\
& - e^{(2/\sigma^2)(c_0 - c_1)\,x}\, e^{-\alpha x_0(t)}\times \\
& \left.\left\{e^{\frac{1}{2}(\alpha x_+ - \beta|x_+|)}\mathrm{erfc}\left(\frac{|x_+| - \beta\tau_0}{2\sqrt{\tau_0}}\right) - e^{\frac{1}{2}(\alpha x_+ + \beta|x_+|)}\mathrm{erfc}\left(\frac{|x_+| + \beta\tau_0}{2\sqrt{\tau_0}}\right)\right\}\right],
\end{aligned}
\tag{7.48}
$$

where erfc(·) is the complementary error function defined by $\mathrm{erfc}(x) := 1 - \mathrm{erf}(x)$ (see Abramowitz and Stegun 1965), and

$$\tau_0 := (\sigma^2/2)\theta_0\,, \tag{7.49}$$

$$\alpha := \frac{\mu - c_0}{\sigma^2/2} - 1\,, \tag{7.50}$$

$$\beta := \sqrt{\alpha^2 + 4\frac{d+h}{\sigma/2}}\,, \tag{7.51}$$

$$x_\pm := x \pm x_0(t)\,. \tag{7.52}$$

To repeat, it is understood that $x = \ln(s/s_{\min}(t))$.

The derivation follows the paper Malevergne et al. (2013), but it seems that the factor $e^{(2/\sigma^2)(c_0-c_1)\,x}$ in the third line in (7.48) is missing in Eq. (A.29) in the paper.

If one assumes that the entire history of the stochastic process is sufficiently large, namely, τ_0 is large, (7.48) reduces to a simple form depending on the sign of x_-, i.e., depending on the two region $s > s_0(t)$ and $s_0(t) > s$. See Eq. (A32) in Malevergne et al. (2013), but with the above correction.

References

Abramowitz M, Stegun IA (eds) (1965) Handbook of mathematical functions with formulas, graphs, and mathematical tables, 9th edn. Dover Publications, New York

Aoki M (1996) New approaches to macroeconomic modeling: evolutionary stochastic dynamics, multiple equilibria, and externalities as field effects. Cambridge University Press, Cambridge

Aoki M, Yoshikawa H (2007) Reconstructing macroeconomics: a perspective from statistical physics and combinatorial stochastic processes. Cambridge University Press, Cambridge

Aoki M, Yoshikawa H (2012) Non-self-averaging in macroeconomic models: a criticism of modern micro-founded macroeconomics. J Econ Interac Coord 7(1):1–22
Aoyama H, Fujiwara Y, Ikeda Y, Iyetomi H, Souma W (2010) Econophysics and companies: statistical life and death in complex business networks. Cambridge University Press, Cambridge
Aoyama H, Fujiwara Y, Ikeda Y, Iyetomi H, Souma W, Yoshikawa H (2017) Macro-econophysics: new studies on economic networks and synchronization. Cambridge University Press, Cambridge
Arata Y (2014) Firm growth and laplace distribution: the importance of large jumps. RIETI discussion paper series, 14-E-033
Axtell RL (2001) Zipf distribution of us firm sizes. Science 293(5536):1818–1820
Bottazzi G, Secchi A (2003) Why are distributions of firm growth rates tent-shaped? Econ Lett 80(3):415–420
Bottazzi G, Secchi A (2006) Explaining the distribution of firm growth rates. RAND J Econ 37(2):235–256
Fujiwara Y, Di Guilmi C, Aoyama H, Gallegati M, Souma W (2004) Do Pareto-Zipf and Gibrat laws hold true? An analysis with European firms. Physica A 335:197–216
Fujiwara Y (2008) Review on Masanao Aoki and Hiroshi Yoshikawa, Reconstructing macroeconomics: a perspective from statistical physics and combinatorial stochastic processes. Cambridge University Press, 2007. Evol Inst Econ Rev 4:313–317
Fujiwara Y, Aoyama H (2010) Large-scale structure of a nation-wide production network. Eur Phys J B 77(4):565–580
Fujiwara Y, Souma W, Aoyama H, Kaizoji T, Aoki M (2003) Growth and fluctuations of personal income. Physica A 321:598–604
Gabaix X (1999) Zipf's law for cities: an explanation. Q J Econ 114(3):739–767
Gardiner C (2009) Stochastic methods: a handbook for the natural and social sciences, 4th edn. Springer, Berlin
Ijiri Y, Simon HA (1977) Skewed distributions and the sizes of business firms. North-Holland, Amsterdam
Kadanoff LP (2000) Statistical physics: statics, dynamics and renormalization. World Scientific Publishing, River Edge
Luttmer EGJ (2007) Selection, growth, and the size distribution of firms. Q J Econ 122(3):1103–1144
Luttmer EGJ (2011) On the mechanics of firm growth. Rev Econ Stud 78(3):1042–1068
Malevergne Y, Saichev A, Sornette D (2013) Zipf's law and maximum sustainable growth. J Econ Dyn Control 37:1195–1212
Redner S (2001) A guide to first-passage processes. Cambridge University Press, Cambridge. See also errata distributed by the author
Rossi-Hansberg E, Wright MLJ (2007a) Establishment size dynamics in the aggregate economy. Am Econ Rev 97(5):1639–1666
Rossi-Hansberg E, Wright MLJ (2007b) Urban structure and growth. Rev Econ Stud 74:597–624
Simon HA (1955) On a class of skew distribution. Biometrika 42:425–440
Simon HA (1960) Some further notes on a class of skew distribution functions. Inf Control 3:80–88
Sornette D (2006) Critical phenomena in natural science; Chaos, fractals, selforganization and disorder: concepts and tools, 2nd edn. Springer, Berlin
Steindl J (1965) Random processes and the growth of firms: study of the Pareto Law. Griffin, London
Sutton J (1997) Gibrat's legacy. J Econ Lit 35(1):40–59

Part III
Economic Agents and Interactions

Chapter 8
The Law of Proportionate Growth and Its Siblings: Applications in Agent-Based Modeling of Socio-Economic Systems

Frank Schweitzer

In memory of Masanao Aoki

Abstract The law of proportionate growth simply states that the time-dependent change of a quantity x is proportional to x. Its applicability to a wide range of dynamic phenomena is based on various assumptions for the proportionality factor, which can be random or deterministic, constant or time dependent. Further, the dynamics can be combined with additional additive growth terms, which can be constants, aggregated quantities, or interaction terms. This allows to extent the core dynamics into an agent-based modeling framework with vast applications in social and economic systems. The chapter adopts this overarching perspective to discuss phenomena as diverse as saturated growth, competition, stochastic growth, investments in random environments, wealth redistribution, opinion dynamics and the wisdom of crowds, reputation dynamics, knowledge growth, and the combination with network dynamics.

Keywords Multiplicative growth · Social influence · Reputation · Reciprocity · Wisdom of crowds

8.1 Introduction

Stochastic systems and their application to economic dynamics have always been at the heart of Masanao Aoki (Aoki and Yoshikawa 2011). His aim was to reconstruct macroeconomic dynamic behavior from a large collection of interacting agents (Aoki 2002), with a particular focus on the dynamics of firms. Already early on, Aoki has combined such studies with decentralized optimization problems

F. Schweitzer (✉)
Chair of Systems Design, ETH Zurich, Zurich, Switzerland
e-mail: fschweitzer@ethz.ch

H. Aoyama et al. (eds.), *Complexity, Heterogeneity, and the Methods of Statistical Physics in Economics*, Evolutionary Economics and Social Complexity Science 22,
https://doi.org/10.1007/978-981-15-4806-2_8

(Aoki 1973). What makes his work appealing to me is the clarity, the rigor, and the accessibility of his modeling approach. Linking economic behavior back to generalized stochastic dynamics allows to bridge different scientific disciplines, including applied mathematics and statistical physics.

Such achievements made Aoki a forerunner in agent-based modeling, the way we want it to be: Away from mere, and often arbitrary, computer simulations based on ad-hoc assumptions about agent's behavior, towards a formal, tractable and still insightful analysis of interacting systems. Current trends in *econophysics* (Aoyama et al. 2017) and *sociophysics* (Schweitzer 2018b) point into this direction.

In the spirit of Aoki's approch, I will sketch how a *class of multiplicative models* can be fruitfully applied to various dynamic problems in the socio-economic domain. The core of this model class is the *law of proportionate growth* proposed by R. Gibrat in 1931 for the *growth of firms*. The size of a firm is described by a (positive) variable $x_i(t)$. The law of proportionate growth then states that the growth of a firm, expressed by the time derivative $\dot{x}_i(t)$, is proportional to $x_i(t)$. But for the proportionality factor various assumptions can be made. In its original version, growth rates have been proxied by random variables, so it is a *stochastic model*. It is also an *agent-based model* because the dynamics focuses on individual firms. But, as in other agent-based models, the aim is *not* to capture the growth of a particular firm in the most precise manner. Instead, the research interest is in correctly reproducing the *aggregated*, or macro behavior of an ensemble of firms.

It is interesting that, despite its simplicity, the law of proportionate growth is indeed able to reproduce so-called *stylized facts* about the dynamics of firms. At the same time, it misses one important modeling ingredient, namely, *interactions* between agents. This sets the ground for the following discussions. We will extend the basic model by introducing *direct* interactions, but also *indirect* interactions via global couplings, for example redistribution mechanisms. These different interaction terms are combined with different expressions for the *growth term*, which can become also negative. Further, in addition to the multiplicative growth term, we consider an *additive term* and, for these two terms, combine *stochastic* and *deterministic* dynamics in different ways.

With these assumptions, we obtain various agent-based models that all describe the dynamics of *agents*, via $x_i(t)$. Eventually, we combine this dynamic for the agent variable with another dynamics that changes the *interaction structure* of agents. This way, we arrive at a whole ensemble of agent-based models, which all inherit from the same basic dynamics, namely, proportional growth, but additional model components allow to capture a plethora of socio-economic phenomena.

8.2 Basic Dynamics: Multiplicative Growth

8.2.1 Exponential Growth: Short Time Horizons

In the following, we consider a number of agents $i = 1, \ldots, N$, each of which is described by a time dependent quantity $x_i(t)$. Thus, the system's dynamics results from N concurring dynamic processes. x is *continuous* and *positive*, i.e., $x_i(t) \geq 0$. The law of proportionate growth states that the increase in time of $x_i(t)$ is proportional to the current value

$$\frac{dx_i(t)}{dt} = \alpha_i x_i(t) \; ; \qquad x_i(t) = x_i(0) \exp\{\alpha_i t\} \tag{8.1}$$

It describes a self-reinforcing process which for the growth factor $\alpha_i > 0$ leads to exponential growth and for $\alpha_i < 0$ to exponential decay of $x_i(t)$. Instead of a continuous time t, we can also consider a discrete formulation $t, t+\Delta t, t+2\Delta t, \ldots$. With $\Delta t = 1$, the growth dynamics then reads:

$$x_i(t+1) = x_i(t)\,[1+\alpha_i] \tag{8.2}$$

The exponential growth dynamics is shown in Fig. 8.2a.

Applications

Using this dynamics in a plain manner has the problem that, for *long* times, the result becomes either *unrealistic*, because with $\alpha_i > 0$ the values of x_i exceed any limit, or it becomes *uninteresting*, because with $\alpha_i < 0$ the values of x_i converge to zero. Nevertheless, for *intermediate* times, we can still find exponential growth/decay in real systems. Exponential growth has been observed in OTC derivatives market of the US (Nanumyan et al. 2015), but also in the growth of open source software platforms such as `Sourceforge` (Schweitzer et al. 2014) (see Fig. 8.1).

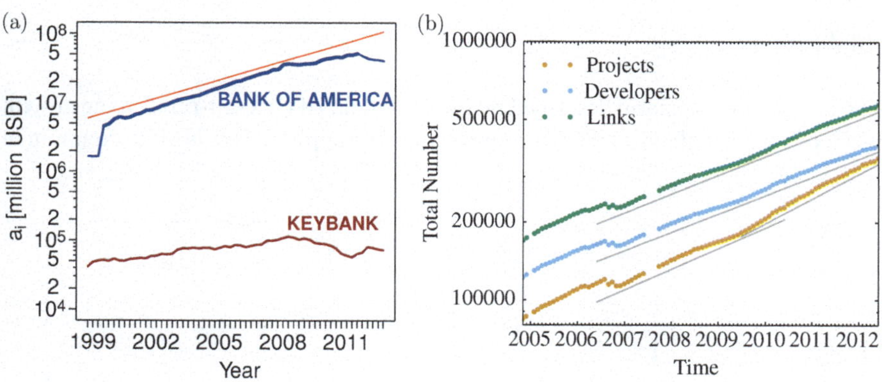

Fig. 8.1 Exponential growth in real systems: (**a**) Value of OTC derivatives of the Bank of America (Nanumyan et al. 2015), (**b**) Number of developers registered on the platform `Sourceforge` (Schweitzer et al. 2014)

8.2.2 *Relative Growth: Competition*

If we consider concurring processes, it is useful to introduce relative variables, or fractions, $y_i(t) = x_i(t)/\sum_i x_i(t)$ for which a conservation holds: $\sum_i y_i(t) = 1$. Let us further assume some direct or indirect coupling that may affect the growth rate $\alpha_i = \alpha_i(\ldots, x_i, x_j, \ldots)$. For example, the growth of quantity x_i occurs via an interaction between agents i and j. Specifically, it depends on the *relative advantage* $(a_i - a_j)$ of i over j and the respective quantity $x_j(t)$. If all agents are allowed to interact, for the growth of i results:

$$\alpha_i(\ldots, x_i, x_j, \ldots) = \sum_i (a_i - a_j)\, x_j \tag{8.3}$$

For the growth dynamics of agent i we then find, in terms of the relative variable:

$$\frac{dy_i(t)}{dt} = y_i(t)\,[a_i - \langle a(t)\rangle] \;; \quad \langle a(t)\rangle = \frac{\sum_i a_i x_i(t)}{\sum_i x_i} = \sum_i a_i y_i(t) \tag{8.4}$$

This selection equation, also known as Fisher-Eigen equation (Feistel and Ebeling 2011), states that, despite the $x_i(t)$ of all agents grow exponentially, their share relative to the total population only grows as long as their advantage (or fitness) a_i is larger than the average fitness $\langle a(t)\rangle$. The latter, however, increases over time because the $y_i(t)$ of agents with a fitness *below average* shrink. This way, each agent i receives indirect information about its performance with respect to the average performance. In the end, this competition dynamics leads to an outcome where only one agent survives – the one with the highest advantage a_i. This is illustrated in Fig. 8.2b.

Applications

The competition scenario described by Eq. (8.4) holds if (i) a self-reinforcing growth mechanism is involved, and (ii) a conservation law applies. This is quite common in

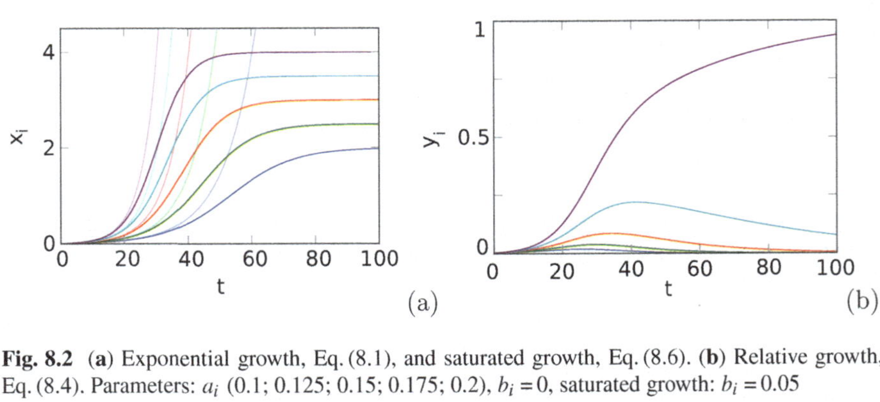

Fig. 8.2 (**a**) Exponential growth, Eq. (8.1), and saturated growth, Eq. (8.6). (**b**) Relative growth, Eq. (8.4). Parameters: a_i (0.1; 0.125; 0.15; 0.175; 0.2), $b_i = 0$, saturated growth: $b_i = 0.05$

socio-economic systems, where, e.g., products compete for customers via their cost price (Feistel and Ebeling 2011). Also, market shares cannot grow independently because they are coupled to the market size (Schweitzer 1998). The same dynamics can be also found for competing strategies in a game-theoretical setting (Schweitzer et al. 2013) or in cluster formation (Schweitzer and Schimansky-Geier 1994).

8.2.3 Size Dependent Growth Factor: Saturation

Long-term exponential growth is a quite unrealistic scenario if limited resources are considered. Therefore, for the growth factor α_i usually some quantity dependent decrease is assumed. A very common assumption is

$$\alpha_i(x_i) = a_i - b_i x_i \tag{8.5}$$

where b_i is assumed to be small. In this case, we observe saturated growth (see also Fig. 8.2a)

$$\frac{dx_i(t)}{dt} = a_i x_i - b_i x_i^2 \; ; \quad x_i(t \to \infty) = \frac{a_i}{b_i} \tag{8.6}$$

which is known as the *logistic equation*, originally proposed by P. Verhulst in 1838, rediscovered by R. Pearl in 1920 and by A. Lotka in 1925.

Applications

In *population dynamics* many realistic growth processes are described by the logistic equation, where the saturation reflects a limited *carrying capacity*. Surprisingly, also the growth of *donations* empirically matches this dynamics (Schweitzer and Mach 2008). Here, the limited resource is not only the money available, but also the number of people willing to donate.

An important application of the dynamics of Eq. (8.6) comes from its discretized version. Using the transformation $t \to n$, $z_n = x(t)\, b/r$ with $r = a + 1$, we arrive at the famous *logistic map*

$$z_{n+1} = r\, z_n(1 - z_n) \tag{8.7}$$

This is one of the paragons to study *deterministic chaos*, provided that $3.57 < r < 4$.

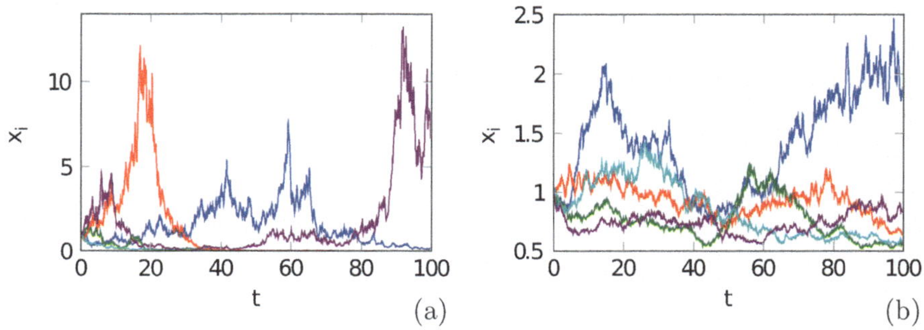

Fig. 8.3 (**a**) Random growth, Eq. (8.8), (**b**) Coupled random growth, Eq. (8.10). Parameters: $\mathcal{N}(\mu_\eta, \sigma_\eta^2)$ with μ_η=0, σ_η^2=1

8.2.4 Time Dependent Growth Factor: Randomness

An important variant of the law of proportionate growth assumes random growth factors instead of fixed ones, i.e., $\alpha_i \to \eta_i(t)$, where $\eta_i(t)$ is a random number draw from, e.g., a normal distribution with mean μ_η and variance σ_η^2:

$$\eta_i(t) \sim \mathcal{N}(\mu_\eta, \sigma_\eta^2) \tag{8.8}$$

Because of stochastic influences the most successful agent cannot be predicted from the outset, as shown in Fig. 8.3a. Instead, one finds that the quantity x follows a log-normal distribution $P(x, t)$ which changes over time as

$$P(x, t) = \frac{1}{\sqrt{2\pi\sigma_\eta^2 t}} \frac{1}{x} \exp\left\{-\frac{\left[\log(x) - \mu_\eta t\right]^2}{2\sigma_\eta^2 t}\right\} \tag{8.9}$$

We note that this probability distribution does not reach a steady state. Its mean value and variance increase over time as $\mu_x \propto t$, $\sigma_x^2 \propto t$. However, if $\mu_\eta < 0$, for long times and sufficiently large x the tail of the distribution can be approximated by a power law: $P(x) \propto x^{-|\mu_\eta|}$.

Applications

Historically, this dynamic was first used by R. Gibrat in 1931 to describe the growth of companies (Sutton 1997). This has found mixed empirical evidence (Aoyama et al. 2017). But other quantities that can be approximately described by a time-dependent log-normal distribution, for instance, the wealth distribution, have been also modeled with this approach (Yakovenko and Rosser 2009). Eventually, also the growth of cities has been described by the law of proportionate growth (Malevergne et al. 2011).

8.2.5 Coupled Random Growth: Fraction Dependent Fluctuations

The dynamics $\dot{x}_i(t) = \eta_i(t)x_i(t)$ with a randomly drawn growth rate η_i assumes that agents are subject to fluctuations in the same manner, regardless of their value $x_i(t)$. If x_i denotes for example the size of a firm, then it is empirically known that *larger* firms should be subject to *smaller* fluctuations (Aoyama et al. 2017). This can be considered by a size dependent variance, $\sigma^2(x) \propto x^{-\beta}$, where $\beta \approx 0.2$.

Focusing on the size only, however, completely ignores the market structure. Firms with a larger market share, for instance, face a stronger competition, which should result in larger fluctuations. One way of achieving this is a global coupling via $\sum_i x_i(t)$, for example:

$$\frac{dx_i(t)}{dt} = \eta_i(t)\frac{x_i(t)}{\sum_i x_i(t)} = \eta_i(t)y_i(t) \tag{8.10}$$

which is illustrated in Fig. 8.3b. Here, the growth is proportional to the relative influence of agent i, i.e., to the *fraction* $y_i(t)$ obtained in the system. For sufficiently chosen μ_η, σ_η^2, the total quantity $\sum_i x_i(t)$ may grow over time, which results in a smaller and smaller impact of the further growth *if* the market share of i is small. I.e., in the course of time, for those agents we observe a comparably stable value of $y_i(t)$. For agents with a large $x_i(t)$, and hence a large fraction $y_i(t)$, we still observe remarkable fluctuations, although not comparable to those without a global coupling, as shown in Fig. 8.3a.

In comparison to Eq. (8.3), which already introduced such a global coupling between the different growth processes, the existence of large fluctuations prevents the system from converging to an equilibrium state where "the winner takes it all." We note that both dynamics of Eqs. (8.4) and (8.10) belong to the class of so-called *frequency dependent processes*, where the dynamics depends on the relative share y_i, determined either in a local neighborhood or globally. Examples of important frequency-dependent processes are the (non-linear) *voter model* (Schweitzer and Behera 2009) and the Polya process.

Applications

This dynamic allows to combine two processes: (a) the indirect interaction via an evolving mean value, which is the essence of a competition process, and (b) fluctuations in the growth process that depend on the relative influence, or the *ranking*, of the agent. This combination prevents the system from converging to an uninteresting equilibrium state, but still considers the "comparative advantage" of agents.

8.3 Multiplicative and Additive Growth

8.3.1 *Lossy Multiplicative Growth: Geometric Versus Arithmetic Mean*

The outcome of a discrete dynamics of the type

$$x_i(t+1) = x_i(t)[1+\eta_i(t)] = \lambda_i(t)x_i(t) \tag{8.11}$$

very much depends on the *parameters* of the distribution $\mathcal{N}(\mu_\lambda, \sigma_\lambda^2)$ of the randomly drawn growth rates λ_i. We can express these parameters as follows:

$$\mu_\lambda = \langle\lambda\rangle \;; \quad \sigma_\lambda^2 = \left\langle\lambda^2\right\rangle - \langle\lambda\rangle^2 \tag{8.12}$$

Equation (8.11) can be rewritten as

$$\log x_i(t+1) = \log\lambda_i(t) + \log x_i(t) = \sum_{s=0}^{t} \log\lambda_i(s) \tag{8.13}$$

with the parameters for the distribution of the random variable $(\log\lambda)$:

$$\mu_{\log\lambda} = \langle\log\lambda\rangle \;; \quad \sigma_{\log\lambda}^2 = \left\langle\log\lambda^2\right\rangle - \langle\log\lambda\rangle^2 \tag{8.14}$$

Applying the central limit theorem to Eq. (8.13) implies that the distribution of the random variable $x(t)$ over time gets closer to a log-normal distribution, Eq. (8.9) or, equivalently, the random variable $\log x(t)$ gets closer to a normal distribution with the parameters

$$\mu_{\log x}(t) = t\; \mu_{\log\lambda} \;; \quad \sigma_{\log x}^2(t) = t\; \sigma_{\log\lambda}^2 . \tag{8.15}$$

This means that the *expected value*, i.e., the maximum of the probability distribution, still grows in time. On the other hand, one can show (Lorenz et al. 2013) that individual growth trajectories x_i disappear if

$$\mu_{\log\lambda} < 0 < \log\mu_\lambda \quad \Rightarrow \quad \langle\lambda\rangle_{\text{geo}} = \exp(\mu_{\log\lambda}) < 1 < \mu_\lambda = \langle\lambda\rangle \tag{8.16}$$

where $\langle\lambda\rangle_{\text{geo}}$ denotes the *geometrical mean*, which has to be smaller than the *arithmetic mean* $\langle\lambda\rangle$. The fact that $x_i(t) \to 0$ is remarkable because it is also counter intuitive. So, there is a need to also use agent-based modeling in addition to an analysis of aggregated measures, such as distributions, because it allows us to better understand what happens on the microscopic/individual level.

Applications

The above insights can be directly applied to multiplicative growth processes with random time-dependent growth factors discussed already in Sect. 8.2.4. Hence, they help to better understand under which conditions a decline in firm sizes, city sizes, or individual wealth (Slanina 2004) can be expected if the underlying stochastic dynamics holds. The same dynamics was also applied to model the growth, more precisely the decline, of individual human capital which follows a life cycle over time (Grochulski and Piskorski 2010).

8.3.2 *Constant Additive Growth: Stationarity*

To avoid a scenario where individual growth trajectories disappear, one can add a term ω_i to the dynamics:

$$x_i(t+1) = \lambda_i(t)x_i(t) + \omega_i(t) \tag{8.17}$$

$\omega_i(t)$ can have different forms as discussed below: it can be a small positive constant, $\omega_i(t) \equiv A > 0$, it can be a time-dependent function that further depend on the state of other agents, or it can be fluctuating, like an additive noise term.

The mere existence of such an additive term changes the properties of the underlying dynamics. For $\omega_i = A$, we find a *stationary* distribution:

$$P^s(x) = \frac{(A/\sigma_\lambda^2)^{\mu_\lambda}}{\Gamma(\mu_\lambda)} x^{-(1-\mu_\lambda)} \exp\left\{-\frac{A}{\sigma_\lambda^2 x}\right\} \tag{8.18}$$

where $\Gamma(x)$ is the Gamma function. This distribution is plotted in Fig. 8.4. The most probable value, i.e., the maximum of the distribution, is given by $x^{\mathrm{mp}} \approx A/\langle\lambda^2\rangle$.

We note that Eqs.(8.17) and (8.18) are special cases of a more general framework for multiplicative processes (Richmond 2001)

$$\Delta x(t) = \eta(t)G[x(t)] + F[x(t)] \tag{8.19}$$

with the general (non-normalized) solution

$$P^s(x) = \frac{1}{G^2(x)} \exp\left\{\frac{2}{D}\int^x \frac{F(x')}{G^2(x')}\mathrm{d}x'\right\} \tag{8.20}$$

Our case is covered by $G(x) = x$ and $F(x) = A$.

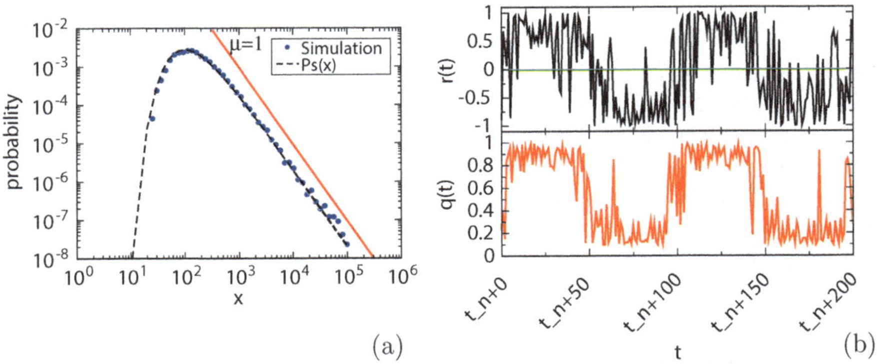

Fig. 8.4 (**a**) Stationary distribution $P^s(x)$, Eq. (8.18) (dashed line), agent-based simulations, Eq. (8.17) (dots) (Navarro et al. 2008a), (**b**) Detecting an optimal investment $q_i(t)$ in a noisy market by means of a genetic algorithm (Navarro et al. 2008b)

Applications

This dynamics is frequently used to model stock market behavior (Richmond 2001) or investments in random environments, in general (Navarro et al. 2008a,b). The stochasticity can come from fluctuating yields, e.g., $\eta_i(t) = r(t)q_i(t)$, where $0 \leq q_i(t) \leq 1$ is the wealth fraction that agent i decides to invest in a volatile market and $r(t)$ is the *return on investment*, i.e., the random variable. $r(t)$ is independent of the agents and describes the market dynamics, with a lower bound of -1, i.e., full loss of the investment, but no upper bound. Investment decisions are then modeled by forecasting the best value $q_i(t)$ given some information about previous values of $r(t)$ from time series data. Here, machine learning algorithms can be used to determine the dynamics for $q_i(t)$, as demonstrated in Fig. 8.4b.

8.3.3 Variable Additive Growth: Redistribution

Instead of a fixed (small) amount added to the individual growth dynamics, one can also consider a changing amount that depends on the overall growth. Let us assume that $x_i(t)$ denotes the individual wealth of agent i, which is taxed by a a central authority (the government) at a fixed tax rate a, known as *proportional tax* scenario.

From the total amount of taxes, $T(t) = a\sum_i x_i(t)$, the government withholds a fraction b to cover the costs for its administration, and *redistributes* the remaining fraction $(1 - b)$ equally to all N agents as a subsidy (Lorenz et al. 2013). The wealth of each agent still evolves independently according to the stochastic growth dynamics of Eq. (8.14). Together with the taxation and the subsidy, the total wealth of an agent at time $t+1$ is therefore given as:

$$x_i(t+1) = x_i(t)\,[\lambda_i(t) - a] + \frac{a[1-b]}{N} \sum_i x_i(t) \qquad (8.21)$$

Let us now assume that the conditions of Eq. (8.16) hold, i.e., that due to the stochastic dynamics alone the individual wealth will disappear over time. This is realized by choosing $\langle\lambda\rangle_{\text{geo}} = 2/3 < 1 < 3/2 = \langle\lambda\rangle$. The larger the spread of these two values, the larger the "risk" associated with the "production of wealth." The question then is: under which conditions could the proposed redistribution mechanism prevent the decay of wealth? Could it even lead to an *increase*, instead of a decrease, of individual wealth over time?

The answer is *yes*, and the simplicity of the agent-based model allows to study these conditions in a simulation approach. Figure 8.5a shows sample trajectories of the *total wealth* $\sum_i x_i(t)$ for varying parameters a, b, N. The colors refer to three different taxation schemes (see Lorenz et al. (2013) for details), the blue curve holds for proportional tax. The straight black lines show two limit cases: The lower line is for "no tax," where the individual wealth evolves in time proportional to $[\langle\lambda\rangle_{\text{geo}}]^t$, i.e., it decays exponentially. The upper line is for "full tax," where the individual wealth evolves over time proportional to $[(1-ba)\,\langle\lambda\rangle]^t$, i.e., it increases exponentially. Realistic redistribution scenarios have to be between these two limit cases and further depend on the size of the agent population, N. The larger the

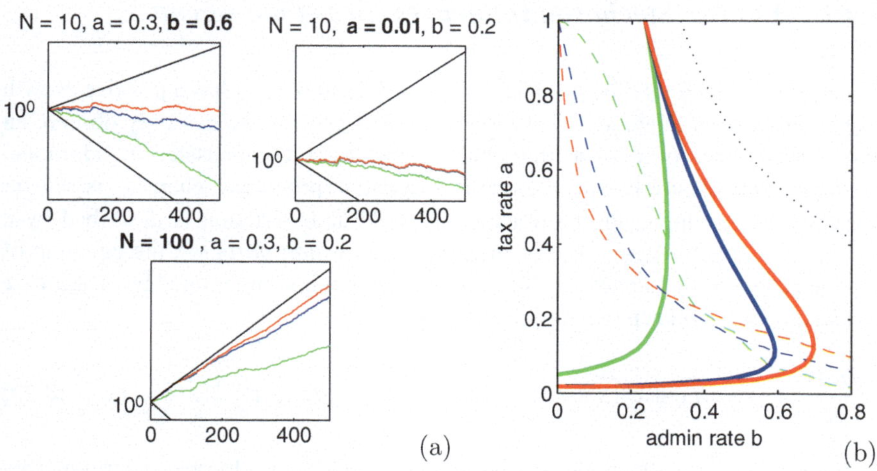

Fig. 8.5 (**a**) Sample trajectories of the total wealth $\sum_i x_i(t)$ (y-axis, in log scale) over time t (x-axis, in normal scale) for three different parameter settings a, b, N. Tax schemes: (blue) proportional tax, (red) progressive tax (no tax if wealth is below a threshold), (green) regressive tax (fixed tax for everyone), see Lorenz et al. (2013) for details. (**b**) Solid lines divide zones of wealth growth (to the left) and wealth destruction (to the right). Dashed lines $a_{\text{opt}}(b)$ are optimal tax rates for a given administration cost, which maximize the growth of total wealth. Above the black dotted line only wealth destruction can happen

population, the better the redistribution effect. Obviously, the value of the tax rates, a, is not to be chosen independently of the value of the administration cost, b. Figure 8.5b shows, for fixed values of N and $\langle\lambda\rangle$, $\langle\lambda\rangle_{\mathrm{geo}}$, the range of parameters which could possibly lead to an increase of total wealth.

Applications

The redistribution model allows to study the impact of different *tax scenarios* on the wealth of a population. As shown in Fig. 8.5, two other realistic scenarios of tax collection, progressive tax and regressive tax, have been discussed in Lorenz et al. (2013). Further, the impact of different *redistribution mechanisms* can be studied and additional economic constraints, such as conservation of money, can be included.

From a more general perspective this redistribution model has much in common with other models studying the *portfolio effect* in *investment* science (Marsili et al. 1998; Slanina 1999). The positive impact of rebalancing gains and losses, first discussed by JL Kelly in 1956, is rediscovered from time to time in different contexts (Yaari and Solomon 2010).

8.4 Multiplicative Decay and Additive Growth

8.4.1 Additive Stochastic Influences: Brownian Agents

So far, we assumed that the proportional growth term $\alpha_i x_i(t)$ has a positive growth rate α_i at least *on average*. Otherwise, instead of growth, we can only observe an exponential decay of x_i over time, which needs to be compensated by additional *additive terms*. There is a whole class of dynamic processes where α_i is *always* negative. For example, the motion of a particle under friction is described by a friction coefficient $\alpha_i \equiv -\gamma$. For the case of *Brownian particles*, the equation of motion proposed by Langevin posits that this friction is compensated by an *additive stochastic force*, to keep the particle moving:

$$\frac{dv(t)}{dt} = -\gamma\, v(t) + \sqrt{2S}\,\xi(t)\ ; \quad \langle\xi(t)\rangle = 0\ ; \quad \left\langle\xi(t')\xi(t)\right\rangle = \delta(t'-t) \tag{8.22}$$

S denotes the strength of the stochastic force and is, in physics, determined by the *fluctuation-dissipation theorem*. $\xi(t)$ is Gaussian white noise, i.e., it has the expectation value of zero and only delta-correlations in time. $v(t)$ denotes the continuous *velocity* of the Brownian particle, which can be positive or negative. The positive quantity $x_i(t) = |v_i(t)|$ then has the physical meaning of a speed and follows the same equation.

We assume that the *agent dynamics* is described by a set of stochastic equations which resemble the Langevin equation of Browian motion, therefore the notion of *Brownian agents* has been established (Schweitzer 2003). For our further consideration in an *agent-based model*, the *structure* of Eq. (8.22) is important. The agent dynamics results from a *superposition* of two different types of influences, deterministic and stochastic ones. In Eq. (8.17), the first term $\lambda_i(t)x_i(t)$ is the stochastic term, while the second term $\omega_i(t)$ is the deterministic term. In Eq. (8.22), on the other hand, the first term denotes *deterministic* forces. This is, in the most simple case of Eq. (8.22), the relaxation term which defines a temporal scale of the agent dynamics. The second term denotes *stochastic* forces which summarize all influences that are *not* specified on these temporal or spatial scales.

To develop Eq. (8.22) into the dynamics of a Brownian *agent*, this picture still misses *interactions* between agents. These can be represented by additional additive terms:

$$\frac{dx_i(t)}{dt} = -\gamma\, x_i(t) + \mathcal{G}(\mathbf{x}, \mathbf{w}, \mathbf{u}) + D_i \xi_i(t) \tag{8.23}$$

The function $\mathcal{G}(\mathbf{x}, \mathbf{w}, \mathbf{u})$ fulfills several purposes. First, with $\mathbf{x}$ as the vector of all variables $x_i(t)$, it describes interactions between agents via couplings between $x_i(t)$ and any $x_j(t)$. Second, $\mathcal{G}$ is, in general, a *nonlinear* function of x_i itself, $\sum_{k=0}^{n} \beta_k(\mathbf{w}, \mathbf{u})\, x_i^k(t)$ (Schweitzer 2018a), which allows to consider dynamic feedback processes such as self-reinforced growth. Third, the coefficients $\beta_k(\mathbf{w}, \mathbf{u})$ of such a nonlinear function can consider additional couplings to other variables $w_i(t)$ of the agents, which are summarized in the vector $\mathbf{w}$. $\mathbf{u}$ eventually represents a set of *control parameters* to capture, e.g., the influence of the environment. D_i defines the individual susceptibility of agent i to stochastic influences.

Applications

The concept of *Brownian agents* (Schweitzer 2003) has found a vast range of applications at different levels of organization: physical, biological, and social. Specifically, active motion and clustering in biological systems (Schweitzer and Schimansky-Geier 1994; Ebeling et al. 1999; Garcia et al. 2011; Ebeling and Schweitzer 2003), self-wiring of networks, and trail formation based on chemotactic interactions (Helbing et al. 1997; Schweitzer et al. 1997; Schweitzer and Tilch 2002) and emotional influence in online communications (Schweitzer and Garcia 2010; Garas et al. 2012; Garcia et al. 2014, 2016; Tadic et al. 2017) are studied both from a modeling and a *data-driven* perspective.

An important application for the additional coupling between agent variables considers the variable $w_i(t)$ as the *internal energy depot* of an agent. It allows for different activities that go beyond the level defined by the fluctuation-dissipation theorem. This has resulted into an unifying agent-based framework to model *active matter* (Schweitzer 2018a). As other types of self-organizing systems, active matter

(Bechinger et al. 2016) relies on the take-up of energy that can be used for example for active motion or structure formation. Our theoretical description is based on the coupling between *driving* variables, $w_i(t)$, to describe the take-up, storage and conversion of energy, and *driven* variables, $x_i(t)$, to describe the energy consuming activities. Modified Langevin equations reflect the stochastic dynamics of both types of variables. System-specific hypotheses about their coupling can be encoded in additional nonlinear functions.

8.4.2 Wisdom of Crowds: Response to Aggregated Information

The additive stochastic dynamics discussed above can be used to model the opinion dynamics of agents. Here, $x_i(t)$ denotes the continuous opinion of agent i. Let us consider the so-called *wisdom of crowds* (WoC) effect, where the values of x are usually mapped to the positive space, $x \geq 0$. Agents are given a particular question with a definite answer, unknown to them, for example: "What is the length of the border of Switzerland?" (Lorenz et al. 2011). Their opinion $x_i > 0$ then denotes their individual estimates about this length. The WoC effect states that if one takes N *independent* estimates, the average $\langle x \rangle = (1/N) \sum_i x_i$ is close to the true value x^T. I.e., the WoC effect is a purely statistical phenomenon, where the "wisdom" is on the population level. It only works if the distribution of estimates $P(x)$ is sufficiently *broad*, i.e., the variance, or the *group diversity* of opinions, should be high.

In case of *social influence*, e.g., information exchange between agents, estimates are no longer independent and the variance can reduce considerably. One can argue that social influence could help agents to converge to a mean value closer to the truth. On the other hand, social influence could also help agents to converge to a mean value much further *away* from the truth – without recognizing it. That means, agents can collectively convince each other that the *wrong* opinion should be the *right* one.

Because this is a real-world problem for all social decision processes, it has been studied both experimentally (Lorenz et al. 2011; Rauhut et al. 2011; Mavrodiev et al. 2013) and theoretically (Mavrodiev et al. 2012). In a controlled experiment, agents are given the same question a number of times. They form an independent initial estimate $x_i(0)$. After each subsequent time step, agents are given additional information about the estimates of other agents, which allows them to correct their own estimate, i.e., $x_i(t)$ becomes a function of time. This can be described by the dynamics:

$$\frac{dx_i(t)}{dt} = \gamma \left[x_i(0) - x_i(t)\right] + \sum\nolimits_j \mathcal{F}(x_j, x_i) + D\xi_i(t) \tag{8.24}$$

which is a modification of Eq. (8.23). The relaxation term $-\gamma x_i$ is now corrected by the initial estimate. That means, without any social influence $x_i(t)$ has the tendency to converge to $x_i(0)$, rather than to zero. γ is the strength of an agent's *individual conviction*. Thus, the first term describes the tendency of an agent to stick to the original opinion.

$\mathcal{F}(x_j, x_i)$ describes the *interaction* between agents, specifically between their opinions. In a controlled experiment (Lorenz et al. 2011), agents can for example at each time step get information about the estimates $x_j(t)$ of *all other agents* (full information regime), or only information about the *average estimate* $\langle x(t)\rangle$ (aggregated information regime). These regimes are expressed in different forms of $\mathcal{F}$. A general ansatz reads:

$$\mathcal{F}(x_j, x_i) = \left[x_j(t) - x_i(t)\right] w_{ij} \tag{8.25}$$

Different forms of w_{ij} encode how much weight agent i attributes to the opinion of agent j. For the aggregated information regime, the quantity w_{ij} is a constant, $w_{ij} = \alpha/N$, where α denotes the strength of the *social influence*. With this, we can rewrite the dynamics of Eq. (8.24) as:

$$\begin{aligned} \frac{dx_i(t)}{dt} &= \gamma\,[x_i(0) - x_i(t)] + \alpha\,[\langle x(t)\rangle - x_i(t)] + D\xi_i(t) \\ &= -\gamma' x_i(t) + \alpha\,\langle x(t)\rangle + \gamma x_i(0) + D\xi_i(t) \end{aligned} \tag{8.26}$$

with $\gamma' = \gamma + \alpha$. Equation (8.26) highlights the *coupling* to the *"mean field"* formed by all agents, because all agents interact and have the same w_{ij}. The stochastic equation for the mean opinion (Mavrodiev et al. 2012):

$$\frac{d\,\langle x(t)\rangle}{dt} = \gamma\,[\langle x(0)\rangle - \langle x(t)\rangle] + \frac{D}{\sqrt{N}}\,\langle \xi(t)\rangle \tag{8.27}$$

describes a so-called *Ornstein-Uhlenbeck process* and has an analytic solution.

To better understand the role of the two model parameters, individual conviction γ and social influence α, one can run agent-based simulations with the dynamics of Eq. (8.26) (Mavrodiev et al. 2012). Figure 8.6 shows how well the wisdom of crowds performs in reaching the (known) truth x^T, dependent on the *initial conditions*, $x_i(0)$. Figure 8.6a illustrates a starting configuration, where $\ln x^T < \langle \ln x(0)\rangle$. In this case, a *larger* social influence *always* leads to a *worse* performance of the WoC (indicated by the monotonous color change from red to blue). Figure 8.6b, on the other hand, illustrates a starting configuration, where $\ln x^T > \langle \ln x(0)\rangle$. Here we find instead a *non-monotonous* color change. While for very small values of the social influence the performance is lower (yellow), it increases for medium values of α (red), before it declines again for large values of α (blue). Hence, in a region *A* increasing social influence can help the wisdom of crowds, while in a region *B* increasing social influence rather distorts the WoC effect.

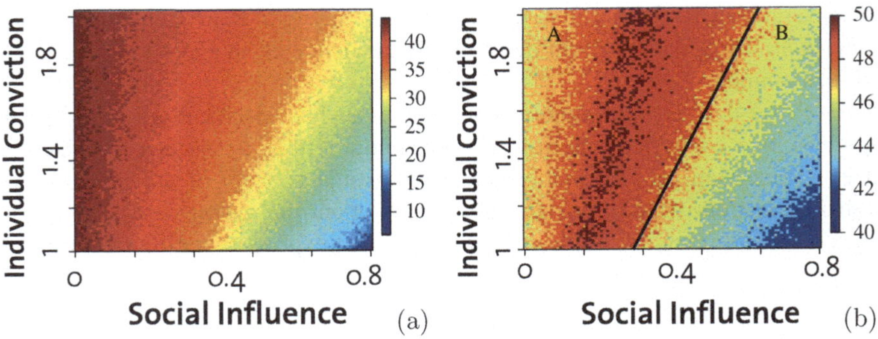

Fig. 8.6 WoC effect for a parameter sweep of individual conviction γ and social influence α. Different initial conditions: (**a**) $\ln x^T < \langle \ln x(0) \rangle$, (**b**) $\ln x^T > \langle \ln x(0) \rangle$. The color code indicates how close the wisdom of crowds approaches the known truth: 50 (red) is the best performance (Mavrodiev et al. 2012)

Applications

It is quite remarkable how well the agent-based dynamics of Eq. (8.26) describes the empirical results for the aggregated information regime (Mavrodiev et al. 2013) obtained in controlled experiments with humans (Lorenz et al. 2011). It was found that the adjustment of individual opinions depends *linearly* on the distance to the *mean* of all estimates, even though the correct answers for different questions differ by several orders of magnitude.

8.4.3 Bounded Confidence: Consensus Versus Coexistence of Opinions

The redistribution model and the WoC model both assume that agents in a population interact via an aggregated variable. This is different in the so-called "bounded confidence" model (Lorenz 2007). Here, the continuous values of x represent opinions which are mapped to the positive space, $x \geq 0$, and transformed to the unit interval [0, 1]. The model assumes that two randomly chosen agents i and j can interact only if they are sufficiently close in their values $x_i(t)$, precisely if $|x_i(t) - x_j(t)| < \varepsilon$, i.e., below a given threshold ε, which defines a *tolerance* for other's opinions. Thanks for their interaction, agents adjust their opinions towards each other, which is motivated by social arguments:

$$\frac{dx_i(t)}{dt} = \gamma \left[x_j(t) - x_i(t)\right] \Theta[z_{ij}(t)] \; ; \quad z_{ij}(t) = \varepsilon - \left|x_j(t) - x_i(t)\right| \tag{8.28}$$

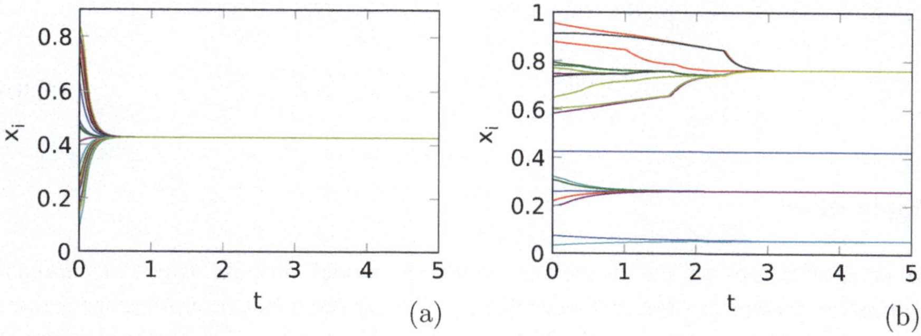

Fig. 8.7 Bounded confidence dynamics, Eq. (8.28) for $\gamma = 0.5$ and different threshold values: (**a**) $\varepsilon = 0.5$, (**b**) $\varepsilon = 0.1$

Here, $\Theta[z]$ is the Heaviside function, which returns $\Theta[z] = 1$ if $z \geq 0$ and $\Theta[z] = 0$ otherwise. The parameter $0 < \gamma \leq 0.5$ basically defines the time scale at which the opinions of the two agents converge, provided that $z_{ij}(t) \geq 0$. If $\gamma = 0.5$, both agents immediately adjust their $x_i(t)$, $x_j(t)$ towards the common mean.

Because at each time step, only two randomly chosen agents can interact, the sequence of interactions matters for the final outcome and the *collective opinion dynamics* becomes a path dependent process. The main research question addressed with this type of model regards *consensus formation*, i.e., the conditions under which a population of agents with randomly chosen initial opinions $x_i(0) \in [0, 1]$ converges to *one* final opinion. While γ only determines the time scale for convergence, the threshold ε mainly decides about the outcome. Figure 8.7 shows examples for two different values of ε. For $\varepsilon = 0.5$, we indeed find consensus, while for $\varepsilon = 0.1$ we observe the *coexistence of two final opinons*. It was shown (Deffuant et al. 2000) that convergence towards consensus can be expected for $\varepsilon \geq 0.25$. If the interaction threshold is below this critical value, we observe instead the convergence towards multiple stationary opinions. This reminds on the period doubling scenario, i.e., the multiplicity of solutions found for the logistic map, Eq. (8.7), when varying the control parameter r. Similar to that example, in the bounded confidence model we also observe "windows" in which convergence to one stationary value is observed.

Instead of a sequence of dyadic interactions of agents, one can also consider *group interactions*, in which many agents interact simultaneously. The dynamics then changes into:

$$\frac{dx_i(t)}{dt} = \frac{\gamma}{\mathcal{N}_i(\varepsilon, t)} \sum_j \left[x_j(t) - x_i(t)\right] \Theta[z_{ij}(t)] \; ; \quad \mathcal{N}_i(\varepsilon, t) = \sum_j \Theta[z_{ij}(t)] \tag{8.29}$$

where the normalization $\mathcal{N}_i$ depends on all agents' opinions and therefore on time, but also on the threshold ε. For $\varepsilon \to 1$, $\mathcal{N}_i(\varepsilon, t) \to N$, we obtain again an agent dynamics which is coupled to the *mean*, with $\gamma' = \gamma/N$:

$$\frac{dx_i(t)}{dt} = -\gamma' x_i(t) + \gamma' \langle x(t) \rangle \tag{8.30}$$

Applications

Most applications of the bounded confidence model propose ways to *enhance consensus formation*, for instance, by introducing *asymmetric* confidence values $\varepsilon^{\text{left}}$, $\varepsilon^{\text{right}}$ (Hegselmann et al. 2002). Consensus can be also fostered using a *hierarchical* opinion dynamics (Perony et al. 2012, 2013) as shown in Fig. 8.8a. During a first time period, all agents adjust their opinions according to the bounded confidence model, Eq. (8.28), such that groups with distinct opinions are formed. During a second period, these group opinions are represented by *delegates* that follow the same dynamics, but have a larger threshold than "normal" agents, $\varepsilon_2 > \varepsilon_1$. Therefore, these delegates are likely to find a consensus even in cases where the original agent population fails to converge to a joint opinion

Another application of the bounded confidence model explains the emergence of so-called *local cultures* that denote a commonly shared behavior within a cluster of firms (Groeber et al. 2009). The basic assumption is that agents *keep partnership relations* from past interactions and this way form so-called *in-groups* $I_i(t)$. The opinions of agents from the in-group continue to influence an agent's opinion, this

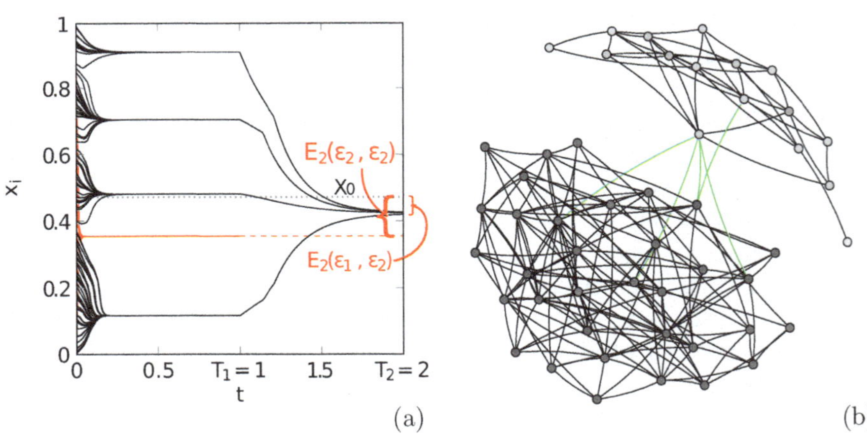

Fig. 8.8 (**a**) Hierarchical opinion dynamics with $\varepsilon_1 = 0.1$, $\varepsilon_2 = 1$. Additionally, in the dynamics an asymmetric preference for opinions closer to zero is assumed (Perony et al. 2013). (**b**) Opinion dynamics with in-group influence, Eqs. (8.31) and (8.32), with $\varepsilon = 0.3$. Green links indicate that agents would *not* interact *without* the influence of their in-groups (Groeber et al. 2009)

way leading to an *effective opinion*

$$x_i^{\text{eff}}(t) = [1 - \alpha_i(t)]\, x_i(t) + \alpha_i(t)\, \langle x \rangle_i^I\,(t) \tag{8.31}$$

Here $\langle x \rangle_i^I\,(t)$ is the mean opinion of agents in the in-group of i, and $\alpha_i(t)$ weights this influence against the "native" opinion $x_i(t)$ of agent i, considering the size of the in-group, $|I_i(t)|$:

$$\langle x \rangle_i^I\,(t) = \frac{1}{|I_i(t)|} \sum_{j \in I_i(t)} x_j(t)\ ; \quad \alpha_i(t) = \frac{|I_i(t)|}{|I_i(t)| + 1} \tag{8.32}$$

While agents adjust their opinions $x_i(t)$ according to the bounded confidence model, Eq. (8.28), their effective opinions $x_i^{\text{eff}}(t)$ decide about their interactions, i.e., $z_{ij}(t) = \varepsilon - \left| x_j^{\text{eff}}(t) - x_i^{\text{eff}}(t) \right|$ Only if interaction takes place, i.e., $z_{ij}(t) \geq 0$, j is added to the in-group of i and a link between agents i and j is formed. Because a change of $\langle x \rangle_i^I\,(t)$ can occur even if i does not interact, this impacts $x_i^{\text{eff}}(t)$ continuously. So, two agents i and j randomly chosen at different times may form a link later, or may remove an existing link because of their in-groups' influence, as illustrated in Fig. 8.8b. This feedback between agents' opinions and their in-group structure sometimes allows to obtain consensus, or a common "local culture," even in cases where the original dynamics would fail.

8.4.4 Bilateral Encounters: Reputation Growth from Battling

In opinion dynamics, the variable $x_i(t)$ does not assume any intrinsic value, i.e., it is not favorable to have a larger or smaller $x_i(t)$. This changes if we consider that $x_i(t)$ represents the *reputation* of agent i, where "higher" means "better." Reputation, in loose terms, summarizes the "status" of an agent, as perceived by others. It can be seen as a social capital and influences for example the choice of interaction partners. For firms, reputation is an *intangible asset*, that means, it is difficult to quantify, but at the same time influences the decisions of investors or customers (Zhang and Schweitzer 2019). Even if the measurement of reputation is a problem, it is obvious that reputation has to be maintained, otherwise it fades out. This can be captured by the dynamics already discussed:

$$\frac{dx_i(t)}{dt} = -\gamma x_i(t) + \sum\nolimits_j \mathcal{F}(x_j, x_i) \tag{8.33}$$

The multiplicative term describes the exponential decay of reputation over time. To compensate for this requires a continuous effort, expressed in the interaction term $\mathcal{F}(x_j, x_i)$. This assumes that reputation can be (only) built up in interactions with other agents j. One could include into the dynamics of Eq. (8.33) another source term for reputation which solely depends on the efforts of agent i, but its justification remains problematic. One could argue that, for example, the reputation of scientists depends on their effort writing publications. But this individual effort can hardly be quantified and compared across scientists. More importantly, not the effort matters for the reputation, but the attention the publication receives from *other* scientists (Sarigol et al. 2014), as quantified, e.g., by the number of citations.

Equation (8.33) is similar to the general dynamics proposed in Eq. (8.24), just that no additive stochastic influence is explicitly considered here and no intrinsic reputation $x_i(0)$ is assumed. For the interaction term, we can in the following separately discuss two different *limit cases*: (i) Reputation is obtained solely during direct battles between two agents, where the winner gains in reputation and the looser not. (ii) Reputation is obtained solely from interacting with other agents and increases with their reputation.

In case of individual battles, we assume that during each time step each agent i has a *bilateral* interaction with any other agent j. For the interaction term we propose (Schweitzer et al. 2020):

$$\mathcal{F}(x_j, x_i) = \frac{1}{N}\sum\nolimits_j \rho(x_i, x_j)\Big\{g + h\Delta_{ji}\,\Theta\left[\Delta_{ji}\right]\Big\}\,; \quad \Delta_{ji} = x_j(t) - x_i(t) \tag{8.34}$$

$\rho(x_i, x_j)$ is a function that decides which agent will be the winner in an interaction between any two agents i and j. It depends on the reputation of both agents, but additionally also considers random influences (Schweitzer et al. 2020). The expression in curly brackets determines the reputation gain for the winner. It consists of two contributions. g is a constant reward for every winner. It accounts for the fact that engaging in such fights is a costly action that should be compensated. $h\Delta_{ji}$ is a bonus reward that applies only if agent i was the one with the lower reputation, $x_i < x_j$, and still won the fight. This is expressed by the Heavyside function $\Theta[\Delta_{ji}]$. Note that, in this model, only the reputation of the *winning agent* will be changed, the loosing agent does not additionally loose in reputation.

Applications

Fights between individuals are ubiquitous in the animal kingdom to establish reputation. In a biological setting, reputation differences translate into *dominance relations*. Hence, this model has a particular relevance to explain social hierarchies in animal societies (Bonabeau et al. 1999). It allows to test whether hierarchies in social organizations are an *emerging phenomenon* or whether they result from the reinforcement of *intrinsic advantages* of individuals. Subsequently, an interaction model allows to test different feedback mechanisms. If the winner is rewarded *and* the looser is punished, this results in a double reinforcement, and the model displays a strong *lock-in effect*. That is, the outcome is almost entirely determined by the first few interactions, initial random differences are just amplified. To obtain realistic

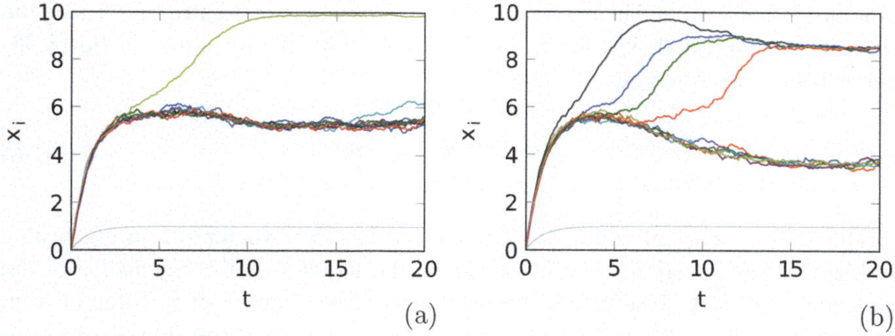

Fig. 8.9 Reputation dynamics from bilateral encounters, Eqs. (8.33) and (8.34). Variance of the normal distribution, from which random influences are drawn: **(a)** $\sigma^2 = 1.4$, **(b)** $\sigma^2 = 1.2$ (Schweitzer et al. 2020)

hierarchies, it is sufficient to only reward the winner (Schweitzer et al. 2020). For hierarchies with different levels the mentioned function $\rho(x_i, x_j)$ plays a particular role. It reflects random influences, the magnitude of which is expressed by the variance σ^2 of a normal distribution. For large values of σ^2 egalitarian regimes are obtained, for intermediate values one agent dominates (despotic hierarchy), as shown in Fig. 8.9a, while for small values layered hierarchies can be obtained as shown in Fig. 8.9b.

8.4.5 *Network Interactions: Reputation Growth Through Feedback Cycles*

The second limit case, where reputation is obtained solely from interacting with other agents, can be expressed by the following interaction term:

$$\mathcal{F}(x_j, x_i) = \sum\nolimits_j l_{ji}\, x_j(t) \tag{8.35}$$

The coefficients l_{ji} are unweighted, but directed *links* between agents j and i. $l_{ji}(t) = 1$ if there is a link from j to i, i.e., agent j can boost the reputation of i proportional to its own reputation. This is a very common feedback mechanism, also used to define *eigenvector centrality* (Bonacich 1987), with many applications. For example, in an online social network (OSN) like `Twitter`, a link $j \to i$ indicates that j is a *follower* of i, and the prominence of j impacts the prominence of i. $l_{ji}(t) = 0$ if no directed link exists, and $l_{ii}(t) = 0$ because an agent cannot boost its own reputation.

With these considerations, the multi-agent system can be represented as a *complex network*, $G(E, V)$ (graph), where *nodes*, V (vertices), represent agents and directed *links*, E (edges), between nodes their directed interactions. The network structure is then encoded in an *adjacency matrix* **A** with matrix entries l_{ji}. Using the interaction term, Eq. (8.35), the *stationary solution* for the dynamics of Eq. (8.33) can be formally written as:

$$x_i^{\text{stat}} = \frac{1}{\gamma} \sum_j l_{ji} x_j^{\text{stat}} \tag{8.36}$$

This defines a set of coupled equations and has the structure of an eigenvalue problem. It has a stationary solution only if the factor γ is the *eigenvalue* of the adjacency matrix **A**. That means, for arbitrarily chosen values of γ different from an eigenvalue, the $x_i(t)$ will either grow too fast (small γ) or too slow (large γ) to be balanced by the other $x_j(t)$, this way resulting in a nonstationary solution. For a stationary solution, usually the *largest* eigenvalue is taken because it guarantees that all solutions are positive (if the matrix **A** is non-negative).

One can eliminate γ by transforming the absolute reputation values $x_i(t)$ into *relative reputations*, $y_i(t) = x_i(t)/\sum_j x_j(t)$. This also has a practical implication: absolute values are hard to know and, to *compare* agents, relative values are sufficient. Under most practical circumstances, however, one would also not be able to obtain a complete normalization, $\sum_j x_j(t)$. But it is sufficient (Schweitzer et al. 2020) if we can normalize by the largest reputation: $y_i(t) = x_i(t)/x_z^{\max}(t)$.

$$\frac{dy_i}{dt} = \sum_j l_{ji}\, y_j(t) - y_i(t) \sum_j l_{jz}\, y_j(t) \tag{8.37}$$

where z is the index of the agent with highest absolute reputation $x_z^{\max}(t)$ at time t, which is for instance often known in a OSN. Its scaling impact on the relative reputation is summarized in the second term of Eq. (8.37). This represents the reputation *decay* for agent i with a strength equal to the total boost in reputation that agent z receives. One can show (Schweitzer et al. 2020) that an equilibrium solution for $x_i(t)$, Eqs. (8.33) and (8.35), is also an equilibrium solution for $y_i(t)$ (with either normalization) up to a scaling factor. Specifically, for an eigenvector $\mathbf{y}^\lambda$ of the adjacency matrix **A**, the corresponding eigenvalue λ is given by: $\sum_j l_{jz}\, y_i = \lambda$.

Whether *non-trivial solutions* for the stationary reputation values, $x_i(t) \to x_i^{\text{stat}}$, exist, strongly depends on the *adjacency matrix*, as illustrated in Fig. 8.10. Specifically, if an agent has no incoming links that boosts its reputation, $x_i(t)$ will go to zero. Therefore, even if this agent has an outgoing link to other agents j, it cannot boost their reputation. Nontrivial solutions depend on the existence of *cycles* which are formally defined as subgraphs in which there is a closed path from every node in the subgraph back to itself. The shortest possible cycle involves two agents, $1 \to 2 \to 1$. This maps to *direct reciprocity*: agent 1 boosts the reputation of agent 2, and vice versa. Cycles of length 3 map to *indirect reciprocity*, for example, $1 \to 2 \to 3 \to 1$. In this case, there is *no* direct reciprocity between any two agents, but all of them benefit regarding their reputation because they are part of the cycle. In order to obtain a nontrivial reputation, an agent not necessarily has to be part of a cycle, but it has to be connected to a cycle.

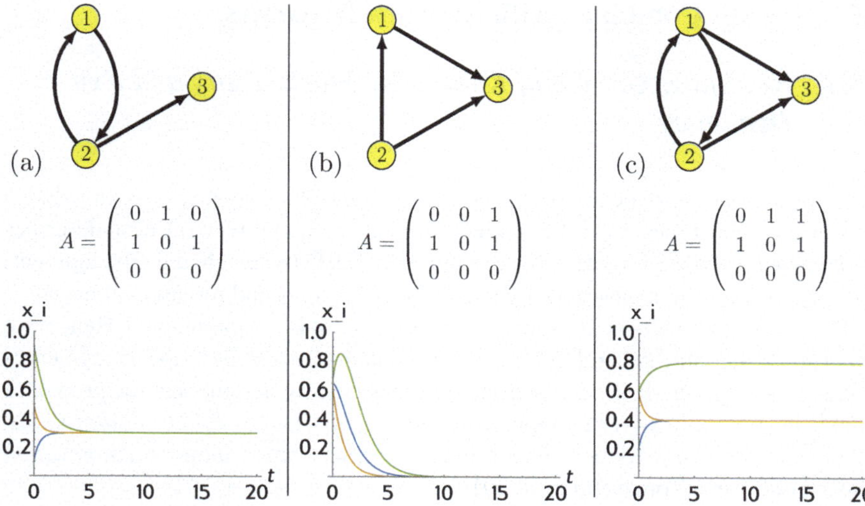

Fig. 8.10 Impact of the adjacency matrix on the reputation $x_i(t)$ of three agents. Only if cycles exist and agents are connected to these cycles, a non-trivial stationary reputation can be obtained. The chosen $\gamma = 1$ is indeed an eigenvalue of the adjacency matrix in (**a**) and (**c**). This is not the case for (**b**), hence we do not observe a stationary solution, just a convergence to zero (Casiraghi and Schweitzer 2020)

Applications

The type of feedback dynamics discussed above is widely used to characterize the importance of nodes in a network. Already `Google's` early version of the `PageRank` algorithm built on this. A related measure, *DebtRank* was introduced to quantify the importance of institutions in a financial network (Battiston et al. 2012). Further, the approach has found an important application to model online social networks (OSN) (Schweitzer et al. 2020). For example in `Twitter` or `Instagram`, the reputation of users is not just determined by the *number* of followers, but also by their *reputation*. It makes all the difference, whether individual i is a follower of the famous actor z, or the other way round.

Social networks are often characterized by a *core-periphery* structure, where the core contains a subset of well-connected users. This is important for the application of this model, as it relies on the existence of cycles. These cycles can be of any length, even structures of interlocking cycles can be present. Their existence, as reflected in the *adjacency matrix*, then impacts the corresponding eigenvalues and hence the (relative) reputation of users. It is computationally hard to detect such interlocking cycle structures in real social networks. In a case study of 40 million `Twitter` users, reputation was therefore measures by means of a *D-core decomposition* (Garcia et al. 2017).

8.5 Growth Combined with Network Dynamics

8.5.1 Nonlinear Growth of Knowledge Stock: Entry and Exit Dynamics

Not only reputation depends on the feedback from other agents, also knowledge growth crucially relies on it. Let us assume that the quantity $x_i(t)$ now describes the *knowledge stock* of agent i, for example, the R&D (research and development) experience of a firm, measurable by its number of patents and research alliances.

The value of knowledge continuously decreases if it is not maintained. Hence, we can propose the same general Eq. (8.33) for reputation to also describe the dynamics of the knowledge stock. To compensate for the decay, we assume that the growth of knowledge is mainly driven by input from *other agents*, i.e., by *R&D collaborations*, rather than by own activities. This reflects empirical observations for *innovation networks* of firms (Tomasello et al. 2016).

Different from reputation growth, for which no upper limit needs to be assumed, it is reasonable to consider a *saturation* for the growth of knowledge stock, similar to the quadratic term used for saturated growth, Eq. (8.6). At higher levels of knowledge stock, it becomes more difficult to "absorb" new knowledge, i.e., to incorporate it into a firm, simply because of the internal complexity associated with the way knowledge is stored and linked internally. Because of this absorptive capacity, we propose the following dynamics for the knowledge stock (Koenig et al. 2009):

$$\frac{dx_i(t)}{dt} = -\gamma\, x_i(t) + \nu \sum\nolimits_j l_{ji}\, x_j(t) + \nu^{\text{ext}} \sum\nolimits_j p_{ji}\, x_j(t) - \kappa \sum\nolimits_j l_{ij}\, x_i^2(t) \tag{8.38}$$

The knowledge growth is mainly determined by the knowledge stock of agents j that have a *direct link* to agent i, as expressed by the l_{ji}. But we can additionally consider that some links, denoted by p_{ji}, provide direct input to i from particular valuable agents. For example, instead of obtaining *indirect* knowledge input from an agent k via other agents j, agent i would much more benefit if k had a *direct* link to i. So, if $p_{ji} = 1$, in addition to the usual benefit ν there will be an extra benefit ν^{ext} from interacting with this valuable agent. As we have already noticed the importance of *indirect reciprocity* in the growth of x_i, such extra benefit could also arise from links that contribute to closing *cycles* in the interaction network. This would allow feedback cycles for instance in the development of a technology.

With or without the additional saturation and growth terms, under certain conditions for the parameters Eq. (8.38) will lead to a *stationary* solution for the knowledge stock of all agents, as discussed in Sect. 8.4.5. An evaluation of the stationary solutions of Eq. (8.38) that corresponds to Fig. 8.10 can be found in Koenig et al. (2009). To make the dynamics of the system more realistic, we can further consider an *entry and exit* dynamics. Not successful agents may leave the system, whereas new agents enter. This is associated with *rewiring the network* that represents the collaboration interactions, i.e., some links are removed and others are newly formed.

As an implication, the dynamics is then described by *two different time scales*: there is a dynamics *on* the network at time scale t, and a dynamics *of* the network at time scale T, and we assume that they can be *separated*. On the shorter time scale, t, agents interact and in conclusion obtain a stationary value of their knowledge stock, x_i^{stat}. On the longer time scale, T, the *entry and exit dynamics* takes place, specifically *after* the stationary solution for $x_i(t)$ was reached. That means, the interaction structure given by the network evolves on time scale T, whereas the knowledge stock of agents evolves on time scale t.

At each time step T a different (quasi-)stationary value $x_i^{\text{stat}}(T)$ is obtained. This can be used to distinguish between successful and not successful agents, i.e., to measure *performance*. We can *rank* agents against their obtained stationary knowledge stock, $x_i^{\text{stat}}(T)$ taken at time T, *before* the network is changed. As already explained in Fig. 8.10, agents without incoming links will likely have a knowledge stock of zero, as well as agents that are not part of a cycle of direct or indirect reciprocity. Only agents that are part of collaboration cycles will reach a high value of $x_i^{\text{stat}}(T)$. That means, agents well integrated into collaborations are clearly distinguishable from less integrated ones.

Applications

There are different ways to apply the above combination of nonlinear growth and entry and exit dynamics. Using economic arguments, different nonlinear expressions can be motivated (Koenig et al. 2009), in particular with respect to externalities, ν^{ext}, and saturation effects. The impact of these assumptions on the resulting knowledge stock distribution can then be evaluated.

More important is the study of *different entry and exit dynamics*. Its simplest form is a so-called *extremal dynamics*: from the least performing agents with the lowest knowledge stock one is randomly chosen and removed from the system together with all its collaboration links. This agent is then replaced by a new agent, which is randomly connected to the remaining agents. Because of the large degree of randomness involved, this type of entry and exit dynamics would describe a network disruption based on perturbations rather than an economic process. Nevertheless, the dynamic outcome is quite insightful. Figure 8.11a illustrates that the overall performance of the system, measured by means of an average knowledge stock, follows different stages: Initially, it is very low because collaboration structures, i.e., cycles of direct and indirect reciprocity have not yet established. After that, $\langle x \rangle$ constantly increases because these structures gradually improve by better integrating agents. But if *all* agents reach high performance, the extremal dynamics will eventually destroy such structures because it removes agents from existing cycles. This eventually leads to *crashes* in the system performance which are followed by new stages of *recovery*. This way, the system never reaches an equilibrium.

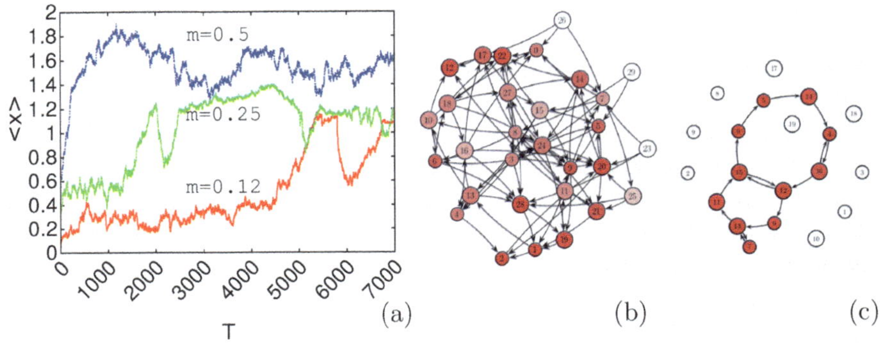

Fig. 8.11 (**a**) Evolution of the average knowledge stock at time scale T, involving network disruptions (Seufert and Schweitzer 2007). (**b, c**) Different nonlinearities in Eq. (8.38) combined with different mechanisms for link deletion and creation result in different network structures: (**b**) Extremal dynamics, no externalities. (**c**) Random unilateral link creation, optimal unilateral link deletion, externalities ν^{ext} give higher weights to links contributing to cycles, this way fostering indirect reciprocity (Koenig et al. 2009)

An extension of the extremal dynamics explicitly considers that entry and exit involve more than one agent. Instead of choosing randomly one of the agents with lowest performance, one can consider to remove a *fraction* of least performing agents (Schweitzer et al. 2020) and compensate this with the entry of many more new agents. This implies to define a threshold for the performance, which interestingly has a nontrivial impact on the overall stability of the system. Small threshold values are able to *improve* the stability by reducing the number of crashes over time (Schweitzer et al. 2020).

8.5.2 Linear Growth of Knowledge Stock: Rational Decisions

The simplified entry and exit dynamics described above does not involve any decisions of agents, because they are replaced by stochastic perturbations of the system. In socioeconomic systems, however, agents make decisions about creating or deleting links to other agents, based on their *utility*. This considers the *benefits* and *costs* of interactions. To calculate these, agents need information, e.g., about the knowledge stock of their collaborators, which is not always fully available. Therefore, decisions are based on *bounded rationality*, i.e., in the absence of information also random decisions about link creation or deletion govern the dynamics. In our case, the benefits of interactions are clearly given by the *growth* of the own knowledge stock, whereas the costs result from maintaining collaborations with other agents. The latter should be proportional to the number of links an agent has. But here we have to consider that agents maintain *outgoing* links, i.e., links that contribute to the knowledge growth of *other* agents, whereas benefits depend on *incoming* links from other agents (which are not necessarily the same).

This precisely describes the *dilemma*: why should agents maintain links if they do not see a direct benefit from this? *Reciprocity* would be the appropriate argument for this, but only *direct* reciprocity can be easily observed by an agent. To detect *indirect* reciprocity would require knowledge about the interaction structure in the broader neighborhood, in case of larger cycles even knowledge about the full system. This becomes increasingly unrealistic. Yet, system wide collaboration structures are empirically observed, and indirect reciprocity is an established mechanism is many social systems.

Agent-based models allow to study the conditions under which such collaboration structures *emerge* despite individual utility considerations would stand against them. We define the utility of agent i as

$$u_i(t) = B_i[\mathbf{A}, \mathbf{x}(t)] - C_i[\mathbf{A}, \mathbf{x}(t)] \tag{8.39}$$

$\mathbf{x}(t)$ is the vector of knowledge stock values $x_i(t)$ of all agents and $\mathbf{A}$ is the adjacency matrix that describes the current interaction structure. Both benefits B_i and costs C_i depend on these, as follows. Benefits are assumed to be proportional to the *growth* of knowledge stock, i.e., $B_i(t) \propto \dot{x}_i(t)/x_i(t)$ (Koenig et al. 2008, 2011, 2012). The dynamics of the knowledge stock is described by Eq. (8.38), but here we drop the last two terms, i.e., we neglect saturation ($\kappa = 0$) and externalities ($\nu^{\text{ext}} = 0$), making this a linear dynamics in x. One can then prove (Koenig et al. 2008) that $\lim_{t\to\infty} \dot{x}_i(t)/x_i(t) = \lambda^{\text{PF}}(G_i)$, where $\lambda^{\text{PF}}(G_i)$ is a property of the *adjacency matrix* $\mathbf{A}$, precisely the largest real eigenvalue, also known as Perron-Frobenius (PF) eigenvalue, of the connected component G_i agent i is part of.

For the costs C_i, we consider that all outgoing links have to be maintained at a cost c, i.e., $C_i = c\sum_j l_{ij} = c\,k_i^{\text{out}}$, where k_i^{out} is the *out-degree* of agent i. This leads to the following expression for the agent utility:

$$u_i(t) = \frac{\dot{x}_i(t)}{x_i(t)} - c\,k_i^{\text{out}} \quad \Rightarrow \quad u_i(T) = \lim_{t\to\infty} u_i(t) = \lambda^{\text{PF}}(G_i) - c\,k_i^{\text{out}} \tag{8.40}$$

We still have to define how agents make use of the information derived from their utility, to decide about link formation and link deletion. We posit that these decisions are driven by *utility maximization*. If a pair (i, j) of agents is selected at random, then a link $(i, j) \notin E(G)$, that is not part of the set of links, E, of the network G is *created* if the link (i, j) increases either $u_i(T)$ or $u_j(T)$ (or both) and none decreases. This selection scheme is known as *incremental improvement*. As an alternative, one could also consider a random *unilateral* link creation, i.e., a link to a randomly chosen agent j is already created if only $u_i(T)$ increases.

Further, if a pair (i, j) of agents is selected at random, then an existing link $(i, j) \in E(G)$ is *deleted* if at least one of the two agents increases its utility from removing this link. This is known as *optimal unilateral* link deletion. An alternative could be the *optimal bilateral* link deletion, which considers both agents similar to the incremental improvement scheme.

Applications

There are different ways to extent this model. First, one could consider alternatives for *calculating the utilities*, e.g., by modifying the information taken into account for the calculation, or by including nonlinear terms to reflect saturation effects, etc. Second, one may consider alternatives for *calculating the decisions* made on these utilities. Incremental improvement just picks the *first* randomly selected pair of agents with a positive utility increase to create a link. A different scheme would be *best response*. It creates the link only between the pair of agents that will give the *highest* increase of utility. This would require (i) to have access to all agents and to have full information about their knowledge stocks and (ii) to postpone decisions until all possible pairs have been considered. It can be shown that such a scenario, even with more information, not necessarily leads to a better outcome regarding the collaboration structure. Because of path-dependent decision processes, the agent population can get trapped in *suboptimal* system states (Koenig et al. 2008).

A realistic modification is to consider that link deletion involves a *severance cost* (Koenig et al. 2011). I.e., agents that have invested in establishing a collaboration will lose part of this investment when they decide to cancel the collaboration. If these additional costs become high, agents will be more reluctant to change their collaboration structure. Again, the system can then be trapped in suboptimal states.

8.6 Conclusions

As we have demonstrated, the law of proportionate growth is a very versatile dynamics, in particular when combined with additional dynamic assumptions. The core dynamics simply states that the growth of a quantity x_i, i.e., dx_i/dt, is proportional to x_i. The formal solution of this basic dynamics is exponential growth or exponential decay, dependent on the proportionality constant. It has been observed that such a dynamic with suitable modifications can explain a larger range of empirical phenomena observed in socioeconomic systems. Notably, the "law of proportionate growth" was first related to the observed *size distribution of firms* by R. Gibrat in 1931 (Sutton 1997).

Distributions refer to *systemic* (or "macroscopic") properties, while the underlying dynamics is proposed for the ("microscopic") system elements, or agents. Hence, such agent-based models are capable of establishing the *micro-macro link*, if they can explain the emergence of systemic properties from the interaction of the system elements. Already the application by Gibrat illustrates that it needs additional assumptions to make this happen. It is *not* simply the exponential growth that reproduces the firm size distribution. It further needs specific assumptions about the proportionality factor – its underlying normal distribution, nonstationarity, and randomness – that only allows to obtain the correct systemic property. Hence, what constitutes the essence of the particular phenomenon can be understood from the *deviations* from the simple exponential dynamics. And these "deviations" are in fact the ingredients that make a particular dynamic model an economic or a social one. They often allow for an interpretation in a socioeconomic context, as Gibrat's example witnesses.

The various applications discussed in this chapter illustrate that in agent-based models, the law of proportionate growth often acts at two different levels: First, there is the growth (or the decay) dx_i/dt proportional to the *own* quantity $x_i(t)$, with the growth of firm sizes or individual wealth as typical examples. Second, there is *additionally* the growth dx_i/dt proportional to the quantities $x_j(t)$ of *other* agents, with the dynamics of opinions, reputation, or knowledge stock as examples. The latter requires *interactions* between agents, for which different forms have been discussed. There are *direct* interactions between any two agents, as in the example of battling. There are interactions *restricted* by the existence of links, as in the case of networks, or thresholds, as in the bounded confidence model. Eventually, there are also *indirect* interactions resulting from the coupling to aggregated variables, for example, in the wealth redistribution model or in the wisdom of crowds.

The versatility of the agent-based models discussed also results from the combination of different deterministic and stochastic growth assumptions. There are *random* proportionality factors sampled from different distributions that determine whether individual agents experience growth or decay in the long run. Examples are the growth of firm sizes or of individual wealth. There are *deterministic* proportionality factors, which can be either positive or negative, constant or time dependent. Examples are saturated growth, the decay of reputation or knowledge stock. Even more, these assumptions about growth factors can be combined in an *additive* or a *multiplicative* manner. This was illustrated in the simple investment model and in the wealth redistribution model, which both combine multiplicative and additive growth.

Despite the richness of the models that result from combining such assumptions, we still have to remark their simplicity and accessibility. As demonstrated, in many cases, we are able to formally analyze such models, to derive insights about systemic properties and critical parameter constellations. This is in fact one of the main reasons to base our agent-based models on the law of proportionate growth as the core dynamics. Constructing models this way allows us to *derive expectations* about the *collective* dynamics, and often to generate hypotheses, while agent-based simulations *illustrate* the dynamics from an individual perspective.

Acknowledgments The author thanks Nicola Perony for providing Figs. 8.2, 8.3, 8.7, and 8.9.

References

Aoki M (1973) On decentralized linear stochastic control problems with quadratic cost. IEEE Trans Autom Control 18(3):243–250

Aoki M (2002) Modeling aggregate behavior and fluctuations in economics: stochastic views of interacting agents. Cambridge University Press, Cambridge

Aoki M, Yoshikawa H (2011) Reconstructing macroeconomics: a perspective from statistical physics and combinatorial stochastic processes. Cambridge University Press, Cambridge

Aoyama H, Fujiwara Y, Ikeda Y, Iyetomi H, Souma W, Yoshikawa H (2017) Macro-econophysics: new studies on economic networks and synchronization. Cambridge University Press, Cambridge

Battiston S, Puliga M, Kaushik R, Tasca P, Caldarelli G (2012) DebtRank: too central to fail? Financial networks, the FED and systemic risk. Sci Rep 2:541

Bechinger C, Di Leonardo R, Löwen H, Reichhardt C, Volpe G, Volpe G (2016) Active particles in complex and crowded environments. Rev Mod Phys 88(4):045006

Bonabeau E, Theraulaz G, Deneubourg JL (1999) Dominance orders in animal societies: the self-organization hypothesis revisited. Bull Math Biol 61(4):727–757

Bonacich P (1987) Power and centrality: a family of measures. Am J Sociol 92(5):1170–1182

Casiraghi G, Schweitzer F (2020) Improving the robustness of online social networks: a simulation approach of network interventions. Front Robot AI 7:57

Deffuant G, Neau D, Amblard F, Weisbuch G (2000) Mixing beliefs among interacting agents. ACS Adv Complex Syst 3:87–98

Ebeling W, Schweitzer F (2003) Self-organization, active brownian dynamics, and biological applications. Nova Acta Leopold 88:169–188

Ebeling W, Schweitzer F, Tilch B (1999) Active Brownian particles with energy depots modeling animal mobility. Biosystems 49(1):17–29

Feistel R, Ebeling W (2011) Physics of self-organization and evolution. Wiley, New York

Garcia V, Birbaumer M, Schweitzer F (2011) Testing an agent-based model of bacterial cell motility: how nutrient concentration affects speed distribution. Eur Phys J B 82(3–4):235–244

Garcia D, Garas A, Schweitzer F (2014) Modeling collective emotions in online social systems. In: von Scheve C, Salmela M (eds) Collective emotions. Oxford University Press, Oxford, pp 389–406

Garcia D, Kappas A, Kuster D, Schweitzer F (2016) The dynamics of emotions in online interaction. R Soc Open Sci 3:160059

Garcia D, Mavrodiev P, Casati D, Schweitzer F (2017) Understanding popularity, reputation, and social influence in the Twitter society. Policy Internet 9(3):343–364

Garas A, Garcia D, Skowron M, Schweitzer F (2012) Emotional persistence in online chatting communities. Sci Rep 2:402

Grochulski B, Piskorski T (2010) Risky human capital and deferred capital income taxation. J Econ Theory 145(3):908–943

Groeber P, Schweitzer F, Press K (2009) How groups can foster consensus: the case of local cultures. J Aritif Soc Soc Simul 12(2):1–22

Hegselmann R, Krause U et al (2002) Opinion dynamics and bounded confidence models, analysis, and simulation. J Artif Soc Soc Simul 5(3):2

Helbing D, Schweitzer F, Keltsch J, Molnár P (1997) Active Walker model for the formation of human and animal trail systems. Phys Rev E 56(3):2527–2539

Koenig MD, Battiston S, Napoletano M, Schweitzer F (2008) On algebraic graph theory and the dynamics of innovation networks. Netw Heterog Media 3(2):201–219

Koenig MD, Battiston S, Schweitzer F (2009) Modeling evolving innovation networks. In: Pyka A, Scharnhorst A (eds) Innovation networks: new approaches in modelling and analyzing. Springer, Berlin, pp 187–267

Koenig MD, Battiston S, Napoletano M, Schweitzer F (2011) Recombinant knowledge and the evolution of innovation networks. J Econ Behav Organ 79(3):145–164

Koenig MD, Battiston S, Napoletano M, Schweitzer F (2012) The efficiency and stability of R&D networks. Games Econ Behav 75(2):694–713

Lorenz J (2007) Continuous opinion dynamics under bounded confidence: a survey. Int J Mod Phys C 18(12):1819–1838

Lorenz J, Rauhut H, Schweitzer F, Helbing D (2011) How social influence can undermine the wisdom of crowd effect. Proc Natl Acad Sci (PNAS) 108(22):9020–9025

Lorenz J, Paetzel F, Schweitzer F (2013) Redistribution spurs growth by using a portfolio effect on risky human capital. PLoS One 8(2):e54904

Malevergne Y, Pisarenko V, Sornette D (2011) Testing the Pareto against the lognormal distributions with the uniformly most powerful unbiased test applied to the distribution of cities. Phys Rev E 83(3):036111

Marsili M, Maslov S, Zhang Y-C (1998) Dynamical optimization theory of a diversified portfolio. Phys A 253(1–4):403–418

Mavrodiev P, Tessone CJ, Schweitzer F (2012) Effects of social influence on the wisdom of crowds. In: Proceedings of the conference on collective intelligence CI-2012. https://arxiv.org/html/1204.2991

Mavrodiev P, Tessone CJ, Schweitzer F (2013) Quantifying the effects of social influence. Sci Rep 3:1360

Nanumyan V, Garas A, Schweitzer F (2015) The network of counterparty risk: analysing correlations in OTC derivatives. PLoS One 10:e0136638

Navarro E, Cantero R, Rodrigues JAF, Schweitzer F (2008a) Investments in random environments. Phys A 387(8–9):2035–2046

Navarro JE, Walter FE, Schweitzer F (2008b) Risk-seeking versus risk-avoiding investments in noisy periodic environments. Int J Mod Phys C 19(6):971–994

Perony N, Pfitzner R, Scholtes I, Schweitzer F, Tessone CJ (2012) Hierarchical consensus formation reduces the influence of opinion bias. In: Proceedings of the 26th European conference on modelling and simulation – ECMS 2012, pp 662–668

Perony N, Pfitzner R, Scholtes I, Tessone CJ, Schweitzer F (2013) Enhancing consensus under opinion bias by means of hierarchical decision making. ACS Adv Complex Syst 16:1350020

Rauhut H, Lorenz J, Schweitzer F, Helbing D (2011) Reply to Farrell: improved individual estimation success can imply collective tunnel vision. Proc Natl Acad Sci 108(36):E626

Richmond P (2001) Power law distributions and dynamic behaviour of stock markets. Eur Phys J B 20(4):523–526

Sarigol E, Pfitzner R, Scholtes I, Garas A, Schweitzer F (2014) Predicting scientific success based on coauthorship networks. EPJ Data Sci 3:9

Schweitzer F (1998) Modelling migration and economic agglomeration with active Brownian particles. ACS Adv Complex Syst 1(1):11–37

Schweitzer F (2003) Brownian agents and active particles: collective dynamics in the natural and social sciences. Springer, Berlin

Schweitzer F (2018a) An agent-based framework of active matter with applications in biological and social systems. Eur J Phys 40(1):014003

Schweitzer F (2018b) Sociophysics. Phys Today 71(2):40–46

Schweitzer F, Behera L (2009) Nonlinear voter models: the transition from invasion to coexistence. Eur Phys J B 67(3):301–318

Schweitzer F, Garcia D (2010) An agent-based model of collective emotions in online communities. Eur Phys J B 77(4):533–545

Schweitzer F, Mach R (2008) The epidemics of donations: logistic growth and power-laws. PloS One 3(1):e1458

Schweitzer F, Schimansky-Geier L (1994) Clustering of active Walkers in a two-component system. Phys A 206(3–4):359–379

Schweitzer F, Tilch B (2002) Self-assembling of networks in an agent-based model. Phys Rev E 66(2):1–10

Schweitzer F, Lao K, Family F (1997) Active random walkers simulate trunk trail formation by ants. Biosystems 41(3):153–166

Schweitzer F, Mavrodiev P, Tessone CJ (2013) How can social herding enhance cooperation? ACS Adv Complex Syst 16:1350017

Schweitzer F, Nanumyan V, Tessone CJ, Xia X (2014) How do OSS projects change in number and size? A large-scale analysis to test a model of project growth. ACS Adv Complex Syst 17:1550008

Schweitzer F, Mavrodiev P, Seufert AM, Garcia D (2020, submitted) Modeling user reputation in online social networks: the role of costs, benefits, and reciprocity. Comput Math Organ Theory

Schweitzer F, Casiraghi G, Perony N (2020, submitted) Modeling the emergence of hierarchies from dominance interactions. Bull Math Biol

Seufert AM, Schweitzer F (2007) Aggregate dynamics in an evolutionary network model. Int J Mod Phys C 18(10):1659–1674

Slanina F (1999) On the possibility of optimal investment. Phys A Stat Mech Appl 269(2–4):554–56

Slanina F (2004) Inelastically scattering particles and wealth distribution in an open economy. Phys Rev E 69(4):046102

Sutton J (1997) Gibrat's legacy. J Econ Lit 35(1):40–59

Tadic B, Suvakov M, Garcia D, Schweitzer F (2017) Agent-based simulations of emotional dialogs in the online social network MySpace. In: Holyst JA (ed) Cyberemotions: collective emotions in cyberspace. Springer, Cham, pp 207–229

Tomasello MV, Napoletano M, Garas A, Schweitzer F (2016) The rise and fall of R&D networks. ICC Ind Corp Chang 26(4):617–646

Yaari G, Solomon S (2010) Cooperation evolution in random multiplicative environments. Eur Phys J B 73(4):625–632

Yakovenko VM, Rosser JB Jr (2009) Colloquium: statistical mechanics of money, wealth, and income. Rev Mod Phys 81(4):1703

Zhang Y, Schweitzer F (2019) The interdependence of corporate reputation and ownership: a network approach to quantify reputation. R Soc Open Sci 6:190570

Chapter 9
Collective Phenomena in Economic Systems

Hiroshi Iyetomi

Abstract We have recently carried out empirical studies on collective phenomena as encountered in economics systems, including stock market behavior, business cycles, and inflation/deflation. A new methodology, the complex Hilbert principal component analysis combined with the random matrix theory or the rotational random shuffling, which we have developed, was so successful in demonstrating the existence of collective behaviors of entities in the economic systems. We take this opportunity to review some of those works with new additional results for missing the loss of Professor Masanao Aoki. In fact, we have been led by his insightful question of "what about interactions among agents?" against the central dogma of the current mainstream economics.

Keywords Collective phenomena · Stock market · Business cycles · Price changes · Complex Hilbert principal component analysis

9.1 Introduction

To explain the motivation of this article, let us begin with quoting a passage from the preface by the late Professor Masanao Aoki for his book (Aoki and Yoshikawa 2011) written with Professor Hiroshi Yoshikawa:

> For your information here is a bit of my intellectual meander to writing this book. I remember vividly my shock when I first encountered representative agent models at an NSF workshop. I was very puzzled by this representative agent assumption that many papers were using. I kept asking myself "what about interactions among agents?"

This is a very natural question which comes to mind of physicists. Because interactions among basic entities such as atoms and molecules, including Newton's

H. Iyetomi (✉)
Department of Mathematics, Niigata University, Niigata, Japan

The Canon Institute for Global Studies, Tokyo, Japan
e-mail: hiyetomi@sc.niigata-u.ac.jp

H. Aoyama et al. (eds.), *Complexity, Heterogeneity, and the Methods of Statistical Physics in Economics*, Evolutionary Economics and Social Complexity Science 22,
https://doi.org/10.1007/978-981-15-4806-2_9

law of universal gravity, play a crucial role in forming this world. In fact, Professor Aoki studied physics when he was an undergraduate and master's degree student in Tokyo. It is no exaggeration to say that the terminology "econophysics," coined to refer to fruitful collaboration of economics and physics, is for him. I also studied physics at the same university from which he graduated. I have thus advanced my research on econophysics along the line laid down by him. Unfortunately, I could not have enough opportunities to learn a number of his creative ideas from him in a direct way.

Here we pay attention to macroeconomic phenomena such as stock market behavior, business cycles, and inflation/deflation. If the physicist's view is adopted, those are regarded as collective phenomena arising from interactions among economic agents on the analogy of the fact that the sea wave is an outcome of interactions between water molecules. It should be noted that macroeconomic phenomena could not be trivial at all even if microeconomic interactions were exactly known; macroeconomics and microeconomics are both important. Figure 9.1 provides readers with an illustrative example for this remark. It is absolutely true that the sea wave is made from water molecules. At the microscopic level, we observe that water molecules move just at random colliding each other. Macroscopically, however, we recognize collective motion of water molecules as wave. For a surfer, it is sufficient to know just how the sea wave behave, not necessary to know microscopic dynamics of water molecules.

We have recently carried out empirical studies on collective phenomena as encountered in economics systems, including stock market behavior (Arai et al. 2015), business cycles (Iyetomi et al. 2020), and inflation/deflation (Kichikawa et al. 2020). In the course of those studies, we have developed a methodology

Fig. 9.1 Macroscopic and microscopic views on the sea. This illustration is based on one of the ukiyoe series, Fugaku Sanjūrokkei (Thirty-six Views of Mount Fuji), by Hokusai (https://en.wikipedia.org/wiki/The_Great_Wave_off_Kanagawa)

for multivariate analysis, that is, complex Hilbert principal component analysis combined with the random matrix theory or rotational random shuffling. The new tool was so successful as to verify existence of collective behaviors of entities in the economic systems. The objective of this chapter is to miss the loss of Professor Masanao Aoki by reviewing some of our recent works with new additional results. The rest of the chapter is organized as follows. The second section recalls the Yule-Slutsky effect (Slutzky 1937; Yule 1927). A moving average of time series may generate oscillatory behavior even if none exists in the original data. We have to be careful to avoid such a ghost pattern when coarse-graining microscopic information to predict macroscopic properties. The third section is devoted to brief introduction of the new methodology which we have developed to extract collective motion embedded in noisy multivariate time series. In the fourth through sixth sections, we demonstrate how powerful is the methodology by applying it to collective behavior of stock prices in a financial market, business cycles, and comovement of POS (point of sale) prices, respectively. The final section is devoted to concluding remarks for this article.

9.2 Real or Fake

Figure 9.2 shows time variation of the leading, coincident, and lagging indexes of business conditions in Japan over the last 35 years, monthly published by the government (Cabinet Office, Government of Japan 2016). Those are designed to be a useful tool for detecting peaks and troughs in the cyclic behavior of the economic activity of the nation. As observed in Fig. 9.2, the business cycle indicators have well-established lead-lag relations mutually in real time. That is, the leading index

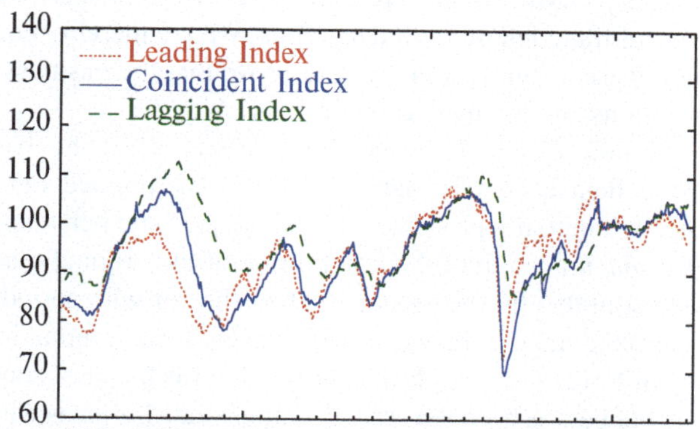

Fig. 9.2 Time variation of the leading (dotted line), coincident (solid line), and lagging (dashed line) indexes of business conditions in Japan

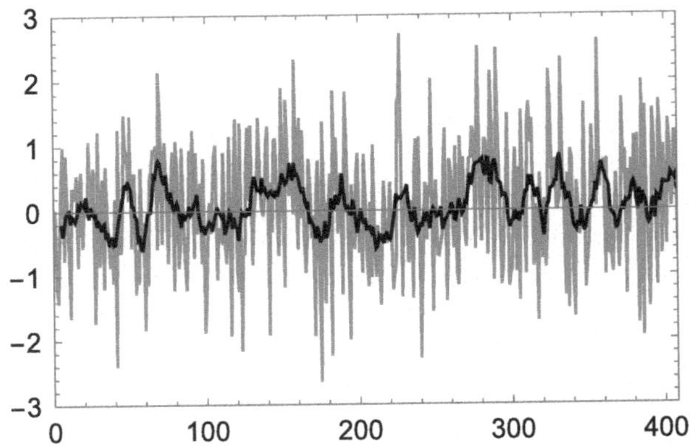

Fig. 9.3 Demonstration of the Yule-Slutsky effect (Slutzky 1937; Yule 1927). A random time series of the same length as the time series in Fig. 9.2, depicted by thin gray line, was generated from the standardized normal distribution. The thick solid line shows its 10-term moving average

leads the coincident index by a few months on average, and the coincident index, in turn, leads the lagging index by about 6 months (Cabinet Office, Government of Japan 2016). It looks like we have confirmed the emergence of business cycle as collective motion of many variables in macroeconomy. It is not so simple though.

At this point we should recall the caution by Slutzky (1937) and Yule (1927). In fact, a moving average may generate an irregular oscillatory pattern even if none exists in the original data. The Slutzky-Yule effect is visible in Fig. 9.3. It is a manifestation of the arcsine law (Feller 1968) for simple random walk; once a gambler stands on a winner side, he/she tends to stay on the side for a long time. This finding led main-stream economists to explain business cycles as the cumulative effects of various random shocks hitting the economic system, resulting in the real business cycle theory (Kydland and Prescott 1982). We thus learn that study of a single time series of finite length is so dangerous. We are thereby required to carry out a careful multivariate analysis in order to prove that the business cycles really arise from interactions among many economic variables.

In passing, we note that there is another spurious effect involved in random time series. More than a century ago, Terada (1916) pointed out that random number sequence without any processes may show periodic behavior, as shown in Fig. 9.4. It is just magnification of the first portion of the original random series in Fig. 9.3. We can certainly observe pseudo-cyclic behavior with periodicity of about 3. In fact, the expected interval between two adjacent local minima is theoretically calculated (Husimi 1942) as 3. Terada may be regarded as father of complex systems science in Japan, but he was born too early to demonstrate his ideas with a computer. He left the following concluding remark at the end of the paper (Terada 1916):

> The present note is chiefly intended to draw attention of seismologists and meteorologists to the existence of the apparent quasi-periodicity of accidental phenomena, which sometimes might be mistaken for a periodicity with a real physical significance.

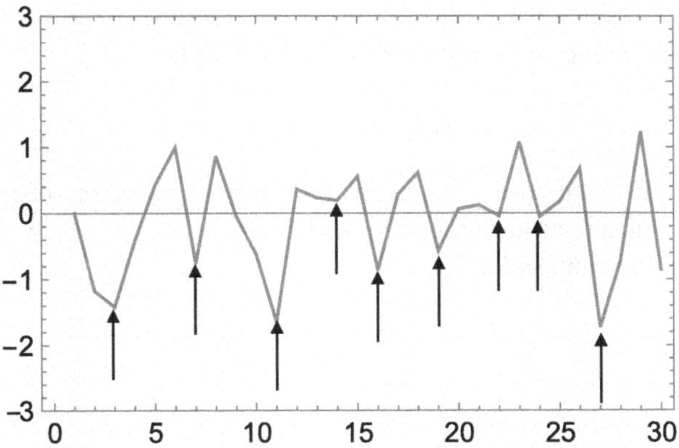

Fig. 9.4 Apparent periodicity of random time series (Terada 1916). The first portion of the original random sequence in Fig. 9.3 is magnified with arrows designating its local minima

9.3 Complex Hilbert Principal Component Analysis

The complex Hilbert principal component analysis (CHPCA) is a powerful tool for detecting genuine collective motion with lead-lag relations embedded in a dataset of multivariate time series. And the random matrix theory (RMT) or the rotational random shuffling (RRS) collaborates with the CHPCA to remove harmful noises out of the data. As will be seen, in fact, economic data are so noisy that it is a critical problem how to get rid of the Yule-Slutsky effect. For details of the methodology, we refer readers to our recent book (Aoyama et al. 2017). Here we just present the notations necessary for discussion in the following sections.

The CHPCA begins with complexifying each real time series using the Hilbert transformation for its imaginary part. Let us suppose that we have N time series $w_\alpha(t)$ of length T ($\alpha = 1, 2, \cdots N$; $t = 0, 1, \cdots, T$), where $w_\alpha(t)$ may be logarithmic difference or simple difference of an original time series depending on whether it is composed of positive definite values or not. According to our definition for the Fourier decomposition, the resulting complex time series $\widetilde{w}_\alpha(t)$ rotates clockwise in its complex plane. The complex correlation coefficient is then defined as

$$C_{\alpha\beta} := \langle \widetilde{w}_\alpha(t) \widetilde{w}_\beta(t)^* \rangle_t \,, \tag{9.1}$$

where $\widetilde{w}_\alpha(t)$ are assumed to have been standardized already, and the asterisk and $\langle \dots \rangle_t$ stand for complex conjugate and time average operations, respectively. The absolute value of $C_{\alpha\beta}$ measures the strength of correlation between time series α and β. On the other hand, its phase $\theta_{\alpha\beta}$ gives information on the lead-lag relation between the two variables; if $\theta_{\alpha\beta}$ is positive, time series α leads β.

To explore collective behavior of multiple time series, we solve the eigenvalue problem for the complex correlation matrix $\boldsymbol{C} = (C_{\alpha\beta})$:

$$\boldsymbol{C}\,\boldsymbol{V}^{(\ell)} = \lambda_\ell \boldsymbol{V}^{(\ell)}, \tag{9.2}$$

where λ_ℓ and $\boldsymbol{V}^{(\ell)}$ are the ℓ-th eigenvalue and eigenvector, respectively. The eigenvalues are arranged in descending order, $\lambda_1 \geqslant \lambda_2 \geqslant \cdots \geqslant \lambda_N \geqslant 0$, and satisfy the following sum rule:

$$\sum_{\ell=1}^{N} \lambda_\ell = N\,. \tag{9.3}$$

The eigenvectors constitute an orthonormal complete basis set in N dimensional complex vector space:

$$\boldsymbol{V}^{(\ell)\dagger}\boldsymbol{V}^{(m)} = \delta_{\ell m}\,, \tag{9.4}$$

where $\boldsymbol{V}^{(\ell)\dagger}$ is the Hermitian conjugate of $\boldsymbol{V}^{(\ell)}$. Any time series vector $\widetilde{\boldsymbol{w}}(t) = (\widetilde{w}_\alpha(t))$ is therefore decomposable in terms of the eigenmodes as

$$\widetilde{\boldsymbol{w}}(t) = \sum_{\alpha=1}^{N} \widetilde{w}_\alpha(t)\boldsymbol{e}_\alpha = \sum_{\ell=1}^{N} a_\ell(t)\boldsymbol{V}^{(\ell)}\,, \tag{9.5}$$

with

$$a_\ell(t) = \boldsymbol{V}^{(\ell)\dagger}\,\widetilde{\boldsymbol{w}}(t)\,. \tag{9.6}$$

We refer to the expansion coefficient $a_\ell(t)$ in Eq. (9.5) as *mode signal* of the ℓ-th eigenmode. The mode signal represents temporal behavior of the eigenmode and its strength is measured by

$$I_\ell(t) = |a_\ell(t)|^2\,. \tag{9.7}$$

The total intensity $I(t)$ of fluctuations of the complex time series, given by $I(t) = \|\widetilde{\boldsymbol{w}}(t)\|^2 = \widetilde{\boldsymbol{w}}(t)^\dagger\widetilde{\boldsymbol{w}}(t)$, is decomposed into individual contributions of the eigenmodes:

$$I(t) = \sum_{\ell=1}^{N} I_\ell(t)\,. \tag{9.8}$$

This is due to the mutual orthogonality of $\boldsymbol{V}^{(\ell)}$'s. Taking time average of Eq. (9.8) recovers the sum rule, Eq. (9.3), for the eigenvalues with $\langle I(t)\rangle_t = N$ and $\langle I_\ell(t)\rangle_t = \lambda_\ell$. Finally, we note that the normalized mode signal $\hat{a}_\ell(t)$ as defined below is equivalent to the cosine similarity (generalized for complex vectors) between $\tilde{\boldsymbol{w}}(t)$ and $\boldsymbol{V}^{(\ell)}$:

$$\hat{a}_\ell(t) := \frac{a_\ell(t)}{\|\tilde{\boldsymbol{w}}(t)\|} = \frac{\boldsymbol{V}^{(\ell)\dagger}\,\tilde{\boldsymbol{w}}(t)}{\|\tilde{\boldsymbol{w}}(t)\|} \,. \tag{9.9}$$

The relative intensity $\hat{I}_\ell(t) := |\hat{a}_\ell(t)|^2$ of the ℓ-th mode thereby satisfies the following sum rule:

$$\sum_{\ell=1}^{N} \hat{I}_\ell(t) = 1 \,. \tag{9.10}$$

In order to find significant eigenmodes that represent statistically significant comovements (signals), one may invoke on the the random matrix theory (RMT) (Laloux et al. 1999; Plerou et al. 1999, 2002; Utsugi et al. 2004; Kim and Jeong 2005). Even in the ordinary principal component analysis (PCA), one faces the same problem of how to extract significant eigenmodes. According to the RMT, in the limit of $N, T \to \infty$ with $Q := T/(2N)$ fixed, the eigenvalue distribution $\rho(\lambda)$ of the complex correlation matrix for random time series is given (Arai et al. 2013, 2015; Aoyama et al. 2017) by

$$\rho(\lambda) = \frac{Q}{2\pi}\frac{\sqrt{(\lambda_+ - \lambda)(\lambda - \lambda_-)}}{\lambda} + (1-Q)\Theta(1-Q)\delta(\lambda) \,, \tag{9.11}$$

with

$$\lambda_\pm = \left(1 \pm \sqrt{1/Q}\right)^2 \,, \tag{9.12}$$

where $\delta(x)$ is the Dirac delta function and $\Theta(x)$ is its integral, that is, the Heaviside step function. The probability distribution function for components of the eigenvector associated with any of the eigenvalues obeys (Arai et al. 2015) a two-dimensional Gaussian form:

$$\rho(u, v) = \frac{N}{\pi}\exp\left(-N(u^2 + v^2)\right) , \tag{9.13}$$

where u and v denote the real part and imaginary part of eigenvector components, respectively. Since the eigenvalues for random data are bounded by $\lambda_- \leqslant \lambda \leqslant \lambda_+$, the eigenvalues larger than λ_+ for actual data represent statistically meaningful correlations in them.

Recently we have worked out an alternative significance test for the eigenmodes in the PCA and CHPCA called rotational random shuffling (RRS) (Iyetomi et al. 2011a,b; Arai et al. 2013). In the RRS simulation, each time-series is randomly and independently rotated in a form of ring with its head and end joined, and then the eigenvalues are numerically calculated for the randomized data. Any eigenvalues above the corresponding RRS eigenvalues observed by comparison of the two results rank by rank is identified to be associated with significant comovements. The RRS simulation is superior to the RMT method which suffers from nontrivial effects due to autocorrelation and finiteness of time series. In contrast to the RMT, the RRS simply destroys cross correlations between time series keeping autocorrelations intact, so that it is applicable to any time series.

Using the significant eigenmodes approved by the RMT or RRS, one can construct the significant part of the complex correlation matrix as

$$C_{\alpha\beta}^{(\mathrm{sig})} = \sum_{\ell=1}^{S} \lambda_\ell V_\alpha^{(\ell)} V_\beta^{(\ell)*} \quad (\alpha \neq \beta), \tag{9.14}$$

where S is the number of the significant eigenmodes and $C_{\alpha\alpha}^{(\mathrm{sig})} = 1$.

Before leaving this section, we address how effective is the CHPCA method in detecting collective motion of multivariate time series with lead-lag relations. For the purpose we prepare the following synthetic multivariate time series into which definite lead-lag relations are incorporated:

$$x_\alpha(t) = \sin\left(\frac{2\pi}{P}t - \phi_\alpha\right) + \epsilon z_\alpha(t), \tag{9.15}$$

where $\alpha = 1, 2, \cdots, N$ and $t = 0, 1, \cdots, T$. The first term in the right-hand side of Eq. (9.15) represents a sinusoidal signal of period P with a given phase ϕ_α, which is randomly chosen in the range $(-\pi/2, \pi/2)$. The second term plays a role of random noises disturbing the signal. The parameter ϵ determines the relative strength of noises as compared with the signal and $z_\alpha(t)$ is generated randomly according to the standard normal distribution. We then apply the CHPCA to the test time series by taking difference for each of them:

$$\Delta x_\alpha(t) = x_\alpha(t) - x_\alpha(t-1). \tag{9.16}$$

The signal-to-noise ratio S/N in $\Delta x_\alpha(t)$ is approximately given by

$$S/N = \frac{P_\mathrm{S}}{P_\mathrm{N}} = \frac{1}{4\epsilon^2}\left(\frac{2\pi}{P}\right)^2, \tag{9.17}$$

where P_S and P_N are the signal power and the noise power, respectively. This formula is derived by noting that the difference of $x_\alpha(t)$ can be replaced by its derivative in the condition of $P \gg 2\pi$:

$$\Delta x_\alpha(t) \simeq \frac{2\pi}{P}\cos\left(\frac{2\pi}{P}t - \phi_\alpha\right) + \epsilon z_\alpha(t) - \epsilon z_\alpha(t-1). \tag{9.18}$$

Taking ensemble average of Eq. (9.18) over noises, we obtain

$$\left\langle \Delta x_\alpha(t)^2 \right\rangle \simeq \left(\frac{2\pi}{P}\right)^2 \cos^2\left(\frac{2\pi}{P}t - \phi_\alpha\right) + 2\epsilon^2. \tag{9.19}$$

The time average of Eq. (9.19) finally leads to

$$\overline{\left\langle \Delta x_\alpha(t)^2 \right\rangle} \simeq \frac{1}{2}\left(\frac{2\pi}{P}\right)^2 + 2\epsilon^2, \tag{9.20}$$

where the first and second terms in the right-hand side of Eq. (9.20) give P_{S} and P_{N}, respectively.

The validation analysis of the CHPCA has been carried out using the data, Eq. (9.15), synthesized with $N = 87$, $T = 383$, and $m = 5$, and hence $P = 76.6$. This parameter set for the artificial data is relevant to the previous work (Kichikawa et al. 2020) on price dynamics in Japan. We summarize the results of the test in Fig. 9.5. The correlation coefficient ρ between the given phases and the extracted phases from the first eigenvector is adopted to measure to what extent the CHPCA is effective; as ρ is closer to 1, the CHPCA works better. Below the signal-to-noise

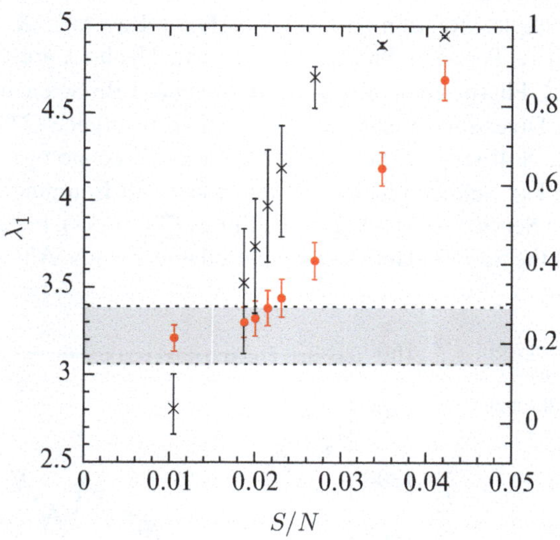

Fig. 9.5 Capability of the CHPCA method to reproduce the lead-lag relations incorporated into the artificial data, Eq. (9.15), as a function of the signal-to-noise ratio S/N, where $N = 87$, $T = 383$, and $m = 5$, and hence $P = 76.6$. The solid circles represent the mean of the largest eigenvalue λ_1 of the complex correlation matrix over 100 samples; their error bars the standard deviation. The crosses represent the corresponding median of the correlation coefficient ρ between the given phases and the extracted phases from the first eigenvector; their error bars the interquartile range. The gray region shows the 2σ range of the largest eigenvalue determined by the RRS simulation with 1000 samples

ratio $\simeq$ 0.025, the largest eigenvalue is not distinguishable any more from that of the corresponding randomized data. Almost at the same time, the CHPCA loses its capability of extracting the genuine information on the lead-lag relations. Thus, the above test strongly supports the postulate that the lead/lag relations among time series data detected from the eigenvectors of the CHPCA are reliable once their corresponding eigenvalues are judged to be statistically significant.

9.4 Collective Behavior in Financial Markets

In this section, we discuss collective behavior of stock price changes in financial markets as the first application of the CHPCA.

We have recently analyzed (Arai et al. 2015) a database from the S&P 500 index in the USA using the CHPCA method. We considered a one-day log return for a 4-year period from 2008 to 2011 ($T = 1009$ days), and extracted 483 ($= N$) stocks from the database that were priced for all business days in that period. These data contain 24 industry groups: Energy (39 stocks), Materials (29 stocks), Capital Goods (40 stocks), Commercial & Professional Services (11 stocks), Transportation (9 stocks), Automobiles & Components (4 stocks), Consumer Durables & Apparel (14 stocks), Consumer Services (14 stocks), Media (15 stocks), Retailing (32 stocks), Food & Staples Retailing (9 stocks), Food Beverage & Tobacco (21 stocks), Household & Personal Products (6 stocks), Health Care Equipment & Services (31 stocks), Pharmaceuticals, Biotechnology & Life Sciences (19 stocks), Banks (15 stocks), Diversified Financials (27 stocks), Insurance (21 stocks), Real Estate (16 stocks), Software & Services (28 stocks), Technology Hardware & Equipment (26 stocks), Semiconductors & Semiconductor Equipment (16 stocks), Telecommunication Services (8 stocks), and Utilities (33 stocks). Figure 9.6 depicts temporal change of the S&P 500 index in the period under study. Although the large

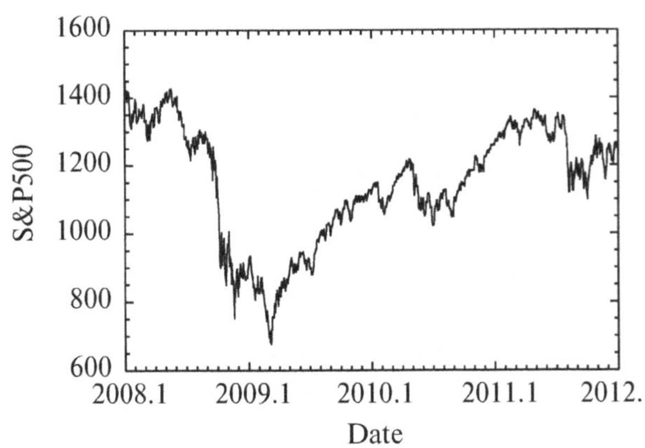

Fig. 9.6 Temporal change of the S&P 500 index in the period of Jan. 1, 2008 through Dec. 30, 2011

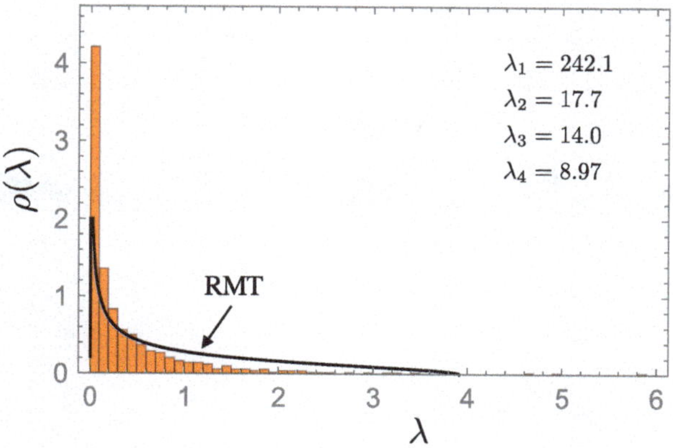

Fig. 9.7 Probability distribution of the eigenvalues of the complex correlation matrix for the daily stock price data of S&P 500 collected in the period of Jan. 1, 2008 through Dec. 30, 2011, compared with the corresponding result predicted by the RMT. One can infer that the seven largest eigenvalues, exceeding the upper limit of the RMT, are statistically meaningful

shock stemming from the Lehman crisis is involved in the stock price data, all of the log returns well pass the unit root test confirming their stationarity.

Figure 9.7 displays the probability distribution of the eigenvalues obtained for the S&P 500 dataset. One can identify the seven largest eigenvalues above $\lambda_+ (= 3.916)$ in Eq. (9.12). The RRS simulation does not change the number of the significant eigenmodes. Figure 9.8 depicts the eigenvectors in the complex plane up to the one associated with the ninth largest eigenvalue. The stock prices move very coherently almost like a point particle in the first eigenmode with the largest eigenvalue λ_1, which explains about half of the total intensity of the stock price fluctuations, $\lambda_1 \simeq N/2$. The first eigenmode apparently corresponds to the overall market behavior represented by the S&P 500 index. The higher significant eigenmodes arise from group correlations of the stock price changes. In the previous paper (Arai et al. 2015), we projected the extracted information on dynamic correlations of the stock prices onto a synchronization network in which pairs of stocks with phase difference smaller than certain threshold were linked with strength of their correlations as weight. We then detected communities of comoving stocks in the network and also elucidated lead-lag relationship between those communities. The obtained results indicate that frustrated triangle correlations among the stock groups exist dynamically behind the overall market behavior. This affirms the previous results (Yoshikawa et al. 2013; Aoyama et al. 2017) based on a static correlation network constructed with the conventional PCA.

Here we focus on the market mode as represented by $\boldsymbol{V}^{(1)}$, which was dismissed by us in the previous study (Arai et al. 2015). We should reiterate that the eigenvectors rotate clockwise as time passes owing to our definition of the Fourier transform. Taking a closer look at $\boldsymbol{V}^{(1)}$ in Fig. 9.8, we find that the stock prices comove but with certain lead-lag relations among themselves even in the market

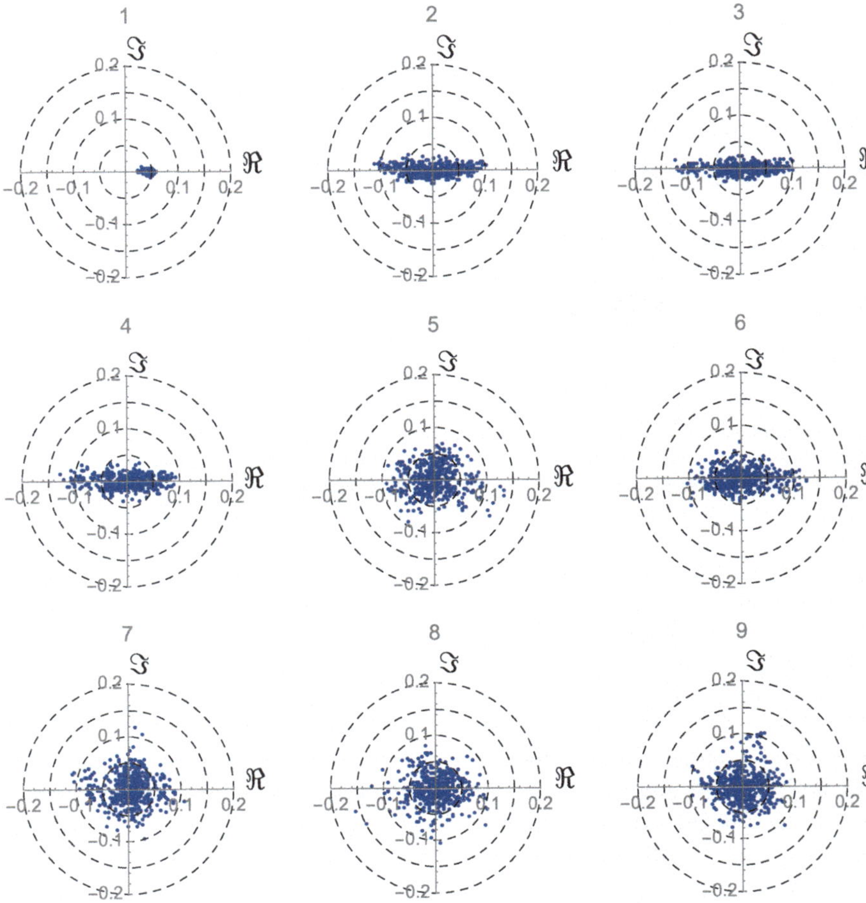

Fig. 9.8 Eigenvectors $\boldsymbol{V}^{(\ell)}$ of the complex correlation matrix for the S&P 500 stock price data up to $\ell = 9$, the components of which are represented in the complex plane

mode. Figure 9.9 is a box-and-whisker diagram showing distribution of the phases of the stocks in each of the ten major sectors. The leading sectors are Financials (Banks, Diversified Financials, Insurance, Real Estate) and Consumer Staples (Food & Staples Retailing, Food Beverage & Tobacco, Household & Personal Products). On the other hand, the lagging sectors include Telecommunication Services, Energy, and Health Care (Health Care Equipment & Services, Pharmaceuticals, Biotechnology & Life Sciences). Tables 9.1 and 9.2 give more specific information on the lead-lag relations among the stocks in the market mode, listing the top 10 leading and lagging stocks. We thus see the power of the CHPCA.

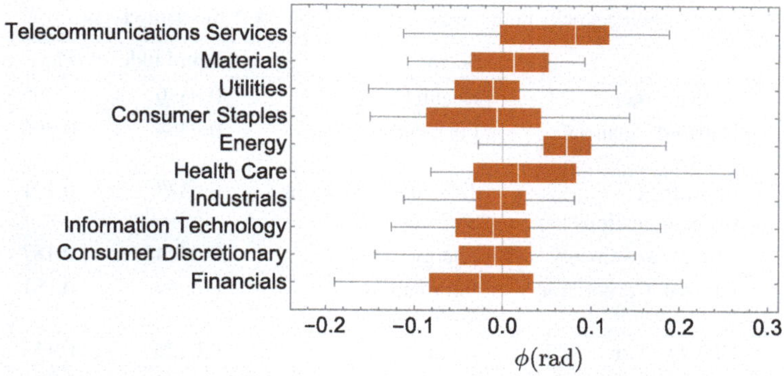

Fig. 9.9 Lead-lag relations among the ten major sectors in the market mode for the S&P 500 stocks during Jan. 1, 2008 through Dec. 30, 2011. Distribution of the phases measured in units of radian for the stocks within each sector is displayed in a box-and-whisker diagram

Table 9.1 Top 10 *leading* stocks in the market mode of the S&P 500 dataset

Ticker	Firm	Sector	Amplitude	Phase (rad)
EQR	Equity Residential	Financials	0.0485	−0.187
HCN	Health Care REIT	Financials	0.0483	−0.173
PSA	Public Storage	Financials	0.0513	−0.168
SCHW	Charles Schwab	Financials	0.0506	−0.155
PCL	Plum Creek Timber Co.	Financials	0.0512	−0.153
DUK	Duke Energy	Utilities	0.0426	−0.149
SO	Southern Co.	Utilities	0.0402	−0.148
PEP	PepsiCo Inc.	Consumer Staples	0.0416	−0.148
HRB	Block H&R	Consumer Discretionary	0.0398	−0.142
COST	Costco Co.	Consumer Staples	0.0448	−0.140

9.5 Business Cycles

Let us recall the discussion about business cycles as has been given in Sect. 9.2. The economy should be regarded as a system of closely interrelated components. This is a fundamental idea of complexity science which was established in early 1980s. Mutual interactions of microscopic entities give rise to completely new phenomena such as collective motion of the components at a macroscopic scale; for instance, life is an outcome of coherent behavior of molecules. Microeconomics and macroeconomics used to stand in parallel as two independent disciplines. These days, however, macroeconomics is absorbed into microeconomics. This is because macroeconomics is lacking concrete empirical evidences which illustrates its necessity.

Table 9.2 Top 10 *lagging* stocks in the market mode of the S&P 500 dataset

Ticker	Firm	Sector	Amplitude	Phase (rad)
HUM	Humana Inc.	Health Care	0.0330	0.265
HIG	Hartford Financial Svc.Gp.	Financials	0.0368	0.206
PCS	MetroPCS Communications Inc.	Telecommunications Services	0.0333	0.191
CHK	Chesapeake Energy	Energy	0.0444	0.187
SNDK	SanDisk Corporation	Information Technology	0.0359	0.181
CI	CIGNA Corp.	Health Care	0.0420	0.155
GS	Goldman Sachs Group	Financials	0.0473	0.153
DISCA	Discovery Communications	Consumer Discretionary	0.0411	0.153
AMD	Advanced Micro Devices	Information Technology	0.0396	0.152
MU	Micron Technology	Information Technology	0.0424	0.146

The leading, coincident, and lagging indexes of business conditions in Japan, the temporal behaviors of which are shown in Fig. 9.2, are constructed from aggregation of more fundamental macroeconomic variables as listed in Table 9.3 ($N = 30$). We quest for collective motion of the constituting macroeconomic variables in the period of January 2000 through December 2014 ($T = 179$); the collection of the constituents is regularly updated. Very recently, we have also carried out a similar study on relationship between macroeconomic indicators and economic cycles in the USA (Iyetomi et al. 2020).

Figure 9.10 displays the eigenvalue distribution obtained by the CHPCA for the dataset of the Japanese indexes of business conditions as well as that by the conventional PCA. This rank by rank comparison of the actual eigenvalues with the null model results identify how many eigenmodes are statistically meaningful: two in the CHPCA, whereas three in the PCA. The two eigenvectors corresponding to the first and second largest eigenvalues of the CHPCA are depicted in complex plane in Fig. 9.11. The first eigenvector apparently represents collective motion of the constituents for the indexes of business conditions. On the whole, the result conforms to the assignment of leading, coincident, and lagging to each of the macroeconomic indicators by the Japanese government. However, there are some indicators which might be misclassified; for instance, the roles of Effective Job Offer Rate (#21) and Contractual Cash Earnings (#28) might be interchanged. Also one can use information of the magnitude of each component when judging whether it is appropriate as a constituent for the representative indexes or not. The second eigenvector, in which Index of Producer's Inventory (#30) makes the largest contribution, represents a mode for dynamics of inventory.

Table 9.3 Macroeconomic variables constituting the indexes of business conditions in Japan (Cabinet Office, Government of Japan 2016). Asterisk (*) indicates an inversely-cycled variable, so that the sign of its logarithmic difference is changed in the analysis. Dagger (†) indicates a variable which is not positive definite or is change from previous year; the simple difference is applied to such a variable instead of the logarithmic difference

No.	Constituents
	Leading Indicators
1*	Index of Producer's Inventory Ratio of Finished Goods (Final Demand Goods)
2*	Index of Producer's Inventory Ratio of Finished Goods (Producer Goods For Mining and Manufacturing)
3	New Job offers (Excluding New School Graduates)
4	New Orders for Machinery at Constant Prices (Manufacturing)
5	Total Floor Area of New Housing Construction Started
6	Consumer Confidence Index
7	Nikkei Commodity Price Index (42 items)
8†	Money Stock (M2) (Change From Previous Year)
9	Stock Prices (TOPIX)
10†	Index of Investment Climate (Manufacturing)
11†	Sales Forecast DI of Small Businesses
	Coincident Indicators
12	Index of Industrial Production (Mining and Manufacturing)
13	Index of Producer's Shipments (Producer Goods for Mining and Manufacturing)
14	Index of Producer's Shipment of Durable Consumer Goods
15	Index of Non-Scheduled Worked Hours (Industries Covered)
16	Index of Producer's Shipment (Investment Goods Excluding Transport Equipments)
17†	Retail Sales Value (Change From Previous Year)
18†	Wholesale Sales Value (Change From Previous Year)
19	Operating Profits (All Industries)
20	Index of Shipment in Small and Medium Sized Enterprises
21	Effective Job Offer Rate (Excluding New School Graduates)
	Lagging Indicators
22	Index of Tertiary Industry Activity (Business Services)
23†	Index of Regular Workers Employment (Change From Previous Year)
24	Business Expenditures for New Plant and Equipment at Constant Prices (All Industries)
25†	Living Expenditure (Workers' Households) (Change From Previous Year) (not including agricultural, forestry and fisheries households)
26	Corporation Tax Revenue
27*	Unemployment Rate
28	Contractual Cash Earnings (Manufacturing)
29†	Consumer Price Index (All items, less fresh food) (Change From Previous Year)
30	Index of Producer's Inventory (Final Demand Goods)

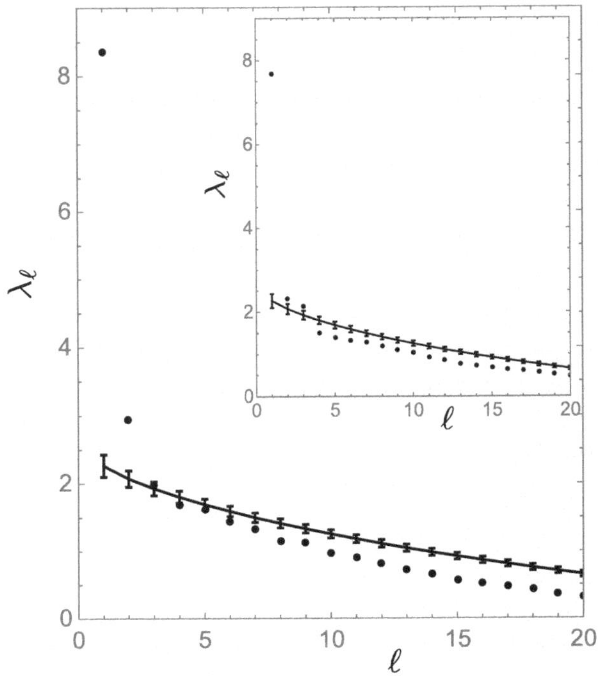

Fig. 9.10 Eigenvalues of the CHPCA obtained for the dataset of the indexes of business conditions in Japan collected during January 2000 through December 2014, compared with those of the RRS simulation, where their mean values are connected by line with associated error bars representing their 2σ deviations. The inset shows the corresponding results of the conventional PCA

We are now in a position to establish relationship between the results of the CHPCA and those of the ordinary PCA.[1] The readers may be curious about why the numbers of significant eigenmodes are different between the two PCA's. The panels (a) and (b) in Fig. 9.12 compare the second eigenvector $\boldsymbol{V}^{(2)}$ in the PCA and the real vector $\Re'[\widetilde{\boldsymbol{V}}^{(2)}]$ composed of the complex components of the second eigenvector in the CHPCA which are projected onto the optimized real part axis in Fig. 9.11b. The panels (c) and (d) compare $\boldsymbol{V}^{(3)}$ in the PCA and $\Im'[\widetilde{\boldsymbol{V}}^{(2)}]$ in the CHPCA. The cosine similarity $\cos\theta$ between $\boldsymbol{V}^{(2)}$ and $\Re'[\widetilde{\boldsymbol{V}}^{(2)}]$ is $\cos\theta = 0.930$. The similarity between $\boldsymbol{V}^{(3)}$ and $\Im'[\widetilde{\boldsymbol{V}}^{(2)}]$ is also very close to 1, $\cos\theta = 0.879$. As a matter of fact, the optimized real and imaginary axes were determined by maximizing the sum of squares of the two cosines. We thus see that the second and third eigenmodes in the PCA just reflect two orthogonal aspects of a single eigenmode in the CHPCA. This is one of the examples illustrating superiority of the CHPCA to the ordinary PCA.

---

[1] In this paragraph, the eigenvectors of the CHPCA are designated as $\widetilde{\boldsymbol{V}}^{(\ell)}$ to distinguish them from those of the ordinary PCA.

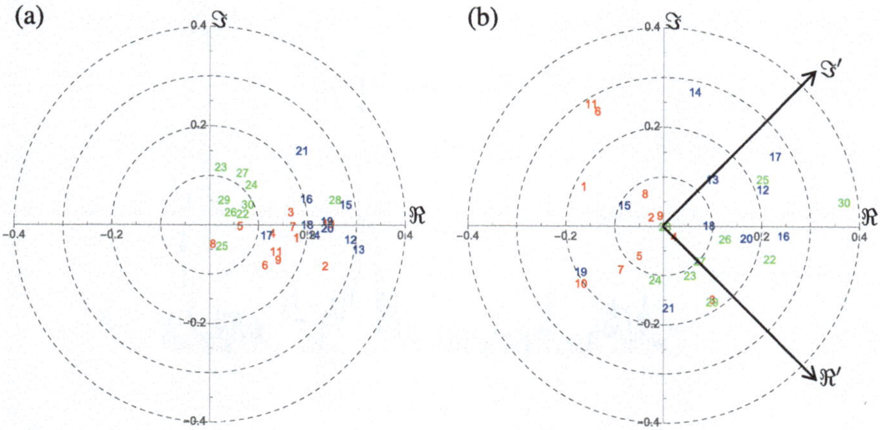

Fig. 9.11 Complex plane representation of the eigenvectors associated with the first (**a**) and second (**b**) largest eigenvalues of the CHPCA for the dataset of the indexes of business conditions in Japan. The panel (**b**) also has the optimized real part and imaginary part axes, designated by $\Re'$ and $\Im'$ respectively, to be used for establishing the relationship between the CHPCA and PCA as given in Fig. 9.12

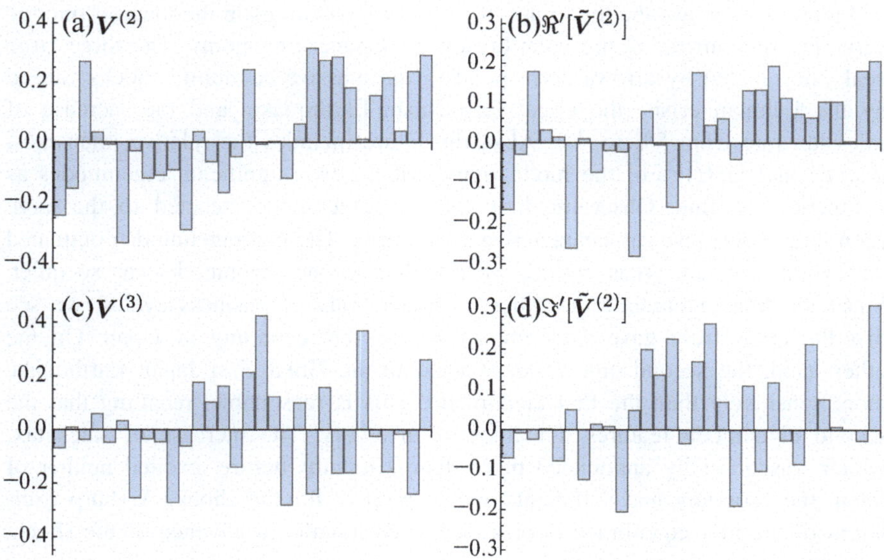

Fig. 9.12 Relationship between the CHPCA and PCA in the case of the dataset of the indexes of business conditions in Japan. Refer to the text for the meanings of the designations used here

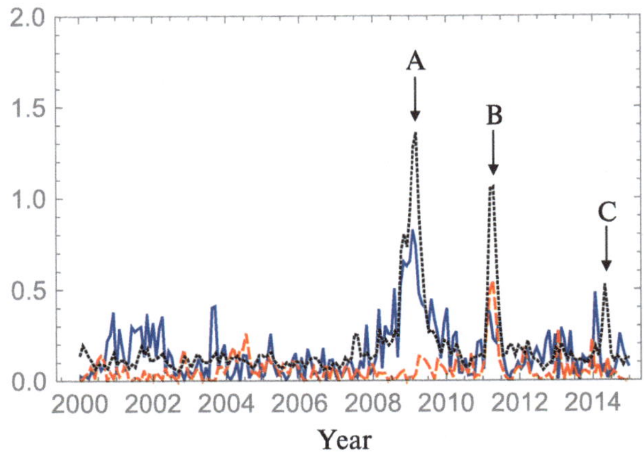

Fig. 9.13 Relative intensity $\hat{I}_\ell(t) = |\hat{a}_\ell(t)|^2$ of the first (solid blue line) and second (dashed red line) eigenmodes along with the total intensity $I(t)$ (dotted black line) of fluctuations of the constituting macroeconomic variables for the indexes of business conditions. The three arrows A, B, and C designate massive economic shocks caused by the Lehman crisis, the Great East Japan Earthquake, and the increase of sales tax rate from 5% to 8%, respectively

Figure 9.13 shows the total intensity $I(t)$ of fluctuations in the macroeconomic variables, demonstrating the volatility of the Japanese economy. The three large peaks designated by arrows correspond to the massive economic shocks caused by the Lehman crisis, the Great East Japan Earthquake, and the increase of sales tax rate from 5% to 8%. Also, the figure includes the relative intensities, $|\hat{a}_1(t)|^2$ and $|\hat{a}_2(t)|^2$, of the mode signals of the two significant eigenmodes as a function of time. Observing how the two eigenmodes reacted to the large economic shocks, we can characterize their nature. The first eigenmode dominated during the Lehman crisis period, whereas the second eigenmode was so quiet. Since the first eigenmode describes the main body of business cycles, we see that the crisis truly gave deep impact on the real economy in Japan. On the other hand, the second eigenmode reacted to the Great East Japan Earthquake more sensitively than the first eigenmode. This is reasonable, recalling that the second eigenmode features dynamics of inventory. The increase of sales tax, which was officially announced more than 9 months before, excited neither of them; the economy had sufficient time to prepare for the shock. A sharp excitation of the first eigenmode is observed three months in advance of the shock, though.

The mode signals $a_\ell(t)$'s enable us to see to what extent business cycles are described by the significant eigenmodes. We first construct representative leading, coincident, and lagging indexes by averaging the standardized log-difference or simple difference of the original data over each of the three categories. The results are given in Fig. 9.14a, where the representative indexes are successively accumulated in the time direction. The corresponding results obtained by selecting the first and second eigenmodes alone are shown in Fig. 9.14b. The essential features

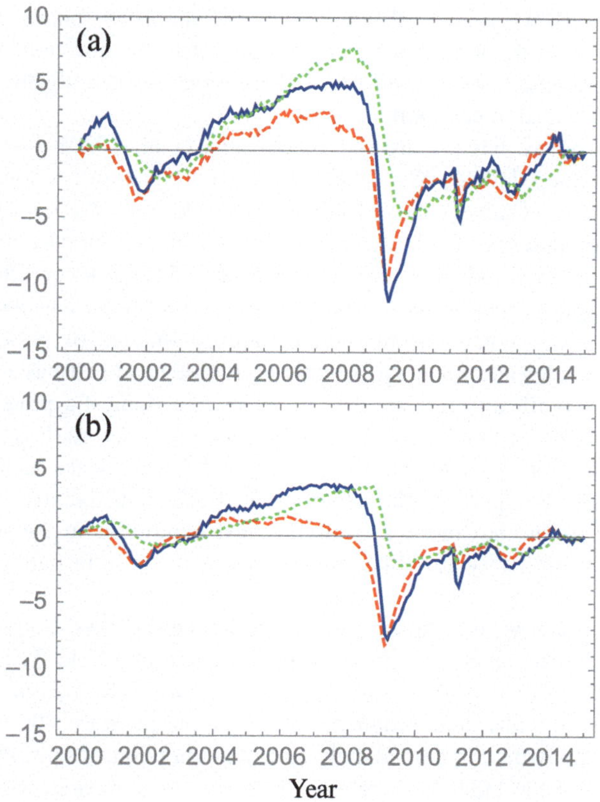

Fig. 9.14 Comparison of the representative leading (dashed line), coincident (solid line), and lagging (dotted line) indexes with the equivalent indexes described by the dominant eigenmodes alone. The panel (**a**) shows temporal accumulation of the standardized log-difference or simple difference of the original data averaged over the leading, coincident, and lagging categories. The panel (**b**) shows the corresponding results obtained by adopting the first and second eigenmodes

of the business cycles including the large shock due to the Lehman crisis are well explained by the two eigenmodes. Since $(\lambda_1+\lambda_2)/N = 11.31/30 \simeq 0.377$, roughly speaking, about 60% of the total intensity of fluctuations of the marcoeconomic variables is ascribed to random noises independent of the business cycles.

9.6 Comovement of POS Prices

The Phillips curve (Phillips 1958) is the earliest empirical indication of close relationship between aggregated price dynamics (as measured by inflation rate) and economic conditions (as measured by unemployment rate). It is an urgent issue for the Japanese economy how to get rid of the long-standing deflation. The

Bank of Japan (BOJ) is drastically increasing the supply of money with inflation targeting. However, no one has a conclusive answer to the question: *Which comes first, inflation/deflation or economic growth/recession?* Apparently, the BOJ expects that inflation is ahead of economic growth.

Very recently, we have addressed (Kichikawa et al. 2020) this fundamental problem using the CHPCA. We collected a set of Japanese economic data over the last 32 years, from January 1985 through December 2016, composed of individual price indexes of middle classification level (imported goods, producer goods, consumption goods and services), indices of business conditions (leading, coincident, lagging), yen-dollar exchange rate, money stock, and monetary base. The CHPCA gives a new insight into dynamical linkage of price movements with business cycles and financial conditions. A statistical test based on the RRS identified two significant eigenmodes, in which the domestic prices move in a collective way with certain lead-lag relations among themselves. It is indicated that the collective motion of prices is intrinsic because the dynamical structures of prices in the two modes are quite similar. However, it is driven differently, that is, by the exchange rate in the first mode and the business conditions in the second mode. In contrast, the monetary variables play an important role in neither of the two modes.

The UTokyo Daily Price Index, now called Nikkei-UTokyo Daily Price Index, is a new price index constructed by Tsutomu Watanabe and Kota Watanabe (2014). Their construction of the price index is based on daily information on the prices and quantities of individual products sold at approximately 300 supermarkets throughout Japan, which is immediately collected via point of sale (POS) systems. The advantage of the index is thereby its freshness as compared with the official price index, announced on a monthly base.

Having this fashionable trend in our mind, we turn attention to the POS price data in Japan. We analyze a set of monthly averaged POS price indexes for 202 consumer goods and 8 macroeconomic variables ($N = 210$), compiled (UTokyo Daily Price Project 2015; Cabinet Office, Government of Japan 2016) during the period of January 1991 through February 2015 ($T = 289$). The POS price dataset is composed of 44 prices of chilled foods, 99 prices of shelf-stable foods, 5 prices of frozen foods, and 54 prices of household commodities. The dataset of macroeconomic variables includes indices of business conditions (leading, coincident, lagging), money stock, contractual cash earnings in the manufacturing sector, index of producer's inventory for final demand goods, consumer price index (CPI) for all items except fresh foods, and yen-dollar exchange rate.

Figure 9.15 shows the eigenvalue distribution of the CHPCA[2] on the POS price data combined with the macroeconomic indicators, which is compared with

[2]In this analysis, we stationalized all of the time series by taking difference between consecutive observations.

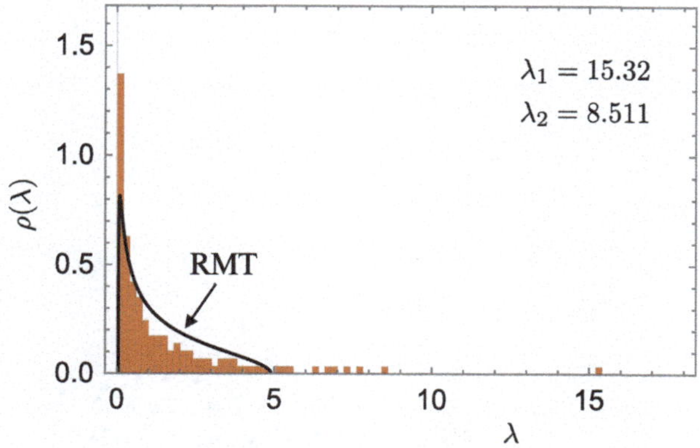

Fig. 9.15 Eigenvalue distribution of the CHPCA on the POS price dataset with the corresponding RMT result

that predicted by the RMT. One can identify 10 significant eigenmodes whose eigenvalues are larger than the upper limit of the RMT. Figure 9.16 depicts the first eigenvector in complex plane as usual. Clearly, the POS prices move in a coherent fashion, led by the indexes of business conditions together with contractual cash earnings in the manufacturing sector. This dynamical linkage between the POS prices and the business conditions is quite similar to that found in the case of the official data of prices (Kichikawa et al. 2020). In Fig. 9.16, the position (0.0521, −0.0011) of the official CPI agrees excellently with the center of gravity for all of the POS prices given by (0.0563, −0.0001). This fact indicates that the POS price data is as reliable as the official price data as far as the collective motion of prices is concerned. In other words, if inflation/deflation is defined in terms of the collective motion of prices, the two complementary data on prices give observations on the current economy which should be consistent to each other. At the same time, we should remark that the first mode gives only a small portion of contribution to the total intensity of fluctuations of the POS data; in fact, $\lambda_1/N = 15.32/210 \simeq 0.073$. This means that comparison between the two price data in a raw form does not make sense. The final remark on the empirical findings in the first mode is that the supply of money does not excite the collective motion of prices to a large extent, which is a reminiscence of the result that we have for the official price data. Instead of keeping the easy monetary policy, therefore, how to increase income of individuals is more important for giving rise to inflation in Japan. In passing, we note that one cannot directly convert the phase differences between variables in Fig. 9.16 to lead-lag relations between them in real time. This is because multiple Fourier components are generally involved in their dynamics. In the present case, however, we have the business cycle indicators which have well-established lead-lag relations in real time. That is, the leading index leads the coincident index by a few months on average, and the coincident index, in turn, leads the lagging index by about six months (Cabinet

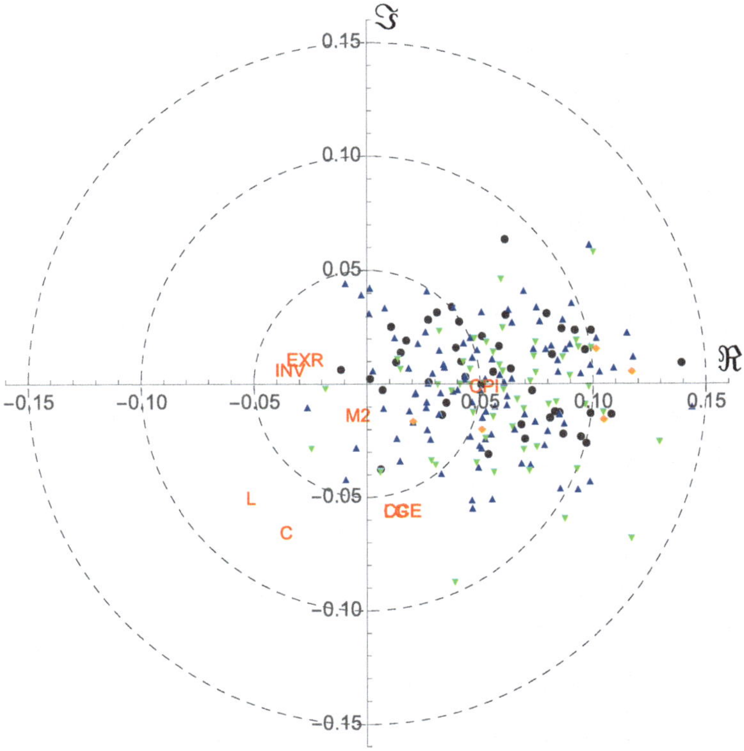

Fig. 9.16 The first eigenvector corresponding to the largest eigenvalue in Fig. 9.15. Its components are displayed in complex plane, where the gray filled circles represent POS prices of chilled foods, the blue filled triangles represent those of shelf-stable foods, the orange filled diamonds represent those of frozen foods, and the green filled inverted triangles represent those of household commodities. Also the macroeconomic variables included in this analysis are referred to by their acronyms: L, C, and LG denote the leading, coincident, and lagging indexes of business conditions, respectively; M2, money stock; CCE, contractual cash earnings in the manufacturing sector; INV, index of producer's inventory for final demand goods; CPI, consumer price index for all items, less fresh foods; EXR, dollar-yen exchange rate. Note that LG and CCE are almost overlapped

Office, Government of Japan 2016). Thus we can estimate that the lagging index and the contractual cash earnings in the manufacturing sector move almost one year in advance of the consumer price index.

The second eigenmode is shown in Fig. 9.17. Since the lagging index of business condition and index of producer's inventory for final demand goods dominate this mode among the macroeconomic variables, it may be assigned as an inventory mode. Also, we note that the prices of shelf-stable foods tend to be anticorrelated to those of household commodities in this mode.

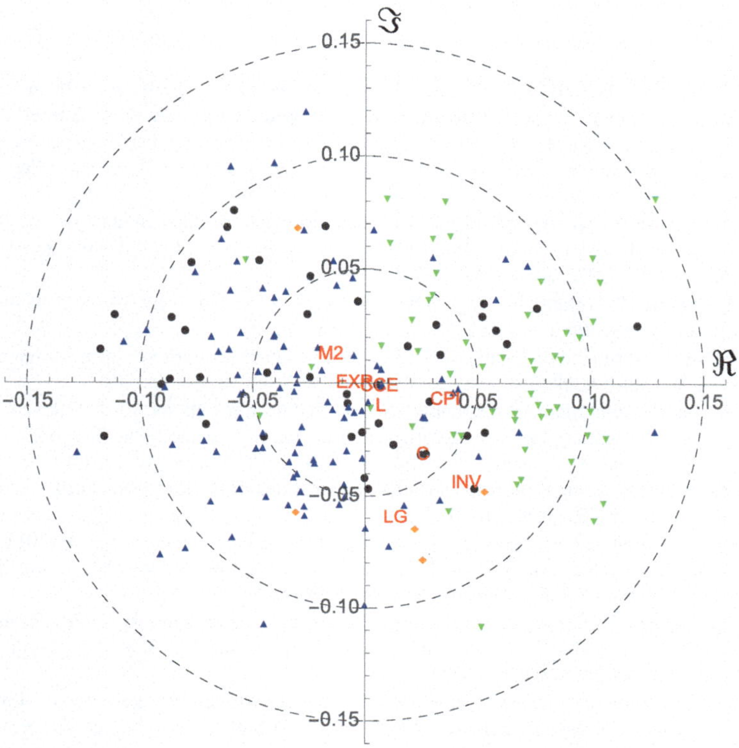

Fig. 9.17 Same as Fig. 9.16, but for the second eigenvector

9.7 Concluding Remarks

I took this opportunity to review our recent empirical studies on the collective phenomena in the economic systems with new additional results for missing the loss of Professor Masanao Aoki. Once again I realize that we have been led by his insightful question of "what about interactions among agents?" against the central dogma of the current mainstream economics. I hope the readers would agree that the CHPCA combined with the RMT or the RRS turned out to be a promising powerful tool to answer the question empirically. This chapter is devoted to the great man who were totally free from the authority.

Acknowledgments This study has been conducted as a part of the project "Large-scale Simulation and Analysis of Economic Network for Macro Prudential Policy" undertaken at the Research Institute of Economy, Trade and Industry (RIETI). It was also supported by MEXT as Exploratory Challenges on Post-K computer (Studies of Multilevel Spatiotemporal Simulation of Socioeconomic Phenomena). I highly appreciate continual collaboration with my colleagues, Hideaki Aoyama, Yuji Aruka, Yuta Arai, Yoshi Fujiwara, Ryohei Hisano, Yuichi Ikeda, Yuichi Kichikawa, Wataru Souma, Irena Vodenska, Hiroshi Yoshikawa, Takeo Yoshikawa, and Tsutomu Watanabe, on this and related topics in econophysics.

References

Aoki M, Yoshikawa H (2011) Reconstructing macroeconomics: a perspective from statistical physics and combinatorial stochastic processes. Cambridge University Press, Cambridge

Aoyama H, Fujiwara Y, Ikeda Y, Iyetomi H, Souma W, Yoshikawa H (2017) Macro-econophysics: new studies on economic networks and synchronization. Cambridge University Press, Cambridge

Arai Y, Yoshikawa T, Iyetomi H (2013) Complex principal component analysis of dynamic correlations in financial markets. Intell Decis Technol Front Artif Intell Appl 255:111–119. https://doi.org/10.3233/978-1-61499-264-6-111

Arai Y, Yoshikawa T, Iyetomi H (2015) Dynamic stock correlation network. Proc Comput Sci 60:1826–1835. https://doi.org/10.1016/j.procs.2015.08.293

Cabinet Office, Government of Japan (2016) Indexes of business conditions. https://www.esri.cao.go.jp/en/stat/di/di-e.html

Feller W (1968) An introduction to probability theory and its applications, vol 1. Wiley, New York

Husimi K (1942) Probability theory and statistics, in Japanese. Kawadeshobo, Tokyo

Iyetomi H, Nakayama Y, Aoyama H, Fujiwara Y, Ikeda Y, Souma W (2011a) Fluctuation-dissipation theory of input-output interindustrial relations. Phys Rev E 83(1):016103. https://doi.org/10.1103/PhysRevE.83.016103

Iyetomi H, Nakayama Y, Yoshikawa H, Aoyama H, Fujiwara Y, Ikeda Y, Souma W (2011b) What causes business cycles? Analysis of the Japanese industrial production data. J Jpn Int Econ 25(3):246–272. https://doi.org/10.1016/j.jjie.2011.06.002

Iyetomi H, Aoyama H, Fujiwara Y, Souma W, Vodenska I, Yoshikawa H (2020) Relationship between macroeconomic indicators and economic cycles in U.S. Scientific Reports www.nature.com/articles/s41598-020-65002-3

Kichikawa Y, Iyetomi H, Aoyama H, Fujiwara Y, Yoshikawa H (2020) Interindustry linkages of prices – Analysis of Japan's deflation. PLoS ONE, 15(2):e0228026. https://doi.org/10.1371/journal.pone.0228026

Kim DH, Jeong H (2005) Systematic analysis of group identification in stock markets. Phys Rev E 72:046133. https://doi.org/10.1103/PhysRevE.72.046133

Kydland FE, Prescott EC (1982) Time to build and aggregate fluctuations. Econometrica 50:1345–1370. https://doi.org/10.2307/1913386

Laloux L, Cizeau P, Bouchaud JP, Potters M (1999) Noise dressing of financial correlation matrices. Phys Rev Lett 83:1467–1470. https://doi.org/10.1103/PhysRevLett.83.1467

Phillips AW (1958) The relation between unemployment and the rate of change of money wage rates in the United Kingdom, 1861–1957. Economica 25:283–299. https://doi.org/10.1111/j.1468-0335.1958.tb00003.x

Plerou V, Gopikrishnan P, Rosenow B, Nunes Amaral LA, Stanley HE (1999) Universal and nonuniversal properties of cross correlations in financial time series. Phys Rev Lett 83:1471–1474. https://doi.org/10.1103/PhysRevLett.83.1471

Plerou V, Gopikrishnan P, Rosenow B, Amaral LAN, Guhr T, Stanley HE (2002) Random matrix approach to cross correlations in financial data. Phys Rev E 65:066126. https://doi.org/10.1103/PhysRevE.65.066126

Slutzky E (1937) The summation of random causes as the source of cyclic processes. Econometrica 5(2):105–146. Reprinted in English from *Problems of Economic Conditions*, edited by The Conjuncture Institute at Moskow, Vol. 3, No. 1 (1927). https://doi.org/10.2307/1907241

Terada T (1916) Apparent periodicities of accidental phenomena. Proc Tokyo Math Phys Soc 8:566–570

UTokyo Daily Price Project (2015) Item-Level Indexes. https://www.cmdlab.co.jp/price_u-tokyo/monthly-item-tm_e/

Utsugi A, Ino K, Oshikawa M (2004) Random matrix theory analysis of cross correlations in financial markets. Phys Rev E 70:026110. https://doi.org/10.1103/PhysRevE.70.026110

Watanabe K, Watanabe T (2014) Estimating daily inflation using scanner data: A progress report. CARF Working Paper CARF-F-342. https://www.carf.e.u-tokyo.ac.jp/en/research/2197/

Yoshikawa T, Arai Y, Iyetomi H (2013) Comparative study of correlations in financial markets. Intell Decis Technol Front Artif Intell Appl 255:104–110. https://doi.org/10.3233/978-1-61499-264-6-104

Yule GU (1927) On a method of investigating periodicities disturbed series, with special reference to Wolfer's sunspot numbers. Philos Trans R Soc Lond Ser A 226:267–298. https://doi.org/10.1098/rsta.1927.0007

Chapter 10
Clusters of Traders in Financial Markets

Rosario N. Mantegna

Abstract In this chapter we discuss Aoki's work on the description of clusters of economic agents acting in a market. Specifically, we briefly discuss his work on the Ewens distribution and its application in a model of stock market with heterogeneous agents. We then review recent empirical analyses on the heterogeneity of financial market participants and make a working hypothesis for an empirical study on the distribution of the number of clusters of market participants in a real stock market monitored with a resolution down to the shadowed identity of market participants.

Keywords Stock market · Ewens distribution · Representative agent · Behavioral finance · Individual investor

10.1 Introduction

The concept of representative agent is a key concept in economics dating back to Marshall (1961), and it is one of the most common assumptions used in modern theoretical economics (Hartley 1996). In spite of its widespread use, the concept has been criticized under different perspectives. A classic study summarizing critics on the concept of representative agent is Kirman's 1992 paper (Kirman 1992). Since the publishing of this seminal paper, the limits of the representative agent have motivated many researchers to consider the nature and role of heterogeneity of

R. N. Mantegna (✉)
Dipartimento di Fisica e Chimica – Emilio Segrè, Università degli Studi di Palermo, Palermo, Italy

Complexity Science Hub Vienna, Vienna, Austria

Computer Science Department, University College London, London, UK
e-mail: rosario.mantegna@unipa.it

H. Aoyama et al. (eds.), *Complexity, Heterogeneity, and the Methods of Statistical Physics in Economics*, Evolutionary Economics and Social Complexity Science 22,
https://doi.org/10.1007/978-981-15-4806-2_10

economic actors in economic systems and problems (see, e.g., Gallegati and Kirman 2012).

Heterogeneity of economic actors impacts many areas of economics (see Hommes and LeBaron (2018) for a recent collection of papers covering macroeconomics, finance, experimental economics, and networks, among others). Dynamics and heterogeneity of economic actors were aspects of major interest in most of works of Masanao Aoki (some prominent examples of his interests, results, models, and conclusions about the role of dynamics and heterogeneity of complex systems are summarized in Aoki (1996, 2002a) and Aoki and Yoshikawa (2011)). Empirical studies of several markets provide an overwhelming evidence that dynamics and heterogeneity are present in a large number of markets. In this contribution, I will focus on dynamics and distributional properties of clusters of economic actors acting in financial markets (Aoki 2002b) by considering observations and models proposed by Masanao Aoki (2000, 2002a,b). Specifically, in Sect. 10.2, I will recall Masanao Aoki's studies about heterogeneity of market participants; in Sect. 10.3, I will review recent studies analyzing the behavior and trading choices of agents acting in financial markets; and in Sect. 10.4, I will present a working hypothesis for a research project motivated by the approach proposed by Masanao Aoki. In Sect. 10.5, I present some conclusions.

10.2 Heterogeneity in Markets

The essential role of heterogeneity of economic actors in markets has been discussed in several papers. As authoritatively pointed out by Kirman in his paper (Kirman 1992), markets are modeled by using the representative agent concept "*..., instead of being a hive of activity and exchange, are frequently, as Varian (1987) points out, ones in which no trade at all takes place. Indeed, one can cite a whole series of "no trade" theorems (Rubenstein, 1975; Hakansson et al., 1982; Milgrom and Stokey, 1982; and others). In such a world there would be no meaningful stock market, distributional considerations could not enter government policy and the very idea of asymmetric information would make little sense.*" Aoki was among the first scholars to note that markets require some form of coordination effect of heterogeneous economic agents for their functioning. Moreover, he pointed out that externalities might play an essential role in several market choices. This two basic observations strongly support the abandon of the concept of representative agent and the buildup of an approach describing dynamics of heterogeneous interacting economic agents (Aoki 1996).

Masanao Aoki investigated heterogeneity in markets in several papers. His view was that many markets see economic agents participating to the market partitioned in clusters (i.e., in groups characterized by similar features). Specifically, he defined clusters by saying (Aoki 2000) "*We consider a collection of a large number of interacting economic agents, such as firms, households, and sectors of economies, or even countries. To simplify our exposition suppose that there are a fixed number n of them. They belong to a potentially large number of different types. Here, the word "type" should be broadly interpreted. For example, firms belong to different categories in terms of capitalization, size of employees, or plants and equipments. Households may be classified into different categories or types by their income levels, places they purchase various goods, or more generally by their demand patterns for some goods or services, and so on. The word could even mean that agents are classified by the kinds of algorithms they use in their decision making, searches for jobs, and so on. The types generally change over time. Agents may change their mind in their stock purchase patterns and switch their strategies, or may become bearish from bullish or vice versa."*

Having highlighted the importance of heterogeneity and dynamics in the modeling of markets, one proposal of Aoki's was to use the framework of the Ewens sampling formula originally proposed in the field of genetics (Ewens 1972) for the characterization of clusters of economic agents having reached a dynamical equilibrium (i.e., a stationary state) in a specific market. The Ewens distribution (or Ewens sampling formula) states that

$$P(\mathbf{z}) = \frac{n!}{\theta^{[n]}} \prod_{i=1}^{n} \left(\frac{\theta}{i}\right)^{z_i} \frac{1}{z_i!}, \tag{10.1}$$

where n is the number of agents, $\theta > 0$, $\theta^{[n]} = \theta(\theta + 1)\cdots(\theta + n - 1)$ is the Pochhammer symbol, and $\mathbf{z} = (z_1, \ldots, z_n)$ is the partition vector. In the partition vector, z_i is the number of clusters with exactly i agents. The total number of clusters is k. With these definitions $k = \sum_{i=1}^{n} z_i$ and $n = \sum_{i=1}^{n} i z_i$. For fixed n, Ewens distribution has θ as a single parameter.

Since Ewens' seminal paper (Ewens 1972), the Ewens distribution has been derived by following different approaches. Garibaldi et al. use a finitary approach (Garibaldi et al. 2004), i.e., they assume that the number of agents is finite and that the state of agents changes over discrete times as some agents move from cluster to cluster. Within this approach, the parameter θ has a simple interpretation. By indicating with $\nu < n$ the total weight of joining existing clusters (i.e., a herding choice), and with θ the total weight of founding a new cluster (i.e., to start a new type of grouping). At each step of the temporal evolution, a new cluster can be created with innovation probability $u = \theta/(\theta + \nu)$ (Garibaldi et al. 2004; Costantini et al. 2005).

The study of clusters of economic agents in markets has primarily focused on the classic problem of firm size (Costantini et al. 2005) and to a much less extent to the topic of clusters of traders acting in a stock market (Aoki 2002b). The abstract of Aoki (2002b) summarizes Aoki's approach. Specifically, it states *"This paper examines a share market by using a jump Markov process to model entries, exits and switchings of trading rules by a large number of interacting participants in the market. The paper examines stationary distributions of clusters of agents by strategies. We concentrate on situations where behavior of market participants are positively correlated. In these cases about 95 percent of the market participants can be shown to belong to two largest subgroups of agents with two trading rules. Contributions of the remaining 5 percent or so of participants are ignored in examining the market behavior as a whole. Market excess demand and price dynamics are examined in this framework. At the end a possibility for the existence of a power law is raised."* In other words, Aoki is interested in building up a dynamical description of trading strategies taken by different market participants. The dynamics is modeled by jump Markov processes, and a stationary distribution is hypothesized under different assumptions of the switching transition probabilities. A similar discussion applied to firm size can be found in Costantini et al. (2005).

When Aoki (2002b) was published, an empirical analysis of clusters of traders active in a stock market was unfeasible along the line of concepts and tools discussed in the paper. In recent years, a number of studies have characterized the simultaneous presence of distinct trading strategies among heterogeneous participants trading in a stock market. In the next section, I will review some of these empirical investigations.

10.3 Empirical Analysis of Heterogeneity in Stock Markets

The financial crisis of October 1987 triggered a number of studies deviating from the classic efficient market hypothesis and modeling an equity market in terms of a stylized representation of different types of market participants. One of the first papers along this line (used as reference in Aoki's work of 2002 (Aoki 2002b)) was Day and Huang's paper (Day and Huang 1990). In this paper, three stylized types of market participants were defined. They were called α-investors, β-investors, and the market maker. α-investors were the prototype of investors focusing on the fundamentals of the traded stock whereas β-investors were assumed to rely on simple heuristics (being later sometime addressed as "noise traders"); the last type of market participant was described as the market maker (a figure that was inspired by the so-called specialist of the New York Stock Exchange (Madhavan and Sofianos 1998)). Approximately during the same years, the field of market microstructure started. In the theoretical and empirical development of this research area, market microstructure scholars hypothesize the presence of different types of traders in their models, e.g., informed, non-informed, and market makers (see, e.g., Kyle 1985; O'hara 1995).

Behavioral finance has also pointed out stylized regularities of households investors (Shiller 2003; Thaler 2005) puzzling several aspects of current financial theory (Campbell 2006). The most famous evidence of behavioral bias of households investors is the so-called disposition effect, i.e., the stylized fact that retail investors show a preference to sell stocks that keep going up in price and hold those that keep going down (Odean 1998; Feng and Seasholes 2005; Dorn et al. 2008). Another robust stylized observation concerns the limited degree of portfolio diversification (Grinblatt and Keloharju 2000; Campbell 2006).

Starting from 2010, the investigation of investors acting in financial markets has also been performed within econophysics (Mantegna and Stanley 1999). Morton de Lachapelle and Challet (2010) studied quantitatively the heterogeneity of the average portfolio value of individual investors trading through the largest online Swiss broker. Tumminello et al. (2012) were able to detect clusters of investors taking similar trading decisions by devising a specific statistical test that is using tools and concepts of network science. Specifically, the amount of similarity of trading decisions between pairs of investors was assessed with a well-defined statistical test (Tumminello et al. 2011), and clusters of investors were obtained by using community detection techniques developed in the study of complex networks (Rosvall and Bergstrom 2007). Fei and Zhou (2013) investigated the trading decisions of series of market orders traded by two broad categories of investors operating in the Chinese stock market. Challet and Morton de Lachapelle performed a study of investment decisions of investors, companies, and asset managers that were using a leading online broker and detected robust evidence of the contrarian profile of retail investors (Challet and Morton de Lachapelle 2013). Bohlin and Rosvall (2014) studied the relationship between the similarity of portfolios and the similarity in trading decisions of Swedish investors. Lillo et al. (2015) investigated the relationship between exogenous news about a given stock and the trading decisions of different categories of investors. Musciotto et al. (2016) detected clusters of investors characterized by similar trading decisions with methods using hierarchical clustering (Mantegna 1999) and statistically validated networks (Tumminello et al. 2011).

In the last 2 years, several studies dealing with investors' choices have been published. Baltakys et al. (2018) developed a procedure for multilayer aggregation based on a form of statistical validation applied to an investor network. With their multilayer methodology, authors were able to find that investors in the capital of Finland (the country they investigated) have high centrality in investor networks suggesting that they are skillful and well-informed investors. Ranganathan et al. (2018) investigated the correlation between inventory of investors trading Nokia stock around the dot-com bubble. They used the minimum spanning tree approach (Mantegna 1999) to characterize the trading profiles of different categories of investors and concluded that households can have a pronounced herding tendency around bubbles. Musciotto et al. (2018) investigated daily trading decisions of investors and were able to detect time-evolving clusters of investors characterized by similar trading profiles. Their findings are compatible with the existence of an ecology of investors where groups (i.e., clusters) of traders are always competing, adopting, using, and eventually discarding new investment strategies. We will discuss their results in more detail in the next section. Challet et al. (2018) inferred a lead-lag network of investors trading in the foreign exchange market. They verified that the inferred networks are remarkably persistent and lead-lag relationships suggest that most of the trading activity has a market endogenous origin. Sueshige et al. (2018) focus on how traders submit limit and market order in the foreign exchange market. They are able to detect some limit-order and market-order strategies, and they interpret their roles in the market from an ecological perspective. Specifically, they note that trading strategies can be classified by their response pattern to historical price changes. Gutiérrez-Roig et al. (2019) use mutual information and transfer entropy to identify a network of synchronization and anticipation relationships between financial traders. They apply their methodology to a dataset of 566 non-professional investors of a private investment firm trading on 8 different stocks of the Spanish market during a period of time from 2000 to 2008. They conclude that individual's reaction to daily price changes explains around 20% of the links in the synchronization network. Baltakienė et al. (2019) investigate trading co-occurrences of investors for 69 securities that had their initial public offerings (IPOs) during the years from 1995 to 2007. They construct multilink networks covering 2 years after their IPOs. Starting from networks, they obtain clusters of investors characterized by synchronization in the timing of trading decisions. By cross-validating investor clusters on IPO securities with the investor clusters of more mature stocks, authors conclude that persistent clusters observed in Musciotto et al. (2018) are not limited to highly liquid companies, but they are also observable in securities during the first years after their IPO. Cordi et al. (2019) propose a method to detect lead-lag networks between the states of traders determined at different timescales. They apply their method to two investor resolved foreign exchange data sets and detect quantifiable asymmetric influence of timescales on the structure of lead-lag networks. They observe that institutional and retail traders have a totally different causality structure of the lead-lag networks.

10.4 Working Hypothesis for an Empirical Analysis

In this section, I propose a working hypothesis for an investigation of the dynamics and distributional properties of clusters of investors trading in a stock market. I base the feasibility of my proposal on some results recently obtained in Musciotto et al. (2018).

Due to limited access to data and confidentiality problems, the majority of empirical investigations of the trading decisions of investors is performed by covering relatively limited periods of time (from a few months to a few years). Musciotto et al. (2018) were able to overcome the problem and they studied a long-term dynamics of trading decisions of all Finnish investors investing into the Nokia stock. Their study covers the 15 year time period from 1/1995 to 12/2009. During the investigated years, Nokia stock was one of the most capitalized and liquid stock traded at the Nordic Stock Exchange. By using a database collected by Euroclear, the authors were able to analyze trading decision of investors on a daily basis (see the section of dataset and methodology of Musciotto et al. (2018) for details). In their study, investors are defined as unique legal entities, and a number of features categorizing them are available (different types of legal entities, postal code of the official address, gender and age for natural persons, etc.).

By using the tool of statistically validated networks (Tumminello et al. 2011), Musciotto et al. (2018) detect groups (i.e., clusters) of investors that are characterized by similar daily trading decisions (categorized in terms of a daily action classified as "primarily buying," "primarily selling," "buying and selling without setting up inventory," and "inactive"). Their investigation considered investors (i.e., unique legal entities) making more than five market transactions per year. The clustering procedures was performed yearly from 1995 to 2009, and they were able to discover that market participants trading Nokia shares can be described in terms of an ecology of clusters of investors. Moreover, the clusters are evolving over time. In fact, a cluster forms, expands, and then disappears with a specific time scale. The time scales of different clusters are heterogeneous, and they are ranging from 1 year (i.e., the shortest time scale associated with the detection methodology) up to several years.

In other words, the empirical results of Musciotto et al. (2018) are fully consistent with Aoki's modeling hypothesis that investors can be "*... classified by the kinds of algorithms they use in their decision making, searches for jobs, and so on. The types generally change over time. Agents may change their mind in their stock purchase patterns and switch their strategies, or may become bearish from bullish or vice versa (Aoki 2000).*"

I therefore propose the following working hypothesis for an analysis of the dynamics of clusters of investors trading in a financial market: Trading decisions of investors can be tracked over time and used to detect the presence of clusters using identical or similar trading decisions over a selected time window. The main object of the research will focus on the distribution of clusters over time. Is the Ewens distribution describing well the cluster distribution? Does the cluster distribution depend on the way clusters are defined and/or statistically detected? Is the cluster distribution stationary? Can the dynamics of clusters be modeled in terms of Markov processes?

Although it is difficult to access data about trading decisions of a large number of investors acting in a financial market at the micro level, today these types of data are potentially accessible and studies about the working research questions listed above are feasible in some markets. The results obtained from these studies would certainly highlight the nature, role, and function of heterogeneity in financial markets.

10.5 Conclusion

Recent econophysics studies have shown that heterogeneity of economic actors trading in a financial market (both in stock and in the foreign exchange market) can be empirically tracked by monitoring large samples of investors (up to the size of an entire country) active for several years. Today it is therefore possible to study the nature and role of heterogeneity of economic actors in financial markets from different perspectives. Under the key assumption that the concept of representative agent is not adequate for the economic description of markets composed by heterogeneous agents: (a) it is possible to develop a theoretical modeling of the process of price discovery of a financial asset performed by heterogeneous agents,

(b) it is possible to develop agent based models, and (c) it is possible to perform empirical analysis tracking and modeling the dynamics of heterogeneous agents in a market.

The modeling of a financial market with the basic assumption of heterogeneity of investors has a direct counterpart in the concept of market ecology of different traders (Farmer and Lo 1999; Farmer 2002). The modeling of heterogeneity of market participants under the lenses of an ecological system was implicitly present in Aoki's proposal to use Ewens distribution in the description of the stationary distribution of clusters of investors (Aoki 2002a,b). An ecological setting considers "species" of investors and studies the nature and distribution of trading decisions (including the dynamics of these decisions). The observation of a market ecology of investors is also compatible with the adaptive markets hypothesis (AMH) (Lo 2004, 2017). In the AMH, financial markets are dynamically evolving settings and groups of traders are competing among themselves by first inventing, than adopting, using, modifying, and eventually discarding specific investment strategies.

Today it is possible to perform a study to evaluate stylized facts of the distribution and dynamics of clusters of traders and model them with a genuine interdisciplinary approach taking advantage of tools and concepts originated in different disciplines such as finance, econometrics, statistics, biology, genetics, ecology, statistical physics, etc. Masanao Aoki was an outstanding scholar interested in a genuine interdisciplinary approach to the model of economic and social complex systems. His work has been and will be an authoritative guide in the study of the nature and role of heterogeneity of economic actors in economic and social systems and specifically in financial markets.

References

Aoki M (1996) New approaches to macroeconomic modeling: evolutionary stochastic dynamics, multiple equilibria, and externalities as field effects. Cambridge University Press, Cambridge

Aoki M (2000) Cluster size distributions of economic agents of many types in a market. J Math Anal Appl 249:32–52

Aoki M (2002a) Modeling aggregate behavior and fluctuations in economics: stochastic views of interacting agents. Cambridge University Press, Cambridge

Aoki M (2002b) Open models of share markets with two dominant types of participants. J Econ Behav Organ 49:199–216

Aoki M, Yoshikawa H (2011) Reconstructing macroeconomics: a perspective from statistical physics and combinatorial stochastic processes. Cambridge University Press, Cambridge

Baltakienė M, Baltakys K, Kanniainen J, Pedreschi D, Lillo F (2019) Clusters of investors around initial public offering. Palgrave Commun 5:129

Baltakys K, Kanniainen J, Emmert-Streib F (2018) Multilayer aggregation with statistical validation: application to investor networks. Sci Rep 8:8198

Bohlin L, Rosvall M (2014) Stock portfolio structure of individual investors infers future trading behavior. PloS one 9:e103006

Campbell JY (2006) Household finance. J Financ 61:1553–1604

Challet D, Morton de Lachapelle D (2013) A Robust Measure of Investor Contrarian Behaviour. In: Abergel F, Chakrabarti B, Chakraborti A, Ghosh A (eds) Econophysics of Systemic Risk and Network Dynamics. New Economic Windows. Springer, Milano, pp 105–118
Challet D, Chicheportiche R, Lallouache M, Kassibrakis S (2018) Statistically validated lead-lag networks and inventory prediction in the foreign exchange market. Adv Complex Syst 21:1850019
Cordi M, Challet D, Kassibrakis S (2019) The market nanostructure origin of asset price time reversal asymmetry. arXiv preprint arXiv:1901.00834
Costantini D, Donadio S, Garibaldi U, Viarengo P (2005) Herding and clustering: Ewens vs. Simon? Yule models. Physica 355:224–231
Day RH, Huang W (1990) Bulls, bears and market sheep. J Econ Behav Organ 14:299–329
Dorn D, Huberman G, Sengmueller P (2008) Correlated trading and returns. J Financ 63:885–920
Ewens WJ (1972) The sampling theory of selectively neutral alleles. Theor Popul Biol 3:87–112
Farmer JD (2002) Market force, ecology and evolution. Ind Corp Chang 11:895–953
Farmer JD, Lo AW (1999) Frontiers of finance: evolution and efficient markets. Proc Natl Acad Sci 96:9991–9992
Fei R, Zhou WX (2013) Analysis of trade packages in the Chinese stock market. Quant Financ 13:1071–1089
Feng L, Seasholes MS (2005) Do investor sophistication and trading experience eliminate behavioral biases in financial markets? Rev Financ 9:305–351
Gallegati M, Kirman A (2012) Reconstructing economics: agent based models and complexity. Complex Econ 1:5–31
Garibaldi U, Costantini D, Viarengo P (2004) A finitary characterization of the Ewens sampling formula. Adv Complex Syst 7:265–284
Grinblatt M, Keloharju M (2000) The investment behavior and performance of various investor types: a study of Finland's unique data set. J Financ Econ 55:43–67
Gutiérrez-Roig M, Borge-Holthoefer J, Arenas A, Perelló J (2019) Mapping individual behavior in financial markets: synchronization and anticipation. EPJ Data Sci 8:10
Hartley JE (1996) Retrospectives: the origins of the representative agent. J Econ Perspect 10:169–177
Hommes CH, LeBaron BD (eds) (2018) Handbook of computational economics, vol 4. North Holland, Amsterdam
Kirman AP (1992) Whom or what does the representative individual represent? J Econ Perspect 6:117–136
Kyle AS (1985) Continuous auctions and insider trading. Econometrica 53:1315–1335
Lillo F, Miccichè S, Tumminello M, Piilo J, Mantegna RN (2015) How news affects the trading behaviour of different categories of investors in a financial market. Quant Financ 15:213–229
Lo AW (2004) The adaptive markets hypothesis. J Portf Manag 30:15–29
Lo AW (2017) Adaptive markets. Financial evolution at the speed of thought. Princeton University Press, Princeton
Madhavan A, Sofianos G (1998) An empirical analysis of NYSE specialist trading. J Financ Econ 48:189–210
Mantegna RN (1999) Hierarchical structure in financial markets. Eur Phys J B-Condens Matter Complex Syst 11:193–197
Mantegna RN, Stanley HE (1999) Introduction to econophysics: correlations and complexity in finance. Cambridge University Press, Cambridge
Marshall A (1961) Principles of economics, 9th edn. Reprint. Macmillan and Co., London
Morton de Lachapelle D, Challet D (2010) Turnover, account value and diversification of real traders: evidence of collective portfolio optimizing behavior. New J Phys 12:075039
Musciotto F, Marotta L, Miccichè S, Piilo J, Mantegna RN (2016) Patterns of trading profiles at the Nordic Stock Exchange. A correlation-based approach. Chaos Solitons Fractals 88:267–278
Musciotto F, Marotta L, Piilo J, Mantegna RN (2018) Long-term ecology of investors in a financial market. Palgrave Commun 4:92
Odean T (1998) Are investors reluctant to realize their losses? J Financ 53:1775–1798

O'hara M (1995) Market microstructure theory, vol 108. Blackwell, Cambridge, MA

Ranganathan S, Kivelä M, Kanniainen J (2018) Dynamics of investor spanning trees around dot-com bubble. PloS one 13:0198807

Rosvall M, Bergstrom CT (2007) An information-theoretic framework for resolving community structure in complex networks. Proc Natl Acad Sci 104:7327–7331

Shiller RJ (2003) From efficient markets theory to behavioral finance. J Econ Perspect 17:83–104

Sueshige T, Kanazawa K, Takayasu H, Takayasu M (2018) Ecology of trading strategies in a forex market for limit and market orders. PloS one 13:0208332

Thaler RH (ed) (2005) Advances in behavioral finance, vol 2. Princeton university press, Princeton

Tumminello M, Miccichè S, Lillo F, Piilo J, Mantegna RN (2011) Statistically validated networks in bipartite complex systems. PloS one 6:e17994

Tumminello M, Lillo F, Piilo J, Mantegna RN (2012) Identification of clusters of investors from their real trading activity in a financial market. New J Phys 14:013041

Chapter 11
Economic Networks

Hideaki Aoyama

Abstract After briefly mentioning encounter with Prof. Aoki, recent developments in economic network analysis are described, with stress on those made of time-series. In order to analyse network made of correlations with time delay, we bring in methodologies made of CHPCA, RRS, Hodge decompositions. Several results are also described.

Keywords Pareto · Income distribution · Gibra'ts law · CHPCA · Hodge decomposition

11.1 Introduction

I believe that I met Professor Masanao Aoki sometime in early 2000 or so, soon after I started my research in economics by chance.

I am a theoretical physicist. While I was at Caltech as a Ph.D. candidate in theoretical high-energy physics group, I heard interesting tales of research outside the physics by Richard Feynman, Murray Gell-Mann, and George Zweig, all of whom were great names. Encouraged by them, I did research in condensed matter physics and linguistics before then, and loved my findings (but that is another story).

One day at a PC shop in Akiharabara ("Electric Town") in Tokyo, I came across a database of Japanese people who paid income tax of more than 10 million yen the year before. This was before the age of privacy act. So, those peoples' names, addresses, and even phone numbers were posted in each tax offices, as a praise of their valuable contribution to the country. A database company collected those data by visiting the tax offices one by one and created the database. The result was sold

H. Aoyama (✉)
Kyoto University, Kyoto, Japan

Research Institute of Economy, Trade and Industry, Tokyo, Japan

H. Aoyama et al. (eds.), *Complexity, Heterogeneity, and the Methods of Statistical Physics in Economics*, Evolutionary Economics and Social Complexity Science 22,
https://doi.org/10.1007/978-981-15-4806-2_11

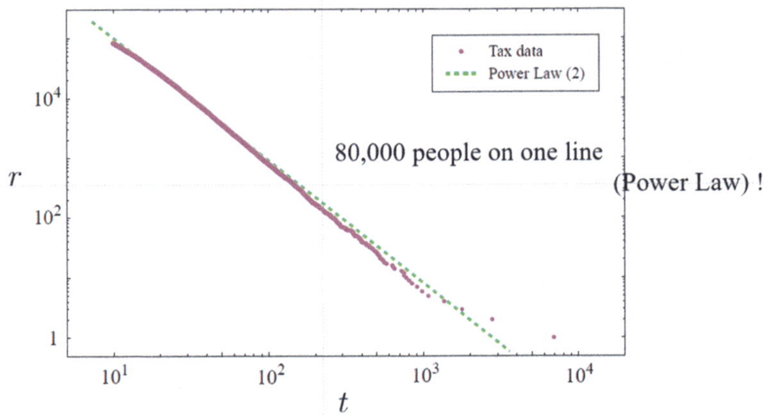

Fig. 11.1 Rank-size distribution of personal income

on CD for about 18,000 yen (some 150 USD) to general public, to be used for mailing direct advertisements.

With a vague idea on its importance in economic issues, I bought it with my pocket money, plotted its distribution as a Rank-Size plot, and found Fig. 11.1. This was quite a surprising result to me then: There are some 80,000 people in this database, which means that there are some 80,000 points in this plot. This population is quite inhomogeneous: There are baseball players, musicians, TV personalities, company owners, and executives, people who were just lucky this year and what not. They got this much of income for diverse reasons. Yet, they form an almost perfect line in this log-log plot.

Mesmerized by this straight line, I ventured into the world of big data in economy. What supported me was this deep feeling that there are hidden laws in economic phenomena, which must be based on some hidden basic laws.

Dr. Wataru Souma, my then research fellow in the particle physics group (now an associate professor at Nihon University), joined forces with me and extended my analysis to lower incomes and to other years.

Sometime before then, I met Prof. Masanao Aoki. He warmly welcomed and encouraged us, theoretical physicists with no background on economics, for further research. We received advice on several points on our income research, main points of this is to extend our scope to include real estate index and stock market indices. It was not only very heartwarming but also very critical in extending our view of economic research.

Later, encouraged by Prof. Aoki's advice, Dr. Yoshi Fujiwara joined us and we found various regularities, some of which are associated with names like Pareto and Gibrat.

That is how I started my research on economics.

11.2 Economic Network

This is the year 2020. Twenty years has passed since my first research on economics. Most of the analytical methods we invented and/or refined and the results of our research are described in our two books, Aoyama et al. (2010, 2017). So, let me describe what is new since 2017 in this chapter.

Economics networks were in my mind even when I started my research, as they are the base space on which economic phenomena occurs, much like the three-dimensional space for Galilean classical mechanics, four-dimensional space–time for Einstein's general relativistic world, or ten or eleven-dimensional space-time for superstring theories. I and Wataru even constructed a network model of people's income at the very early stage, which was not that much convincing because of the narrow perspective of the model (only people was the network agents and it missed the sources of income) and remain unpublished. Still I believe it was one of the earliest work where economic network model was proposed.

Anyhow, at this stage of research, I believe that the following two classifications is useful in explaining the economic networks.[1]

Type A Network whose agents are real, visible. Examples are:

- Share-holding network. (Japanese) Companies hold shares of each other. Network nodes are companies and directed links (edges) are amount of share held.
- Interbank network. Banks are the nodes and links can be loans and other ties between banks.
- Bank-firm network. Two-layer networks, made of a layer on which nodes are banks and another layer of firms. Links between the layers are made of loans (shot-term and long-term), among others. Data for this network exist in Japan for listed firms only.
- Interfirm network. Nodes are firms and links are trade relationship. In Japan, data for some active firms are available, but with no amount of trade. There are, however, data with the trade amount partially.
- International trade network. Nodes are countries and links are amount of import/export for goods and services.
- Crypto asset network. Nodes are the internet nodes or users (buyer/seller) and links are amount of trade (such as Bitcoin). Research on this network is rapidly expanding currently due to the increasing money value of crypto assets.

Type B Networks whose notes are quantities or properties and links are hidden relations between them, such as Correlation. Some examples are:

- Prices of goods/services. Nodes are time-series of goods/services and links are made of correlation.
- Consumer's behavior. Nodes are time-series of a product and links are made of correlation.

[1]Caution: This is my proposal and nobody is using these "Type A/B" classification.

- Stock market. Nodes are time-series of stock and links are made of correlation.
- Economic indices. Nodes are the economic indices, linked by correlation with time lag.

In the following, I will describe a most notable Type A network, the interfirm network. Then I will explain our toolbox we have developed to analyze some of the Type B networks, where links are correlations as stated above, and therefore we need solid methodology to extract useful information.

11.3 Type A Network: Interfirm Network

The most notable network in Type A is the interfirm network first studied in Fujiwara and Aoyama (2010). It has almost all the active firms in Japan, about one million of them, which is the main engine, core of the country's economy. Its scale, importance, and the uniqueness, as it is rare to have such REAL data among all the countries of the world, make the study of these data most fascinating. (On the other hand, these data were collected and put together by a commercial company, Tokyo Shoko Research. Because of the huge amount of resource needed for the construction of these data, their price is prohibitively huge. Some of us were lucky in obtaining these data through RIET and other funds.)

A partial view of this network, three degrees of Toyota motor, is in Fig. 11.2 (Chakraborty et al. 2018).

There are a series of papers written on this network. Among the latest results, I find the one shown in Fig. 11.3 most interesting, a key stone of the research (Chakraborty et al. 2018).

Here the red points are firms that belong to "IN" components, green are "GSCC," and blue are "OUT." Traditionally, this kind of network was thought to have "bow tie" structure, whose "IN" and "OUT" are extended away from "GSCC" like in wings of a bird flying, but it is not. We named this kind of structure as "Walnut," because of the two tight shells formed from "IN" and "OUT."

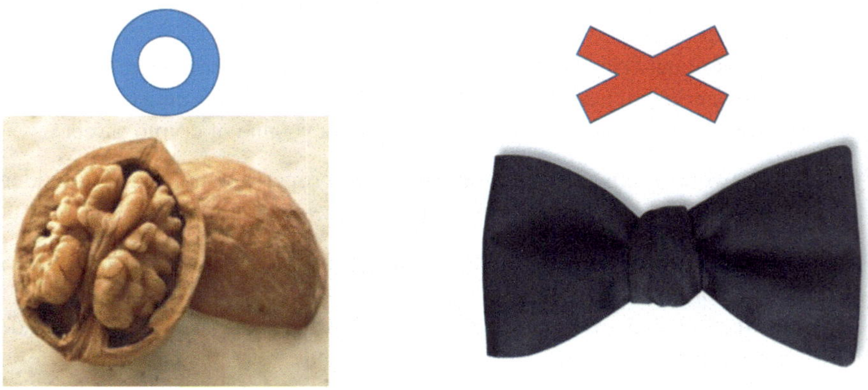

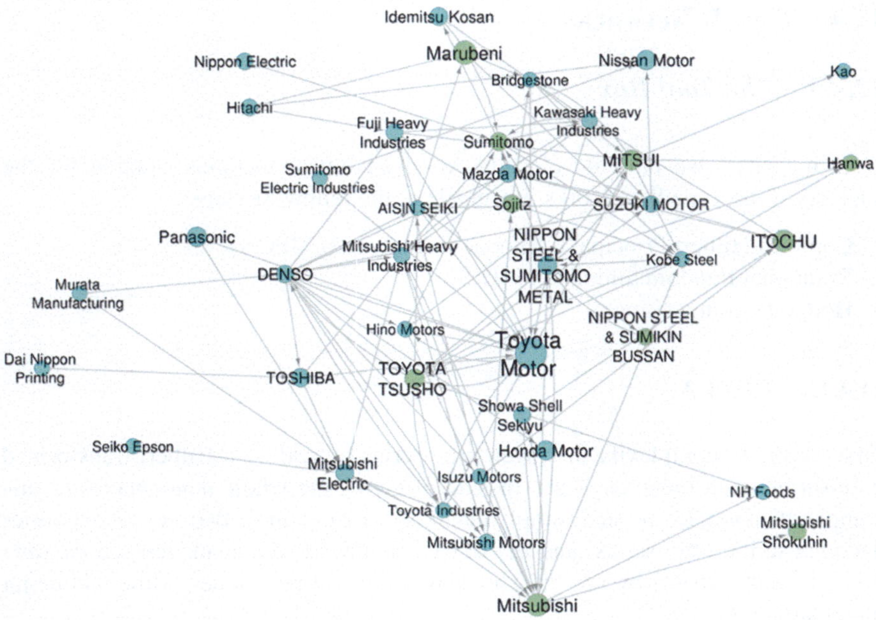

Fig. 11.2 A partial view of the Japanese interfirm network

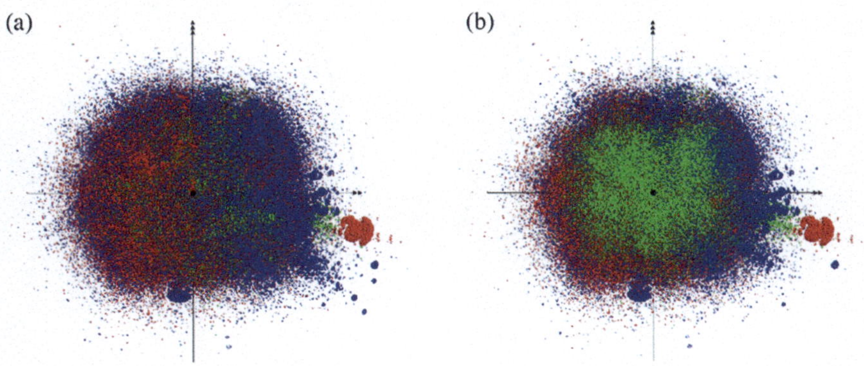

Fig. 11.3 Walnut structure of the Japanese interfirm network

Furthermore community structure was analyzed in the paper, as communities form basic grain of the whole complex network.

Further research using this network is being done, modeling of business cycles, propagation of economic shocks, among others. For the former, I would like to draw readers' attention to work on economic shocks due to natural disasters, (Inoue and Todo 2017).

11.4 Type B Networks

11.4.1 The Tool Box

Over the years we have developed several analytical methods suitable for the analysis of the Type B networks. It is made of the following steps:

1. Complex Hilbert Principal Component Analysis (CHPCA)
2. Rotational Random Simulation (RRS)
3. Hodge Decomposition

11.4.1.1 CHPCA

First step is to complexify the given time-series by adding a Hilbert-transformed time-series as an imaginary part. Instead of giving the whole mathematics of this complexification, let me state simply that it is made of simple two steps: (1) Fourier decompose the time series, and (2) in each Fourier component, replace $cos(\omega t)$ by $e^{-i\omega t}$ and $sin(\omega t)$ by $ie^{-i\omega t}$. This leaves the real part intact, while adding an imaginary part.

One example is illustrated below.

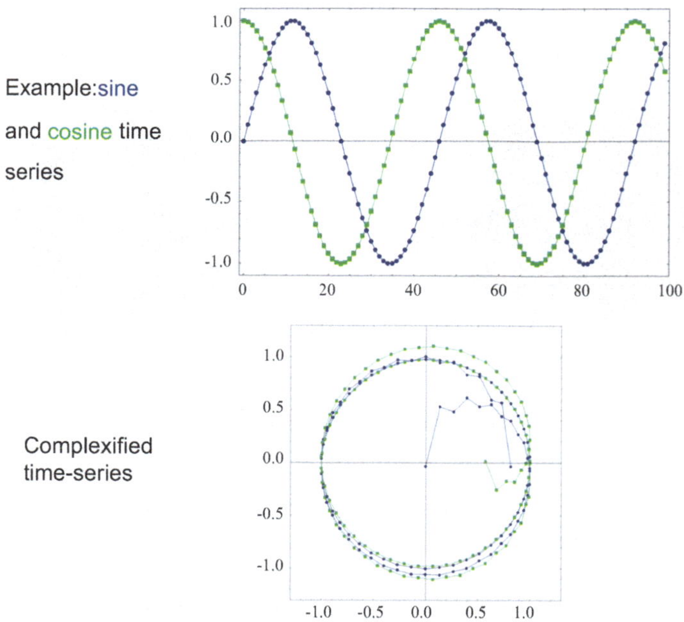

Here, original two time series in the upper panel are complexified and rotated clockwise as in the lower panel, where their motion on the complex plane is drawn. Readers may think that this is trivial as a simple replacement. But look closely, it is not: The time-range in the upper panel is not an integer multiple of the period of the sine and cosine: The Fourier decomposition is made of infinite components. Yet, this complexification makes them nearly perfect rotation in the complex plane. (If we used simple derivative instead of the Hilbert transformation, extra factor of ω makes it sensitive to the higher-components and it does not yield this beautiful behavior. Furthermore, it would make a noisy time-series more noisy.)

Now, the correlation matrices obtained from the ordinary PCA and the one obtained from this complexified time-series are given below. The PCA results have a very small off-diagonal element, reflecting the fact that the sin and cosine curves have $\pi/2$ phase difference. If they are continuous data, their equal-time correlation is exactly zero. Only because they are discrete, we have a small but non-zero correlation.

PCA detects no correlation. $$C = \begin{pmatrix} 1 & 0.049 \\ 0.049 & 1 \end{pmatrix}$$

CHPCA detects the correlation with lead/lag.

$$\tilde{C} = \begin{pmatrix} 1 & 0.981e^{0.484\pi i} \\ \underline{0.981}e^{-\boxed{0.484\pi} i} & 1 \end{pmatrix}$$

Strong Correlation time-lag

But look at the lower panel: Complex correlation matrix has a significant (12) component. Its absolute value is close to one, indicating that correlation is almost perfect. Its phase is close to $\pi/2$, indicating the time difference between them.

This is the power of CHPCA. It allows us to detect the correlation with time lag.

11.4.1.2 RRS

Using CHPCA and calculating its eigensystem, we identify independent co-movement modes. For data with N time-series, we find N modes. But not all of them are signal, because our time-series is limited in time-period: If our time-series is infinitely long, all the noise part have zero eigenvalues. But that is not a reality.

Those of the readers who know this kind of business may say "Ah, Random Matrix Theory (RMT) can deal with it!"

But it does not. For RMT to be applicable, several conditions has to be met. Notorious among them is the lack of auto-correlation, which real-world data do not have. So, RRS was invented.

Simply put, it randomly rotates each time-series (made to a ring by the head and the tail connected) against each other. This is just rotating the rings (numbers) on a dial lock.

This process destroys the correlation between the time-series, while autocorrelation intact. Then, through CHPCA the eigensystem of complex correlation matrix are obtained. By doing so many times, we obtain the distribution of eigenvalues from RRS and compare them with the original eigenvalues.

Following is an example of such a calculation.

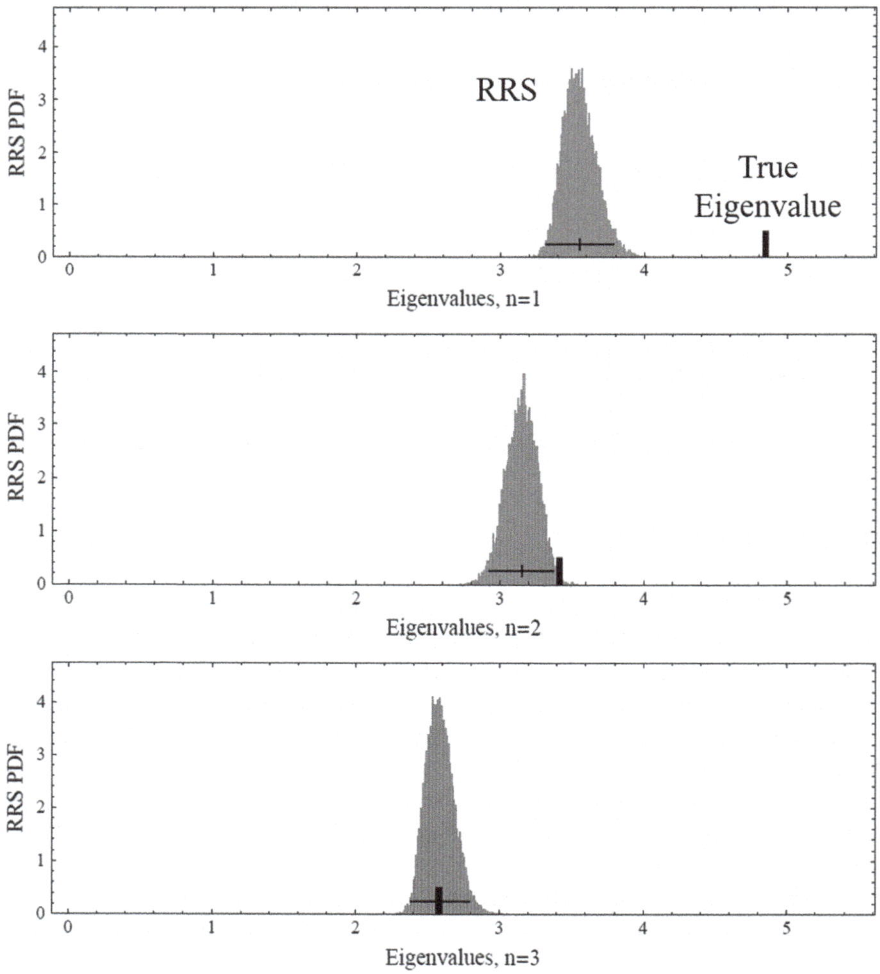

Here, at the top most panel we are looking at the largest eigenvalue (as it represents the co-movement who has the most presence). The eigenvalue of the original data noted by a short thick bar is close to 5. On the other hand, RRS gives the distribution far smaller then 5. Thus we conclude that the true eigenmode is due to the correlation between time-series and represents a co-movement.

Same is (almost) true on the second eigenmode as seen in the middle panel. But in the third panel, the true eigenvalue is completely buried in the RRS distribution. Thus, this third mode cannot be a true co-movement. So we conclude the top two modes are significant in this example.

This way, we identify the significant eigenmodes and by limiting the summation of the eigenmodes in the complex correlation matrix, we construct the significant part of it, as illustrated below.

Complex Correlation Matrix (CCM), EigenSystem

$$\tilde{\boldsymbol{C}}\boldsymbol{V}^{(n)} = \lambda^{(n)}\boldsymbol{V}^{(n)} \qquad \boldsymbol{V}^{(n)\dagger} \cdot \boldsymbol{V}^{(m)} = \delta_{nm}, \quad \sum_{n=1}^{N} \lambda^{(n)} = N$$

Significant CCM (S=Number of significant mode, identified by RRS)

$$\tilde{C}^{(\mathrm{sig})}_{\alpha\beta} = \sum_{n=1}^{S} V^{(n)}_{\alpha} V^{(n)*}_{\beta}$$

Phase as the Flow

Remember

$$\tilde{C} = \begin{pmatrix} 1 & 0.981e^{0.484\pi i} \\ 0.981e^{-0.484\pi i} & 1 \end{pmatrix}$$

Strong Correlation time-lag

11.4.1.3 Hodge Decomposition

Once we obtain the significant complex correlation matrix, it is time to construct the economic network it represents. I named it "Hodge Correlation Network."

But first, let me explain the Hodge decomposition itself, as it exists in the domain of general network theory.

A good example of its outcome in the following:

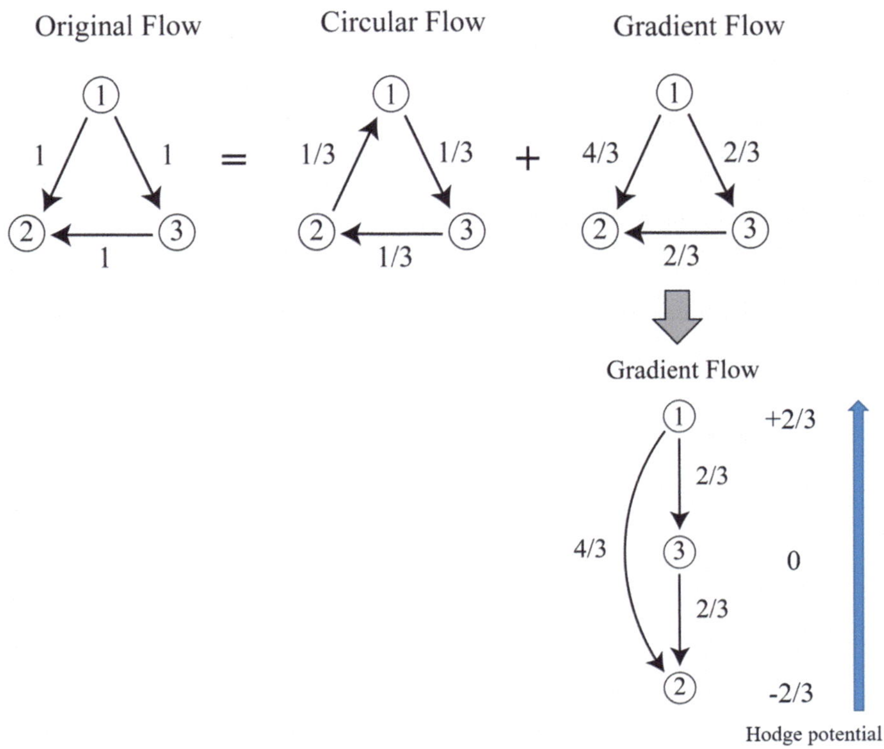

The original network with directed flow is at the left. The purpose of the Hodge decomposition is to sort out the hierarchy of the nodes: clarifying who is at the top of the network and so on, quantitatively. The result is the decomposition to the two networks, one with circular flow and the other with gradient flow. Addition of the flows (with its direction taken into account) reproduces original flow. Circular flow are just circular, going around. The gradient flow is equal to the difference of the Hodge potential assigned to each node as illustrated in the bottom right. For example, the Hodge potential of the node 1 is +2/3, and the node 2 has 0, difference being 2/3 which is the gradient flow from the node 1 to the node 2.

So, we establish the hierarchical order of the nodes by the value of the Hodge potential.

The following are some of the nontrivial results, where left panels are the original network where links are directed and has strength one, visualized with the well-known charge-string method. The right panels are the same networks, in which each node's vertical coordinates are fixed to be their Hodge potential and horizontal coordinates are determined by the charge-string method.

I hope that the readers see the value of Hodge decomposition in these examples.

Example no.1

7918

$$\begin{pmatrix} 0 & 1 & 0 & 0 & 1 & 1 \\ 0 & 0 & 0 & 1 & 1 & 0 \\ 0 & 0 & 0 & 0 & 0 & 1 \\ 0 & 0 & 0 & 0 & 0 & 1 \\ 0 & 1 & 0 & 0 & 0 & 0 \\ 0 & 0 & 0 & 0 & 0 & 0 \end{pmatrix}$$

Adjacent Matrix

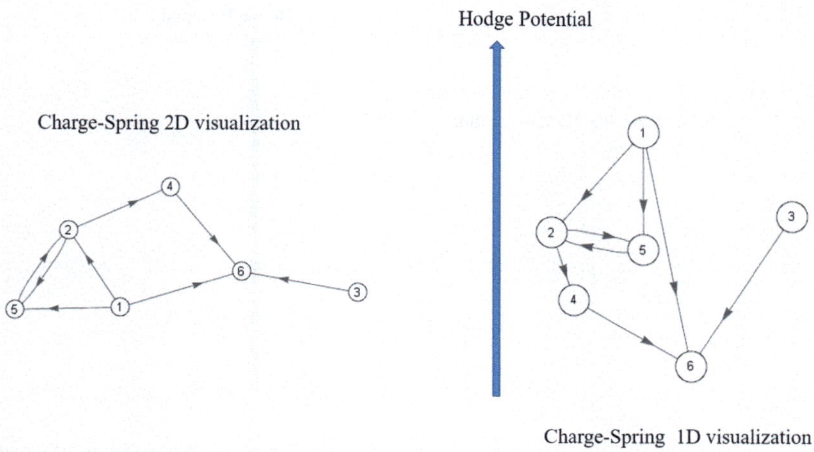

Example no.2

464575

$$\begin{pmatrix} 0 & 0 & 0 & 1 & 1 & 1 \\ 0 & 0 & 0 & 1 & 1 & 1 \\ 0 & 1 & 0 & 0 & 1 & 1 \\ 0 & 0 & 0 & 0 & 1 & 1 \\ 0 & 0 & 0 & 1 & 0 & 1 \\ 0 & 0 & 0 & 1 & 0 & 0 \end{pmatrix}$$

Adjacent Matrix

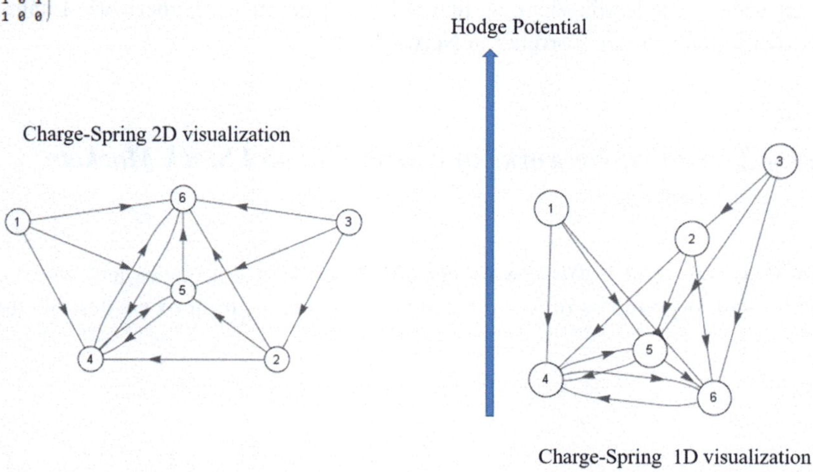

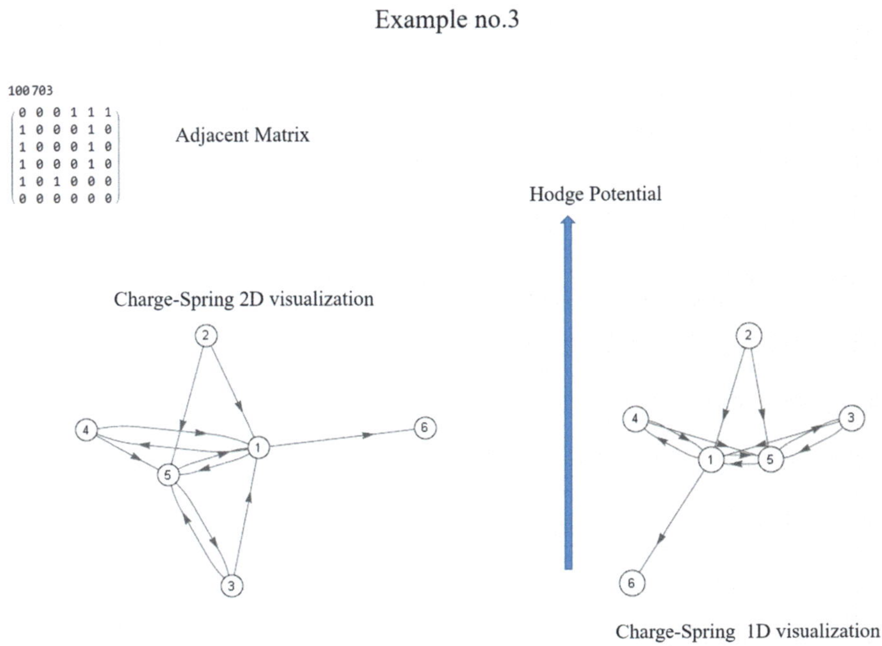

Now, in using this Hodge methods to our CHPCA+RRA results, we choose the phase of the significant complex correlation matrix, as it is the time-lag of their correlation: For a pair of time-series, the larger the phase, the larger the time-lag, and larger the difference between their Hodge potentials. (The sign of the phase tells which node is lagging and which node is leading.) So, the network constructed this way reflects the leading/lagging hierarchical structure of the network. I named this network "The Hodge Correlation Network."

11.4.2 Global Networks of Currencies and Stock Market Indices

In Vodenska et al. (2016), we analyzed network of currencies and stock market indices of 48 countries of world listed below, using the toolbox we described above.

No.	Country	Stock Index	Currency
1	UK	UKX	Pound Sterling
2	Austria	ATX	Euro
3	Belgium	BEL20	Euro
4	Finland	HEX25	Euro
5	France	CAC	Euro
6	Germany	DAX	Euro
7	Ireland	ISEQ	Euro
8	Italy	FTSEMIB	Euro
9	Netherlands	AEX	Euro
10	Portugal	PSI20	Euro
11	Spain	IBEX	Euro
12	Greece	ASE	Drachma, then Euro since Jan. 2001
13	Malta	MALTEX	Maltese Lira, then Euro since Jan. 2008
14	Slovakia	SKSM	Slovak Koruna, then Euro since Jan. 2009
15	Norway	OBX	Norwegian Krone
16	Sweden	OMX	Swedish Krona
17	Iceland	ICEXI	Icelandic Krona
18	Switzerland	SMI	Swiss Franc
19	Czech	PX	Czech Koruna
20	Denmark	KFX	Danish Krone
21	Hungary	BUX	Forint
22	Poland	WIG	Zloty
23	Russia	INDEXCF	Ruble
24	USA	SPX	US Dollar
25	Canada	SPTSX	Canadian Dollar
26	Mexico	MEXBOL	Mexican Peso
27	Brazil	IBOV	Real
28	Argentina	MERVAL	Argentine Peso
29	Chile	IPSA	Chilean Peso
30	Peru	IGBVL	Nuevo Sol
31	Venezuela	IBVC	Bolivar
32	India	SENSEX	Indian Rupee
33	Sri Lanka	CSEALL	Sri Lankan Rupee
34	Indonesia	JCI	Indonesian Rupiah
35	Japan	NKY	Yen
36	South Korea	KOSPI	South Korean Won
37	Malaysia	FBMKLCI	Ringgit
38	Thailand	SET	Baht
39	Philippine	PCOMP	Philippine Peso
40	Hong Kong	HSI	Hong Kong Dollar
41	Australia	AS51	Australian Dollar
42	Israel	TA-25	Shekel
43	Pakistan	KSE100	Pakistani Rupee
44	Saudi Arabia	SASEIDX	Saudi Riyal
45	South Africa	TOP40	Rand
46	Oman	MSM30	Rial
47	Qatar	DSM	Riyal
48	Mauritius	SEMDEX	Mauritian Rupee

		Whole Period	
No.	Country	Stock	Currency
1	UK	1	2
2	Austria	1	2
3	Belgium	1	2
4	Finland	1	2
5	France	1	2
6	Germany	1	2
7	Ireland	1	2
8	Italy	1	2
9	Netherlands	1	2
10	Portugal	1	2
11	Spain	1	2
12	Greece	1	2
13	Malta	3	2
14	Slovakia	1	2
15	Norway	1	2
16	Sweden	1	2
17	Iceland	3	2
18	Switzerland	1	2
19	Czech	1	2
20	Denmark	1	2
21	Hungary	1	2
22	Poland	1	2
23	Russia	1	3
24	USA	1	3
25	Canada	1	2
26	Mexico	1	3
27	Brazil	1	2
28	Argentina	1	3
29	Chile	1	3
30	Peru	1	3
31	Venezuela	1	3
32	India	3	3
33	Sri Lanka	4	3
34	Indonesia	4	3
35	Japan	4	2
36	Korea	3	3
37	Malaysia	4	3
38	Thailand	4	3
39	Philippine	4	3
40	Hong Kong	4	3
41	Australia	4	2
42	Israel	1	3
43	Pakistan	4	3
44	Saudi Arabia	4	3
45	South Africa	1	2
46	Oman	4	3
47	Qatar	4	3
48	Mauritius	4	3

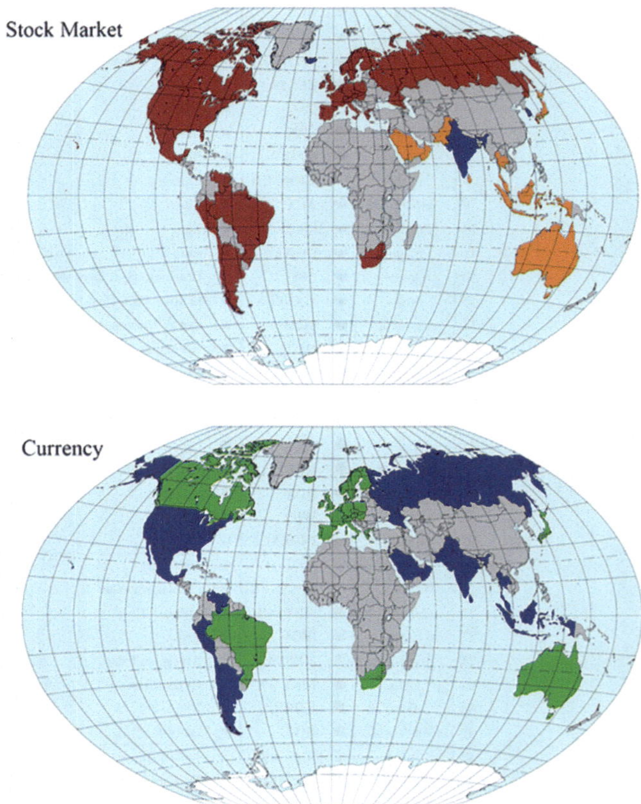

Fig. 11.4 World map of community decomposition

The community decomposition of these $48 \times 2 = 96$ time-series is illustrated in Fig. 11.4.

11.4.3 Prices

In Kichikawa et al. (2019), we analyzed network of prices of goods and services in Japan. At the most micro-level, individual prices behave as in Fig. 11.5

There are both systematic price changes and also individual deviation from it. What needs to be found is the former, and its relation to the macroeconomic indicators. In order to do this task, we have analyzed the mid-classification level

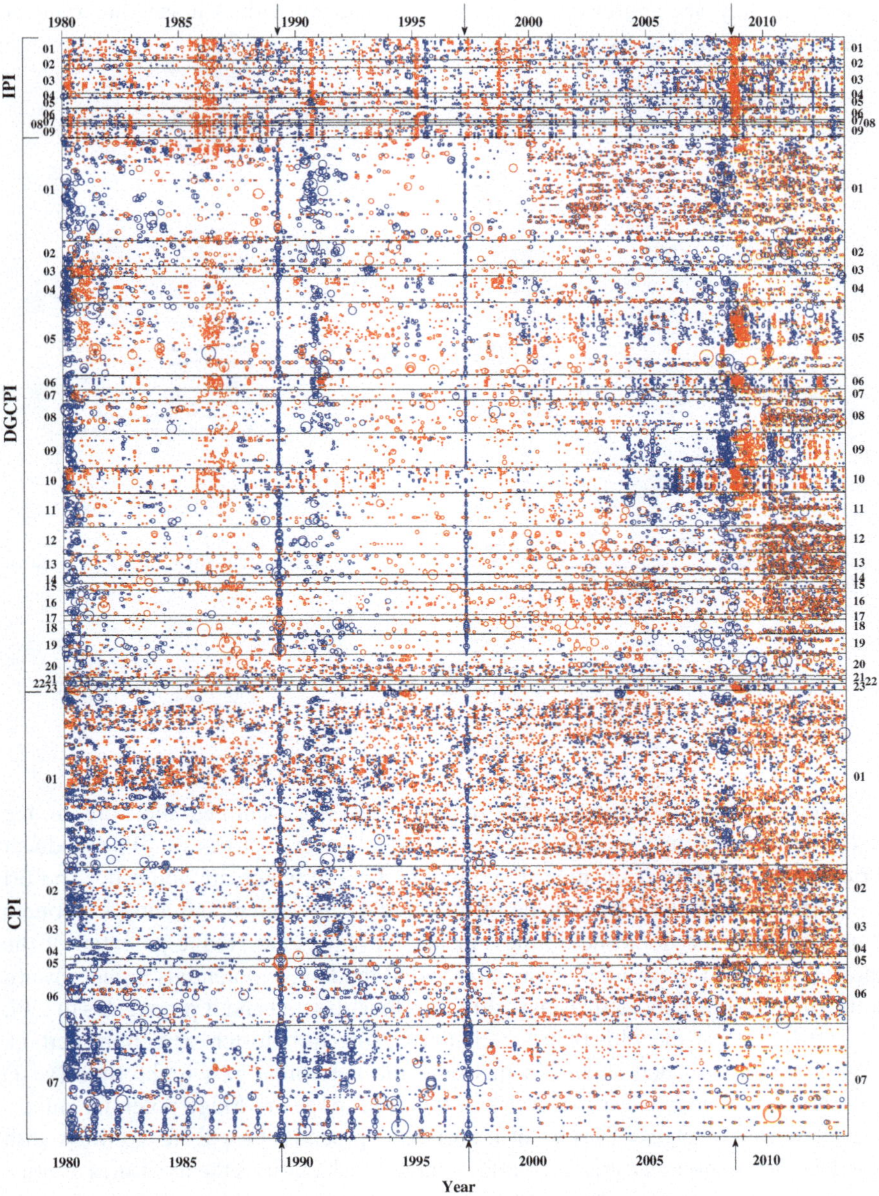

Fig. 11.5 Behavior of micro prices

prices (as they are aggregated to some level and individual noises are reduced somewhat) and indicators listed below:

Mid-aggregate level

1 IPI Foodstuffs & feedstuffs
2 IPI Textiles
3 IPI Metals & related products
4 IPI Wood, lumber & related products
5 IPI Petroleum, coal & natural gas
6 IPI Chemicals & related products
7 IPI General purpose, production & business oriented machinery
8 IPI Electric & electronic products
9 IPI Transportation equipment
10 IPI Other primary products & manufactured goods
11 PPI Food, beverages, tobacco & feedstuffs
12 PPI Textile products
13 PPI Lumber & wood products
14 PPI Pulp, paper & related products
15 PPI Chemicals & related products
16 PPI Petroleum & coal products
17 PPI Plastic products
18 PPI Ceramic, stone & clay products
19 PPI Iron & steel
20 PPI Nonferrous metals
21 PPI Metal products
22 PPI General purpose machinery
23 PPI Production machinery
24 PPI Business oriented machinery
25 PPI Electronic components & devices
26 PPI Electrical machinery & equipment
27 PPI Information & communications equipment
28 PPI Transportation equipment
29 PPI Other manufacturing industry products
30 PPI Agriculture, forestry & fishery products
31 PPI Minerals
32 PPI Electric power, gas & water
33 PPI Scrap & waste

34 CPI Cereals
35 CPI Fish & seafood
36 CPI Meats
37 CPI Dairy products & eggs
38 CPI Vegetables & seaweeds
39 CPI Fruits
40 CPI Oils, fats & seasonings
41 CPI Cakes & candies
42 CPI Cooked food
43 CPI Beverages
44 CPI Alcoholic beverages
45 CPI Meals outside the home
46 CPI Rent
47 CPI Repairs & maintenance
48 CPI Electricity
49 CPI Gas
50 CPI Other fuel & light
51 CPI Water & sewerage charges
52 CPI Household durable goods
53 CPI Interior furnishings
54 CPI Bedding
55 CPI Domestic utensils
56 CPI Domestic non-durable goods
57 CPI Domestic services
58 CPI Clothes
59 CPI Shirts, sweaters & underwear
60 CPI Footwear
61 CPI Other clothing
62 CPI Services related to clothing
63 CPI Medicines & health fortification
64 CPI Medical supplies & appliances
65 CPI Medical services
66 CPI Public transportation
67 CPI Private transportation
68 CPI Communication
69 CPI School fees
70 CPI School textbooks & reference books for study
71 CPI Tutorial fees
72 CPI Recreational durable goods
73 CPI Recreational goods
74 CPI Books & other reading materials
75 CPI Recreational services
76 CPI Personal care services
77 CPI Toilet articles
78 CPI Personal effects
79 CPI Tobacco
80 CPI Other miscellaneous

Macro Indices

81 US Dollar to Japanese Yen Exchange Rate
82 Index of Business Condition Leading Index
83 Index of Business Condition Coincident Index
84 Index of Business Condition Lagging Index
85 M2(seasonal adjusted)
86 Monetary base(seasonal adjusted)
87 Contractual cash earnings (Manufacturing)

What we found is summarized in Fig. 11.6: We identified the core of the collective motion in this data set. It is made of several prices of PPI (Producer Price Index) and CPI (Consumer Price Index), both of which are domestic. The IPI (Imported Price Index) are outside of this core co-movement and acts as a source that stimulates the domestic co-movement. Top left is the Hodge potential of the indices in this co-movement mode. Notice that the Hodge potentials higher toward left, where PPIs are located. That is, PPIs are first affected and it propagates to CPI.

Left-bottom is the plot of price changes using the cluster-extraction method, which is not explained above. In this plot, the horizontal axis is the time (year) and the vertical axis is for the prices in the order of their Hodge potential values. It is clear that changes of prices of high Hodge potential propagates to those with low Hodge potential in time. This kind of plot, which clarifies the dynamics of price changes, was made possible for the first time by using our tool set. The right plot is the network of this co-movement, where the vertical axis is the Hodge potential of each price, and the horizontal coordinate is determined by the charge-string optimization scheme of network visualization.

I would refer interested readers to the original paper.

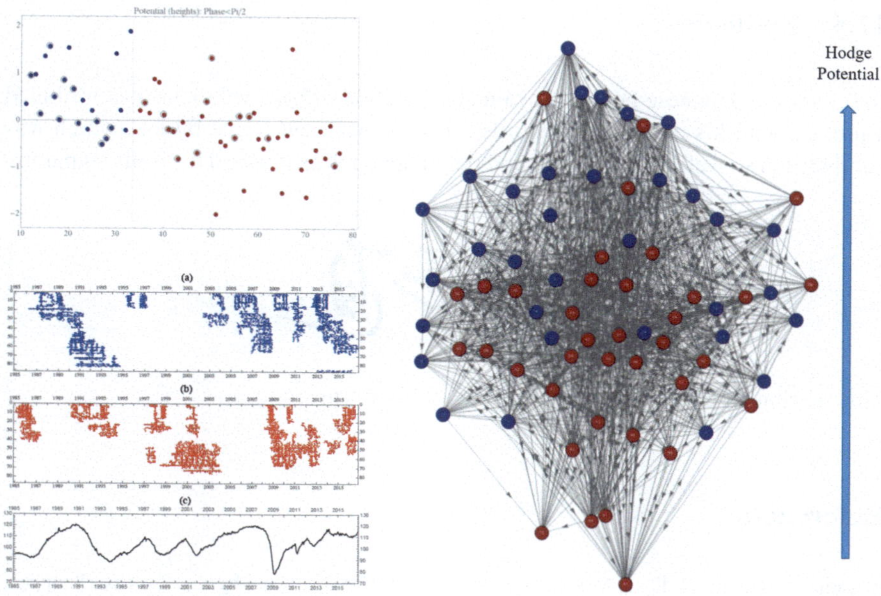

Fig. 11.6 Summary of the results of price analysis

11.4.4 Outlook

What is described above is a very small part of the research efforts currently going on. With our tool box, which is expanding with introduction of new techniques now, many hidden correlation structures will be found.

Especially important is the expansion to the multi-layer economic networks. Readers must have noticed that we are looking at the whole economy from different angles, picking up parts by parts, and revealing what kind of structure/dynamics they have. This is just a starting point. The whole economy is huge. They way to understand it is the multi-layer network of individuals, households, firms, banks, countries, each with a magnitude of interactions within each layer and between layers. Data are limited to construct this ultimate economics network, and I feel that we do not have a tool box to handle it. But we are making progress steadily.

I have this quote posted in front of my work desk.

> We are at the beginning of time for the human race. It is not unreasonable that we grapple with problems. But there are tens of thousands of years in the future. Our responsibility is to do what we can, learn what we can, improve the solutions, and pass them on. – Richard Feynman

11.5 Epilogue

In one of our Japanese books, Aoyama et al. (2008), Prof. Aoki kindly contributed a preface with his encouraging words for us. It was sent to me by fax, which was handwritten so well that I scanned and put in the book as it was. This is his signature.

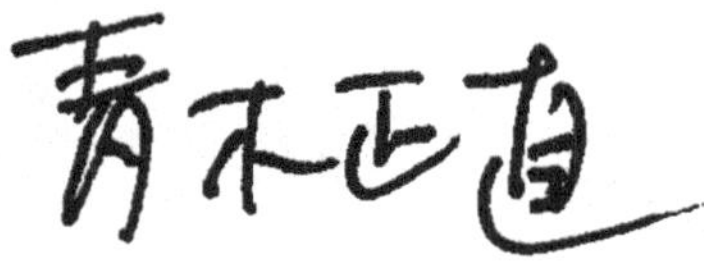

This is what he left for us, reminding me of his warm smile.

References

Aoyama H, Iyetomi H, Ikeda Y, Souma W, Fujiwara Y (2008) Econophysics. Kyoritsu Shuppan, Inc., Tokyo

Aoyama H, Fujiwara Y, Ikeda Y, Iyetomi H, Souma W (2010) Econophysics and companies – statistical life and death in complex business networks. Cambridge University Press, Cambridge

Aoyama H, Fujiwara Y, Ikeda Y, Iyetomi H, Souma W, Yoshikawa H (2017) Macro-econophysics – new studies on economic networks and synchronization. Cambridge University Press, Cambridge

Chakraborty A, Kichikawa Y, Iino T, Iyetomi H, Inoue H, Fujiwara Y, Aoyama H (2018) Hierarchical communities in the walnut structure of the Japanese production network. PloS one 13(8):e0202739

Fujiwara Y, Aoyama H (2010) Large-scale structure of a nation-wide production network. Eur Phys J B 77(4):565–580

Inoue H, Todo Y (2017) Propagation of negative shocks through firm networks: evidence from simulation on comprehensive supply-chain data. Available at SSRN 2932559

Kichikawa Y, Iyetomi H, Aoyama H, Fujiwara Y, Yoshikawa H (2019) Interindustry linkages of prices-analysis of Japan's deflation. Available at SSRN 3400573

Vodenska I, Aoyama H, Fujiwara Y, Iyetomi H, Arai Y (2016) Interdependencies and causalities in coupled financial networks. PloS one 11(3):e0150994

Chapter 12
An Interacting Agent Model of Economic Crisis

Yuichi Ikeda

Abstract Most national economies are linked by international trade. Consequently, economic globalization forms a massive and complex economic network with strong links, that is, interactions arising from increasing trade. Various interesting collective motions are expected to emerge from strong economic interactions in a global economy under trade liberalization. Among the various economic collective motions, economic crises are our most intriguing problem. In our previous studies, we have revealed that the Kuramoto's coupled limit-cycle oscillator model and the Ising-like spin model on networks are invaluable tools for characterizing the economic crises. In this study, we develop a mathematical theory to describe an interacting agent model that derives the coupled limit-cycle oscillator model and the Ising-like spin model by using appropriate approximations. Our interacting agent model suggests phase synchronization and spin ordering during economic crises. We confirm the emergence of the phase synchronization and spin ordering during economic crises by analyzing various economic time series data. We also develop a network reconstruction model based on entropy maximization that considers the sparsity of the network. Here network reconstruction means estimating a network's adjacency matrix from a node's local information. The interbank network is reconstructed using the developed model, and a comparison is made of the reconstructed network with the actual data. We successfully reproduce the interbank network and the known stylized facts. In addition, the exogenous shock acting on an industry community in a supply chain network and financial sector are estimated. Estimation of exogenous shocks acting on communities of in the real economy in the supply chain network provide evidence of the channels of distress propagating from the financial sector to the real economy through the supply chain network.

Y. Ikeda (✉)
Graduate School of Advanced Integrated Studies in Human Survivability, Kyoto University, Kyoto, Japan
e-mail: ikeda.yuichi.2w@kyoto-u.ac.jp

H. Aoyama et al. (eds.), *Complexity, Heterogeneity, and the Methods of Statistical Physics in Economics*, Evolutionary Economics and Social Complexity Science 22,
https://doi.org/10.1007/978-981-15-4806-2_12

Keywords Global economy · International trade · Economic crisis · Collective motion · Kuramoto model · Ising model · Network reconstruction · Interbank network · Supply chain network

12.1 Introduction

Most national economies are linked by international trade. Consequently, economic globalization forms a massive and complex economic network with strong links, that is, interactions due to increasing trade. In Japan, several small and medium enterprises would achieve higher economic growth by free trade based on the establishment of economic partnership agreement, such as the Trans-Pacific Partnership. Various collective motions exist in natural phenomena. For instance, a heavy nucleus that consists of a few hundred nucleons is largely deformed in a highly excited state and subsequently proceeds to nuclear fission. This phenomenon is a well-known example of quantum mechanical collective motion due to strong nuclear force between nucleons. From the analogy with the collective motions in natural phenomena, various interesting collective motions are expected to emerge because of strong economic interactions in a global economy under trade liberalization. Among the various economic collective motions, economic crises are our most intriguing problem.

12.1.1 Business Cycle

There have been several theoretical studies on the concept of the "business cycle" (Von Haberler 1937; Burns and Mitchell 1964; Granger and Hatanaka 1964). In recent times, the synchronization (Huygens 1966) of international business cycle as an example of the economic collective motion has attracted economists and physicists (Krugman 1996). Synchronization of business cycles across countries has been discussed using correlation coefficients between GDP time series (Stock and Watson 2005). However, this method remains only a primitive first step, and a more definitive analysis using a suitable quantity describing business cycles is needed. In an analysis of business cycles, an important question is the significance of individual (micro) versus aggregate (macro) shocks. Foerster et al. (2011) used factor analysis to show that the volatility of U.S. industrial production was largely explained by aggregate shocks and partly by cross-sectoral correlations from the individual shocks transformed through the trade linkage. The interdependent relationship of the global economy has become stronger because of the increase in international trade and investments (Tzekinaa et al. 2008; Barigozzi et al. 2011; He and Deem 2010; Piccardi and Tajoli 2012).

We took a different approach to analyze the shocks to explain the synchronization in international business cycles. We analyzed the quarterly GDP time series for

Australia, Canada, France, Italy, the United Kingdom, and the United States from Q2 1960 to Q1 2010 to determine the synchronization in international business cycles (Ikeda et al. 2013a). The followings results were obtained.

(1) The angular frequencies ω_i estimated using the Hilbert transform are almost identical for the six countries. Therefore, frequency entrainment is observed. Moreover, the phase locking indicator $\sigma(t)$ shows that partial phase locking is observed for the analyzed countries, representing direct evidence of synchronization in international business cycles.
(2) A coupled limit-cycle oscillator model was developed to explain the synchronization mechanism. A regression analysis showed that the model is a very good fit for the phase time series of the GDP growth rate. The validity of the model implies that the origin of the synchronization is the interaction resulting from international trade.
(3) We also showed that information from economic shocks is carried by phase time series $\theta_i(t)$. The comovement and individual shocks are separated using the random matrix theory. A natural interpretation of the individual shocks is that they are "technological shocks". The present analysis demonstrates that average phase fluctuations well explain business cycles, particularly recessions. Because it is highly unlikely that all of the countries are subject to common negative technological shocks, the results obtained suggest that pure "technological shocks" cannot explain business cycles.
(4) Finally, the obtained results suggest that business cycles may be understood as comovement dynamics described by the coupled limit-cycle oscillators exposed to random individual shocks. The interaction strength in the model became large in parallel with the increase in the amounts of exports and imports relative to GDP. Therefore, a significant part of comovements comes from international trade.

We observed various types of collective motions for economic dynamics, such as synchronization of business cycles (Ikeda et al. 2013a,b, 2014), on the massive complex economic network. The linkages among national economies play important roles in economic crises and during normal economic states. Once an economic crisis occurs in a certain country, the influence propagates instantaneously toward the rest of the world. For instance, the global economic crisis initiated by the bankruptcy of Lehman Brothers in 2008 is still fresh in our minds. The massive and complex global economic network might show characteristic collective motion during economic crises.

12.1.2 Economic Crisis

Numerous preceding studies attempted to explain the characteristics of stock market crash using spin variables in the econophysics literature. First, we note some content and mathematical descriptions from previous studies (Sornette et al. 2014; Bouchaud 2013). In particular, we note studies by Kaizoji and Sornette (Kaizoji et al. 2002; Kaizoji 2000; Bornholdt 2001; Sornette and Zhou 2006; Harras and Sornette 2011; Vikram and Sinha 2011; Johansen et al. 2000; Nadal et al. 2005) in which investor strategies (buy or sell) are modeled as spin variables, with stock prices varying depending on the differences in the number of spin-ups. In addition, the feedback effect on an investor's decision making through a neighbor's strategies can explain bubble formations and crashes. For instance, the temporal evolution is simulated by adding random components in Sornette and Zhou (2006). Most papers adopted two-state spin variables; however, the study by Vikram and Sinha (2011) adopted three-state spin variables. Note that the purpose of these studies was to reproduce the scaling law and not explain phase transitions.

In contrast, economics journals aim to explain the optimality of investors' decision making (Harras and Sornette 2011). In Nadal et al. (2005), phase transition is discussed, starting with discrete choice theory. Many papers have similar discussions on phase transitions, with slight variations in optimization and profit maximization. Although empirical studies using real data are relatively few, Wall Street market crash in 1929, 1962, and 1987 and the Hong Kong Stock Exchange crash in 1997 were studied in Johansen et al. (2000). Note that elaborate theoretical studies exist on phase transition effects on networks and the thermodynamics of networks (Aleksiejuk et al. 2002; Dorogovtsev et al. 2002, 2008; Ye et al. 2015). Furthermore, preceding studies on macroprudential policy exist that mainly focus on time series analyses of macroeconomic variables (Borio and Zhu 2012; Borio et al. 2014; Borio 2011).

Although the market crash is an important part of an economic crisis, our main interest is that the real economy consists of many industries in various countries. We analyzed industry-sector-specific international trade data to clarify the structure and dynamics of communities that consist of industry sectors in various countries linked by international trade (Ikeda et al. 2016). We applied conventional community analysis to each time slice of the international trade network data: the World Input Output Database. This database contains industry-sector-specific international trade data on 41 countries and 35 industry sectors from 1995 to 2011. Once the community structure was obtained for each year, the links between communities in adjoining years were identified using the Jaccard index as a similarity measure between communities in adjoining years.

The identified linked communities show that six backbone structures exist in the international trade network. The largest linked community is the Financial Intermediation sector and the Renting of Machines and Equipments sector in the United States and the United Kingdom. The second is the Mining and Quarrying sector in the rest of the world, Russia, Canada, and Australia. The third is the Basic Metals and Fabricated Metal sector in the rest of the world, Germany, Japan, and the United States. These community structures indicate that international trade is actively transacted among the same or similar industry sectors. Furthermore, the robustness of the observed community structure was confirmed by quantifying the variations in the information for perturbed network structure. The theoretical study conducted using a coupled limit-cycle oscillator model suggests that the interaction terms from international trade can be viewed as the origin of the synchronization.

The economic crisis of 2008 showed that the conventional microprudential policy to ensure the soundness of individual banks was not sufficient, and prudential regulations to cover the entire financial sector were desired. Such regulations attract increasing attention, and policies related to such regulations are called a macroprudential policy that aims to reduce systemic risk in the entire financial sector by regulating the relationship between the financial sector and the real economy. We studied channels of distress propagation from the financial sector to the real economy through the supply chain network in Japan from 1980 to 2015 using a Ising-like spin model on networks (Ikeda and Yoshikawa 2018). An estimation of exogenous shocks acting on communities of the real economy in the supply chain network provided evidence of channels of distress propagation from the financial sector to the real economy through the supply chain network. Causal networks between exogenous shocks and macroeconomic variables clarified the characteristics of the lead lag relationship between exogenous shocks and macroeconomic variables when the bubble bursts.

12.2 Interacting Agent Models

The coupled limit-cycle oscillator model and the Ising-like spin model on networks are invaluable tools to characterize an economic crisis, as described in Sect. 12.1. In this section, we develop a mathematical theory to describe an interacting agent model that derives the aforementioned two models using appropriate approximations.

12.2.1 Interacting Agent Model on Complex Network

12.2.1.1 Hamiltonian Dynamics

Our system consists of N company agents and M bank agents. The states of the agents are specified by multi-dimensional state vectors $\boldsymbol{q}_i$ and $\boldsymbol{q}_j$ for companies and banks, respectively. If we consider (1) security indicators: (1-1) total common equity divided by total assets and (1-2) fixed assets divided by total common equity; (2) profitability indicators: (2-1) operating income divided by total assets and (2-2) operating income divided by total revenue; (3) capital efficiency indicator: total revenue divided by total assets, and (4) growth indicator: operating income at time t divided by operating income at time $t-1$ as variables to the soundness of companies, state vectors $\boldsymbol{q}_i$ are expressed in six dimensional space. The agents interact in the following way:

$$H_{\mathrm{int}}(\boldsymbol{q}) = -\sum_{i\in C} \boldsymbol{H}_{C,i}\boldsymbol{q}_i - \sum_{j\in B} \boldsymbol{H}_{B,j}\boldsymbol{q}_j - J_C \sum_{i\in C, j\in C} a_{ij}\boldsymbol{q}_i\boldsymbol{q}_j - J_{CB} \sum_{i\in C, j\in B} b_{ij}\boldsymbol{q}_i\boldsymbol{q}_j, \tag{12.1}$$

where H_C, H_B, J_C, J_{CB}, a_{ij}, and b_{ij} represent the exogenous shock acting on companies, the exogenous shock acting on banks, the strength of the inter-company interactions, the strength of company-bank interactions, the adjacent matrix of the supply chain network, and the adjacent matrix of the bank to company lending network, respectively. The Hamiltonian $H(\boldsymbol{q}, \boldsymbol{p})$ of the system is the sum of the kinetic energy of th e companies (the first term), the kinetic energy of the banks (the second term), and the interaction potential $H_{\text{int}}(\boldsymbol{q})$:

$$H(\boldsymbol{q}, \boldsymbol{p}) = \sum_{i \in C} \frac{\boldsymbol{p}_i^2}{2m} + \sum_{j \in B} \frac{\boldsymbol{p}_j^2}{2m} + H_{\text{int}}(\boldsymbol{q}), \tag{12.2}$$

where $\boldsymbol{p}_i$ and m are the multi-dimensional momentum vector and the mass of agent i. Here, we set $m = 1$ without loss of generality. We obtain the canonical equations of motion for agent i:

$$\frac{\partial H(\boldsymbol{q}, \boldsymbol{p})}{\partial \boldsymbol{p}_i} = \dot{\boldsymbol{q}}_i, \tag{12.3}$$

$$\frac{\partial H(\boldsymbol{q}, \boldsymbol{p})}{\partial \boldsymbol{q}_i} = -\dot{\boldsymbol{p}}_i. \tag{12.4}$$

From Eq. (12.3), we obtain

$$\frac{\boldsymbol{p}_i}{m} = \dot{\boldsymbol{q}}_i. \tag{12.5}$$

By substituting Eq. (12.5) into Eq. (12.4), we obtain the equation of motion of the company agent i:

$$\ddot{\boldsymbol{q}}_i = \boldsymbol{H}_{C,i} + J_C \sum_{j \in C} \left(a_{ij} + a_{ji}\right) \boldsymbol{q}_j + J_{CB} \sum_{j \in B} b_{ij} \boldsymbol{q}_j, \tag{12.6}$$

and the equation of motion of bank agent j:

$$\ddot{\boldsymbol{q}}_j = \boldsymbol{H}_{B,j} + J_{CB} \sum_{i \in C} b_{ij} \boldsymbol{q}_i. \tag{12.7}$$

12.2.1.2 Langevin Dynamics

Hamiltonian dynamics are applicable to a system in which its total energy is conserved. However, to be noted is that the economic system is open and no quantity is conserved accurately. Considering this point, we add a term for constant energy inflow $\boldsymbol{P}_i$ and a term for energy dissipation outside the system $-\alpha\dot{\boldsymbol{q}}_i$ to the equation of motion for company agent i in Eq. (12.6):

$$\ddot{\boldsymbol{q}}_i = \boldsymbol{P}_i - \alpha\dot{\boldsymbol{q}}_i + \boldsymbol{H}_{C,i} + J_C \sum_{j\in C} \left(a_{ij} + a_{ji}\right) \boldsymbol{q}_j + J_{CB} \sum_{j\in B} b_{ij}\boldsymbol{q}_j, \tag{12.8}$$

where we assume that energy dissipation is proportional to the velocity of agent $\dot{\boldsymbol{q}}_i$. The stochastic differential equation in Eq. (12.8) is called the Langevin equation.

Similarly, way, we obtain the Langevin equation for bank agent j:

$$\ddot{\boldsymbol{q}}_j = \boldsymbol{P}'_j - \alpha'\dot{\boldsymbol{q}}_j + \boldsymbol{H}_{B,j} + J_{CB} \sum_{i\in C} b_{ij}\boldsymbol{q}_i, \tag{12.9}$$

If a system's inertia is very large and thus $\ddot{\boldsymbol{q}}_i \simeq 0$, we obtain the following first order stochastic differential equation for company agent i:

$$\dot{\boldsymbol{q}}_i = \frac{\boldsymbol{P}_i}{\alpha} + \frac{\boldsymbol{H}_{C,i}}{\alpha} + \frac{J_C}{\alpha} \sum_{j\in C} \left(a_{ij} + a_{ji}\right) \boldsymbol{q}_j + \frac{J_{CB}}{\alpha} \sum_{j\in B} b_{ij}\boldsymbol{q}_j. \tag{12.10}$$

Similarly, we obtain the first order stochastic differential equation for bank agent j:

$$\dot{\boldsymbol{q}}_j = \frac{\boldsymbol{P}'_j}{\alpha'} + \frac{\boldsymbol{H}_{B,j}}{\alpha'} + \frac{J_{CB}}{\alpha'} \sum_{i\in C} b_{ij}\boldsymbol{q}_i. \tag{12.11}$$

12.2.2 *Ising Model with Exogenous Shock*

12.2.2.1 Underlying Approximated Picture

Suppose that $\boldsymbol{q}_i$ is a one dimensional variable, and we assume that magnitude $|q_i|$ varies slowly compared with orientation s_i. We approximate the magnitude as $|q_i| \approx$ $const.$ and obtain:

$$s_i = \mathrm{sgn}\frac{q_i}{|q_i|}, \tag{12.12}$$

$$\frac{\partial}{\partial q_i} = \frac{\partial}{\partial s_i}\frac{\partial s_i}{\partial q_i} = \frac{1}{|q_i|}\frac{\partial}{\partial s_i}. \tag{12.13}$$

12.2.2.2 Derived Model

Stock price $x_{i,t}(i = 1, \cdots, N(or M), t = 1, \cdots, T)$ is assumed to be a surrogate variable to indicate the soundness of companies or banks. The one-dimensional spin variable $s_{i,t}$ was estimated from the log return of daily stock prices, $r_{i,t}$:

$$s_{i,t} = +1 \quad \left(q_{i,t} = \log x_{i,t} - \log x_{i,t-1} \geq 0\right) \tag{12.14}$$

$$s_{i,t} = -1 \quad \left(q_{i,t} = \log x_{i,t} - \log x_{i,t-1} < 0\right) \tag{12.15}$$

Here spin-up: $s_{i,t} = +1$ indicates that company i is in good condition; on spin-down: $s_{i,t} = -1$ indicates that company i is in bad condition. The macroscopic order parameter $M_t = \sum_i s_{i,t}$ is an indicator of the soundness of the macro economy, which is regarded as an extreme simplification to capture the soundness of the economy. In addition to this simplification, spin variables include noise information because we have various distortions in the stock market caused by irrational investor decision making. The spin variables of companies interact with the spins of other companies through the supply chain network and interact with banks through the lending network. Those interactions between companies and banks are mathematically expressed as Hamiltonian. A Hamiltonian is written as follows:

$$H_{\text{int}}(s) = -H_C \sum_{i \in C} s_{i,t} - H_B \sum_{i \in B} s_{i,t} - J_C \sum_{i \in C, j \in C} a_{ij} s_{i,t} s_{j,t} - J_{CB} \sum_{i \in C, j \in B} a_{ij} s_{i,t} s_{j,t} \tag{12.16}$$

where H_C and H_B are the exogenous shocks acting on companies and banks, respectively. a_{ij} represents the elements of adjacency matrix A of the supply chain network that is treated as a binary directed network.

When spins are exposed for exogenous shock H_{ext}, an effective shock of

$$H_{\text{eff}} = H_{\text{ext}} + H_{\text{int}} \tag{12.17}$$

acts on each spin. By calculating interaction H_{int} of the Hamiltonian of Eq. (12.16), exogenous shock H_{ext} was estimated by considering the nearest neighbor companies in the supply chain network

$$\frac{M_t}{N\mu} = \tanh\left(\frac{\mu H_{\text{ext}}}{kT} + \frac{J}{kT}\frac{\sum_{ij}(a_{ij} + a_{ji})s_{i,t}}{N}\mu\right) \tag{12.18}$$

where T represents temperature as a measure of the activeness of the economy, which is considered proportional to GDP per capita. We note that supply chain network data are a prerequisite condition for estimating exogenous shock H_{ext}.

In the current model, the interactions between banks

$$\sum_{i \in B, j \in B} J_{BB} t_{ij} s_{i,t} s_{j,t} \tag{12.19}$$

were ignored because of a lack of data for interbank network t_{ij}. This lack of data caused by the central bank not making public the data on transactions between banks. A method to reconstruct the interbank network is described in Sect. 12.3.

12.2.3 *Kuramoto Model with Exogenous Shock*

12.2.3.1 Underlying Approximated Picture

When $\boldsymbol{q}_i$ is a two-dimensional variable, we treat this quantity as if it is a complex variable. We assume that amplitude $|\boldsymbol{q}_i|$ varies slowly compared with phase θ_i. We approximate the amplitude as $|\boldsymbol{q}_i| \approx const.$ and, thus, obtain:

$$\boldsymbol{q}_i = |\boldsymbol{q}_i| e^{i\theta_i}, \tag{12.20}$$

$$\frac{\partial}{\partial \boldsymbol{q}_i} = \frac{\partial}{\partial \theta_i} \frac{\partial \theta_i}{\partial \boldsymbol{q}_i}. \tag{12.21}$$

12.2.3.2 Derived Model

The business cycle is observed in most industrialized economies. Economists have studied this phenomenon by means of mathematical models, including various types of linear, nonlinear, and coupled oscillator models.

Interdependence, or coupling, between industries in the business cycle has been studied for more than half a century. A study of the linkages between markets and industries using nonlinear difference equations suggests a dynamical coupling among industries (Goodwin 1947). A nonlinear oscillator model of the business cycle was then developed using a nonlinear accelerator as the generation mechanism (Goodwin 1951). We stress the necessity of nonlinearity because linear models are unable to reproduce sustained cyclical behavior, and tend to either die out or diverge to infinity.

However, a simple linear economic model, based on ordinary economic principles, optimization behavior, and rational expectations, can produce cyclical behavior much like that found in business cycles (Long and Plosser 1983). An important question aside from synchronization in the business cycle is whether sectoral or aggregate shocks are responsible for the observed cycle. This question was empirically examined; it was found that business cycle fluctuations are caused by small sectoral shocks, rather than by large common shocks (Long and Plosser 1987).

As the third model category, coupled oscillators were developed to study noisy oscillating processes such as national economies (Anderson and Ramsey 1999; Selover et al. 2003). Simulations and empirical analyses showed that synchronization between the business cycles of different countries is consistent with such mode-locking behavior. Along this line of approach, a nonlinear mode-locking mechanism was further studied that described a synchronized business cycle between different industrial sectors (Sussmuth 2003).

Many collective synchronization phenomena are known in physical and biological systems (Strogatz 2000). Physical examples include clocks hanging on a wall, an array of lasers, microwave oscillators, and Josephson junctions. Biological examples include synchronously flashing fireflies, networks of pacemaker cells in the heart, and metabolic synchrony in yeast cell suspensions.

Kuramoto established the coupled limit-cycle oscillator model to explain this wide variety of synchronization phenomena (Kuramoto 1975; Strogatz 2000; Acebron et al. 2005). In the Kuramoto model, the dynamics of the oscillators are governed by

$$\dot{\theta}_i = \omega_i + \sum_{j=1}^{N} k_{ji} \sin(\theta_j - \theta_i), \tag{12.22}$$

where θ_i, ω_i, and k_{ji} are the oscillator phase, the natural frequency, and the coupling strength, respectively. If the coupling strength k_{ij} exceeds a certain threshold that equals the natural frequency ω_i, the system exhibits synchronization.

By explicitly writing amplitude $|q_i|$ and phase θ_i, the third term of the R.H.S. in Eq. (12.1) is rewritten as follows:

$$J_C \sum_{i \in C, j \in C} a_{ij} \boldsymbol{q}_i \boldsymbol{q}_j = J_C \sum_{i \in C, j \in C} a_{ij} |\boldsymbol{q}_j| |\boldsymbol{q}_i| \cos(\theta_j - \theta_i). \tag{12.23}$$

The spatial derivative of Eq. (12.23) is obtained:

$$\begin{aligned} \frac{\partial}{\partial \boldsymbol{q}_i} J_C \sum_{i \in C, j \in C} a_{ij} \boldsymbol{q}_i \boldsymbol{q}_j &= \frac{\partial \theta_i}{\partial \boldsymbol{q}_i} \frac{\partial}{\partial \theta_i} J_C \sum_{i \in C, j \in C} a_{ij} |\boldsymbol{q}_j| |\boldsymbol{q}_i| \cos(\theta_j - \theta_i) \\ &= \frac{\partial \theta_i}{\partial \boldsymbol{q}_i} J_C \sum_{j \in C} \left(a_{ij} + a_{ji} \right) |\boldsymbol{q}_j| |\boldsymbol{q}_i| \sin(\theta_j - \theta_i). \end{aligned} \tag{12.24}$$

By substituting Eq. (12.24) into the stochastic differential equation for company agent i of Eq. (12.10), we obtain the following equation:

$$\begin{aligned} \frac{\partial \boldsymbol{q}_i}{\partial \theta_i} \frac{d\theta_i}{dt} &= \frac{\boldsymbol{P}_i}{\alpha} + \frac{\boldsymbol{H}_{C,i}}{\alpha} \\ &\quad + \frac{J_C}{\alpha} \frac{\partial \theta_i}{\partial \boldsymbol{q}_i} \sum_{j \in C} \left(a_{ij} + a_{ji} \right) |\boldsymbol{q}_j| |\boldsymbol{q}_i| \sin(\theta_j - \theta_i) \\ &\quad + \frac{J_{CB}}{\alpha} \frac{\partial \theta_i}{\partial \boldsymbol{q}_i} \sum_{j \in B} b_{ij} |\boldsymbol{q}_j| |\boldsymbol{q}_i| \sin(\theta_j - \theta_i). \end{aligned} \tag{12.25}$$

Consequently, we obtain the stochastic differential equation, which is equivalent to the Kuramoto model of Eq. (12.22) with an additional exogenous shock term:

$$\begin{aligned}\frac{d\theta_i}{dt} &= \frac{1}{|\boldsymbol{q}_i|^2}\left(\frac{\boldsymbol{P}_i}{\alpha} + \frac{\boldsymbol{H}_{C,i}}{\alpha}\right)\frac{\partial \boldsymbol{q}_i}{\partial \theta_i} \\ &+ \frac{J_C}{\alpha}\sum_{j\in C}(a_{ij} + a_{ji})\frac{|\boldsymbol{q}_j|}{|\boldsymbol{q}_i|}\sin(\theta_j - \theta_i) \\ &+ \frac{J_{CB}}{\alpha}\sum_{j\in B} b_{ij}\frac{|\boldsymbol{q}_j|}{|\boldsymbol{q}_i|}\sin(\theta_j - \theta_i).\end{aligned} \tag{12.26}$$

12.3 Network Reconstruction

Network reconstruction estimates a network's adjacency matrix from a node's local information. We developed a network reconstruction model based on entropy maximization and considering network sparsity.

12.3.1 Existing Models

12.3.1.1 MaxEnt Algorithm

The MaxEnt algorithm maximizes entropy S by changing t_{ij} under the given total lending s_i^{out} and the total borrowing s_i^{in} for bank i (Wells 2004; Upper 2011). The analytical solution of this algorithm is easily obtained as

$$t_{ij}^{ME} = \frac{s_i^{\text{out}} s_j^{\text{in}}}{G}, \tag{12.27}$$

$$G = \sum_i s_i^{\text{out}} = \sum_j s_j^{\text{in}}. \tag{12.28}$$

However, noted is that the solution to Eq. (12.27) provides a fully connected network, although real-world networks are often known as sparse networks.

12.3.1.2 Iterative Proportional Fitting

Iterative proportional fitting (IPF) has been introduced to correct the dense property of t_{ij}^{ME} at least partially. By minimizing the Kullback-Leibler divergence between a generic nonnegative t_{ij} with null diagonal entries and the MaxEnt solution t_{ij}^{ME} in

Eq. (12.27), we obtain t_{ij}^{IPF} (Squartini 2018):

$$\min\left(\sum_{ij(i\neq j)} t_{ij}\ln\frac{t_{ij}}{t_{ij}^{ME}}\right)=\sum_{ij(i\neq j)} t_{ij}^{IPF}\ln\frac{t_{ij}^{IPF}}{t_{ij}^{ME}}. \tag{12.29}$$

The solution t_{ij}^{IPF} has null diagonal elements, but does show the sparsity equivalent to real-world networks.

12.3.1.3 Drehmann and Tarashev Approach

Starting from the MaxEnt matrix t_{ij}^{ME}, a sparse network is obtained in the following three steps (Drehmann and Tarashev 2013): First, choose a random set of off-diagonal elements to be zero. Second, treat the remaining nonzero elements as random variables distributed uniformly between zero and twice their MaxEnt estimated value $t_{ij}^{DT} \sim U(0, 2t_{ij}^{ME})$. Therefore, the expected value of weights under this distribution coincides with the MaxEnt matrix t_{ij}^{ME}. Third, the IPF algorithm is run to correctly restore the value of the total lending s_i^{out} and the total borrowing s_i^{in}. However, note that we need to specify the set of off-diagonal nonzero elements. Therefore, accurate sparsity does not emerge spontaneously in this approach.

12.3.2 Ridge Entropy Maximization Model

12.3.2.1 Convex Optimization

We develop a reconstruction model for the economic network and apply it to the interbank network in which nodes and links are banks and lending or borrowing amounts, respectively. First, we maximize configuration entropy S under the given total lending s_i^{out} and total borrowing s_i^{in} for bank i.

Configuration entropy S is written using bilateral transaction t_{ij} between bank i and j as follows,

$$S=\log\frac{\left(\sum_{ij} t_{ij}\right)!}{\prod_{ij} t_{ij}!}\approx\left(\sum_{ij} t_{ij}\right)\log\left(\sum_{ij} t_{ij}\right)-\sum_{ij} t_{ij}\log t_{ij}. \tag{12.30}$$

Here, an approximation is applied to the factorial ! using Stirling's formula. The first term of the R.H.S. of Eq. (12.30) does not change the value of S by changing t_{ij} because $\sum_{ij} t_{ij}$ is constant. Consequently, we have a convex objective function:

$$S=-\sum_{ij} t_{ij}\log t_{ij}. \tag{12.31}$$

Entropy S is to be maximized with the following constraints:

$$s_i^{\text{out}} = \sum_j t_{ij}, \tag{12.32}$$

$$s_j^{\text{in}} = \sum_i t_{ij}, \tag{12.33}$$

$$G = \sum_{ij} t_{ij}. \tag{12.34}$$

Here, constraints Eq. (12.32) and Eq. (12.33) correspond to local information about each node.

12.3.2.2 Sparse Modeling

The accuracy of the reconstruction will be improved using the sparsity of the interbank network. We have two different types of sparsity here. The first is characterized by the skewness of the observed bilateral transaction distributions. The second type of sparsity is characterized by the skewness of the observed in-degree and out-degree distributions. Therefore, a limited fraction of nodes have a large number of links, and most nodes have a small number of links. Consequently, the adjacency matrix of international trade is sparse.

To take into account the first type of sparsity, the objective function of Eq. (12.31) is modified by applying the concept of Lasso (least absolute shrinkage and selection operator) (Tibshirani 1996; Breiman 1995; Hastie et al. 2001) to our convex optimization problem.

By considering this fact, our problem is reformulated as the maximization of objective function z:

$$z(t_{ij}) = S - \sum_{ij} t_{ij}^2 = -\sum_{ij} t_{ij} \log t_{ij} - \beta \sum_{ij} t_{ij}^2 \tag{12.35}$$

with local constraints. Here the second term of R.H.S. of Eq. (12.35) is L2 regularization.

12.3.2.3 Ridge Entropy Maximization Model

In the theory of thermodynamics, a system's equilibrium is obtained by minimizing thermodynamic potential F:

$$F = E - TS \tag{12.36}$$

where E, T, and S are internal energy, temperature, and entropy, respectively. Equation (12.36) is rewritten as a maximization problem as follows:

$$z \equiv -\frac{1}{T}F = S - \frac{1}{T}E. \tag{12.37}$$

We note that Eq. (12.37) has the same structure as Eq. (12.35). Thus, we interpret the meaning of control parameter β and L2 regularization as inverse temperature and internal energy, respectively. In summary, we have a ridge entropy maximization model (Ikeda and Iyetomi 2018; Ikeda and Takeda 2020):

$$\begin{aligned}
\text{maximize} \quad & z(p_{ij}) = -\textstyle\sum_{ij} p_{ij} \log p_{ij} - \beta \sum_{ij} p_{ij}^2 \\
\text{subject to} \quad & G = \textstyle\sum_{ij} t_{ij} \\
& \tfrac{s_i^{\text{out}}}{G} = \textstyle\sum_j \tfrac{t_{ij}}{G} = \sum_j p_{ij} \\
& \tfrac{s_j^{\text{in}}}{G} = \textstyle\sum_i \tfrac{t_{ij}}{G} = \sum_i p_{ij} \\
& t_{ij} \geq 0
\end{aligned} \tag{12.38}$$

12.4 Empirical Validation of Models

The model described in Sect. 12.2 suggests the phase synchronization and the spin ordering during an economic crisis. In this section, we confirm the phase synchronization and the spin ordering by analyizing varilous economic time series data. In addition, the exogenous shock acting on an industry community in a supply chain network and the financial sector are estimated. An estimation of exogenous shocks acting on communities of the real economy in the supply chain network provided evidence of the channels of distress propagation from the financial sector to the real economy through the supply chain network. Finally, we point out that the interactions between banks were ignored in the interacting agent model explained in Sect. 12.2.2 given a lack of transaction data t_{ij} in an interbank network. This lack of data is caused by the central bank not making public the data on transactions between banks. In this section, the interbank network is reconstructed and the reconstructed network is compared with the actual data and the known stylized facts.

12.4.1 Phase Synchronization and Spin Ordering During Economic Crises

We evaluated the phase time series of the growth rate of value added for 1435 nodes (41 countries and 35 industry sectors) from 1995 to 2011 in the World Input Output Database using the Hilbert transform and then estimated the order parameters of the phase synchronization for communities (Ikeda et al. 2016). The order parameter of the phase synchronization is defined by

$$u(t) = r(t)e^{i\phi(t)} = \frac{1}{N}\sum_{j=1}^{N} e^{i\theta_j(t)}. \tag{12.39}$$

The respective amplitude for the order parameter of each community was observed to be greater than the amplitude for all sectors. Therefore, active trade produces higher phase coherence within each community. The temporal change in amplitude for the order parameters for each community are shown in Fig. 12.1 from 1996 to 2011. Phase coherence decreased gradually in the late 1990s but increased sharply in 2002. From 2002, the amplitudes for the order parameter remained relatively high. In particular, from 2002 to 2004, and from 2006 to 2008, we observe high phase coherence. The first period was right after the dot-com crash and lasted from March

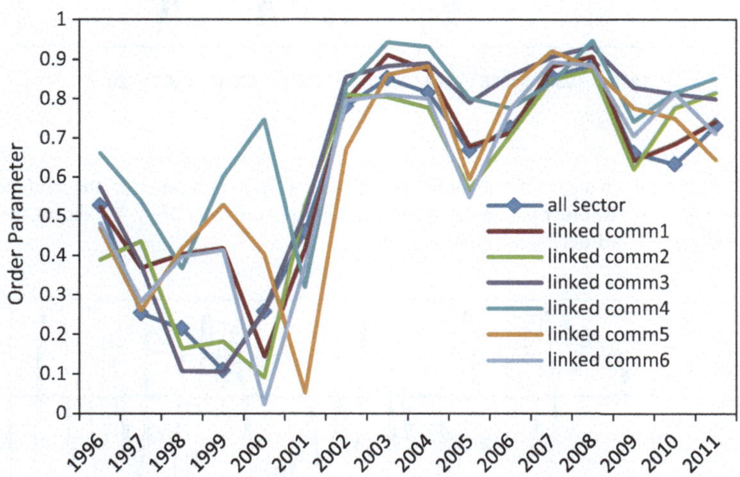

Fig. 12.1 Temporal change in amplitude for the order parameters $r(t)$ of phase synchonization for each community: We applied a conventional community analysis to each time slice of the international trade network data: the World Input Output Database. This database contains the industry-sector-specific international trade data on 41 countries and 35 industry sectors from 1995 to 2011. Once the community structure was obtained for each year, the links between communities in adjoining years was identified by using the Jaccard index as a similarity measure between communities in adjoining years

2000 to October 2002. The second period corresponds to the subprime mortgage crisis that occurred between December 2007 and early 2009. These results are consistent with the results obtained in the previous study (Ikeda et al. 2013a).

The stock price is the daily time series for the period from January 1, 1980 to December 31, 2015. The spin variable $s_{i,t}$ was estimated using Eqs. (12.14) and (12.15). The order parameters of spin ordering are defined by:

$$M_{C,t} = \sum_{i \in C} s_{i,t}. \tag{12.40}$$

$$M_{B,t} = \sum_{i \in B} s_{i,t}. \tag{12.41}$$

for the real economy and the financial sector, respectively. Temporal changes in the order parameter of spin ordering for the real economy (companies) and the financial sector (banks) are shown in Figs. 12.2 and 12.3, respectively. The symbols in Figs.

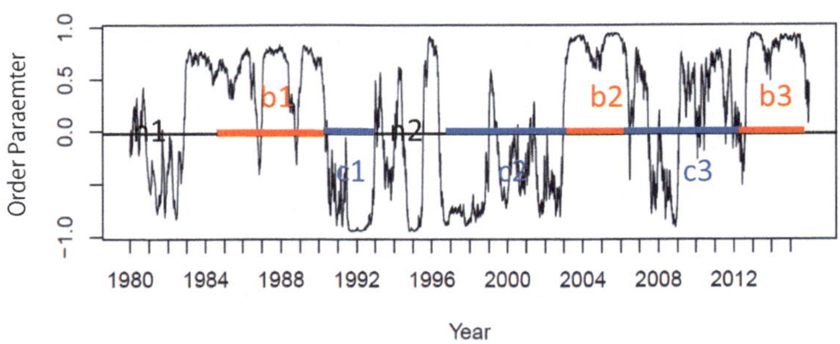

Fig. 12.2 Temporal changes of the order parameter of spin ordering for the real economy (companies) $M_C(t)$: The order parameter shows the high spin ordering $M_{C,t} \approx 1$ during the bubble periods, and $M_{C,t} \approx -1$ during the crisis periods

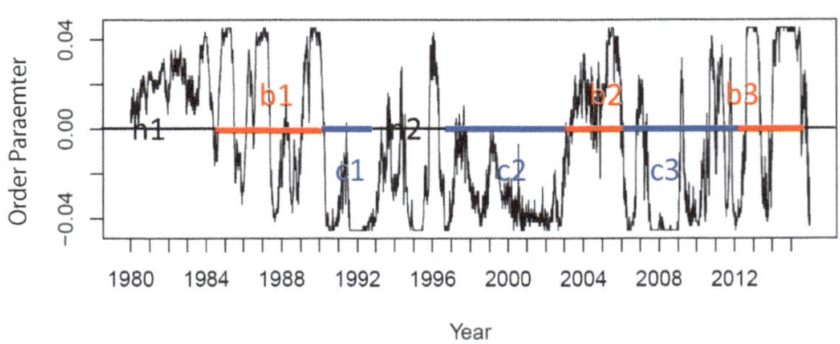

Fig. 12.3 Temporal changes of the order parameter of spin ordering for financial sector (banks) $M_B(t)$: The order parameter shows the high spin ordering $M_{B,t} \approx 1$ during the bubble periods, and $M_{B,t} \approx -1$ during the crisis periods

n1, b1, c1, n2, c2, b2, c3, and b3 show "Normal period: 1980–1985", "Bubble period: 1985–1989", "Asset bubble crisis: 1989–1993", "Normal period: 1993–1997", "Financial crisis: 1997–2003", "Bubble period: 2003–2006", "US subprime loan crisis and the Great East Japan Earthquake: 2006–2012", and "BOJ monetary easing: 2013–present", respectively. The order parameters shows high spin ordering $M_{C,t} \approx M_{B,t} \approx 1$ during the bubble periods, and $M_{C,t} \approx M_{B,t} \approx -1$ during the crisis periods.

In Fig. 12.1, we note that the phase synchronization was observed between 2002 and 2004, and between 2006 and 2008. For these periods, the high spin ordering was observed in Figs. 12.2 and 12.3. The phase synchronization and high spin ordering are explained by the Kuramoto and Ising models, respectively, and are interpreted as the collective motions in an economy. This observation of the phase synchronization and high spin ordering in the same period supports the validity of the interacting agent models explained in Sect. 12.2.

12.4.2 Estimation of Exogenous Shock

Exogenous shocks were estimated using Eq. (12.18), and the major mode of an exogenous shock was extracted by eliminating shocks smaller than 90% of the maximal or the minimal shock. The major mode of exogenous shock acting on the financial sector is shown in Fig. 12.4. The obtained exogenous shock acting on the financial sector indicates large negative shocks at the beginnings of c1 (1989) and c2 (1997) but no large negative shock during period c3 (2008). Therefore, the effect of the U.S. subprime loan crisis on the Japanese economy was introduced through shocks to the real economy (e.g., the sudden decrease of exports to the United States), not through direct shocks in the financial sector.

The major mode of an exogenous shock acting on the community, which consists of construction, transportation equipment, and precision machinery sectors, is shown in Fig. 12.5. For this community, no large negative shock was obtained at

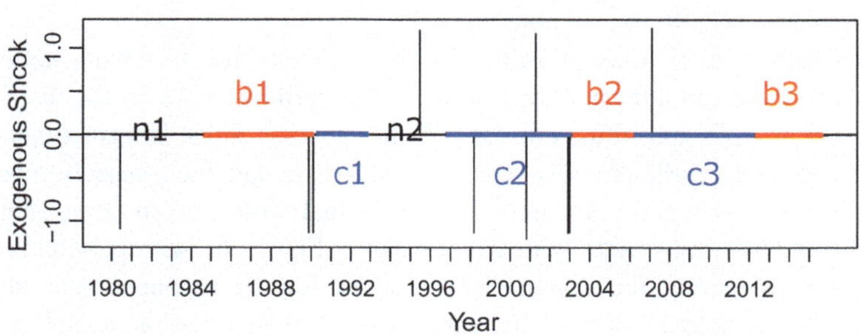

Fig. 12.4 Major mode of exogenous shock acting on the financial sector: The obtained exogenous shock acting on the financial sector indicates large negative shocks at the beginnings of c1 (1989) and c2 (1997), but no large negative shock during period c3 (2008)

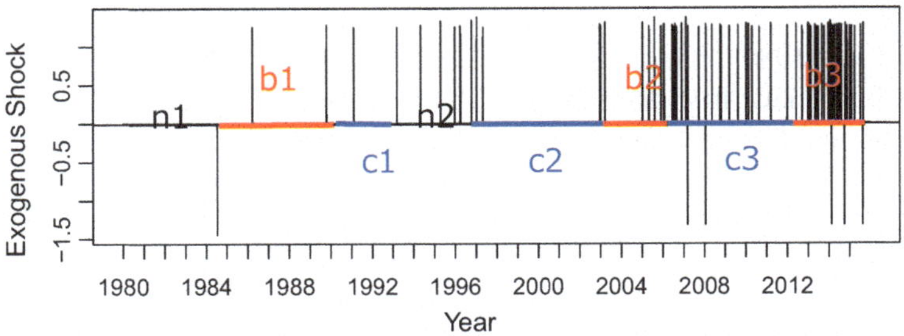

Fig. 12.5 Major mode of exogenous shock acting on the community, which consists of the construction, transportation equipment, and precision machinery sectors: The obtained exogenous shock acting on these sectors indicates no large negative shock at the beginnings of c1 (1989) and c2 (1997), but show a large negative shock during period c3 (2008)

the beginnings of c1 (1989) and c2 (1997). In Fig. 12.2, we note that $M_{C,t} \approx 1$ is observed for this real economy community at the beginnings of c1 (1989) and c2 (1997). This observation is interpreted as the existence of channels of distress propagation from the financial sector to the real economy through the supply chain network in Japan. We observe a negative but insignificant exogenous shock on the real economy at the beginning of the U.S. subprime loan crisis (c3).

12.4.3 Reconstruction of Interbank Network

The interbank network in Japan was reconstructed using the ridge entropy maximization model in Eq. (12.38). The number of banks in each category is 5, 59, 3, and 31 for major commercial bank, leading regional bank, trust bank, and second-tier regional bank, respectively. Call loan s_i^{out} of bank i and call money s_j^{in} of bank j are taken from each bank's balance sheet and are provided as constraints of the model. In addition to the banks, a slack variable is incorporated into the model to balance the aggregated call loan and the aggregated call money. In the objective function in Eqs. (12.38), we assumed $\beta = 15$.

The distribution of transaction t_{ij} for the reconstructed interbank network in 2005 is shown in the left panel of Fig. 12.6. The leftmost peak in the distribution is regarded as zero and, thus, corresponds to spurious links. Transactions t_{ij} for the reconstructed interbank network were used to calculate the transaction between four bank categories and compared with the actual values taken from Table 4 in (Imakubo and Soejima 2010). In the right panel of Fig. 12.6, a comparison is shown of transactions among four categories of banks for the reconstructed interbank network and the actual values. This comparison confirms that the accuracy of the reconstruction model is acceptably good.

For the reconstructed interbank network, we obtain the following characteristics, which are consistent with the previously known stylized facts: the short path

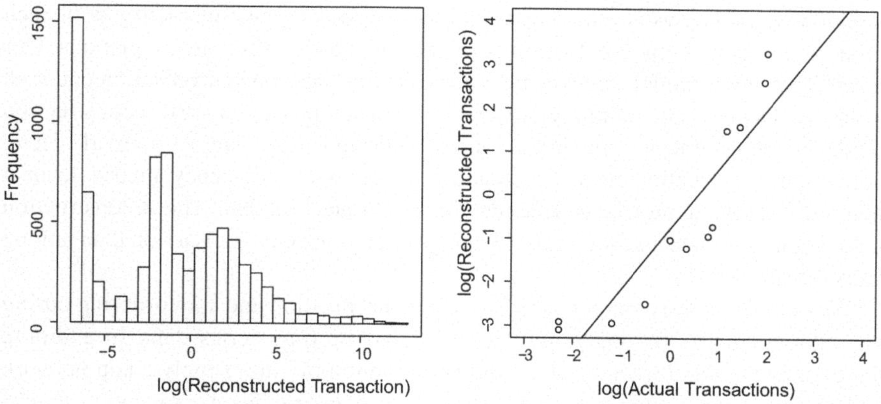

Fig. 12.6 Distribution of transactions t_{ij} for the reconstructed interbank network in 2005 is shown in the left panel. A comparison of transactions between four categories of banks for the reconstructed interbank network and the actual values is shown in the right panel

length, the small clustering coefficient, the disassortative property, and the core and peripheral structure. Community analysis shows that the number of communities is two to three in a normal period and one during an economic crisis (2003, 2008–2013). The major nodes in each community have been the major commercial banks. Since 2013, the major commercial banks have lost the average PageRank, and the leading regional banks have obtained both the average degree and the average PageRank. This observed changing role of banks is considered to be the result of the quantitative and qualitative monetary easing policy started by the Bank of Japan in April 2013.

12.5 Conclusions

Most national economies are linked by international trade. Consequently, economic globalization forms a massive and complex economic network with strong links, that is, interactions resulting from increasing trade. From the analogy of collective motions in natural phenomena, various interesting collective motions are expected to emerge from strong economic interactions in the global economy under trade liberalization. Among various economic collective motions, the economic crisis is our most intriguing problem.

We revealed in our previous studies that Kuramoto's coupled limit-cycle oscillator model and the Ising-like spin model on networks were invaluable tools for characterizing economic crises. In this study, we developed a mathematical theory to describe an interacting agent model that derives these two models using appropriate approximations. We have a clear understanding of the theoretical relationship between the Kuramoto model and the Ising-like spin model on networks. The model describes a system that has company and bank agents interacting with each other under exogenous shocks using coupled stochastic differential equations. Our interacting agent model suggests the emergence of phase synchronization and spin ordering during an economic crisis. We also developed a network reconstruction model based on entropy maximization considering the sparsity of network. Here, network reconstruction means estimating a network's adjacency matrix from a node's local information taken from the financial statement data. This reconstruction model is needed because the central bank has yet to provide transaction data among banks to the public.

We confirmed the emergence of phase synchronization and spin ordering during an economic crisis by analyzing various economic time series data. In addition, the exogenous shocks acting on an industry community in a supply chain network and the financial sector were estimated. The major mode of exogenous shocks acting on a community, which consists of construction, transportation equipment, and precision machinery sectors was estimated. For this community, no large negative shock was obtained during the crises beginning in 1989 and 1997. However, negative spin ordering is observed for this real economy community during crises beginning in 1989 and 1997. Estimation of exogenous shocks acting on communities of the real economy in the supply chain network provided evidence of channels of distress propagation from the financial sector to the real economy through the supply chain network.

Finally, we pointed out that, in our interacting agent model, interactions among banks were ignored because of the lack of transaction data in the interbank network. The interbank network was reconstructed using the developed model, and the reconstructed network and the actual data were compared. We successfully reproduce the interbank network and the known stylized facts.

References

Acebron JA, Bonilla LL, Vicente CJP, Ritort F, Spigler R (2005) The Kuramoto model: a simple paradigm for synchronization phenomena. Rev Mode Phys 77:137–185

Aleksiejuk A, Holyst JA, Stauer D (2002) Ferromagnetic phase transition in Barabasi-Albert networks. Phys A 310:260–266

Anderson HM, Ramsey JB (1999) U.S. and Canadian industrial production indices as coupled oscillators. Economic research reports PR # 99–01, New York University

Barigozzi M, Fagiolo G, Garlaschelli D (2010) Multinetwork of international trade: a commodity-specific analysis. Phys Rev E 81:046104

Barigozzi M, Fagiolo G, Mangionic G (2011) Identifying the community structure of the international-trade multi-network. Phys A 390:2051–2066

Borio C (2011) Implementing the macro-prudential approach to financial regulation and supervision. In: Green CJ (eds) The financial crisis and the regulation of finance. Edward Elgar, Cheltenham/Northhampton, pp 101–117

Borio C, Zhu H (2012) Capital regulation, risk-taking and monetary policy: a missing link in the transmission mechanism? J Financ Stab 8(4):236–251

Borio C, Drehmann M, Tsatsaronis K (2014) Stress-testing macro stress testing: does it live up to expectations? J Financ Stab 12:3–15

Bornholdt S (2001) Expectation bubbles in a spin model of markets: intermittency from frustration across scales. Int J Mod Phys C 12(05):667–674

Bouchaud JP (2013) Crises and collective socio-economic phenomena: simple models and challenges. J Stat Phys 151(3–4):567–606

Breiman L (1995) Better subset regression using the nonnegative garrote. Technometrics 37:373–84. https://doi.org/10.2307/1269730

Burns AF, Mitchell WC (1964) Measuring business cycles, national bureau of economic research. (Studies in business cycles; 2)

Dorogovtsev SN, Goltsev AV, Mendes JFF (2002) Ising model on networks with an arbitrary distribution of connections. Phys Rev E 66:016104

Dorogovtsev SN, Goltsev AV, Mendes JFF (2008) Critical phenomena in complex networks. Rev Mod Phys 80:1275

Drehmann M, Tarashev N (2013) Measuring the systemic importance of interconnected banks. J Financ Intermed 22(4):586–607

Feenstra RC, Lipsey RE, Deng H, Ma AC, Mo H (2005) World trade flows: 1962–2000. NBER Working Paper No. 11040

Filatrella G, Nielsen AH, Pedersen NF (2008) Analysis of a power grid using a Kuramoto-like model. Eur Phys J B 61:485–491

Foerster AT, Sarte PG, Watson MW (2011) Sectoral versus aggregate shocks: a structural factor analysis of industrial production. J Polit Econ 199(1):1–38

Goodwin RM (1947) Dynamical coupling with especial reference to markets having production lags. Econometrica 15:181–204

Goodwin RM (1951) The nonlinear accelerator and the persistence of business cycles. Econometrica 19:1–17

Granger CWJ, Hatanaka M (1964) Spectral analysis of economic time series. Princeton University Press, Princeton

Harras G, Sornette D (2011) How to grow a bubble: a model of myopic adapting agents. J Econ Behav Organ 80(1):137–152

Hastie T, Tibshirani R, Friedman J (2001) The elements of statistical learning. Springer series in statistics. Springer, New York, pp 61–79

He J, Deem MW (2010) Structure and response in theworld trade network. Phys Rev Lett 105:198701

Huygens C (1966) Horologium oscillatorium: 1673. Dawson, Michigan

Ikeda Y, Iyetomi H (2018) Trade network reconstruction and simulation with changes in trade policy. Evol Inst Econ Rev 15:495–513. https://doi.org/10.1007/s40844-018-0110-0

Ikeda Y, Takeda H (2020) Reconstruction of interbank network using ridge entropy maximization model. arXiv:2001.04097v1 [econ.GN] 13 Jan 2020

Ikeda Y, Yoshikawa H (2018) Macroprudential modeling based on spin dynamics in a supply chain network. RIETI discussion paper series 18-E-045, July 2018

Ikeda Y, et al (2013a) Synchronization and the coupled oscillator model in international business cycles. RIETI Discussion Papers, 13-E-089, Oct 2013

Ikeda Y, et al (2013b) Direct evidence for synchronization in Japanese business cycles. Evol Inst Econ Rev 10:1–13

Ikeda Y, et al (2014) Community structure and dynamics of the industry sector-specific international-trade-network. Tenth international conference on signal-image technology and internet-based systems (SITIS), pp 456–461. https://doi.org/10.1109/SITIS.2014.67

Ikeda Y, Aoyama H, Iyetomi H, Mizno T, Ohnishi T, Sakamoto Y, Watanabe T (2016) Econophysics point of view of trade liberalization: community dynamics, synchronization,and controllability as example of collective motions. RIETI Discussion Paper Series 16-E-026, Mar 2016

Imakubo K, Soejima Y (2010) The transaction network in Japan's interbank money markets. Monet Econ Stud 28:107–150

Johansen A, Ledoit O, Sornette D (2000) Crashes as critical points. Int J Theor Appl Finan 3(02):219–255

Kaizoji T (2000) Speculative bubbles and crashes in stock markets: an interacting-agent model of speculative activity. Phys A Stat Mech Appl 287(3):493–506
Kaizoji T, Bornholdt S, Fujiwara Y (2002) Dynamics of price and trading volume in a spin model of stock markets with heterogeneous agents. Phys A Stat Mech Appl 316(1):441–452
Krugman PR (1996) The self-organizing economy. Blackwell Publishers, Cambridge/Oxford
Kuramoto Y (1975) Self-entrainment of a population of coupled nonlinear oscillators. In: Araki H (ed) International symposium on mathematical problems in theoretical physics. Lecture notes in physics no 30. Springer, New York, p 420
Long JB, Plosser CI (1983) Real business cycles. J Polit Econ 91:39–69
Long JB, Plosser CI (1987) Sectoral and aggregate shocks in the business cycle. Am Econ Rev 77:333–336
Nadal J-P, et al (2005) Multiple equilibria in a monopoly market with heterogeneous agents and externalities. Quant Finan 5(6):557–568
Piccardi C, Tajoli L (2012) Existence and significance of communities in the World TradeWeb. Phys Rev E 85:066119
Pikovsky A, Rosenblum M, Kurths J (2001) SYNCHRONIZATION – a universal concept in nonlinear sciences. Cambridge University Press, ISBN: 0521592852
Selover DD, Jensen RV, Kroll J (2003) Industrial sector mode-locking and business cycle formation. Stud Nonlinear Dyn Econom 7:1–37
Sornette D, Zhou WX (2006) Importance of positive feedbacks and overconfidence in a self-fulfilling Ising model of financial markets. Phys A Stat Mech Appl 370(2):704–726
Sornette D (2014) Physics and financial economics (1776–2014): puzzles, Ising and agent-based models. Rep Prog Phys 77(6):062001
Squartini T, et al (2018) Reconstruction methods for networks: the case of economic and financial systems. Phys Rep 757:1–47
Stock JH, Watson MW (2005) Understanding changes in international business cycle dynamics. J Eur Econ Assoc 3(5):968–1006
Strogatz SH (2000) From Kuramoto to Crawford: exploring the onset of synchronization in populations of coupled oscillators. Phys D 143:1–20
Sussmuth B (2003) Business cycles in the contemporary world. Springer, Berlin/Heidelberg
Tibshirani R (1996) Regression shrinkage and selection via the lasso. J R Stat Soc Ser B (methodological) 58:267–288. JSTOR 2346178
Tzekinaa I, Danthi K, Rockmore DN (2008) Evolution of community structure in the world trade web. Eur Phys J B 63:541–545
Upper C (2011) Simulation methods to assess the danger of contagion in interbank markets. J Finan Stab 7(3):111–125
Vikram SV, Sinha S (2011) Emergence of universal scaling in financial markets from mean-field dynamics. Phys Rev E 83(1):016101
Von Haberler G (1937) Prosperity and depression: a theoretical analysis of cyclical movements. League of Nations (Geneva)
Wells S (2004) Financial interlinkages in the United Kingdom's interbank market and the risk of contagion. Bank of England, London
Ye C, Torsello A, Wilson RC, Hancock ER (2015) Thermodynamics of time evolving networks. In: Liu CL, Luo B, Kropatsch W, Cheng J (eds) Graph-based representations in pattern recognition. GbRPR 2015. Lecture notes in computer science, vol 9069. Springer, Cham

Chapter 13
Reactions of Economy Toward Various Disasters Estimated by Firm-Level Simulation

Hiroyasu Inoue

Abstract Social and economic networks can be a channel of negative shocks and thus deteriorate resilience and sustainability of our society. This study focuses on actual supply chains, or supplier–customer networks of firms and examines how production losses caused by disasters. We apply an agent-based model to the actual supply chains of nearly one million firms in Japan and test virtual and actual disasters. As virtual disasters, we test different intensity, substitutability, regions, and sectors of damages. Then, as actual disasters, we estimate the direct and indirect effects of the 2011 Great East Japan earthquake and employ the same model to predict the effect of the Nankai earthquake, a mega earthquake predicted to hit major industrial cities in Japan in the near future.

Keywords Supply chain · Propagation · Simulation · Agent-based model · Negative shock

13.1 Introduction

Human societies embody various types of networks based on, for example, friendships of individuals and business relationships among firms (Barabási 2016). These networks often work as a conduit of information, technology, and behaviors in the society and thus contribute to social development and welfare. However, networks can also propagate negative shocks, such as infectious diseases, software viruses, and financial crises, which can persist in the long run and thus deteriorate sustainability of the society (Watts and Strogatz 1998; Watts 1999; Valente 1995; Banerjee et al. 2013; Kreindler and Young 2014; Acemoglu et al. 2016a; Jackson 2010; Battiston et al. 2012; Thurner and Poledna 2013; Huang et al. 2013). A particular type of such diffusion that influences resilience and sustainability of the

H. Inoue (✉)
Graduate School of Simulation Studies, University of Hyogo, Chuo-ku, Kobe, Hyogo, Japan
e-mail: inoue@sim.u-hyogo.ac.jp

H. Aoyama et al. (eds.), *Complexity, Heterogeneity, and the Methods of Statistical Physics in Economics*, Evolutionary Economics and Social Complexity Science 22,
https://doi.org/10.1007/978-981-15-4806-2_13

economy and society is the propagation of economic shocks through supply chains, namely the production networks of firms linked by supplier–customer relations.

When an economic shock reduces production in a particular region or industry, the suppliers of firms directly affected by the shock must reduce their production because of a lack of demand, and their customers must also shrink production because of a shortage of material, parts, or components (Carvalho et al. 2016; Barrot and Sauvagnat 2016). As a result, a small region- or industry-specific shock can lead to a substantial indirect effect, often more substantial than the direct effect of the shock itself (Tierney 1997; Pelling et al. 2002), and hence large fluctuations across the economy (Acemoglu et al. 2012, 2016b; Bak et al. 1993; Delli Gatti 2005; Lee and Goh 2016).

However, despite recent findings in the network science literature that the structure of networks significantly influences diffusion (Watts and Strogatz 1998; Burt 2004; Centola 2010; Newman 2010; Barabási 2016; Watts 2002), empirical studies of diffusion through supply chains have not fully incorporated the complex nature of the networks among firms (Fujiwara and Aoyama 2010). A notable feature of the network complexity is scale-free property: there are a few giant hubs linked with an extremely large number of firms, and thus most firms are linked indirectly by a few steps through the hubs. If the complexity of actual networks is not fully incorporated, the analysis of propagation of shocks through supply chains is most likely to underestimate the size and persistence of the propagation (Barabási 2016). However, some earlier works rely on inter-industry analysis based on input–output (IO) tables, ignoring firm-level networks (Acemoglu et al. 2012; Haimes and Jiang 2001; Santos and Haimes 2004; Okuyama et al. 2004). Others adopt computable general equilibrium models that assume homogeneous firms in each industry, disregarding substantial variation in the number of links across firms (Rose and Liao 2005). Although several recent studies have incorporated inter-firm supply-chain relations into their analyses, they employ hypothetical networks of firms, whose network complexity is quite different from that of actual networks (Bak et al. 1993; Delli Gatti 2005; Hallegatte 2008, 2012; Henriet et al. 2012).

We utilize the nation-wide supply chain data in Japan and develops an agent-based model in which heterogeneous firms are linked through supply chains and applies it to the actual supplier–customer relations of nearly one million firms in Japan. This chapter is based on two articles already published (Inoue and Todo 2019a,b). The author has proper permission to republish these articles. The two articles report different issues of the simulations of negative shocks. The one is about comprehensive analyses based on artificial networks and shocks. The other is about analyses on actual and predicted earthquakes.

Regarding comprehensive analyses, we address the following issues. First, by comparing outcomes of actual networks with hypothetical ones used in extant literature, we highlight the importance of the network structure in the propagation of shocks through supply chains. Second, we examine how different intensities of direct damages lead to different indirect damages through supply chains. Third, to highlight the importance of substitution of suppliers in the wake of supply chain disruption, we compare the benchmark case with cases wherein substitution is more restricted. Fourth, we examine how direct damages in different regions affect the propagation pattern. Fifth, the effects of direct damages in different sectors are also explored. Finally, we discuss the estimation of indirect damages triggered by a single firm's loss. By these comprehensive analyses, we can discuss the vulnerability and robustness of the economic system that have not been studied until now and reveal the intrinsic nature of the properties of the system.

Regarding actual and predicted earthquakes, we use the Great East Japan earthquake in 2011 (hereafter, the 2011 Japan earthquake) as a source of negative economic shocks to calibrate the model and examine how the shocks propagate through supply chains. We then simulate the model to predict the dynamic effect of the Nankai Trough earthquake (the Nankai earthquake), another mega earthquake expected to hit Japan in the near future. Finally, we experiment with different hypothetical networks to understand what network structure promotes propagation so that we can understand why we have huge indirect loss. We adopt a natural disaster as a source of shocks for two reasons. First, natural disasters, such as the 2011 Japan earthquake, the Thai flood in 2011, and Hurricane Katrina in 2005, have been major causes of economic shocks, and their occurrence is projected to increase because of seismic cycles and climate change (Beroza 2012; Milly et al. 2002). Second, because natural disasters provide shocks independent of economic activities in the pre-disaster period, unlike man-made disasters, such as financial crises, we can analyze the causal effects of shocks on economic activities more accurately.

13.2 Data

13.2.1 Supply-Chain Network

The data used in this study are from the Company Information Database and Company Linkage Database collected by Tokyo Shoko Research (TSR) in 2011. The data are licensed to the Research Institute of Economy, Trade and Industry (RIETI). The former includes detailed firm attributes, whereas the latter includes the suppliers and customers of each firm. Although the maximum number of suppliers and customers reported by each firm is 24, we can capture more than 24 by looking at the supplier–customer relations from the opposite direction. That is, although a large firm (e.g., Toyota Motor Corporation) reports only 24 suppliers, its suppliers are most likely to report the large firm as their customers. Accordingly, we identify the supply chains in Japan to a great extent. The number of firms, or nodes, is 1,109,549, whereas the number of supplier–customer ties, or links, is 5,106,081. This network is directed, as it represents the flows of intermediate goods. The TSR data include the address of the headquarters of each firm. We identify the longitude and latitude of each headquarters by using the geocoding service provided by the Center for Spatial Information Science at the University of Tokyo. One shortcoming of the data is that we cannot identify the location of each branch for firms with multiple branches. In other words, when the headquarters of the firms are not directly damaged by an earthquake, while its branch is destroyed, we assume that the firm is not directly damaged. However, because the share of firms with no branch is 71.8%, we presume that the bias due to this shortcoming is not substantial.

Although the TSR data comprise information about the suppliers and customers of each firm, the relationship information does not include the transaction values of each supplier–customer tie. Because we need these values for the simulations, we estimate them in the following two steps. First, each supplier's sales are divided into customers proportionally, using the sales of customers as weights. This step provides each link with a tentative sales value. In the second step, we employ IO tables for Japan in 2011 (Ministry of Economy, Trade and Industry, Japan 2011) to transform these tentative values into more realistic ones, incorporating the final consumers and the difference between sales and value added. Specifically, we aggregate the tentative values at the firm–pair level to obtain the total sales for each pair of sectors. We then divide the total sales for each sector pair by the transaction values for the corresponding pair in the IO tables. Moreover, we transform the 1,460 sectors in the Japan Standard Industrial Classification (Ministry of Internal Affairs and Communications 2013) used in the TSR data into the 190 industries in the IO tables. The ratio is then used to estimate the transaction values between firms. The final consumption of each sector is allocated to all firms in the sector, using their sales as weights. In this process, we drop firms without sales information. As a result, the number of firms in our simulation is 887,715 and the number of links is 3,223,137. Through the above process, we can obtain the value of damages estimated from our simulation that is reasonably compared with macroeconomic statistics, such as GDP.

13.2.2 Network Structure

The degree of the supply-chain network follows a power-law distribution (see Fig. 13.1), and thus the network is defined as scale-free (Barabási 2016), as is often found in supply-chain networks (Fujiwara and Aoyama 2010). The average path length between firms excluding isolates is 4.8. This path length is consistent with the standard finding in the network science literature: when a network is scale-free, it has ultra-small-world properties and the average path length of the network is short (Barabási 2016). The average path length of the network is theoretically $\ln \ln N$, where N is the number of nodes (Barabási 2016). In our case, $\ln \ln N = 2.6$.

The network has a giant strongly connected component (GSCC) of 47.5% of all firms (i.e., more than 400 thousand firms). An SCC is defined as a sub-network in which any node is reachable from any other node in the sub-network along directed links. Accordingly, nodes form cycles in an SCC. In supply chains, for example, cycles emerge when suppliers of parts and components purchase downstream intermediate goods, such as IC (integrated circuit) chips, or final goods, such as

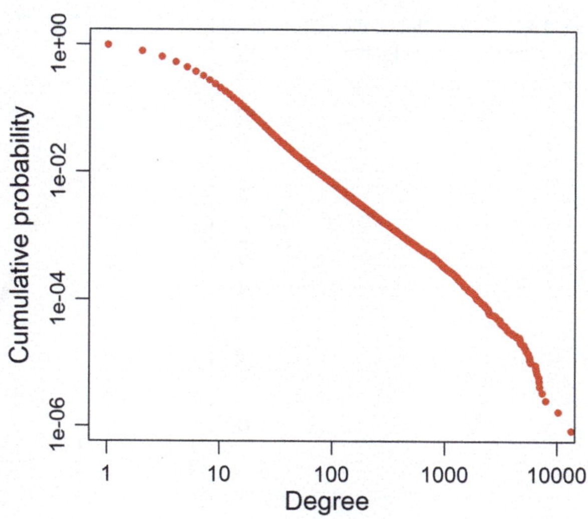

Fig. 13.1 Degree distribution of supply chains in Japan

machinery, for their production. The GSCC in our supply chains is relatively large compared with, for example, the corresponding size for the network of 203 million websites, 27.6% (Broder et al. 2000). The large SCC can be translated as complex cycles in the network. The scale-free property and complexity of cycles in the GSCC are thus the two notable features of this network. The supply chains form a "walnut" structure. Most firms' in- and out-components are connected directly to a GSCC, which can be likened to the shells of a GSCC (Chakraborty et al. 2018).

Further, the network is disassortative. Figure 13.2 shows the relation between the degree and average degree of nearest neighbors. The negative relation between these two indicates disassortativity in the network. That is, firms linked with a larger number of suppliers and customers tend to be connected with those with a smaller number of partners. Disassortative networks are found in many social networks. This disassortativity of the supply chains can be explained by *keiretsu*, where suppliers are classified into groups of firms directly and indirectly connected with large final producers (Aoki 1988). In the *keiretsu* structure, large final producers (e.g., Toyota Motor Corporation and Honda Motor Co., Ltd. in the automobile industry) are less likely to be linked with each other, while their relatively large direct suppliers (e.g., Denso Corporation and Keihin Corporation) are less likely to be linked with each other, too. This *keiretsu* structure can lead to disassortativity in the supply-chain network.

13.2.3 Seismological Background

The 2011 Japan earthquake of magnitude 9.0 was the fourth largest earthquake in the world since 1900. The death toll, including the missing, reached almost

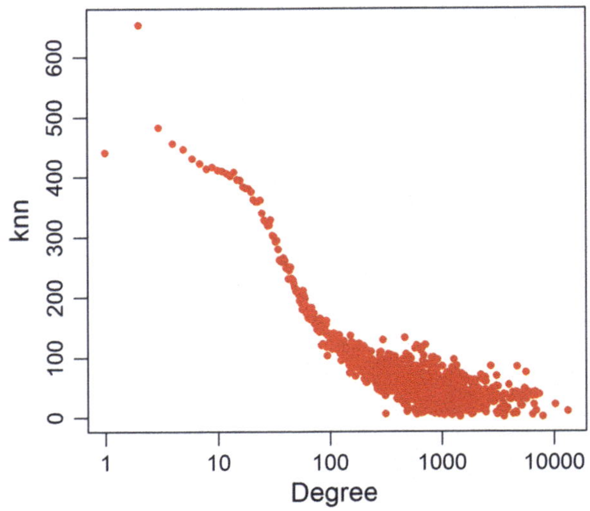

Fig. 13.2 Scatterplot of the degree and nearest neighbor

19,000 (Cabinet Office in Japan 2012). The epicenter was off the coast of the northeastern part of Japan, a relatively backward region where many small- and medium-sized suppliers in the automobile and electric machinery industries are located (Ministry of Economy, Trade and Industry 2011). The areas directly hit by the earthquake are shown in pink in Panel (a) of Fig. 13.13 and those by the tsunami that followed the earthquake are in blue. The direct loss of economic facilities including buildings, utilities, and social infrastructure was estimated to be 16.9 trillion yen, or approximately 212 million US dollars using the exchange rate in 2011 (Cabinet Office in Japan 2012). The Nankai earthquake is a mega earthquake expected to be of approximately magnitude 9 that will hit major industrial clusters in Japan including Tokyo, Nagoya, and Osaka, with a probability of more than 70% within 30 years. The areas predicted to be directly hit by the earthquake and associated tsunamis are shown in pink and blue, respectively, in Panel (a) of Fig. 13.15. Its impact is likely to be enormous. A typical estimation predicts a death toll of 323 thousand and a total direct loss of economic facilities of 98–170 trillion yen (Cabinet Office in Japan 2014).

13.2.4 Model

Our dynamic agent-based model extends existing models in the literature (Hallegatte 2008, 2012; Henriet et al. 2012). Our model improves existing agent-based models used to examine the propagation of shocks by natural disasters through supply chains (Hallegatte 2008) in the three ways, as indicated later in detail. The first improvement is related to the rationing mechanism. Second, the target inventory

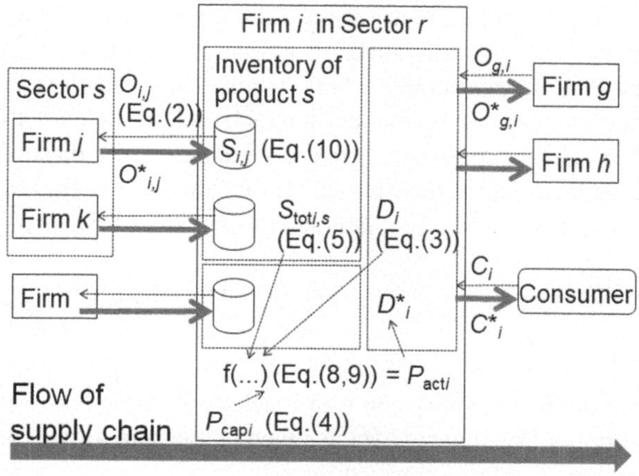

Fig. 13.3 Overview of the agent-based model. Products flow from left to right, whereas orders flow in the opposite direction. The equation numbers correspond to those in Model section

size has a Poisson distribution instead of a common constant. Third, a recovery mechanism is introduced.

In our model, each firm uses a variety of intermediate products as inputs and produces an industry-specific product. Figure 13.3 provides an overview of the model, showing the flows of products to and from firm i in sector r. It is assumed that each firm holds inventories of its intermediates and can substitute an intermediate product from a supplier for that from another current supplier in the same industry, but not from a new supplier. In the wake of a natural disaster, the production capital of firms in a particular region is destroyed to a given extent. The damage for each firm is stochastically assigned based on the actual distributions. Accordingly, suppliers and customers of the directly damaged firms may reduce production because of the shortage of demand and supply, respectively. These negative effects on production propagate through supply chains.

In the comprehensive analyses, i.e., the first part of this article, there is no recovery mechanism. But, in the analyses of actual and predicted earthquakes, it is assumed that the operating production capacity of directly damaged firms is to recover at a given rate, and the negative effect on production becomes smaller after a certain period.

In the initial stage before a disaster affects the economy, the daily trade volume from supplier j to customer i is denoted by $A_{i,j}$, whereas the daily trade volume from firm i to the final consumers is denoted as C_i. Then, the initial production of firm i in a day is given by

$$P_{\text{ini}i} = \Sigma_j A_{j,i} + C_i. \tag{13.1}$$

On day t after the initial stage, the previous day's demand for firm i's product is $D_i^*(t-1)$. The firm thus make orders to each supplier j so that the amount of its product of supplier j can meet this demand, $A_{i,j} D_i^*(t-1)/P_{\text{ini}i}$. We assume that firm i has an inventory of the intermediate goods produced by firm j on day

t, $S_{i,j}(t)$, and aims to restore this inventory to a level equal to a given number of days n_i of the utilization of product of supplier j. The constant n_i is assumed to be Poisson distributed, where its mean is n, which is a parameter. That is, when the actual inventory is smaller than its target, firm i increases its inventory gradually by $1/\tau$ of the gap, so that it reaches the target in τ days, where τ is assumed to be six to follow the original model (Hallegatte 2008). Therefore, the order from firm i to its supplier j on day t, denoted as $O_{i,j}(t)$, is given by

$$O_{i,j}(t) = A_{i,j} \frac{D_i^*(t-1)}{P_{\mathrm{ini}i}} + \frac{1}{\tau} \left[n_i A_{i,j} - S_{i,j}(t) \right], \tag{13.2}$$

where the inventory gap is in brackets. Accordingly, total demand for the product of supplier i on day t, $D_i(t)$, is given by the sum of final demand from final consumers and total orders from customers:

$$D_i(t) = \Sigma_j O_{j,i}(t) + C_i, \tag{13.3}$$

Now, suppose that a disaster hits the economy on day 0 and that firm i is directly damaged. Subsequently, the proportion $\delta_i(t)$ of the production capital of firm i is malfunctioning, although $\delta_i(t)$ decreases over time because of the recovery effort, as we explain in the following paragraph. Hence, the production capacity of firm i, defined as its maximum production assuming no supply shortages, $P_{\mathrm{cap}i}(t)$, is given by

$$P_{\mathrm{cap}i}(t) = P_{\mathrm{ini}i}(1 - \delta_i(t)). \tag{13.4}$$

The production of firm i might also be limited by the shortage of supplies on day 0. Because we assume that firms in the same sector produce the same product, shortage of supplies suffered by firm j in sector s can be compensated for by supplies from firm k in the same sector. Firms cannot substitute new suppliers for damaged ones after the disaster, as we assume fixed supply chains. Thus, the total inventory of the products delivered by firms in sector s in firm i on day t is

$$S_{\mathrm{tot}i,s}(t) = \Sigma_{j \in s} S_{i,j}(t). \tag{13.5}$$

The initial consumption of products in sector s at firm i before the disaster is also defined for convenience:

$$A_{\mathrm{tot}i,s} = \Sigma_{j \in s} A_{i,j}. \tag{13.6}$$

The maximum possible production of firm i limited by the inventory of product of sector s on day t, $P_{\mathrm{pro}i,s}(t)$, is given by

$$P_{\mathrm{pro}i,s}(t) = \frac{S_{\mathrm{tot}i,s}(t)}{A_{\mathrm{tot}i,s}} P_{\mathrm{ini}i}. \tag{13.7}$$

Then, we can determine the maximum production of firm i on day t, considering its production capacity, $P_{\mathrm{cap}_i}(t)$, and its production constraints due to the shortage of supplies, $P_{\mathrm{pro}_{i,s}}(t)$:

$$P_{\mathrm{max}_i}(t) = \mathrm{Min}\left(P_{\mathrm{cap}_i}(t), \mathrm{Min}_s(P_{\mathrm{pro}_{i,s}}(t))\right). \tag{13.8}$$

Therefore, the actual production of firm i on day t is given by

$$P_{\mathrm{act}_i}(t) = \mathrm{Min}\left(P_{\mathrm{max}_i}(t), D_i(t)\right). \tag{13.9}$$

When demand for a firm is greater than its production capacity, the firm cannot completely satisfy its demand, as is denoted by equation (13.9). In this case, firms should ration their production to their customers. Hallegatte proposed a rationing policy where each customer and the final consumer would receive an amount of product that is the same fraction ($P_{\mathrm{act}_i}/P_{\mathrm{ini}_i}$) (Hallegatte 2008). In other words, this rationing policy assumes that the production firm treats all the customers and the final consumer fairly. To understand how this rationing policy influences propagation of shocks, suppose that supplier i in sector r supplies its product to its customers, including customer h in the pre-disaster period. Further suppose that when a disaster hits the economy, other suppliers of product r to customer h are damaged. Then, customer h increases its demand for product r to supplier i because other suppliers of product r reduce their supply to customer h as a result of the disaster. According to this rationing policy, supplier i is compelled to decrease the supply of product r to other customers, even if they are not affected by the disaster. Thus, this rationing policy tends to augment the propagation of negative shocks, leading to a large evaluation of the effects of disasters. For example, 10% damage ($\delta = 0.1$) suffered by a few firms (such as 100 randomly selected firms) can result in the entire supply chain network having the same damage.

To alleviate this possible overvaluation of indirect effects, we propose an alternative rationing policy in which customers and final consumers are prioritized according to their amount of order after the disaster to their initial order, rather than they are treated equally as in the previous work Hallegatte (2008). Suppose that firm i has customers j and a final consumer. Then the ratio of the order from customers j and the final consumer after the disaster to the one before the disaster denoted as $O^{\mathrm{rel}}_{j,i}$ and O^{rel}_{c}, respectively, are determined by the following steps, where $O^{\mathrm{sub}}_{j,i}$ and O^{sub}_{c} are temporal variables to calculate the realized order and set to be zero initially.

1. Get the remaining production r of firm i.
2. Calculate $O^{\mathrm{rel}}_{\mathrm{min}} = \mathrm{Min}(O^{\mathrm{rel}}_{j,i}, O^{\mathrm{rel}}_{c})$.
3. If $r \leq (\sum_j O^{\mathrm{rel}}_{\mathrm{min}} O_{j,i} + O^{\mathrm{rel}}_{\mathrm{min}} C_i)$ then proceed to 8.
4. Add $O^{\mathrm{rel}}_{\mathrm{min}}$ to $O^{\mathrm{sub}}_{j,i}$ and O^{sub}_{c}.
5. Subtract $(\sum_j O^{\mathrm{rel}}_{\mathrm{min}} O_{j,i} + O^{\mathrm{rel}}_{\mathrm{min}} C_i)$ from r.

6. Remove the customer or the final consumer that indicated $O^{\mathrm{rel}}_{\mathrm{min}}$ from the calculation.
7. Return to 2.
8. Calculate O^{rea} that satisfies $r = (\sum_j O^{\mathrm{rea}} O_{j,i} + O^{\mathrm{rea}} C_i)$.
9. Get $O^*_{j,i} = O^{\mathrm{rea}} O_{j,i} + O^{\mathrm{sub}}_{j,i} O_{j,i}$ and $C^*_i = O^{\mathrm{rea}} C_i + O^{\mathrm{sub}}_c C_i$, where the realized order from firm j to supplier i is denoted as $O^*_{j,i}(t)$, and the realized order from a final consumer is C^*_i.
10. Finalize the calculation.

Under this rationing policy, total realized demand for firm i, $D^*_i(t)$, is given by

$$D^*_i(t) = \Sigma_j O^*_{i,j}(t) + C^*_i, \tag{13.10}$$

where the realized order from firm i to supplier j is denoted as $O^*_{i,j}(t)$ and that from the final consumers is C^*_i. According to firms' production and procurement activities on day t, the inventory of firm j's product in firm i on day $t+1$ is updated to

$$S_{i,j}(t+1) = S_{i,j}(t) + O^*_{i,j}(t) - A_{i,j} \frac{P_{\mathrm{act}i}(t-1)}{P_{\mathrm{ini}i}}. \tag{13.11}$$

Finally, we assume a simple process for the recovery of damaged firms. Firm i directly damaged by the disaster stops production for σ days, and thus the proportion of malfunctioning capital declines as follows:

$$\delta_i(t) = (1 - \zeta\gamma)\delta_i(t-1), \tag{13.12}$$

where γ is a parameter and ζ is a damping factor equal to the ratio of healthy neighbor firms to all neighbors. This damping factor is introduced on the basis of the peer effects observed in practice (Todo et al. 2015).

As an important notice, the last process, the recovery, is not incorporated into the first half of the analyses, i.e., the comprehensive analyses. Therefore, we do not see any recovery of the output (value added) in the analyses and the damage is propagated into the system.

13.3 Comprehensive Analyses

Using the model above, we simulate how direct damages, represented by an exogenous reduction in the production capacity of a set of firms, affect the production of the entire economy through the propagation of negative shocks along supply chains. In the simulation, we use the actual supply chains of firms in Japan based on the TSR data. $A_{i,j}$ and C_i are determined using the IO tables and supply chain ties, as described in the section Data. We assume that τ is 6 as per Hallegatte (2008);

the setting of the parameter is ad hoc, although it is desirable for the setting to be supported by empirical data. At the beginning of the simulation, n_i is assigned to each firm from the Poisson distribution with a mean of 15. This parameter also requires empirical support, if it is possible.

In each simulation, exogenous damages are given on day 0. Specifically, our benchmark simulation assumes that 10,000 firms that are randomly selected from 1,109,549 firms lose 50% of their production capacity after the disaster (i.e., δ_i in equation (13.12) is 0.5), although we experiment with other types of shock (explained later). In other words, the benchmark cases assume that approximately 0.5% (10,000 * 0.5/1,109,549) of the total production capacity in the economy is destroyed. Subsequently, we examine how the sum of the value added—or the value of production less the total value of intermediates used for the production—of all firms in the economy changes over time. For each set of parameter values, we conduct a simulation 30 times and show the results graphically. We use a solid line for the average value added, while dotted lines are their standard deviations.

Since the simulation in this study requires substantial computational power due to the presence of more than one million agents and five million ties, we use a supercomputer and run simulations in parallel to minimize the run time. The parallel execution reduces the consumption of wall time. The simulation code is shared on GitHub to ensure readers can run their own agents and networks. The link is https://github.com/HiroyasuInoue/ProductionNetworkSimulator. The code provides abundant variations of simulations.

13.3.1 Benchmark Result

In the benchmark test, 50% of the production losses are assigned to 10,000 randomly chosen firms. Our benchmark result using the actual supply chain network and the parameter values explained above is shown using a red line in Fig. 13.4. The simulation result indicates that the value added declines from 1.154 trillion yen per day before the disaster to 1.148 trillion yen per day on day 0. Subsequently, it declines to 1.062 ($\sigma = 0.007987$) trillion 30 days after the disaster, and then to 0.611 ($\sigma = 0.0006345$) trillion after 200 days. The numbers with parentheses are standard deviations. After roughly 200 days, it becomes almost stable. Although the direct damage was only 0.5% of the value added per day, the loss of value added reaches approximately 8% on day 30, and then reaches 48% on day 200.

The value added monotonically declines over time and converges to a lower level than the pre-disaster level. The monotonic decreases occur because we do not use recovery in the model. In addition, there is other possible recovery mechanism other than the one described in Model section. One of such recoveries is, for example, finding other suppliers or clients.

The recovery is obviously not negligible in the real economy. In the case of the Great East Japan earthquake that occurred in March 2011, firms in the affected areas ceased operations for only five days at the median (Todo et al. 2015). On the other

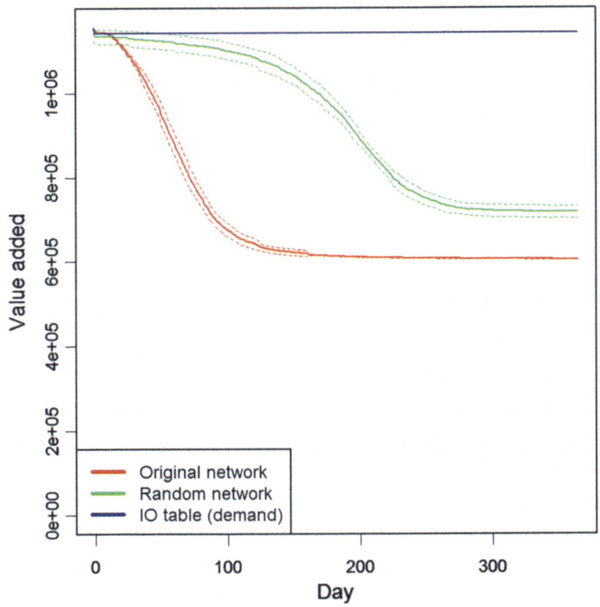

Fig. 13.4 Simulation results for different network structures. The horizontal axis shows days. The vertical axis shows the daily value added of the system. The red lines show the results for the actual network. The green lines show the results for the random networks. The blue line shows the results of the IO table. The solid lines show the average of 30 simulations. The dotted lines show the standard deviations. For all simulations, damages are randomly given to 10,000 firms with 50% production loss ($\delta = 0.5$)

hand, Renesas Electronics, a major producer of microcomputers for automobiles, was heavily hit by the earthquake. It recovered three months later in June 2011. Although some factories involved in the final assemblies of automobiles, which were not directly hit, were compelled to stop operation for a few months due to supply chain disruptions, production of automobiles was restored to the pre-earthquake level in July 2011. Therefore, it is important to consider the recovery process in the model if we want to compare the simulation with the real economy. To fill this gap, the model with recovery will be discussed in the next section.

Therefore, the long-run consequences of our simulation may not indicate actual damages from disasters because it ignores recovery processes. However, it is important to know how fast the propagation is because the pace of the propagation should be considered for government intervention. Therefore, when we interpret the simulation results, we focus on the pace of the decline and the total loss in the long run (one year), depending on the context.

Since we cannot observe the propagation without recovery in the real economy, we only observe it in simulations. Here because we see that the simulation reveals the acute decline, we can interpret the simulation results as indicating how negative shocks propagated with speed. Therefore, we conclude that the indirect effects of disasters through supply chain disruptions are significant.

One may wonder why the value added converges to a certain value in the long run. This is because a steady state is achieved when negative shocks reach all firms that are indirectly connected to directly damaged firms in the supply chains.

13.3.2 Differences with the Random Network and the IO Table

We show differences in the propagation of negative shocks between the actual network and randomly generated networks. Since massive supply-chain data are normally unavailable, random networks are commonly used in the literature. In fact, the original model, upon which we base our model, used a certain type of random network in its simulation (Hallegatte 2008).

The degree distribution (the number of links) in the actual supply chain network in Japan is fat-tailed and follows the power law, as found in Fujiwara and Aoyama (2010) and Inoue (2016). It has been repeatedly discussed that networks with power-law distributions, or scale-free networks, show unique properties in many respects (Barabási 2016). From the viewpoint of supply chains, propagation of negative shocks in the actual network can differ from that in the random networks.

We randomly generate networks with approximately the same number of nodes and links as the actual network (1,109,549 nodes and 5,106,081 links). We thus use the algorithm developed by Gilbert (1959). As mentioned above, the actual and random networks have different degree distributions. In each case, we generate 30 different random networks, and graphically show the average and standard deviation of the change in the value added. In Fig. 13.4, the green lines indicate the results of the random networks. The comparison between the results from the actual and random networks—that is, the red and green lines—clearly show that damages due to indirect effects of the disaster in the short and long run are substantially larger in the actual network than in the random networks. (Here, we use the terms "short run" and "long run" for the first 200 days of the disaster aftermath and the subsequent period, respectively.) Thus, losses are likely underestimated if supply chains are assumed to be random, and hence we should use actual networks in practice.

The difference noted earlier can be explained by differences in path lengths in the network. A path length is the number of steps between two arbitrary nodes in a network, and the average path length is the average of all possible path lengths. The average path length of a random network, $\langle d \rangle$, is proportional to the natural logarithm of the number of nodes, N, or $\langle d \rangle \approx \ln N$. Conversely, a scale-free network, which is the case with the supply chain network in Japan (Fujiwara and Aoyama 2010), has different properties from random networks (Barabási and Albert 1999). Particularly, the average path length is proportional to the log of the log of the number of nodes: $\langle d \rangle \approx \ln \ln N$. In other words, the actual supply chain network has a much shorter average path length than in a random network, suggesting that shocks spread faster in the former network.

Although the path length is longer in the random network, the damages are propagated into the entire network in the end. Thus, one may think that the difference in the final value added of the system should not exist. However, this difference comes from the rationing policy. (Note that the rationing policy is considered realistic.) As shown in Model section, the rationing policy indicates that the demand from affected clients is prioritized over the demand from the final consumer (Demand of the final consumers is not affected by the disaster). Therefore, the demand of the final consumer is relatively postponed, which can help work toward absorbing the supply-driven damages. Importantly, the rationing clients lift production in the successive steps of the supply chains, but the rationing final consumers do not show this effect. Longer path lengths lead to increased absorption of the supply shortage. As a result, damages in the actual network with a shorter average path length are substantially greater than those in random networks with a longer path length.

Another comparison is conducted by using the IO table. We use the same initial damages as our simulations. By solving the inverse matrix, we obtain the damage propagation through the IO table. Here, the damage propagation is considered for the demand side, as conducted generally. The blue line in Fig. 13.4 shows the result. Since the analysis of the IO table does not indicate any temporal transition of the value added, the line is shown horizontally to indicate that the damage occurs on day 0 with no following changes. Evidently, the difference in our simulations is tremendous. This result is natural because the IO table analyses do not consider supply constraints. Since a supply shortage is a key factor that affects production under disaster scenarios, the results are understandable. On the other hand, we can simply use the transposed IO table to ensure that the matrix shows supply-side propagations. Clearly, this result is not significantly different from the one for the demand-side analyses because it is an inter-sectoral analysis that cannot incorporate the supply chain.

13.3.3 Different Intensity of Shocks

Next, we experiment with different intensities of shocks, assuming the following three cases: 50,000 firms lose 10% of their production capacity; 10,000 firm lose 50% of their production capacity, as in the benchmark case; and 5,000 firms lose 100% of their production capacity. Damaged firms are randomly selected in each case. The total capacity loss in the economy—that is, product of the number of firms and the ratio of production losses—is approximately the same across the three cases.

The results from the simulation are shown in Fig. 13.5. The different intensities show different speeds of decay; namely, the decay time decreases with the shock intensity. In particular, the most intensive shock shows 80% daily loss in the end.

The result, i.e., the intensive shock shows the shorter decay time, comes from the inventory of firms. As shown in the model, production is constrained by a minimal

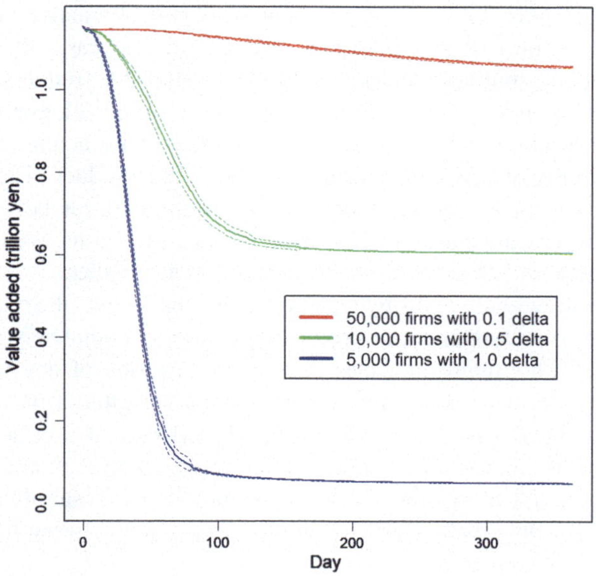

Fig. 13.5 Simulation results for different intensities of shocks. The horizontal axis shows days. The vertical axis shows daily value added of the system. The red lines show the results for 10% production loss ($\delta = 0.1$) in 50,000 firms. The green lines show the results for 50% production loss ($\delta = 0.5$) in 10,000 firms. The blue lines show the results for 10% production loss ($\delta = 0.1$) in 5,000 firms. The solid lines show the average of 30 simulations. The dotted lines show the standard deviations

inventory. Therefore, even if only one supply shows shortage among other plentiful supplies, the firm's production is limited by this shortage. Hence, the intensive shocks show more serious results than the extensive shocks. The case of Renesas Electronics is an example of this: automobile assemblers had to stop production because of a shortage of microcomputers.

13.3.4 Substitution Among Suppliers

Another important issue is substitution of suppliers. It possibly mitigates damages when some intermediate product cannot be provided by a supplier, but other suppliers can provide it. In our model, substitution is realized in equation (13.5). Concretely, our model assumes that when the supplier j of product s, who supplies to firm i, is damaged by a disaster, firm i can substitute supplies from firm j for supplies from firm k, which provides the same product s. Note that the supply chain is fixed and firm i does not find a new supplier. Since the simulation is relatively short (less than one year), this simulation is meaningful. When this kind of substitution is more feasible, indirect damages through supply chains can be mitigated.

To investigate this issue, we experiment with two alternative cases wherein the products (sectors) of suppliers are changed. In one case, the products of firms are randomly shuffled. That is, the distribution of the products is preserved, such as in actual supply chains. Since firms use a variety of intermediates, we expect the substitution to be more difficult compared with actual supply chains. In another alternative case, each firm has a different product. Therefore, there is no substitution. In economics literature, substitutions occur between different products by introducing elasticity. However, in our simulations, we only consider substitutions between the same products from different suppliers.

Figure 13.6 shows the results by using the benchmark case (the red line) and by assuming a random assignment of products (green) and completely differentiated products (blue). This figure indicates that the propagation of negative shocks is substantially faster in the latter two cases wherein substitution is more difficult than in the benchmark case. Therefore, the benchmark case, that is, actual network, substitutes supplies as part of its innate structure, meaning that substitution is an important channel for mitigating shock propagation in actual supply chains. Especially, we can see the innate resistance in the comparison between the benchmark and the random assignment.

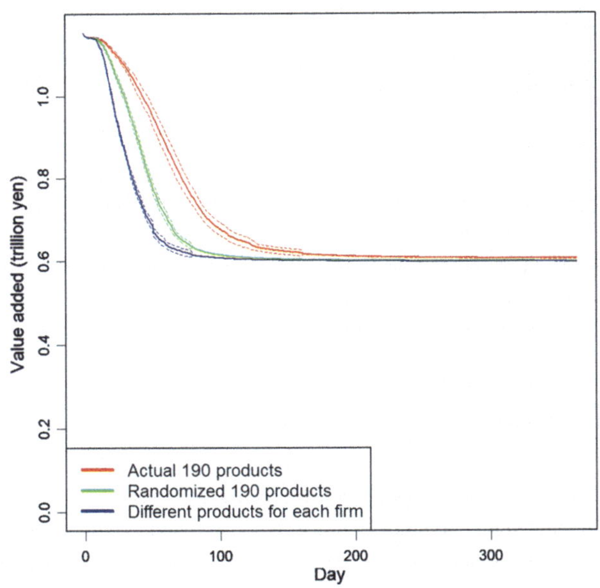

Fig. 13.6 Simulation results to show effect of substitution. The horizontal axis shows days. The vertical axis shows daily value added of the system. The red lines show the results for the actual network. The green lines show the results for the product-randomized networks. The blue lines show the results for no substitution. The solid lines show the average of 30 simulations. The dotted lines show the standard deviations. For all simulations, damages are randomly assigned to 10,000 firms that face 50% production loss ($\delta = 0.5$)

13.3.5 Regional and Sectoral Damages

So far, we assumed that firms affected by the disaster are randomly selected across regions and sectors. However, if we consider natural disasters, such as earthquakes and typhoons, they affect specific regions. Additionally, shocks in the economy may be caused not only by natural disasters but also by financial crises or trade sanctions. These human-made shocks are more likely to be sector-specific. Therefore, we now examine propagation of regional and sectoral shocks.

First, we assume that firms in a particular region are damaged. We divide Japan into eight regions—Hokkaido, Tohoku, Kanto, Chubu, Kinki, Chugoku, Shikoku, and Kyusyu. As in the benchmark simulation, we assume that the 10,000 firms randomly chosen from each region face a 50% loss in production capacity. Results in Fig. 13.7 show that damages in Kanto and Kinki propagate most rapidly, although the total loss in the long run is the same across regional damages. Kanto includes the largest metropolitan area in Japan, such as Tokyo and Yokohama, whereas Kinki includes the second, Osaka. Therefore, when compared with the propagation in remote areas, our results indicate that damages propagate faster when industrial areas are hit. Rapid propagation implies significant damages in the short run.

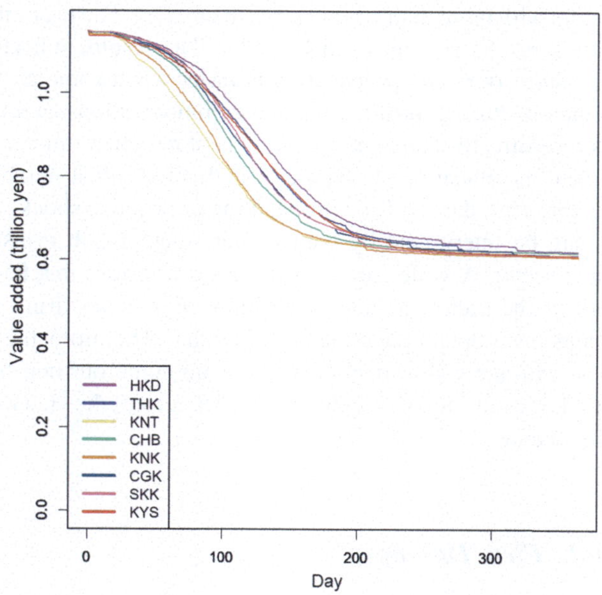

Fig. 13.7 Simulation results for different regional shocks. The horizontal axis shows days, whereas the vertical axis shows daily value added of the system. The solid lines show the average of 30 simulations. It is assumed that 10,000 firms randomly chosen in each of the eight regions—Hokkaido (HKD), Tohoku (THK), Kanto (KNT), Chubu (CHB), Kinki (KNK), Chugoku (CGK), Shikoku (SKK), and Kyusyu (KYS)—face a 50% loss in production capacity. Standard deviations are omitted for visibility

The Great East Japan Earthquake in 2011 hit the Tohoku region, which is less industrialized. On the other hand, the speculation by the Japanese government indicates that a predicted great earthquake, such as the Tokyo Inland Earthquake and the Nankai Trough Earthquake, will hit Kanto or Kinki regions; these regions show faster propagations in the simulations. Therefore, the loss caused by the disasters will be substantially larger than the earthquake in 2011. This issue is revisited in Actual and Predicted Earthquakes section.

On the other hand, the results do not show significant difference in long-run damages between regional shocks. This is because most firms are connected through supply chains. To understand this, Fig. 13.8 illustrates damages on day 30 in the two cases, one in which the Kanto region—the economic center of Japan that includes Tokyo—is directly hit, and the other in which the Tohoku region—a relatively less developed region—is hit. The left and right parts of the figure show the geographical plots of affected firms due to direct damages in Kanto and Tohoku, respectively. In both cases, damages reach most regions of Japan in 30 days. Even in the 30 days, the damages already spread and we do not see an explicit difference. Thus, only immediate intervention, such as governmental aid, can be effective because the damage propagates faster into the entire economy through supply chains.

Second, we assume that firms in a particular sector, among the 190 sectors, are damaged. Since we need more than 10,000 firms in a sector to run the simulation, we focus on 12 sectors with more than 10,000 firms in our data. The list of the 12 sectors and the simulation results are shown in Fig. 13.9. The results indicate substantial variations in the short run—the propagation is faster when some sectors, such as miscellaneous manufacturing, information and communications, and transport and postal services, are directly damaged, while it is slow when others, such as real estate and medical, healthcare and welfare, are affected. Most notably, when the construction sector is hit, there is little propagation of negative shocks.

The results can be interpreted by considering whether hub firms exist in the directly damaged sector. A scale-free network has a few hubs that have numerous links. Therefore, if the sector includes such hubs or includes firms connected to hubs in short steps, then the propagation would be fast. Therefore, the construction sector records an extremely slow decline as there are numerous non-hub firms and they form many layers of closed supply chains. Therefore, the shocks are slow to propagate in this sector.

13.3.6 Single-Firm Damages

It is beneficial to know how a single-firm loss will affect the entire economy, that is, a single firm may cause substantial damage to the entire economy. This is because a single firm can easily shutdown as a result of bankruptcy and suspension, among other reasons. Intuitively, it seems that single-firm loss cannot seriously impact the entire economy, but it is not the case, as shown below.

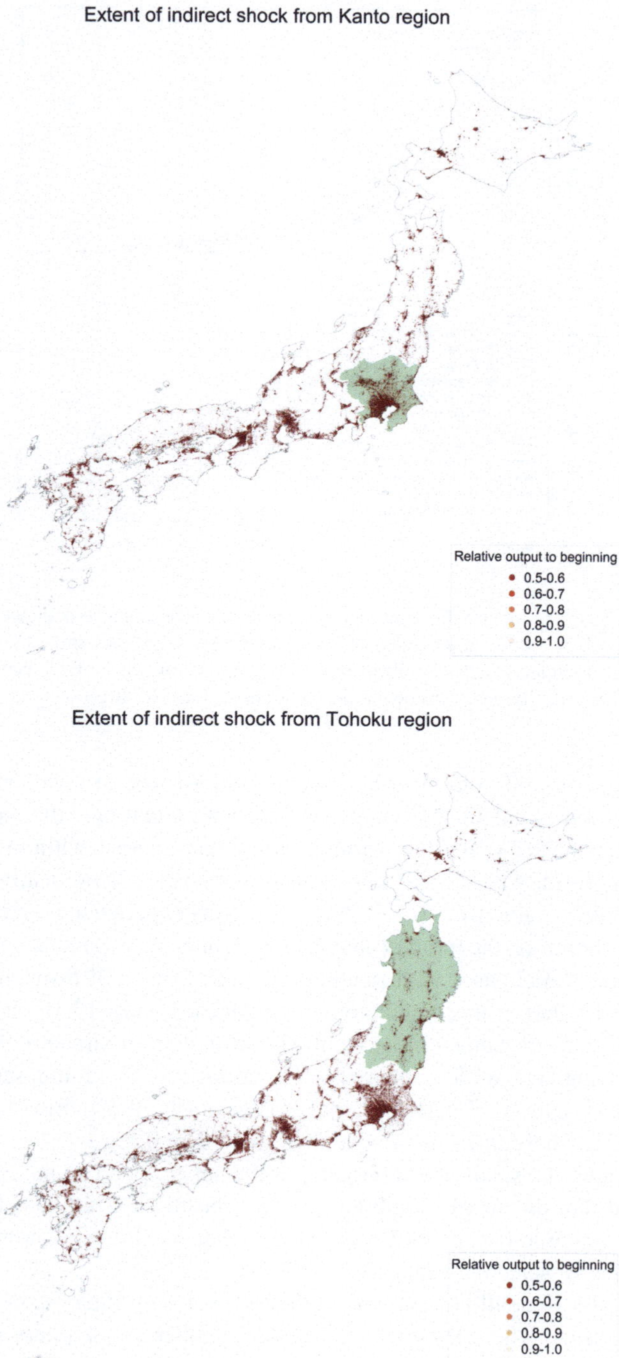

Fig. 13.8 Geographical plots of regional shocks. The left figure shows a snapshot of relative output for the beginning of day 30 in Kanto region, colored in light green. The right figure corresponds to the same simulation for Tohoku region

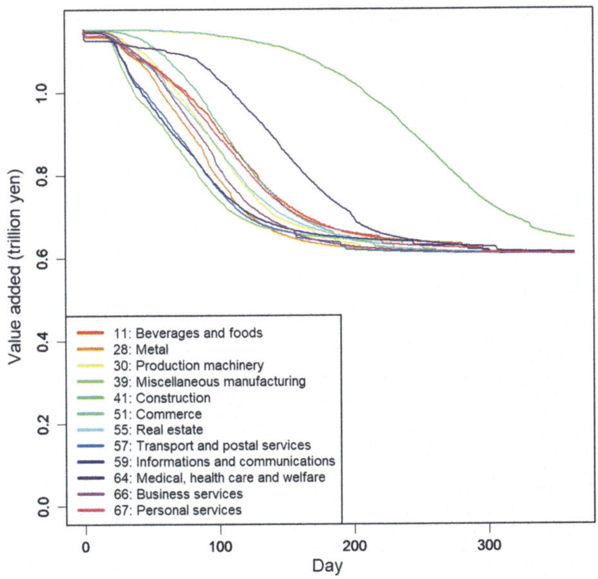

Fig. 13.9 Simulation results for different sectoral shocks. The horizontal axis shows days, whereas the vertical axis shows daily value added of the system. The solid lines show the average of 30 simulations. It is assumed that 10,000 firms randomly chosen from each of 12 sectors face a 50% loss in production capacity. Standard deviations are omitted for visibility

In a simulation, only one firm is completely destroyed at once. The influence of the simulation is calculated using the following equation: (the summation of lost value added in a year)/(the summation of value added without damages in a year). Henceforth, we will call this "system damage." Theoretically, the system damage can take a value from 0 to 1. Note that firms experience no recovery in the simulations. Therefore, the indirect damage monotonously expands as days proceed.

We simulate 7,332 cases with randomly chosen firms. All firms are not tested because of a limitation in computational resources. Figure 13.10 shows the histogram of the system damage. The result shows that approximately 90% of firms show system damage of less than 0.1. Precisely, 86.6% of the sampled firms experience less than 10^{-5} system damage. Conversely, 9.7% firms cause serious system damage. These firms incur a value of more than 0.1.

If we consider the small-world property of the network and no recovery of firms, it can be said that the supply chain has strong robustness. That is, if the failure is random, the systemic risk is not large. On the other hand, the economic system is vulnerable against selective attacks.

We check the Kendall correlation coefficients between the system damage and attributes of firms. The attributes are degree (number of suppliers and clients), in-degree (number of suppliers), out-degree (number of clients), amount of labor, number of institutions, number of factories, sales, and capital. The degree shows 0.326 as the correlation coefficient, which is the largest, and the out-degree shows 0.325, which is the second largest. In contrast, the in-degree shows 0.239.

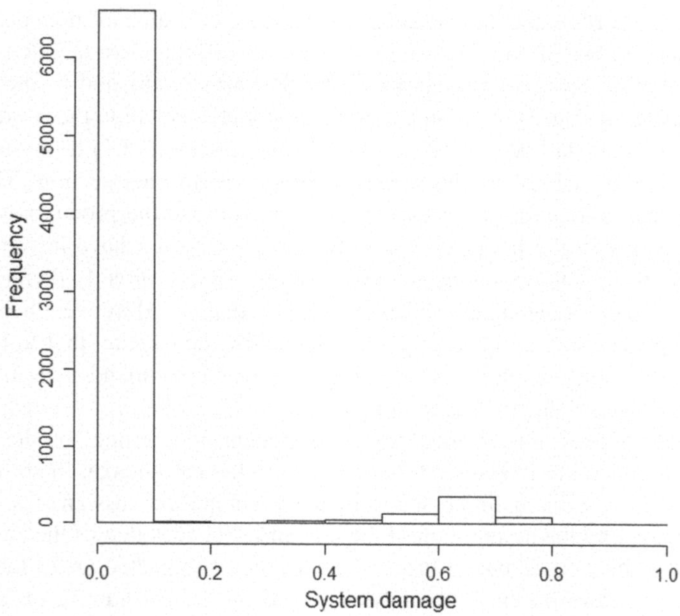

Fig. 13.10 Histogram of system damage: horizontal axis is delimited by 0.1

The results show that the number of suppliers and clients is important for ascertaining risk of single firm failure, among other attributes. Since the out-degree has a larger coefficient, the number of clients, than the number of suppliers, matters more in terms of systemic risk. This finding indicates that the downstream shock is more serious than the upstream shock.

13.4 Actual and Predicted Earthquakes

By calibrating the model to the actual supply chains taken from the TSR data and dynamics of total production, or value added, in Japan after the 2011 Japan earthquake, we determine the parameters in the model. We then use the parameter values to predict the dynamics of production after the Nankai earthquake and examine the network characteristics that affect the propagation of shocks.

13.4.1 Simulation of the 2011 Japan Earthquake

In the simulation analysis, we first calibrate the model by using the case of the 2011 Japan earthquake to accurately predict the actual dynamics of production in

Japan after the earthquake. In particular, we estimate the value of three parameters: n (the mean number of days for which inventories of inputs are targeted to hold), σ (the number of days without recovery after the earthquake), and γ (the recovery rate). We use actual firms in Japan and their supply chains within the country taken from the TSR data and determine $A_{i,j}$ and C_i in equation (13.1) from the supply-chain ties and IO tables, as described in Supply-chain data section. The direct damage of the earthquake is represented by reductions in the production capacity of a set of firms in the impacted areas. Because we do not have information on which firms were actually damaged, we randomly choose directly damaged firms based on the share of damaged firms in the impacted areas. Moreover, there are two types of impacted areas: (i) coastal areas affected by the tsunami that followed the earthquake (the blue area in Panel (a) in Fig. 13.13) and (ii) inland areas affected by the earthquake itself (the pink area in Panel (a) in Fig. 13.13). If a municipality has an earthquake greater than or equal to "seismic intensity 6 strong" on the Japanese scale, the municipality is assigned damage due to the earthquake. In addition, if a municipality has a tsunami higher than 5 m, the municipality is assigned damage due to the tsunami, and the assignment of the tsunami overrides that of the earthquake. By using the share of damaged firms in each type of impacted area (Table 13.1), we randomly determine firms directly damaged by the earthquake on day 0 for each category of damage (Panel (a) in Fig. 13.13). Complete, partial, and some destruction in Table 13.1 translates into 100%, 50%, and 20% losses in production capacity ($\delta = 1.0, 0.5$, and 0.2), respectively.

We then simulate how the sum of value added, or the value of production less the total value of the intermediates used for production, of all the firms in the economy changes over time. For each set of parameter values, we carry out 30 simulations, randomly changing firms initially damaged, and take the average of the simulated value added. The average of the total direct (initial) losses in value added is 1.7 trillion yen. The parameters of the model are calibrated by minimizing the sum of the squared differences between the simulated and actual value added. Because total value added, or gross domestic product (GDP), is available only quarterly, we estimate average value added per day for each month from the industrial production index available monthly and value added taken from the IO tables. The parameter search ranges from 1 to 20 for n, from 0 to 20 for σ, and from 0.005 to 0.100 for γ. The step sizes are 1, 1, and 0.005, respectively. Therefore, combinations of the 8,400 sets composed of the three parameters are tested (Fig. 13.11). This process leads to $n = 9$, $\sigma = 6$, and $\gamma = 0.025$.

Table 13.1 Share of damaged firms in coastal and inland areas by the level of destruction. Data from the Small and Medium Enterprise Agency (2011)

	Complete destruction	Partial destruction	Some destruction
Coastal areas	54.4%	12.7%	28.7%
Inland areas	2.5%	2.7%	82.7%

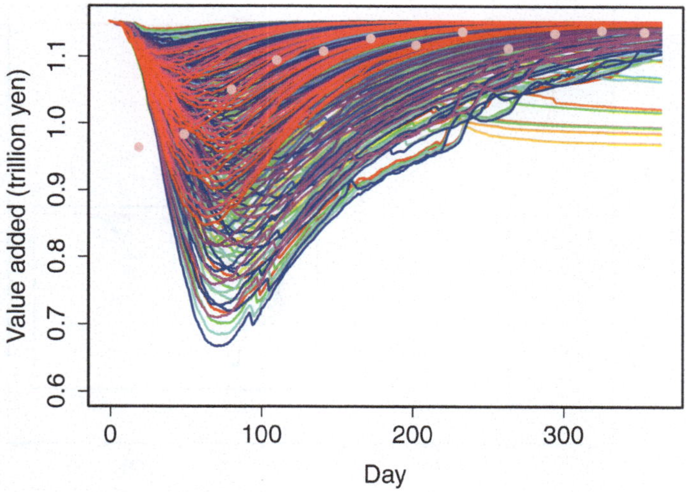

Fig. 13.11 Calibration of the model. Each line shows the simulated dynamics of the total value added of Japan, using a particular set of parameter values. From a large number of value sets, one set is chosen so that the predicted dynamics are closest to the actual dynamics shown by the pink dots

Although the simulated production using these values fits the actual production well 100 days after the earthquake or later, there is a gap between the two in the earlier period (Fig. 13.12) possibly because of power shortages and a consumption slump after the earthquake and tsunami. Because we quantify initial reduction in production due to the disasters by the share of firms damaged by the disasters classified by the levels of damages, our simulations do not incorporate production shrinkage due to the power shortages or the consumption slump. One reason for the omission is that we primarily focus on network structures as determinants of shock propagation, not on these two factors. Moreover, it is difficult to quantify production and consumption shrinkage due to these two factors accurately. First, after the earthquake, energy companies imposed rolling blackouts, i.e., rotating blackouts in a particular region in a particular time period, to their customers. While the rolling blackouts may have reduced the production of firms, it is not easy to estimate the size of the effect. Second, although incorporating the actual final consumption into the model may not be impossible, it is difficult to distinguish between the reduction in consumers' demand and producers' supply because our model does not explicitly incorporate consumers' behaviors.

Table 13.2 shows the parameters and their values used in the present section and the literature. Although the recovery mechanism is introduced in the present section, other models do not assume any recovery mechanism parameter. The value of τ, the inventory adjustment ratio, is not calibrated but taken from the literature because the result is less sensitive to the value of τ than other parameters. Although n, the target inventory size, is given a priori in most previous studies, these values are not far from its value estimated in this study. In addition, since the current model has

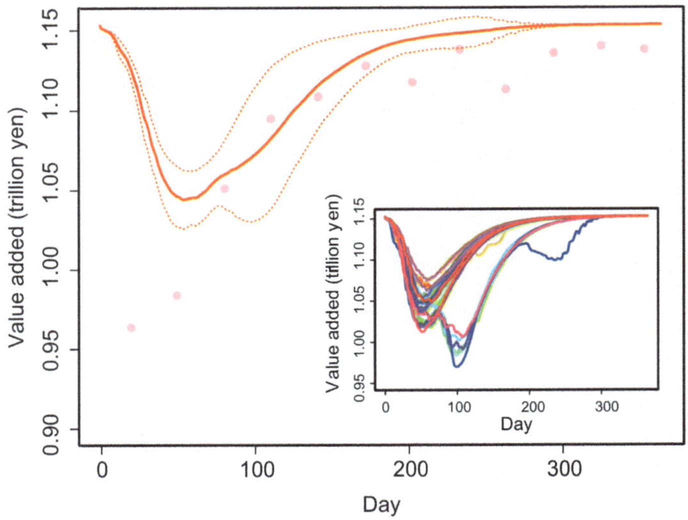

Fig. 13.12 Simulated dynamics of value added after the 2011 Japan earthquake. The horizontal axis shows the number of days after the earthquake. The vertical axis shows total value added per day in trillion yen, while its scale does not start from zero to emphasize its changes over time. The pink dots show actual monthly changes in value added (adjusted to daily values) estimated by the industrial production index. The red line indicates the average of the 30 simulations in which directly damaged firms are randomly changed although the parameter values of the model are fixed. The difference between the red line and dotted red lines represents the standard deviation. In the box, each colored line represents each of the 30 simulations

a recovery mechanism, the calibrated target inventory size can be smaller than the models without any recovery mechanism.

Figure 13.13 shows the geographic propagation of affected firms, or firms whose actual production is less than their pre-disaster capacity, due to the direct or indirect effects of the earthquake. The red dots indicate firms whose production is less than or equal to 20% of their capacity, whereas the light red and orange dots show firms with a more moderate decline in production.

A video is also provided to illustrate the dynamics on a daily basis.[1] Panel (b) in Fig. 13.13 shows that 20 days after the earthquake, its indirect effects propagated to most major cities in Japan that were not directly hit. Panel (d) shows that the indirect effects remained to a large extent even 60 days later. The video shows the simulated geographic propagation of negative shocks directly caused by the 2011 Japan earthquake through supply chains for 100 days after the earthquake. Each dot indicates a firm whose actual production is substantially lower than its production capacity. The color of the dots represents the magnitude of the decline in production, with darker red showing a larger decline and lighter orange a smaller decline.

[1] The URL is https://www.youtube.com/watch?v=IB5a2Ec6iD0

Table 13.2 List of parameters and values from the present study and the literature

Parameters	Inoue & Todo 19 NAT.SUSTAIN (Inoue and Todo 2019b) (Present)	Inoue & Todo 19 PLOS (Inoue and Todo 2019a)	Henriet et al. 12 (Henriet et al. 2012)	Hallegatte 12 (Hallegatte 2012)	Hallegatte & Henriet 08 (Hallegatte and Henriet 2008)
n (Target inventory size)	9[a,b]	15[a]	2–10	90	15
σ (Recovery delay)	6[b]	NA	NA	NA	NA
γ (Recovery rate)	0.025[b]	NA	NA	NA	NA
τ (Inventory adjustment ratio)	6	6	$1/n$	30	6

[a]Poisson distribution's mean
[b]Obtained by calibration

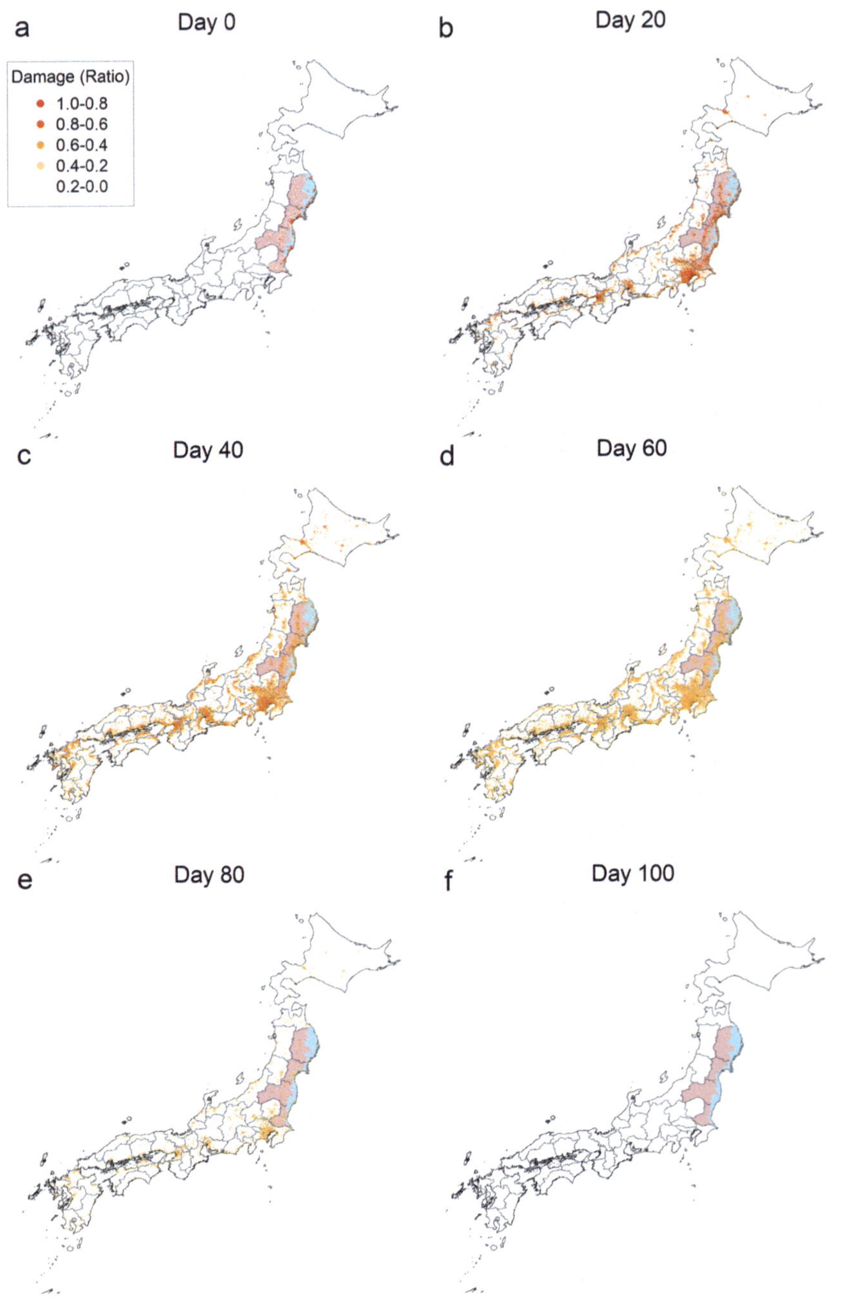

Fig. 13.13 Geographic and dynamic propagation of the shock by the 2011 Japan earthquake. On day 0, directly damaged firms are selected stochastically in each simulation, using the actual share of directly damaged firms by locational characteristics. The red and orange dots indicate firms whose actual production is substantially and moderately, respectively, smaller than their pre-disaster capacity. The parameter values are calibrated to fit the actual value added with the predicted value

Table 13.3 Estimated direct and indirect loss in value added caused by the 2011 Japan and Nankai earthquakes (unit: trillion yen [% of GDP in 2011])

	Direct loss	Indirect loss
2011 Japan earthquake (using the actual network)	0.1 [0.02]	11.4 [2.32]
2011 Japan earthquake (using randomly generated networks)	0.1 [0.02]	1.28 [0.26]
Nankai earthquake	2.3 [0.47]	52.0 [10.6]

To check possible variation across the sets of directly damaged firms assumed in the 30 cases of simulation using the same parameter values, the box in Fig. 13.12 shows the dynamics of value added in each case. The figure indicates that in 6 of these 30 cases, the economy experiences a "second wave" of negative propagation effects approximately 100 days after the earthquake. This second wave is larger than the first wave, even though the production of the entire economy had started to recover approximately 50 days earlier. As a result, the loss in production persists longer in these cases than in others. This simulation result is consistent with the actual observation that total value added (the pink dots in Fig. 13.12) twice fell in the middle of the recovery process, once seven months after the earthquake and again two months later. We discuss the possible persistence more in detail in the later section.

Owing to the propagation of the shock, the total indirect effect of the 2011 Japan earthquake, or the total loss in the value added of firms not directly damaged by the earthquake for one year, is estimated to be 11.4 trillion yen, or 2.3% of GDP. This is more than 100 times the total direct effect, or the total loss in the value added of firms directly damaged by the earthquake (Table 13.3).

13.4.2 Simulation of the Nankai Earthquake

By using the calibrated parameter values, we examine the dynamics of total value added in Japan after the possible Nankai earthquake. We stochastically choose directly damaged firms from the predicted damaged areas, using the observed share of damaged firms (Cabinet Office in Japan 2014), as we did for the 2011 Japan earthquake, to estimate the dynamics of value added in Japan after the earthquake. Figure 13.14 includes the estimated dynamics from the 30 cases of the simulation. Figure 13.15 shows the geographical propagation of the indirect effects through supply chains.

Figure 13.14 compares the dynamics of value added between the 2011 Japan earthquake (red line) and Nankai earthquake (blue line), whereas a video presents the geographic propagation of the indirect effects of the Nankai earthquake.[2] Notes for the video for the 2011 Japan earthquake apply here.

[2]The URL is https://www.youtube.com/watch?v=tUzK280BBIw

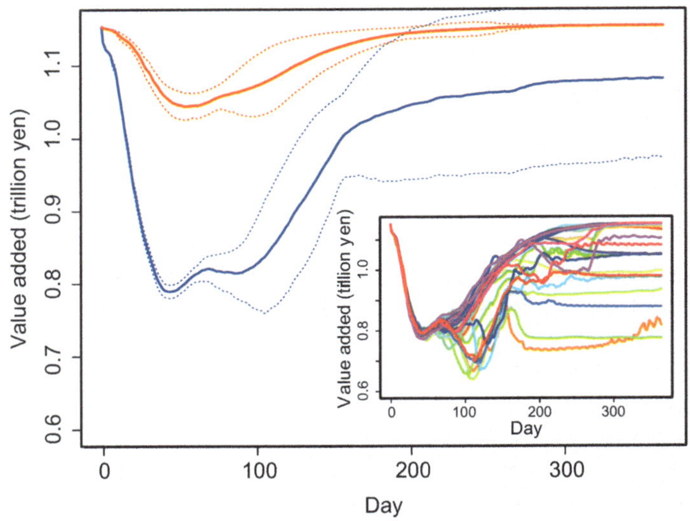

Fig. 13.14 Simulated dynamics of value added after the Nankai earthquake and 2011 Japan earthquake. The horizontal axis shows the number of days after the earthquake. The vertical axis shows total value added per day in trillion yen, while its scale does not start from zero to emphasize its changes over time. The blue line indicates the average of the 30 simulations for the Nankai earthquake. The difference between the blue line and dotted blue lines represents the standard deviation. The red lines indicate the corresponding results for the 2011 Japan earthquake. In the box, each colored line represents each of the 30 simulations for the Nankai earthquake

Figure 13.14 indicates that the effect of the Nankai earthquake is predicted to be substantially larger than that of the 2011 Japan earthquake, although the seismological magnitude of the two is similar. This finding is mostly because the Nankai earthquake and its subsequent tsunamis are predicted to hit major industrial clusters such as Tokyo, Nagoya, and Osaka, as shown in the red and blue areas in Panel (a) of Fig. 13.15. Its estimated total direct and indirect loss in production is 54.3 trillion yen, or 11% of GDP (Table 13.3). As in the case of the 2011 Japan earthquake, the indirect effect of the earthquake is far greater than the direct effect. In addition, many of the 30 cases of the simulation illustrated in the box in Fig. 13.14 show the second wave of negative effects on production, confirming the possibility of persistent economic losses.

13.4.3 Causes of the Large Indirect Effects

The simulation analysis has thus far highlighted two notable features of the propagation of economic shocks through supply chains: (i) the substantial indirect effects and (ii) their possible persistence in the long run. In other words, the mechanisms arising from supply chains can largely affect resilience and sustainability of our economy and society. To examine what the causes of these two features are, we

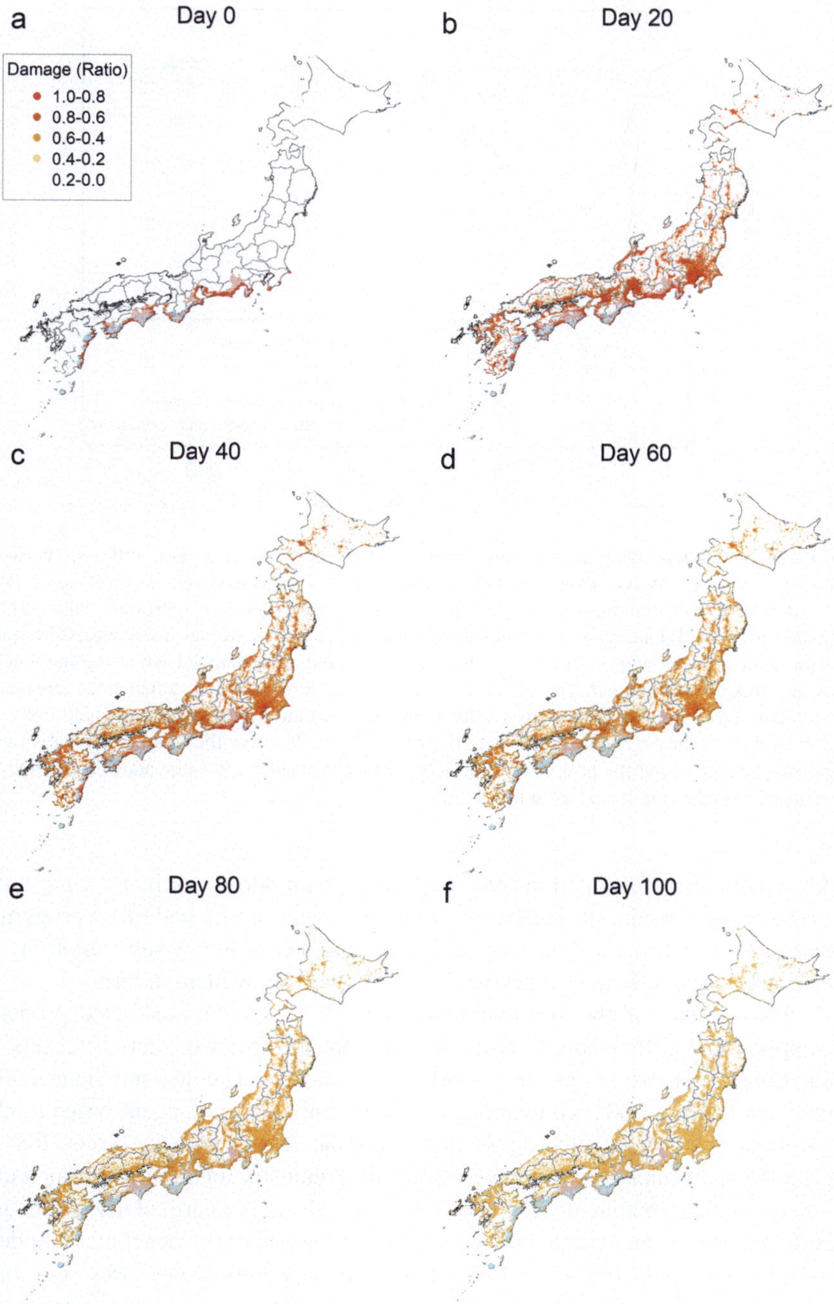

Fig. 13.15 Simulated dynamics of the direct and indirect effects of the Nankai earthquake. On day 0, directly damaged firms are selected stochastically in each simulation, using the actual share of directly damaged firms by locational characteristics. The red and orange dots indicate firms whose actual production is substantially and moderately smaller than their capacity, respectively. The parameter values are calibrated by the simulations of the 2011 Japan earthquake and applied to the Nankai earthquake

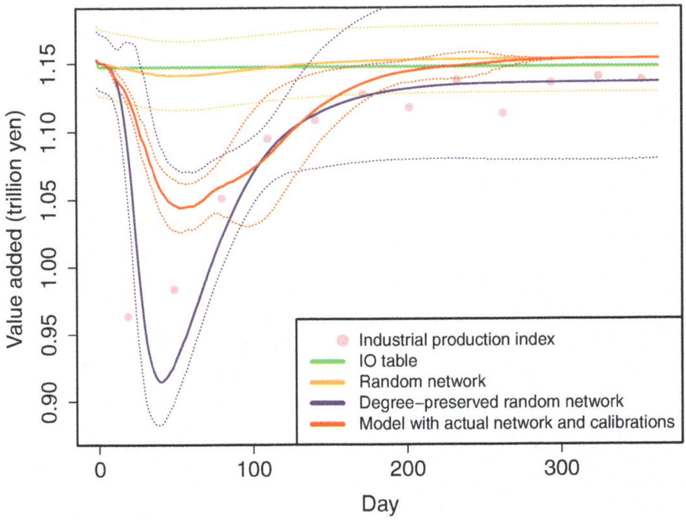

Fig. 13.16 Simulated dynamics of value added using supply chains with different network structures. The vertical axis shows total value added per day in trillion yen, while its scale does not start from zero to emphasize its changes over time. The green line represents value added estimated from the IO analysis. The solid orange line indicates the average value added from the 30 simulations, using supply chains in which links are randomly changed while the number of firms and links is maintained. The difference between the solid line and dotted lines represents the standard deviation. The purple lines indicate results from the supply chains in which links are randomized while the degree distribution is preserved. The red lines are the simulation results using actual supply chains and the pink dots show actual monthly changes in value added estimated by the industrial production index, as in Fig. 13.12

conduct a number of simulations under different assumptions, taking the case of the 2011 Japan earthquake. In particular, we explore the role of scale-free properties (existence of hub firms with an extremely large number of links), substitutability of intermediate products, and cycles in GSCCs. We will show them in turn.

A major cause of the substantial indirect effects is the scale-free property of supply chains. To examine this, we experiment with two alternative sets of simulations. First, we simply use standard IO analysis (Haimes and Jiang 2001; Santos and Haimes 2004; Okuyama et al. 2004) rather than an agent-based model to estimate the loss in value added and show the results with the green line in Fig. 13.16. In this analysis, we only consider inter-industry linkages and completely ignore the complex nature of firm-level networks. The figure particularly shows that the effect of the IO analysis is much smaller than the one of the benchmark model.

Second, we apply our agent-based model to hypothetical networks (i.e., randomly generated supply chains) rather than the actual network. In this experiment, we maintain the total number of nodes and links and randomly determine whether each pair of firms is linked based on the actual probability. Random networks typically have no scale-free property unlike actual supply chains because the distribution of degrees does not follow the power law without any hub node. The orange line in Fig. 13.16 shows the simulation result. The figure highlights that the estimated effect of the earthquake using random networks without any scale-free property is substantially smaller than the benchmark effect using actual supply chains. These smaller effects imply that the scale-free property aggravates the propagation of shocks through supply chains.

This result is in line with the literature on propagation of shocks through artificial networks (Henriet et al. 2012), which creates scale-free networks deduced from actual IO tables and degree distributions, compares them with fully connected artificial networks, and concludes that the scale-free property aggravates the shocks.

In network analyses, degree-preserving random networks are also commonly used to check how characteristics other than the scale-free property affect outcomes, A degree-preserving network of an actual network is defined as a network in which the number of nodes and the distribution of the degree of each node (i.e., the number of links for each node) are the same as in the actual network while the connected nodes are randomly shuffled. In degree-preserving random networks, the scale-free property is retained, but other characteristics may be changed. In our case, in degree-preserving random networks, firms tend to be linked with suppliers in a larger variety of industries and thus find it difficult to substitute damaged suppliers for other current ones than in the actual network in which firms are linked with those in only a few industries. Unlike purely random networks, the simulation using degree-preserving random networks shows greater indirect effects than the actual network. This is because they have scale-free property but the supply-chains' substitutability is comparably low. The role of substitutability will be discussed more in Causes of the persistence of the indirect effects section.

Figure 13.16 shows that there is a huge gap between the IO table analysis and the simulation with the calibrated model. To examine whether this large gap is observed in cases with a smaller shock, we simulate an earthquake of magnitude 7.3 that hit Kumamoto, a western part of Japan, on the 16th April, 2016. By using the same method illustrated in Fig. 13.16, we find that the indirect effect estimated using IO tables and our benchmark simulation is 2.0 and 3.0 trillion yen in a year, respectively. Although we should note that the method using IO tables does not assume recovery of production facilities while our benchmark simulation does, the indirect effect estimated from IO tables should be regarded as the upper limit, it is suggested that as the initial shock becomes smaller, the gap between estimated from the two models becomes smaller.

Another major cause of the substantial indirect effects is the substitutability of intermediate products, as shocks propagate more when inputs are more specific (Hallegatte 2012; Barrot and Sauvagnat 2016). The 2011 Japan earthquake provided many anecdotes that support this conjecture (Fujimoto 2011). To check how this substitutability affects the propagation of shocks, we experiment with three alternative assumptions in our simulations, changing the level of substitutability. First, we assume that each firm produces a firm-specific product, rather than industry-specific, meaning that substitution among intermediates is impossible. The simulation results, shown by the purple line in Fig. 13.17, indicate that the propagation of the disaster shock is substantially faster and larger than in the

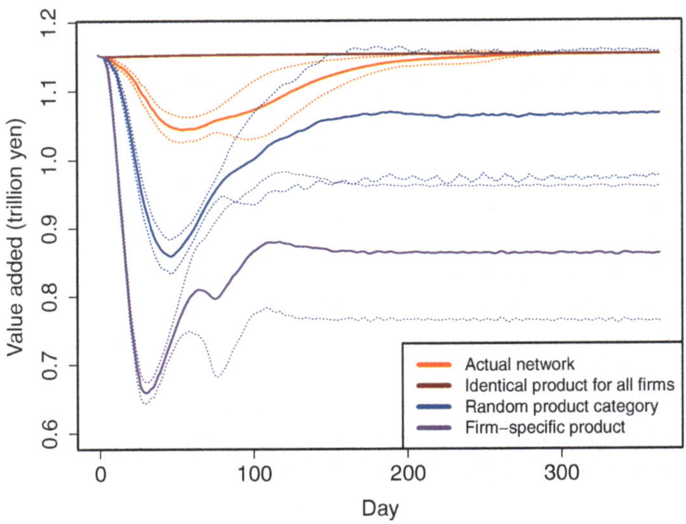

Fig. 13.17 Simulated dynamics of value added using supply chains with different levels of substitution. The vertical axis shows total value added per day in trillion yen, while its scale does not start from zero to emphasize its changes over time. The solid lines indicate the average of value added from the 30 simulations. The difference between the solid line and dotted lines represents the standard deviation. The red, brown, blue, and purple lines are respectively the results from using actual supply chains, those in which all firms produce an identical product (complete substitution of intermediates), those in which the product category (or industry) of each firm is randomly changed (medium substitution), and those in which each firm produces a firm-specific product (no substitution)

benchmark simulation where substitution is allowed. Second, we use actual supply-chain links but change the industry or product category of each firm randomly (the blue line in Fig. 13.17). Under this assumption, products of the suppliers of a firm are less likely to be related to each other or to the product of the firm. Therefore, substitution among intermediates is more difficult in this network than in the actual one. Finally, the brown line in Fig. 13.17 indicates the results assuming complete substitution (i.e., supply chains in which all firms produce an identical product). The blue and purple lines are lower than the red ones, indicating that the indirect effect is larger when the level of substitution is lower. With complete substitution (brown), the negative effect is negligible. The results clearly show that the level of substitutability among inputs is an important determinant of the propagation effects.

13.4.4 Causes of the Persistence of the Indirect Effects

The pink dots in Fig. 13.12 illustrate the drops in actual value added during the recovery from the 2011 Japan earthquake, and the boxes in Figs. 13.12 and 13.14

show the corresponding second waves of negative effects on simulated value added, highlighting that the negative effects of a disaster can persist in the long run. To clarify whether input substitutability affects this possible persistence, the results of the 30 cases in our simulation are shown in Fig. 13.18, assuming complete (Panel b), some (f), and no substitution (h) and using actual supply chains (d). It is clear that as the difficulty of input substitution increases, the negative effect is more likely to persist in the long run mostly because of the second wave, which starts after the short recovery from the first wave.

Another possible cause of the second wave and thus the persistence of the indirect effects is the complexity of cycles in GSCCs because these cycles may lead to the circulation of shocks in a complex manner. To test this conjecture, we simulate our model by using hypothetical supply chains with no cycle among firms. Specifically, starting with actual supply chains, we randomly assign a number to each node sequentially and keep only directional links from a node to another with a smaller number. All other links are dropped. In this tree-like network, products always flow from upstream to downstream firms. In addition, we experiment with the four levels of input substitution using this network with no cycle, as we did in Panels (b), (d), (f), and (h) of Fig. 13.18 using the actual network, and present the results of the 30 simulations in Panels (a), (c), (e), and (g). None of the 30 simulations in these four panels shows a second wave of effects. Therefore, we conclude that the persistence of negative effects does not emerge when there is no cycle in the network, regardless of the level of input substitution. When supply chains have complex cycles because of their scale-free property and sufficiently large GSCC and when substitution between inputs is difficult because of their specificity, the economy is likely to experience a second wave of negative shocks and therefore a persistent decline in production.

13.5 Conclusion

We used Japanese nation-wide supply-chain network data and employed a modified version of Hallegatte's model (Hallegatte 2008). Then, we examined how negative shocks by artificial disasters propagate through supply chains.

First, we analyzed comprehensive shocks and obtained the following results. First, network structures severely affect the speed of propagation in the short run and the total loss in the long run. The scale-free nature of the actual supply-chain network, that is, the power-law degree distribution, leads to faster propagation than the random network. Second, a small number of firms with intense damages cause faster and larger propagation. Third, substitution among suppliers largely contributes to economic resistance. The pace of the propagation of negative shocks increases with an increase in substitution difficulties. Fourth, direct damages in industrial regions promote faster propagation than those in less industrial regions, although the total loss in value added in the long run is the same. Fifth, different sectoral damages cause large differences in the speed of propagation. Particularly,

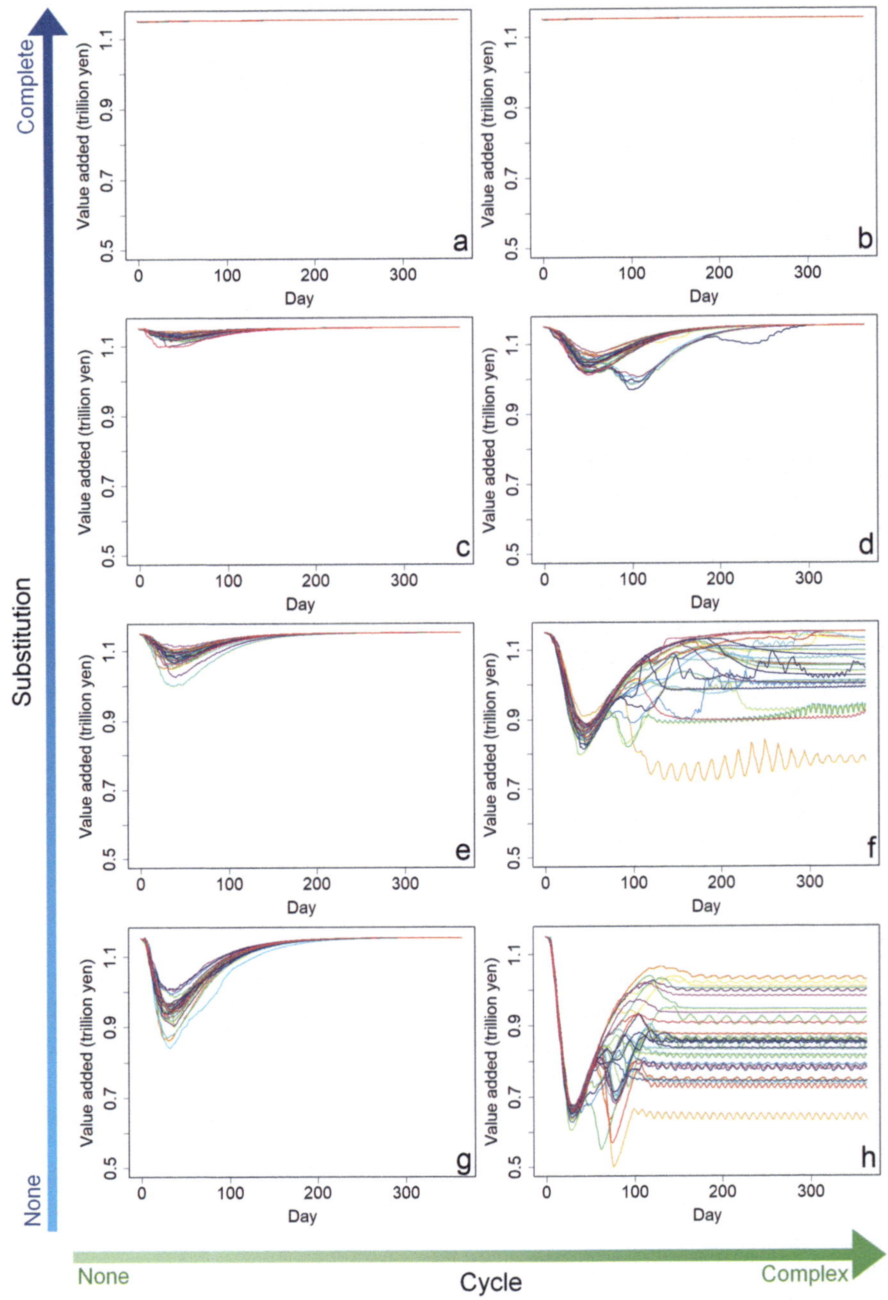

Fig. 13.18 Comparison of the dynamics of value added using different supply chains. The vertical axis shows value added per day, while its scale differs across the panels to highlight the presence or absence of the second wave. The eight sets of the simulation with different assumptions are classified by the level of substitution vertically and the complexity of cycles horizontally. Each color in each box indicates each of the 30 simulations in these eight sets

the effects of direct damages on the construction sector are quite small. Finally, an estimation of the indirect damage triggered by a single-firm loss shows that 86.6% of firms cause less than 10^{-5} of the damage to the entire economy. On the other hand, 9.7% of firms cause more than 10% of the damage to the entire supply chain. Thus, the actual supply chain has strong robustness against random failures, but it is vulnerable to selective attacks. These results imply that we cannot use only the size of direct damages by negative shocks to predict the outcome of the economic loss. Adversely, different initial damages can generate considerably different damages, depending on the property of the supply chain network in the economy.

Then, we simulated the actual and predicted earthquakes. The simulation provide several practical implications for supply-chain resilience to economic shocks and directions for further research. As supply chains are usually complex (scale-free properties and cycles), it is inevitable that economic shocks propagate and are amplified through supply chains, leading to large negative indirect effects across the economy. These negative indirect effects may emerge as a second wave after the recovery process starts and thus be persistent in the long run. In other words, the network complexity deteriorates resilience and sustainability of the economy and society.

We therefore need policy interventions that help those firms directly and indirectly affected by a shock minimize the negative effects. Such interventions can be justified because they also help other firms linked with the firms supported by the interventions (i.e., there are externalities in the propagation process). Supporting only firms directly damaged by the shock is insufficient to prevent propagation. Further research should thus examine efficient network intervention after shocks. Although efficient network intervention has been discussed in other studies (Cohen et al. 2002; Valente 2010, 2017), researchers have rarely adopted this concept in the context of supply-chain analysis.

Our findings suggest that supply chains are more resilient when firms can easily substitute intermediate products. However, because firms benefit from the use of specific inputs that can lead to unique, high value products (Aoki 1988), we must investigate the optimal supply-chain structure that maximizes its benefit and lowers its expected loss due to the propagation of shocks. Although an optimal network structure under the diffusion of information and knowledge has been presented (Alshamsi et al. 2018), no work has thus far been carried out in the context of supply chains.

In addition, one practical implication from our findings is that we need to use actual networks, rather than hypothetical networks, to quantify the diffusion of negative shocks through firm networks. Especially, although we have conducted several experiments, we still do not fully understand how the network complexity affects the behavior of supply chains. Besides, considering the findings in this study, discussions on simple artificial networks may not have any practical implications. However, such actual data are rarely available, particularly those for supply chains in developing countries and global supply chains across countries. Therefore, collecting such supply-chain data more broadly should be required to deepen the understanding of the propagation effect. These three directions are left for future research.

Finally, we can expand the model in terms of the price and equilibrium mechanism. In fact, a preceding paper has discussed the artificial shocks on global supply chains (Otto et al. 2017), which is based on the equilibrium mechanism and the agent based model. Furthermore, by considering the price, we can consider the autonomous choice of trade partners, which generates a more realistic model than a model with a fixed network structure (Gualdi and Mandel 2016).

References

Acemoglu D, Carvalho VM, Ozdaglar A, Alireza T (2012) The network origins of aggregate fluctuations. Econometrica 80(5):1977–2016

Acemoglu D, Akcigit U, Kerr WR (2016a) Innovation network. Proc Natl Acad Sci 113(41):11483–11488

Acemoglu D, Akcigit U, Kerr W (2016b) Networks and the macroeconomy: An empirical exploration. NBER Macroecon Annu 30:273–335

Alshamsi A , Pinheiro FL, Hidalgo CA (2018) Optimal diversification strategies in the networks of related products and of related research areas. Nat Commun 9(1):1328

Aoki M (1988) Information, incentives and bargaining in the Japanese economy: a microtheory of the Japanese Economy. Cambridge University Press, Cambridge

Bak P, Chen K, Scheinkman J, Woodford M (1993) Aggregate fluctuations from independent sectoral shocks: self-organized criticality in a model of production and inventory dynamics. Ricerche Economiche 47(1):3–30

Banerjee A, Chandrasekhar AG, Duflo E, Jackson MO (2013) The diffusion of microfinance. Science 341(6144):1236498–1–7

Barabási A-L (2016) Network science. Cambridge University Press, Cambridge

Barabási AL, Albert R (1999) Emergence of scaling in random networks. Science 286:509–512

Barrot J-N, Sauvagnat J (2016) Input specificity and the propagation of idiosyncratic shocks in production networks. Q J Econ 131(3):1543–1592

Battiston S, Puliga M, Kaushik R, Tasca P, Caldarelli G (2012) Debtrank: too central to fail? Financial networks, the fed and systemic risk. Sci Rep 2:541

Beroza GC (2012) How many great earthquakes should we expect? Proc Natl Acad Sci 109(3):651–652

Broder A, Kumar R, Maghoul F, Raghavan P, Rajagopalan S, Stata R, Tomkins A, Wiener J (2000) Graph structure in the web. Comput Netw 33(1–6):309–320

Burt RS (2004) Structural holes and good ideas. Am J Sociol 110(2):349–399

Cabinet Office in Japan (2012) White paper on disaster management

Cabinet Office in Japan (2014) White paper on disaster management

Carvalho VM, Nirei M, Saito YU, Tahbaz-Salehi A (2016) Supply chain disruptions: evidence from the great east Japan earthquake. Columbia Business School Research Paper 17-5

Centola D (2010) The spread of behavior in an online social network experiment. Science 329(5996):1194–1197

Chakraborty A, Kichikawa Y, Iino T, Iyetomi H, Inoue H, Fujiwara Y, Aoyama H (2018) Hierarchical communities in walnut structure of Japanese production network. PLoS ONE 13(8):1–25

Cohen R, Havlin S, Ben-Avraham D (2002) Structural properties of scale-free networks. In: Handbook of graphs and networks, Wiley-VCH, Weinheim

Delli Gatti D, Di Guilmi C, Gaffeo E, Giulioni G, Gallegati M, Palestrini A (2005) A new approach to business fluctuations: heterogeneous interacting agents, scaling laws and financial fragility. J Econ Behav Organ 56(4):489–512
Fujimoto T (2011) Supply chain competitiveness and robustness: a lesson from the 2011 tohoku earthquake and supply chain “virtual dualization”. Manufacturing Management Research Center
Fujiwara Y, Aoyama H (2010) Large-scale structure of a nation-wide production network. Eur Phys J B 77(4):565–580
Gilbert EN (1959) Random graphs. Ann Math Stat 30(4):1141–1144
Gualdi S, Mandel A (2016) On the emergence of scale-free production networks. J Econ Dyn Control 73:61–77
Haimes YY, Jiang P (2001) Leontief-based model of risk in complex interconnected infrastructures. J Infrastruct Syst 7(1):1–12
Hallegatte S (2008) An adaptive regional input-output model and its application to the assessment of the economic cost of katrina. Risk Anal 28(3):779–799
Hallegatte S (2012) Modeling the roles of heterogeneity, substitution, and inventories in the assessment of natural disaster economic costs. The World Bank, Washington DC
Hallegatte S, Henriet F (2008) Assessing the consequences of natural disasters on production networks: a disaggregated approach. Technical report, Fondazione Eni Enrico Mattei (FEEM)
Henriet F, Hallegatte S, Tabourier L (2012) Firm-network characteristics and economic robustness to natural disasters. J Econ Dyn Control 36(1):150–167
Huang X, Vodenska I, Havlin S, Stanley HE (2013) Cascading failures in bi-partite graphs: model for systemic risk propagation. Sci Rep 3:1219
Inoue H (2016) Analyses of aggregate fluctuations of firm production network based on the self-organized criticality model. Evol Inst Econ Rev 13(2):383–396
Inoue H, Todo Y (2019a) Propagation of negative shocks through firm networks: Evidence from simulation on comprehensive supply-chain data. PLoS ONE 14(3):1–17
Inoue H, Todo Y (2019b) Firm-level propagation of shocks through supply-chain networks. Nat Sustain 2:841–847
Jackson MO (2010) Social and economic networks. Princeton University Press, Princeton
Kreindler GE, Young HP (2014) Rapid innovation diffusion in social networks. Proc Natl Acad Sci 111(Supplement 3):10881–10888
Lee K-M, Goh K-I (2016) Strength of weak layers in cascading failures on multiplex networks: case of the international trade network. Sci Rep 6:26346
Milly PCD, Wetherald RT, Dunne KA, Delworth TL (2002) Increasing risk of great floods in a changing climate. Nature 415(6871):514
Ministry of Economy, Trade and Industry (2011) White paper on international economy and trade. METI Tokyo
Ministry of Economy, Trade and Industry, Japan (2011) The 2011 updated Input-output table
Ministry of Internal Affairs and Communications (2013) The Japan standard industrial classification (JSIC) summary of development of the JSIC and its eleventh revision
Newman M (2010) Networks: an introduction. Oxford University Press Inc., New York
Okuyama Y, Hewings GJD, Sonis M (2004) Measuring economic impacts of disasters: interregional input-output analysis using sequential interindustry model. In: Modeling spatial and economic impacts of disasters. Springer, New York, pp 77–101
Otto C, Willner SN, Wenz L, Frieler K, Levermann A (2017) Modeling loss-propagation in the global supply network: the dynamic agent-based model acclimate. J Econ Dyn Control 83:232–269
Pelling M, Özerdem A, Barakat S (2002) The macro-economic impact of disasters. Prog Dev Stud 2(4):283–305
Rose A, Liao S (2005) Modeling regional economic resilience to disasters: a computable general equilibrium analysis of water service disruptions. J Reg Sci 45(1):75–112
Santos JR, Haimes YY (2004) Modeling the demand reduction input-output (i-o) inoperability due to terrorism of interconnected infrastructures. Risk Anal 24(6):1437–1451

The Small and Medium Enterprise Agency (2011) White paper on small and medium enterprises in Japan
Thurner S, Poledna S (2013) Debtrank-transparency: controlling systemic risk in financial networks. Sci Rep 3:1888
Tierney KJ (1997) Business impacts of the northridge earthquake. J Conting Crisis Manag 5(2):87–97
Todo Y, Nakajima K, Matous P (2015) How do supply chain networks affect the resilience of firms to natural disasters? Evidence from the great east Japan earthquake. J Reg Sci 55(2):209–229
Valente TW (1995) Network models of the diffusion of innovations. Hampton Press, New York
Valente TW (2010) Social networks and health: models, methods, and applications, vol 1. Oxford University Press, New York
Valente TW (2017) Putting the network in network interventions. Proc Natl Acad Sci 114(36):9500–9501
Watts DJ (1999) Small worlds: the dynamics of networks between order and randomness. Princeton University Press, Princeton
Watts DJ (2002) A simple model of global cascades on random networks. Proc Natl Acad Sci 99(9):5766–5771
Watts DJ, Strogatz SH (1998) Collective dynamics of 'small-world' networks. Nature 393:440–442

Chapter 14
The Known (Ex Ante) and the Unknown (Ex Post): Common Principles in Economics and Natural Sciences

Jürgen Mimkes

Abstract In the first part, this chapter discusses a model of the known and unknown elements in science, by which it is possible to select or exclude various mathematical approaches to social and natural sciences. As a result, economics and physics may be formulated by various mathematical fields: differential forms, closed integrals, stochastic theory, non-linear (differential) equations, and chaos theory. All these mathematical fields contain known and unknown elements, and they are not competitive but complementary approaches to science.

The second part applies the results to economics and natural sciences: differential forms in double entry accounting are the basis for the laws of macroeconomics and correspond to the laws of thermodynamics. Closed integrals explain the mechanism of economic cycles and the Carnot cycle in mechanical engineering. Both cycles run on oil! In stochastic theory, entropy leads to the laws of statistical mechanics, microeconomics, and finance. Nonlinear Lotka-Volterra equations and chaos theory are the basis of complexity in economics and natural sciences.

Keywords Accounting · Economic laws · Production function · Entropy · Production cycle · Money · Energy

14.1 Introduction

Prof. Masanao Aoki was an outstanding teacher, an excellent scholar, and a fighter against the walls of thought in science. In his spirit, the following contribution tries to focus on a topic that is common to all sciences: the known and the unknown. This topic has been addressed at several recent economics conferences (Mimkes 2017, 2019). The paper has two different parts:

J. Mimkes (✉)
Physics Department, Paderborn University, Paderborn, Germany
e-mail: juergen.Mimkes@upb.de

H. Aoyama et al. (eds.), *Complexity, Heterogeneity, and the Methods of Statistical Physics in Economics*, Evolutionary Economics and Social Complexity Science 22,
https://doi.org/10.1007/978-981-15-4806-2_14

The first part discusses the known and the unknown in general science and investigates ways to model science of the past and the future by mathematical fields. As the methods for natural sciences are well established, the main object is to find methods to handle social sciences by the proper mathematical fields. The results are compared to the existing mainstream economics theory and to the methods of natural sciences.

The second part uses suitable mathematical fields to discuss economic problems and compares the outcome with data, with standard economics and with natural sciences. This will be the main part of the paper. Few mathematical fields are presented in more detail; other fields are only mentioned.

The final outlook shows the possibilities to apply the future model to many branches of social sciences, economics, sociology, politics, history, and other fields.

14.2 The U–V Model of Science

We teachers may ask ourselves, why we are teaching the knowledge of today, when the students need the knowledge of tomorrow. Is teaching the knowledge of the past useful for the future?

The reason for teaching the known past is hope, the hope that some parts of today's knowledge will still be valid in the future. These parts of knowledge may be called the V-elements of the future. Of course, in the future students will also encounter new and unknown things; these may be called U-elements of the future. Accordingly, the future will consist of the interaction W (V, U) of known V-elements and unknown U-elements. W (V, U) is the general structure of all sciences; we teach the V- elements and we do research for the U-elements.

However, how useful is it to define the U and V elements and the interaction W (U, V), if we cannot look into the future? The answer is simple: Today is the future of yesterday! We may look at our present data and find out what is different from yesterday.

Finally, we must ask whether it will be possible to model the future in social or natural sciences by mathematical theories. How do we solve the contradiction to calculate the future and not to know the outcome for the future?

14.2.1 Examples for the U–V Model of Science

A closer look at different fields of science will show that the U–V model is incorporated in science in general:

Science: Teaching the Known (V) and Doing Research for the Unknown (U)
The U–V model is common to all sciences. In each science we have

V: Teaching the known facts.
U: Research for the unknown.

Economics: Ex Ante (V) and Ex Post (U)
In economics, we find all economic terms are either presently known (ex ante), or they are presently unknown and will perhaps be known in the future (ex post).

V: Ex ante terms like a function $F(x, y)$ are valid (V) in the past and future; we may calculate functions at any time. Another example is a contract. If we have an annual contract for our savings account, we may calculate the interest years in advance.
U: Ex post terms like income or profit are the most common terms in economics. They are only known after we have finished an action: We can file our income tax only at the end of the year, not in the beginning.

In neoclassical theory, there is a widely accepted economic theory, the *Solow Model*:

The Solow model is based on income (Y) as a function of capital (K) and labor (L):

$Y = F(K, L)$. The function $F(K, L)$ is the production function. However, this approach contradicts the U–V model: Income (Y) is an ex post or U term, the function $F(K, L)$ is an ex ante or V term. One cannot calculate an unknown term Y by a known function F! Accordingly, Y and F cannot be equal! The neoclassical theory cannot be valid. We will discuss this point in various instances.

Natural Science: Conservative (V) and Not Conservative (U) Forces
In natural sciences, we have two different kinds of forces. They are either conservative or non-conservative.

V: Conservative systems have no friction; the future is predictable.
U: Non-conservative frictional forces make the future unpredictable. Friction creates heat and leads to the laws of thermodynamics, W (U, V). Thermodynamics is a very general theory and applies in many natural sciences like physics, chemistry, biology, metallurgy, meteorology, or civil engineering.

Astronomy: The Kepler laws of planets are an example for W (0, V): Kepler observed the movement of planets in space without friction, $U = 0$. Accordingly, the Kepler laws of planets are valid in the past and in the future.

Mathematics: Calculus with Exact (V) and Not-Exact (U) Differential Forms
In two-dimensional calculus, differential forms are either exact or not exact.

(V): Exact differential forms (dF) are complete and have a stem function (F), which we may calculate any time.
(U): Not exact differential forms (δM) are incomplete and do not have a stem function (M). A not-exact differential form (δM) may be linked to an exact differential form (dF) by an integrating factor λ: $\delta M = \lambda\, dF$.

Thermodynamics: The first law of thermodynamics is always given by exact and not-exact differential forms: $\delta Q = dE - \delta W$ connects heat (Q) to energy (E) and work (W). Heat and work are not exact; they do not have a stem function. They cannot be calculated unless more information is obtained. In the second law of thermodynamics: $\delta Q = T\,dS$, the not-exact heat (δQ) is linked to an exact function (dS) by an integrating factor (T). The function (S) is called entropy; the integrating factor is the temperature of the economic system.

Mathematics: Closed Line Integrals by Riemann (V) and Stokes (U)
In two-dimensional calculus, we have closed Riemann and closed Stokes line integrals.

(V): Riemann integral: The line integral of an exact differential form (dF) is a Riemann integral. The integral does not depend on the path of integration, and we may calculate the Riemann integral for any boundaries A and B. The closed Riemann integral is always zero, the integrals from A to B and from B to A cancel, as the Riemann integral is path independent. The closed Riemann integral corresponds to a ring.
(U): Stokes integral: The line integral of a not-exact differential form (δM) is a Stokes integral, which depends on the path of integration. The closed Stokes line integral is not zero, the path-dependent integrals from A to B and back from B to A do not cancel.

The closed Stokes integral corresponds to a spiral.

Magnetism: The magnetic field is a Stokes integral and spirals around an electric wire.

Accounting: An account is a Stokes integral: A savings account spirals up to higher profits. A permanently depleted account spirals down to deficit.

Mathematics: Stochastic Theory with "Real" (V) and "Probable" (U) Values
In probability theory, real constraints lead to probable results.

(V): Real functions are often the given constraints in a stochastic theory.
(U): The result of stochastic calculations are probability terms.

Mathematics: Linear (V) and Non-linear (U) Differential Equations
Differential equations are either linear or nonlinear.

(V): Linear differential equations may be solved by various methods.
(U): Non-linear differential equations cannot be solved in general.

This list may be extended to nearly all sciences and fields of mathematics. Some examples of the U–V model have been discussed in the literature (Mimkes 2019).

14.2.2 *Mathematical Fields Representing Economics/Natural Sciences*

The U–V model of science applies to economics, to natural sciences, and to mathematics. This enables us to select proper mathematical fields to represent economics and natural sciences:

V – terms in social or natural sciences must correspond to V – terms in mathematics, and
U – terms in social or natural sciences to U – terms in mathematics.

Line Integrals in Economics or Natural Sciences
Alternatively, we may chose two-dimensional closed-line integrals as a mathematical tool in economics or natural sciences: all ex ante/conservative terms are closed Riemann integrals, and all ex post/not conservative terms are closed Stokes integrals.

Differential Forms in Economics or Natural Sciences
We may chose differential forms in two dimensions as a mathematical tool in economics or natural sciences: all ex ante/conservative terms must correspond to exact differential forms, and all ex post/not conservative terms to not-exact differential forms.

Stochastic Theory in Economics or Natural Sciences
If we chose stochastic theory as a base of economics or natural sciences, all ex ante terms must correspond to real functions, and all ex post terms to probability terms.

Non-linear Differential Equations and Chaos Theory in Economics or Natural Sciences
Economics or natural science theory in differential equations require ex ante and ex post terms to correspond to linear and non-linear differential equations. These equations are the basis of system science, complexity, and chaos theory.

There are two important results of this paragraph:

1. Mathematical fields like calculus, stochastic theory, complexity, or chaos theory do not compete for the theories of economics or natural sciences; they are complementary.
2. The mathematical structures of economics and natural sciences are very similar.

Time
So far, we have discussed the past and the future without mentioning time. A V-element may be a function of time $f(t)$. It is valid in the past and in the future. Its typical example is the field mechanics; here all terms are function of space and time. The laws of mechanics without friction, like in space, are always valid; we may calculate the position of the planets at any time t.

This is not true for the unknown U elements of the future. There are at least two ways to handle time in the future model:

1. Thermodynamics as well as mainstream economics do not contain time as a parameter.
2. Statistical mechanics includes time in non-linear equations like the equations by Fokker Plank, Hamilton, or Lotka-Volterra. However, these equations have complex solutions.

14.3 Applications to Economics

We will now apply the four mathematical fields to model economics and compare the outcome to standard economic theory and to natural sciences. The first two fields, closed integrals and calculus, will be applied to macroeconomics; the third field, stochastic theory to microeconomics and finance; and finally non-linearity to special economic problems.

14.3.1 The Laws of Macroeconomics in Closed Integrals

According to the U–V model, the laws of macroeconomics are given by W (U, V), where V and U may be presented by closed Riemann and Stokes integrals. The problem is now to find the proper equations. A recent paper has derived the integrals of macroeconomics from Luca Pacioli's laws of double entry accounting (Mimkes 2017).

Double Entry Accounting and Macroeconomics

In double entry accounting, Luca Pacioli considers two accounts, the monetary account and be productive account. Accounts can never predicted; they are ex post terms and may be written as closed Stokes integrals.

The monetary account is the surplus or profit (M), the difference between income (Y) and costs (C). The monetary account is ex post and must be presented as closed Stokes integral,

$$\oint \delta M = Y - C = \Delta M \tag{14.1}$$

The monetary account belongs to a household, a company, or an economy and is given in monetary units, in €, US \$, £, ¥, or any other currency.

The productive account (P) is the difference between output of goods (G) like food and input of labor (L). The output of the productive account is also ex post and must be presented as closed Stokes integral,

$$\oint \delta P = G - L = \Delta P \tag{14.2}$$

Labor and food are measured in energy units, in kWh, mega joules, or kcal.

However, in double entry accounting, Luca Pacioli measures labor and food in monetary units and initiates a new science, economics: *The monetary account measures the productive account in monetary units, both accounts add up to zero,*

$$\oint \delta M + \oint \delta P = 0 \tag{14.3}$$

This law is the basis of economic theory.

14.3.2 Differential Forms in Macroeconomics

According to the U–V model, the laws of macroeconomics may also be given by W (U, V), where V and U are presented by exact and not exact differential forms.

First Law of Economics

The first law of economics in differential forms reads.

$$\delta M = dK - \delta P \tag{14.4}$$

Equation (14.4) is the solution of Eq. (14.3). The closed integral of the exact differential *dK* is zero. Equation (14.4) contains three differential forms with the common dimension money:

1. The not-exact monetary term (δM) stands for money, surplus, or losses and relates to a person, a household, a company, a country, or any economic system.
2. (δP) is the ex post term of production or labor input of persons, households, companies, countries, or any economic system.
3. (dK) is an exact term with the dimension "money." (K) refers to money or capital.

All economic terms in Eq. (14.1) are measured in €, US $, £, ¥, or other monetary units.

The Second Law of Economics

According to calculus, we may link a not-exact differential form (δM) with an exact differential form (dF) by an integrating factor λ,

$$\delta M = \lambda\, dF \tag{14.5}$$

(δM) is the inexact or ex post profit, surplus, or loss. The function (F) is the production function, and Eq. (14.5) is the proof of existence of production functions in economics. The dimension of the integrating factor (λ) depends on the production function (F). We will find the production function to be a number (N), and then the integrating factor (λ) has a monetary dimension: (λ) will be the standard of living or the GDP per capita of a country.

Production, Price, and Amount
According to calculus, we may link a not-exact differential form of production or labor input (δP) with an exact differential form (dV) by an integrating factor p,

$$\delta P = -p\, dV \qquad (14.6)$$

(δP) is the inexact differential of production or work, and (dV) the exact differential of volume or amount of the produced item. The integrating factor (p) will be the price of the product (Yakovenko and Rosser 2009).

14.3.3 Differential Forms in Natural Sciences

We can turn Luca Pacioli's law around and measure both accounts in energy units:

The monetary account measures the productive account in energy units; both accounts add up to zero,

$$\oint \delta Q + \oint \delta W = 0 \qquad (14.7)$$

This law is now the basis of economic theory in energy units. Q is the monetary account in energy money. The oil price converts money into energy. W is the work input in energy units.

The First Law of Economics in Energy Units
The first law of economics in differential forms reads.

$$\delta Q = dE - \delta W \qquad (14.8)$$

Equation (14.8) contains three differential forms with the common dimension energy:

1. The not-exact monetary term (δQ) stands for profit in energy units.
2. (δW) is the ex post term of work input in energy units.
3. (dE) is an exact term and refers to capital in energy units.

All terms in Eq. (14.7) are identical to Eq. (14.4), but they are now measured in Joule, calories, kWh, or other energy units.

The Second Law of Economics in Energy Units
According to calculus, we may transform a not exact differential form (δQ) into an exact differential form (dS) by an integrating factor T,

$$\delta Q = T\, dS \qquad (14.9)$$

Equation 14.9 is identical to Eq. 14.5, but is now measured in energy units. (δQ) is the inexact or ex post profit, surplus, or loss in energy units. The function (S) is the production function. The integrating factor (T) has a monetary dimension. Equations 14.7 and 14.8 are also called the first and second law of thermodynamics.

Work, Pressure, and Volume

According to calculus, we may link a not-exact differential form of work (δW) with an exact differential form (dV) by an integrating factor p,

$$\delta W = -p\, dV \tag{14.10}$$

(δW) is the inexact differential of work, and (dV) the exact differential of volume. The integrating factor p will be the pressure of the thermodynamic system.

14.3.4 Equivalence of Macroeconomics and Thermodynamics

As predicted by the U–V model, economics and natural science have the same mathematical structure (Richmond et al. 2013).

Macroeconomics corresponds to thermodynamics and vice versa. In thermodynamics, we call the function S entropy. The laws of macroeconomics and thermodynamics are equivalent.

The sum of capital (K) and amount of goods (V) like houses, property, or other commodities times the price (p) of the goods is the wealth (W) of a person or company:

$$W = K + p\,V \tag{14.11}$$

The difference of capital (K) and production function (F) times mean capital (λ) in Table 14.1 is the Lagrange function (L).

$$L = K - \lambda F \tag{14.12}$$

Table 14.1 shows the close relationship between economic and physical terms. Each term in economics corresponds to a term in thermodynamics.

The equivalence of economics and thermodynamics is not only given by theory, it may also be found by experimental data. In Fig. 14.1, the GDPs per capita of 126 countries are compared to the use of energy per capita. GDP and energy run parallel for nearly all countries. This confirms the equivalence of capital and energy in Table 14.1.

The equivalence of economics and thermodynamics raises the question, whether economics is the physics of markets or whether physics is economics of nature (xx).

Table 14.1 Corresponding terms in economics and thermodynamics

Symbol	Economics	Unit		Symbol	Thermodynamics	Unit
M	Profit, loss	€, \$, £. ¥	↔	Q	Heat	kcal, kWh
K	Capital	€, \$, £. ¥	↔	E	Energy	kcal, kWh
W	Wealth	€, \$, £. ¥	↔	H	Enthalpy	kcal, kWh
P	Production, labor	€, \$, £. ¥	↔	W	Work	kcal, kWh
λ	Mean capital	€, \$, £. ¥	↔	T	Mean energy	kcal, kWh
F	Production function	–	↔	S	Entropy	–
N	Number	–	↔	N	Number	–
p	Price per item	€, \$, £. ¥	↔	p	Pressure	kcal/m^3
V	Volume, amount	–	↔	V	Volume	m^3
L	Lagrange function	€, \$, £. ¥	↔	F	Free energy	kcal, kWh
L_*	LeChatelier function	€, \$, £. ¥	↔	G	Free Enthalpy	kcal, kWh

Most economic terms are measured in monetary units; the corresponding thermodynamic terms are measured in energy units

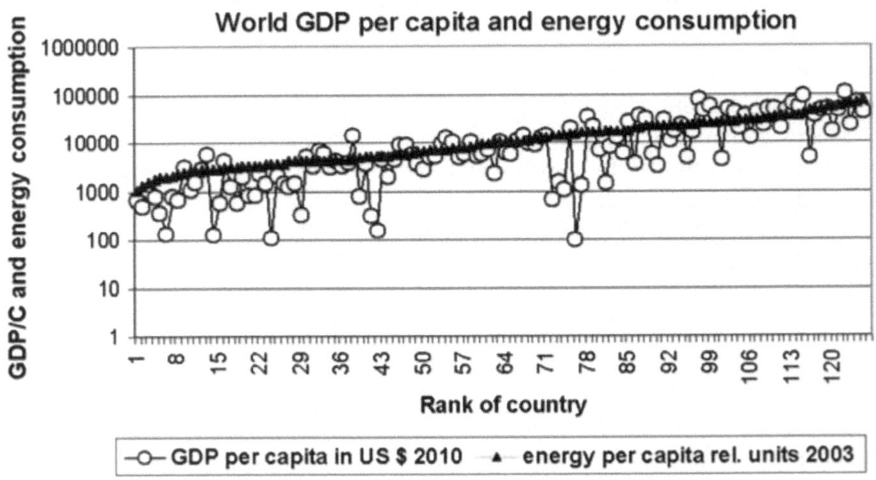

Fig. 14.1 GDP per capita and energy use per capita have been plotted for 126 countries. Both curves are equivalent for nearly all countries

14.3.5 Stokes Integrals: Trade Cycle

The trade cycle of a sales company has four parts: Buying products at a cheap market or producer, e.g., in China; bringing goods to an expensive market, e.g., Europe; and selling goods expensively. The productive cycle is linked to the monetary cycle: Cheap production leads to low costs. Expensive sales lead to high income. One can look either at the monetary cycle or at the productive cycle, Fig. 14.2.

$$\oint \delta M = -\oint \delta P = \oint p\, dV \tag{14.13}$$

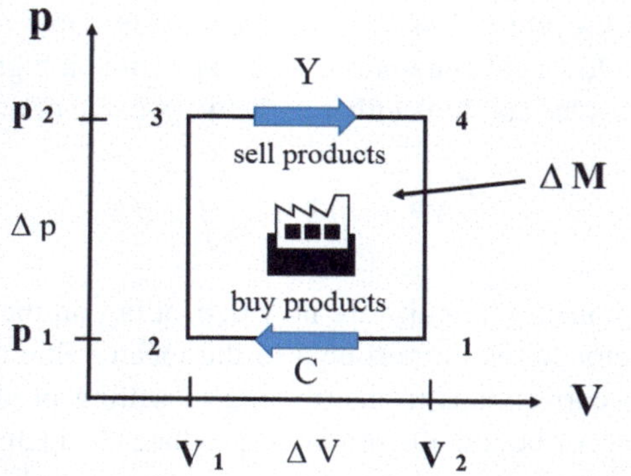

Fig. 14.2 Trade is a two-level process: The merchant buys products cheap at price (P_1) from a wholesale market or by importing directly from a low price country like China and sells the product more expensively at (P_2) in his shop in Europe. The profit (ΔM) of the merchant is based on inequality of prices. In order to make a profit, the merchant has to keep up the difference in prices by separating wholesale and retail prices. Trade companies accomplish the price difference by separating producers and customers by a long trade distance or by market laws. The profit is the inside area of the cycle, Eq. (14.13). The logo indicates the profit of the owner (trade company or merchant)

The merchant brings the products from the farm a market. Here the price of apples (P_2) is higher than at the farm. By changing the location, the merchant has raised the value of the apples. Earning money by trade requires two price levels: cheap – expensive, wholesale – retail, farm – market. Without these two levels, a profit is not possible! In former times, merchants sent ships to far distant places to buy precious goods like spices at a cheap price to sell it back home for a high price. Today merchants buy in China and sell in the USA.

Wealth: By trading, the wealth of the merchant (wealth = capital + value of goods) in Eq. (14.11) has not changed. Trade conserves wealth of buyers and sellers; nobody is robbed in a fair trade!

14.3.6 Stokes Integrals: Production Cycle and Carnot Cycle of Motors

The productive cycle of a company has four parts: cheap production, export, expensive sales, recycling. The productive cycle is linked to the monetary cycle: cheap production leads to low costs. Expensive sales lead to high income. One can look either at the monetary cycle or at the productive cycle. This corresponds to the Carnot cycle of motors.

The Carnot process of a motor has four parts: slow (isothermal) compression at low temperature, fast compression, slow expansion at high temperature, and fast expansion. The work cycle is linked to the heat cycle: slow compression at low temperature leads to low heat generation, slow expansion at high temperature leads to higher heat losses. One can look either at the work cycle or at the heat cycle,

$$-\oint \delta P = \oint \delta M = \oint \lambda \, dF \tag{14.14}$$

Productive and monetary circuits are now depending on the production factors (λ) and (F): the factor (λ) is proportional to the mean value or price, and (F) is the entropy: ($+dF$) corresponds to distributing or selling products and ($-dF$) to collecting, producing, or buying the products: produce cheap and sell expansive. In this way, we obtain four different lines of the line integrals in Fig. 14.2.

Carnot cycle in motors: collect *cold* gas before burning and expelled *hot* gas after burning.

We may divide the production process in Fig. 14.3 into four sections:

1 → 2: Workers in a factory assemble ($-dF$) production parts at constant low standard of living and labor costs (λ_1). Assembling at constant (λ) corresponds to an isothermal process in thermodynamics.

2 → 3: Products are transported (exported) to a region, where the products have a higher value λ due to higher labor costs and standard of living (λ); this corresponds to an adiabatic process in thermodynamics.

3 → 4: At higher value, the products are sold (distributed) to the customers. As selling or distributing the price (λ) stays constant, this corresponds again to an isothermal process in thermodynamics.

4 → 1: After using the products for some time, they will break, and they are transported to recycling centers. The value of the product has declined ($d\lambda < 0$) and this corresponds again to an adiabatic process in thermodynamics.

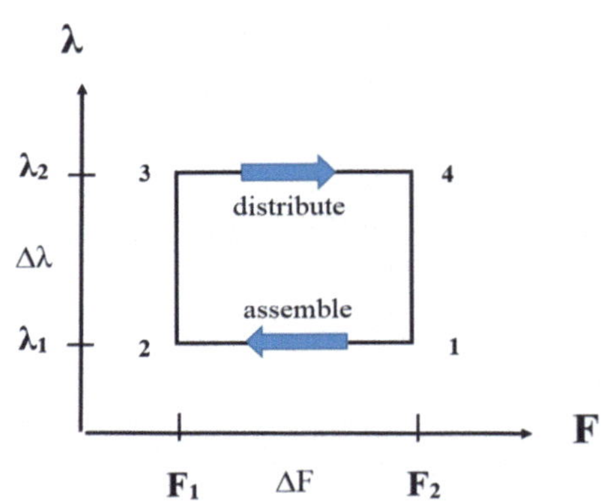

Fig. 14.3 Production circuit: assemble products *cheap* (λ_1) and sell (distribute) expensively (λ_2)!

Efficiency, ROI, and EROI

For efficient economic production and trade, the ratio of returns over input ((ROI) must be larger than 1. In Fig. 14.3, this ratio is given by

$$\mathrm{ROI} = \lambda_2/\lambda_1 > 1 \tag{14.15a}$$

the ratio of income and costs.

For survival of the human race, the energy of food must be larger than the energy of work to obtain this food. The biophysicist Hall (Hall) has called this energy returns over energy input (EROI), and with Fig. 14.3 we obtain

$$\mathrm{EROI} = \lambda_2/\lambda_1 > 1 \tag{14.15b}$$

the *e*nergy *r*eturn *o*ver the energy *i*nput.

The same ratio applies to the efficiency of the Carnot process of a heat pump, where heat is pumped from the cold river (T_1) to a warm house (T_2),

$$\mathrm{EROI} = T_2/T_1 > 1 \tag{14.15c}$$

According to Table 14.1, the mean price λ of economics is now replaced by the temperature T of thermodynamics.

The definition of EROI does not only show the close relationship between economics and thermodynamics, but it also leads to the correct definition of money: We may buy and sell in monetary units, in €, US \$, £, or currencies, but we cannot eat money, we must eat energy. Companies may increase their monetary value at the stock market, and they may pay wages in money, but they run on energy, presently mostly on oil.

This has important consequences for economic costs: If we build a new power plant, we must not ask, how much it costs, but how much energy it will produce compared to the energy that has been invested to build it. This is not only important for power plants but for all items, we produce. All products must be valued in energy terms. For the survival of humankind, the EROI is more important than the ROI. We can live without money, like natural societies, but we cannot live without energy. Energy units like Joule, kWh, or calories are the hard currency, on which every economy is based.

The principle of the known and the unknown has led to new laws of economics, which are closely related to thermodynamics.

14.3.7 Efficiency of State Economies

Efficiency of industry affects the structure of states and countries: countries may by capitalistic, socialistic, or communistic, Fig. 14.4.

Capitalism: Capital favors a high efficiency, $\eta \to$ **max!** This means that high industrial prices and low wages lead to a strong economy and to a rising gap between

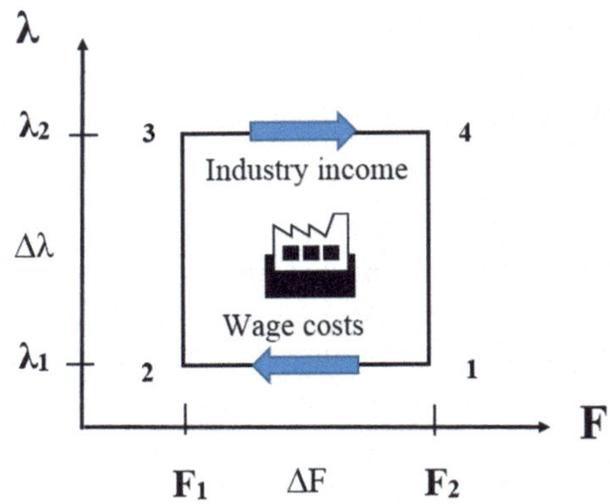

Fig. 14.4 The efficiency of industrial production income versus costs (wages) determines the political state of a country

rich and poor. A good example in Europe is Germany. In order to avoid aggressions between high and low income classes, the government of a strong economy can level out differences in incomes by taxes and by support of unemployed and other problem groups.

Socialism (Labor): Labor favors a lower efficiency, $\eta \rightarrow$ **small!** This means lower industrial prices and higher wages. This leads to a weaker economy and a slowdown of the gap between rich and poor. A good example in Europe seems to be France. Lower income classes still have a rather good standard of living, but the state cannot raise enough taxes to support problem groups like unemployed.

Communism: Communism calls for a one-class society in which the capital is owned by the proletarians. In a one class society ($\lambda_2 = \lambda_1$) the efficiency will be zero, $\eta \rightarrow$ **0!**

This has been observed for all communist states and has led to the downfall of all communist regimes in Europe.

In order to make a refrigerator work, we have to close the door, inside and outside have to be separate. In the same way, rich and poor classes have to be separated to make the economic production process work.

14.3.8 Stochastic Theory in Microeconomics

Microeconomic deals with the amount and price of items bought or sold at a productive market. The standard theory of microeconomics applies utility functions and probability calculations for optimal results. However, standard economics has not been able to link macroeconomics to microeconomics. Again, the U–V model will solve this problem.

Markets with large numbers of goods depend on probability (P) and constraints. The constraints of markets are usually the costs (K). Probability (P) has the property to move from an improbable state to a more probable state,

$$P \rightarrow \text{maximum!} \tag{14.16}$$

This has led Lagrange to formulate the probability law under constraints (K).

$$L* = \ln\ P - K/\lambda \rightarrow \text{Maximum!} \tag{14.17}$$

With P also the logarithm of P will always grow according to the constraints (K).

Like in standard theory, we may start microeconomics with the Lagrange equation,

$$L = C\text{–}\lambda F \rightarrow \text{minimum!} \tag{14.18}$$

(L) represents the Lagrange function, C denotes the costs, λ is the integrating factor, and F is the utility function. However, in contrast to mainstream economics, F is not the *Cobb Douglas* utility function, but according to Table 14.1, the entropy function S. In probability theory, entropy is closely related to the natural logarithm of probability **P**,

$$F = S = \ln \mathbf{P} \tag{14.19}$$

This corresponds to the free energy approach to statistical mechanics.

Equations (13 and 14) link the Lagrange function (L) and probability (**P**) of microeconomics to the Lagrange and entropy functions of macroeconomics in Table 14.1. In contrast to mainstream economics, Eqs. (14.13 and 14.14) are free of any adjustment to elasticity.

14.3.9 Stochastic Theory in Finance: Long Term, Short Term, Strategies

According to the first law in Eq. (14.4), profits (δM) are the result of capital gains (dK) and production input (δP). In closed integrals, Eq. (14.4) now reads

$$\oint \delta M = \oint dK - \oint \delta P \tag{14.20}$$

Profit (δM) comes from production, from labour input (δP). Investing only in capital (dK) will lead to zero output, as capital (dK) is ex ante.

$$\oint dK = 0 \tag{14.21}$$

Capital alone cannot create capital. Figures 14.4 and 14.5 demonstrate profit from long and short-term investments in the (US) stock market.

Long-term investment, e.g., in (US) stocks corresponds to investment in production (δP) and has led to more than 7% annual growth between 1940 and 2010 (Fig. 14.5).

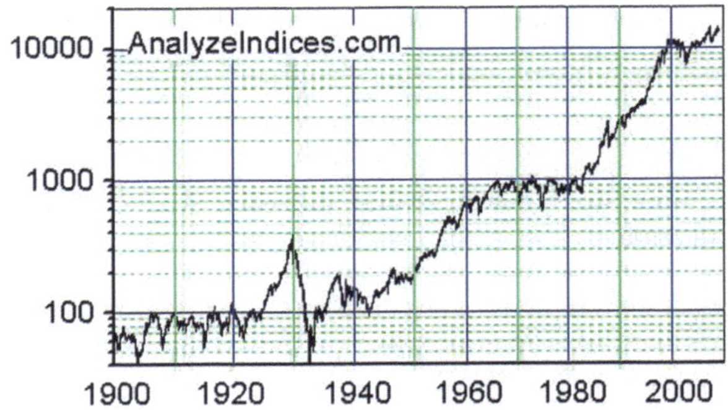

Fig. 14.5 A long-time investment in the (US) stock market corresponds to an investment in production (δP) and shows mean positive returns. [Department of Statistics, Carnegie Mellon University Pittsburgh, PA, 15213, USA (2011)]

Short-time investment corresponds to capital investment (dK). In Fig. 14.4, this may seem more appealing, as much higher returns are possible, like between 1920 and 1929. However, these high growth bubbles finally burst like in the depressions of 1929 and 2009.

Figure 14.6 shows the even distribution of gains and losses of 3-day returns by a bell shaped function with fat tails. Short-term capital investments are similar to gambling and do not contribute to general growth; they only redistribute wealth. A short-term stock market is a legal casino. The only permanent winners are the banks, which collect transfer fees, whether the player wins or loses. Only when banks start investing in financial markets, they will become risky players as well, and they will risk the stability of financial markets.

Strategies try to overcome the risk in financial investments. Without strategies, the investor would lose and win without much profit at the end. Strategies seem to be able to overcome the possibility of losses. A typical example:

Banks start giving credits to risky investors at a high interest. If the investment fails, the next credit to a new investor must be bigger than the first credit, in order to cover the losses. If a bank runs out of money, it will try to borrow more from

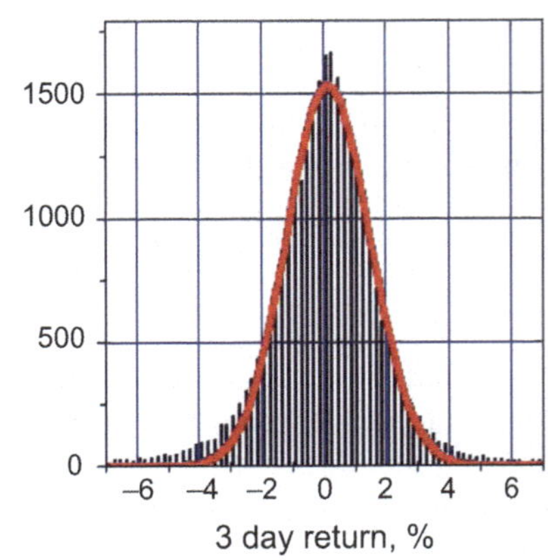

Fig. 14.6 A short-time investment in the stock market corresponds to an investment in capital (dK) and shows a Gauss distribution with symmetric gains and losses. There is no profit in short-time investments. [Department of Statistics, Carnegie Mellon University Pittsburgh, PA, 15213, USA (2011)]

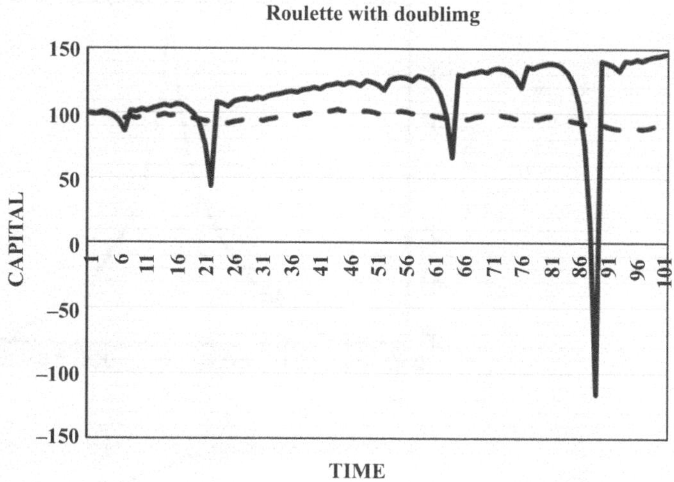

Fig. 14.7 "Winning strategy" of doubling the stake after losses. In the simulation, the capital permanently grows, except for a few spikes

other banks. This strategy is continued until a successful investor finally pays all the losses.

Another strategy is "betting on growing house prices," which led to the world financial crisis in 2008.

We may model these strategies by probability calculations. Figure 14.7 shows the strategy of doubling the stake after loss in a simulated roulette game.

Without strategy, wins and losses are nearly even (dotted line). With strategy, the financial market keeps always growing, except for a few spikes. The market may handle small spikes, if the starting capital is high enough. However, eventually the spikes will be deep enough to let the market crash. This may take some time, but the crash will come to keep the statistics right. The last financial crash took 80 years between 1928 and 2008. However, the time until the crash may come at any time.

14.3.10 Non-linear Differential Equations in Complexity and Chaos Theory

Many financial data, however, do not show a Gaussian distribution of stocks. In contrast to Fig. 14.4, many stock market data show non-Gaussian distributions, so-called fat tails (Fig. 14.8).

The calculation for this non-Gaussian curve is based on time-dependent non-linear Fokker-Planck calculations, which leads to a power law instead of an exponential Boltzmann law for the probability function (Fig. 14.9).

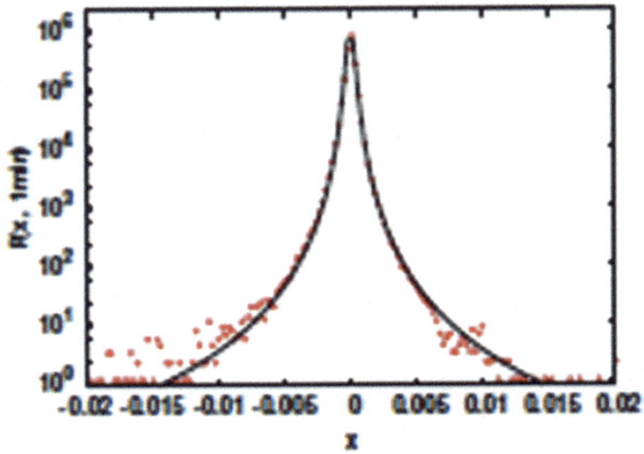

Fig. 14.8 Plot of the probability density distribution for log price returns [Richmond]. For low probability densities, the data show a so-called fat tail and deviate from data in Fig. 14.6

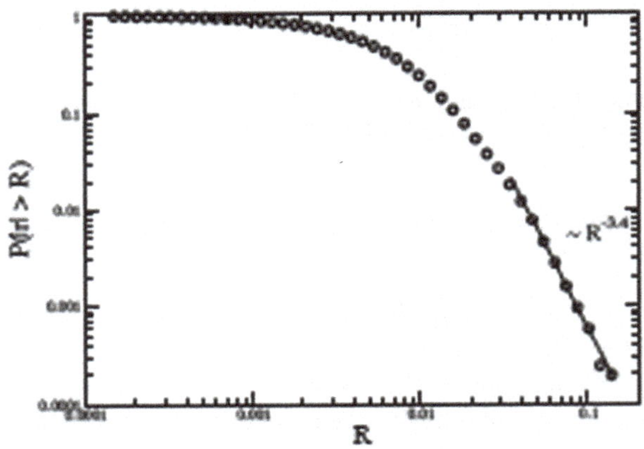

Fig. 14.9 Power law of probability of price returns in a log–log plot [Richmond]. The linear tail indicates a power law and a higher probability of rare events than predicted by a Boltzmann distribution

This power law has first been found for British income distributions by Pareto and has been discussed more recently for the US incomes by Yakovenko. Many researchers have labeled this field of non-linear thermodynamics and statistical mechanics "econophysics" or "complexity."

14.4 Outlook

So far, we have applied the future model of science to economics and natural sciences, using only the fields of calculus and probability. We have presented nonlinearity and chaos theory only in a short paragraph. These fields have been presented in more detail, elsewhere (Giovannini 2008; Gleick 1988; Guckenheimer and Holmes 1983).

In addition, we may also apply the future model to social sciences [xx]. This leads to an insight into the structure of societies, the collective, individual, or global state, which corresponds to the political structure of hierarchy, democracy, and globalism.

Moreover, we may look into the states of integration, segregation, and cooperation, one of the biggest issues of present-day politics.

References

Giovannini E (2008) Understanding economic statistics. OECD Publishing, Paris

Gleick J (1988) chaos: making a new science. Penguin, New York

Guckenheimer J, Holmes P (1983) Nonlinear oscillations, dynamical systems, and bifurcations of vector fields. Springer, New York

Mimkes J (2017) Calculus-based Econophysics with application to the Japanese economy. In: Economic foundations for social complexity science. Springer, Singapore

Mimkes J (2019) Introduction to Econophysics: look back into the future- tomorrow's science by the data of yesterday. IJPMAT 7.1

Richmond P, Mimkes J, Hutzler S (2013) Econophysics and physical economics. Oxford University Press, Oxford

Yakovenko VM, Rosser JB (2009) Colloquium: statistical mechanics of money, wealth and income. Rev Mod Phys 81:1703

Chapter 15
Information, Inattention, Perception, and Discounting

Raymond J. Hawkins, Adrian Yuen, and Lisa Zhang

Abstract We derive a statistical mechanical model of the discount function that extends the information theoretic discount function of Brody and Hughston (Proc R Soc Lond A 457:1343–1363, 2001; Quant Finan 2(1):70–80, 2002) with an adaptation of the quantal response statistical equilibrium model of Scharfenaker and Foley (Entropy 19(444):1–15, 2017) and the Weber-Fechner representation of the distinction between perceived time and objective time proposed by Takahashi (Med Hypotheses 65(4):691–693, 2005). We find that our model, among other things, provides an information-theoretic basis for the β-δ quasi-hyperbolic model often employed in behavioral economics. This, together with the ease of incorporating economic and/or psychological constraints, recommends this approach for general use in economics.

Keywords Term structure model · Hyperbolic discounting · Maximum entropy · Information theory · Weber-Fechner · Time perception · Rational inattention · Behavioral economics

15.1 Introduction

The discount function generates the factor by which the utility of an event (e.g., a cash flow) happening at time τ in the future needs to be reduced so that an individual would be indifferent between that future event and a similar event happing now. For example, if an individual is indifferent between receiving \$100 now and \$105 in two years and if the utility of that individual is linear in money then the value of the discount function at a two-year horizon (or the two-year discount factor) is said to be $D(\tau = \text{two years}) = \$100/\$105 = 0.9524$. By relating future value (e.g., \$105)

R. J. Hawkins (✉) · A. Yuen · L. Zhang
Department of Economics, University of California, Berkeley, CA, USA
e-mail: hawkins@econ.berkeley.edu; adrian_yuen@berkeley.edu; lisazhang@berkeley.edu

H. Aoyama et al. (eds.), *Complexity, Heterogeneity, and the Methods of Statistical Physics in Economics*, Evolutionary Economics and Social Complexity Science 22,
https://doi.org/10.1007/978-981-15-4806-2_15

to present value (e.g., \$100) the discount function plays a key role in economics generally and in financial economics in particular.[1]

Developing and applying the discount function in a given economic context is known as the calibration problem and a particularly compelling solution to the calibration problem is that of Brody and Hughston (2001, 2002) who recast the calibration problem as a variational problem in information theory. Their result was initially compelling because it provided an informationally-coherent basis for an optimal solution to the calibration problem and did so in a computationally-convenient manner. Their result may be even more compelling as recent work by Scharfenaker and Foley (2017) suggests a way of extending it to integrate the decision-theory work of Luce and Suppes (1965) together with the notion of rational inattention developed by Sims (2003), and in so doing establish the behavioral microfoundations of this representation of the discount function. The goal of this chapter is to demonstrate that this is so. To this end we continue in Sect. 15.2 with a review of the approach of Brody and Hughston (2001, 2002) to establish the foundation for our development in Sect. 15.3 of our use of the methodology of Scharfenaker and Foley (2017) to make the results of Brody and Hughston (2001, 2002) consistent with human decision making as discussed by Luce and Suppes (1965). We further establish the behavioral microfoundations of this approach by incorporating the distinction between subjective time and objective time (Takahashi et al. 2008; Zauberman et al. 2009) into our analysis in Sect. 15.4 and close with a discussion and summary in Sect. 15.5.

15.2 Information and Discounting

The relationship between the discount function and information theory was developed by Brody and Hughston (2001, 2002) who noted that two features of the discount function – (i) that it is equal to one when $\tau = 0$ and (ii) that as τ approaches $+\infty$ it approaches zero – suggest that the discount function can be interpreted as a cumulative density function:

$$D(\tau) = \int_{\tau}^{\infty} p(t)dt = \int_{0}^{\infty} \Theta(t-\tau)p(t)dt \tag{15.1}$$

where $\Theta(t-\tau)$ is the Heaviside step function: zero (0) for $t < \tau$, one half (1/2) for $t = \tau$, and one (1) for $t > \tau$. With the introduction of the Heaviside step function, the discount factor is now cast as the expectation of the Heaviside step function and with this a connection to information theory can be made. Since an observed discount factor $D(\tau)$ is the expectation of the associated Heaviside step function $\Theta(t-\tau)$, Brody and Hughston observed that an informationally optimal probability

[1] See, for example, Frederick et al. (2002), Tuckman and Serrat (2011), and references therein.

density $p(t)$ is the density that minimizes the Shannon information (Shannon 1948) information or, equivalently, maximizes the entropy[2]

$$H = -\int p(t) \ln [p(t)]\, dt \tag{15.2}$$

subject to the constraints that (i) the probability be normalized

$$1 = \int p(t) dt \,, \tag{15.3}$$

(ii) that the price of a perpetual annuity ξ be reproduced

$$\xi = \int t p(t) dt \,, \tag{15.4}$$

and (iii) that the observed discount factor be reproduced

$$D(\tau) = \int_0^\infty \Theta(t - \tau) p(t) dt \,. \tag{15.5}$$

The maximum entropy (i.e., minimum Shannon information) solution to this constrained maximization problem is

$$p(t) = \frac{1}{Z} e^{-\lambda_1 t - \lambda_2 \Theta(t-\tau)} \tag{15.6}$$

where the partition function Z is given by

$$Z = \int_0^\infty e^{-\lambda_1 t - \lambda_2 \Theta(t-\tau)} dt \tag{15.7}$$

$$= \frac{1}{\lambda_1} \left(1 - e^{-\lambda_1 \tau} + e^{-\lambda_2} e^{-\lambda_1 \tau}\right) \tag{15.8}$$

and the discount factor is given by

$$D(t) = \frac{1}{\lambda_1 Z} \begin{cases} e^{-\lambda_2} e^{-\lambda_1 t} & \text{for } t \ \geq \tau \\ e^{-\lambda_1 t} - e^{-\lambda_1 \tau} + e^{-\lambda_2} e^{-\lambda_1 \tau} & \text{for } t \ < \tau \end{cases} . \tag{15.9}$$

[2]See, for example, Jaynes (1957, 1968, 2003).

A remarkable feature of this expression for the discount function is that for $t > \tau$ and with the identifications

$$\delta = e^{-\lambda_1 t} \tag{15.10}$$

and

$$\beta = \frac{e^{-\lambda_2}}{(\lambda_1 Z)} \tag{15.11}$$

it is identical to the β-δ model[3] of behavioral economics (Laibson 1997; Frederick et al. 2002). Thus we see that the Brody and Hughston (2001, 2002) model provides an information-theoretic basis for the β-δ model in general and for the functional form of the factor β which was introduced to resolve experimentally observed time inconsistencies (i.e., arbitrage opportunities)[4] with Samuelson's assumption of an exponential discount function (Samuelson 1937).

Our identification of the Brody and Hughston (2001, 2002) model with the β-δ model allows us to leverage the work of McClure et al. (2004) on the neuroanatomical correlates of the β-δ model to get insight into the portions of the brain implicated in the formation of choice by Eqs. (15.10) and (15.11). Specifically, the areas of the brain associated with Eq. (15.10) are the lateral prefrontal and parietal areas commonly associated with higher-level processes and cognitive control, while the areas of the brain associated with Eq. (15.11) are the limbic and paralimbic cortical structures associated with impulsive behavior (McClure et al. 2004).

Since the approach of Brody and Hughston summarized above extends easily to any number of observed discount functions, it readily solves the calibration problem associated with discount factors and expands the β-δ model to multiple observed discount functions. While effective in dealing with the calibration problem and providing an information-theoretic basis for the β-δ model, the economic interpretation of the probability density and the Heaviside function has remained underdeveloped. However, recent work by Scharfenaker and Foley (2017) on the information-theoretic incorporation of quantal response into the description of economic interactions suggests that a reexamination of the experimental elicitation of the discount function from an information-theoretic perspective can provide an economic interpretation of both the probability density and the Heaviside function, and it is to this that we now turn.

[3]This is also known as quasi-hyperbolic discounting.

[4]See Frederick et al. (2002) and references therein.

15.3 Information, Inattention, and Discounting

We consider an elicitation experiment in which a subject is asked to compare the option of (i) receiving a smaller about of money, say \$100, now to that of (ii) receiving a larger amount of money, say \$105, at some future time t. For $t = 0$, the subject will generally take option (ii) since receiving \$105 now is preferred to receiving \$100 now. For small increases in time t, the receipt of \$105 at time t will still be preferred to receiving \$100 now. This is often explained by observing that were the subject to accept \$100 now and invest it in a bank account the amount the subject would have at time t (\$100 plus interest) would be less than \$105, so the subject is better off waiting to receive the \$105. As the length of time between now and when the \$105 is to be received (the horizon) increases, the subject's preference for \$105 in the future will decrease until a horizon, $t = \tau$, is reached when the subject is indifferent between receiving \$100 now or receiving \$105. For all horizons greater than τ, the subject prefers receiving \$100 now. The explanation, as above, is that were the subject to invest \$100 now in a bank account, for all times $t > \tau$ the amount that the subject would have in their account at time t (\$100 plus interest) would be greater than \$105.

The time $t = \tau$ at which the subject is indifferent between receiving \$100 now and receiving \$105 then defines the value of the discount function (also known as the discount factor) at time $t = \tau$, or

$$\$100 = D(\tau)\,\$105 \tag{15.12}$$

The indifference expressed by Eq. (15.12) separates future time into two regions: the time before τ during which the subject will always choose to receive \$105 and the time after τ during which the subject will always choose to receive \$100 now. The basis for this decision is commonly expressed in terms of a utility function which, assumed to be linear in money, is simply the difference between the value of (i) \$100 now and (ii) \$105 in the future, each option being discounted using the value given by the discount function for the time horizon at which these cash flows will be received, or

$$u(t) = D(0) \times \$100 - D(t) \times \$105 \tag{15.13}$$

where that $D(0)$ is assumed to be 1.

This utility function is illustrated in the upper panel of Fig. 15.1 which shows the difference between the present value of \$100 now and \$105 at any time now or in the future for a discount rate r of 2.44%/year and an exponential discount function given by $D(t) = \exp(-rt)$. At $t = 0$ (now) the utility would be $-\$5$ and remains negative until $t = 2$ years at which point the indifference equality expressed in Eq. (15.12) obtains. For $t > 2$ years, the present value of \$105 is less than \$100 and the utility of receiving \$100 now is positive.

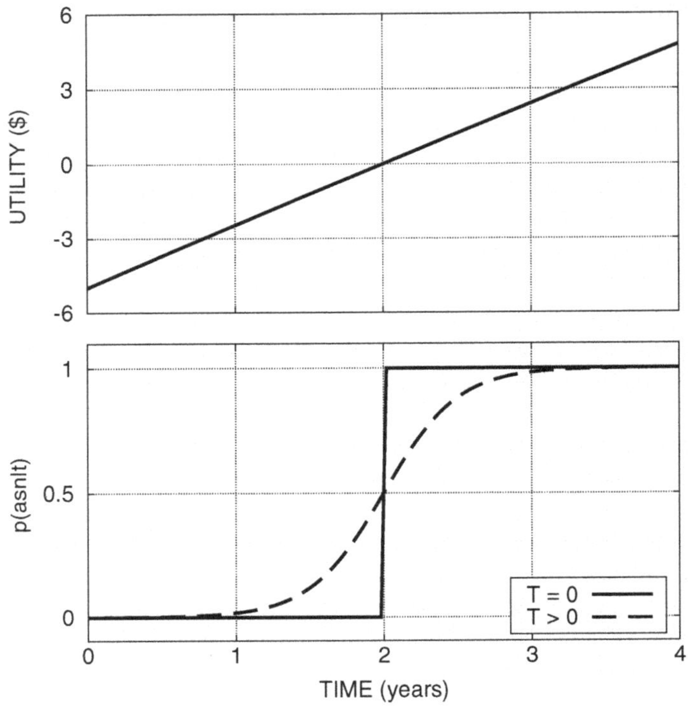

Fig. 15.1 The utility (upper panel) and probability of accepting the smaller amount now (lower panel) as a function of time

The lower panel of Fig. 15.1 shows the associated probability that the subject accepts \$100 now which we generalize to the notion of accepting the smaller amount now (asn). A rational economic agent is assumed to respond solely to the sign of the utility and will always (i) reject the smaller amount now (rsn) for $t \leq \tau < 2$ years, (ii) accept the smaller amount now for $t > \tau = 2$ years, and (iii) be indifferent between the two for $t = \tau = 2$ years as indicated by the solid curve. This suggests that the Heaviside step function in the integral representation of the discount factor developed by Brody and Hughston (2001, 2002) (Eq. (15.1)) can be identified as the conditional probability of accepting the smaller amount now $p(\text{asn}|t)$.

But as experimentally demonstrated and theoretically developed by Luce and Suppes (1965), step function response is not a characteristic of human decision making; rather, a quantal response is seen. This work was built upon significantly in recent work by Scharfenaker and Foley (2017) who employed information theory to incorporate the work of Luce and Suppes (1965) into a model of quantal response statistical equilibrium in which the Heaviside function is generalized to the quantal response function

$$p\,(\text{asn}|t) = \frac{1}{1 + e^{-\frac{t-\tau}{T}}} \tag{15.14}$$

where T is the behavioral temperature[5] which, by smoothing the step function, provides a formal representation of Sims' notion of rational inattention (Sims 2003). For $T = 0$, we recover the Heaviside step function. For $T > 0$, the step function smooths as illustrated by the dashed curve in the lower panel of Fig. 15.1, and this smooth function better replicates experimentally observed human decision making (Luce and Suppes 1965).

To obtain the probability density associated with the discount function, now represented as the expectation of the conditional probability $p\,(\mathrm{asn}|t)$, we employ the approach of Scharfenaker and Foley (2017) and write this as the maximization of the entropy function

$$H = -\int p(t) \ln \left[p(t)\right] dt - \int p(t) H_{T,\tau}(t) dt \tag{15.15}$$

where $H_{T,\tau}(t)$ is the binary entropy function

$$H_{T,\tau}(t) = - \sum_{a \in \{\mathrm{asn},\mathrm{rsn}\}} p(a|t) \ln \left[p(a|t)\right] \tag{15.16}$$

subject to the three constraints mentioned above, but with the discount factor now given by

$$D(\tau) = \int_0^\infty p\,(\mathrm{asn}|t)\, p(t) dt\ , \tag{15.17}$$

and with an additional constraint that follows from an adaptation of the information-theoretic representation by Scharfenaker and Foley (2017) of Adam Smith's theory of capitalist competition. Since individuals tend to choose assets with higher-than-average profit rates, the expectation of profit conditional on acceptance should in general be higher than the average expectation of profit. The act of accepting would, in a trading setting, tend to lower returns as market makers readjust their markets to recent trading activity. The effectiveness of this competitive process can, per Scharfenaker and Foley (2017), be expressed as a constraint on the difference between the expected payoff conditional on accepting and the unconditional expected payoff, or[6]

$$\int \big(p\,(\mathrm{asn}|t) - p\,(\mathrm{rsn}|t)\big) t dt \le \delta_1\ , \tag{15.18}$$

[5]For discussions of the concept of temperature – behavioral, social, economic, etc. – in the social sciences, see Weidlich and Haag (1983), Bahr and Passerini (1998a,b), Weidlich (2000) and Aoki and Yoshikawa (2007).

[6]The coefficient δ_1 is written as δ in Scharfenaker and Foley (2017). We have added the subscript here to avoid confusion with the δ of the β-δ model discussed earlier.

and to this end we follow Scharfenaker and Foley (2017) by introducing the shift parameter μ to the time horizon and write $p(\text{asn}|t)$ as

$$p\left(\text{asn}|t\right) = \frac{1}{1 + e^{-\frac{t-\tau-\mu}{T}}} \tag{15.19}$$

with

$$p(\text{rsn}|t) = e^{-\frac{t-\tau-\mu}{T}} p(\text{asn}|t) \tag{15.20}$$

being the probability that the subject rejects the smaller amount now (rsn). Maximizing the entropy now yields

$$p(t) = \frac{1}{Z} e^{H_{T,\tau}(t) - \lambda_1 t - \lambda_2 p(\text{asn}|t) - \lambda_3 \tanh\left(\frac{t-\tau-\mu}{2T}\right)} \tag{15.21}$$

where the partition function Z is given by

$$Z = \int_0^\infty e^{H_{T,\tau}(t) - \lambda_1 t - \lambda_2 p(\text{asn}|t) - \lambda_3 \tanh\left(\frac{t-\tau-\mu}{2T}\right)} dt. \tag{15.22}$$

In the limit of $T = 0$, we have that $H_{T,\tau}(t) = 0$ and $p\left(\text{asn}|t\right) = \Theta\left(t - \tau\right)$ with which we recover Eq. (15.6) of Brody and Hughston (2001, 2002). In the more general case of $T > 0$, the discount function deviates from the exponential function the informationally-theoretic minimum needed to reproduce observed economic behavior.

15.4 Information, Inattention, Perception, and Discounting

Our development has, so far, treated objective time (i.e., wall-clock time) and subjective time (i.e., perceived time) as being one and the same. This is psychologically incorrect (Kim and Zauberman 2019; Urminsky and Zauberman 2015). Experimental work Takahashi et al. (2008) and Zauberman et al. (2009) has demonstrated that time perception is like many other physiological and cognitive measurement systems in that it maps objective time, t, to subjective time t_{sub} in a logarithmic manner that can be expressed by the Weber-Fechner law (Gescheider 1988, 1997)

$$t_{\text{sub}} = \alpha \ln\left(1 + \beta_1 t\right) \tag{15.23}$$

as proposed by Takahashi (2005).[7]

[7]For further elaboration of the psychophysics of time perception, see Takahashi (2016) and references therein; particularly Han and Takahashi (2012).

Since decisions are made on the basis of subjective time (Kim and Zauberman 2019), our entire theoretical development can be put on psychologically-sound temporal footing by replacing the variable t with t_{sub}, and then substituting Eq. (15.23) to return to the traditional representation in objective time t. After this temporal transformation, in the $T \to 0$ limit the discount function becomes (Takahashi 2005)

$$D(t) = (1 + \beta_1 t)^{-\lambda_1 \alpha} \tag{15.24}$$

which is the well-known hyperbolic form of the discount function with which a wide variety of behavioral-economic phenomena has been represented (Frederick et al. 2002). This temporal transformation also removes from λ_2 the task of creating the deviation between exponential and hyperbolic discounting and allows it to focus on deviations from the implications of perceived time as represented by the Weber-Fechner law.

15.5 Discussion and Summary

Our use of information theory to derive the discount function is a contribution to and a continuation of the approach pioneered by Prof. Masanao Aoki of using statistical mechanics in general and of information theory in particular to develop a macroeconomic models.[8] In this way, we have been able to highlight the behavioral aspects of the model of Brody and Hughston (2001, 2002) and to extend the behavioral reach of the model by adapting the behavioral economic quantal response model of Scharfenaker and Foley (2017) to the development of the theory of the discount factor. The resulting model easily accommodates the difference between subjective and objective time, further incorporating psychological microfoundations. The resulting functional form is both materially different that prior proposed functional forms of the discount function[9] and easily extended to multiple time horizons and to further constraints – economic and/or psychological – that may be discovered in the future.

Acknowledgments We thank Prof. Duncan Foley for his helpful discussions which materially improved this chapter. We also thank Prof. Masanao Aoki – to whose memory this volume is dedicated – for his pioneering work that laid the conceptual and methodological foundation of statistical mechanics and information theory in economics. And, finally, R.J.H. thanks Prof. Aoki for the friendship and collegiality he extended as I made the transition from the finance industry to academia.

[8] See, for example, Aoki (1998, 2001) and Aoki and Yoshikawa (2007).

[9] See, for example, Benhabib et al. (2010), Bleichrodt et al. (2009), Ebert and Prelec (2007), Killeen (2009), Scholten and Read (2006, 2010) and other work discussed in Urminsky and Zauberman (2015).

References

Aoki M (1998) New approaches to macroeconomic modeling: evolutionary stochastic dynamics, multiple equilibria, and externalities as field effects. Cambridge University Press, New York

Aoki M (2001) Modeling aggregate behavior & fluctuations in economics: stochastic views of interacting agents. Cambridge University Press, New York

Aoki M, Yoshikawa H (2007) Reconstructing macroeconomics: a perspective from statistical physics and combinatorial stochastic processes. Japan-U.S. Center UFJ Bank Monographs on International Financial Markets. Cambridge University Press, New York

Bahr DB, Passerini E (1998a) Statistical mechanics of opinion formation and collective behavior: macro-sociology. J Math Sociol 23(1):29–49

Bahr DB, Passerini E (1998b) Statistical mechanics of opinion formation and collective behavior: micro-sociology. J Math Sociol 23(1):1–27

Benhabib J, Bisin A, Schotter A (2010) Present-bias, quasi-hyperbolic discounting, and fixed costs. Games Econ Behav 69(2):205–223

Bleichrodt H, Rohde KI, Wakker PP (2009) Non-hyperbolic time inconsistency. Games Econ Behav 66(1):27–38

Brody DC, Hughston LP (2001) Interest rates and information geometry. Proc R Soc Lond A 457:1343–1363

Brody DC, Hughston LP (2002) Entropy and information in the interest rate term structure. Quant Finan 2(1):70–80

Ebert JEJ, Prelec D (2007) The fragility of time: time-insensitivity and valuation of the near and far future. Manag Sci 53(9):1423–1438

Frederick S, Loewenstein G, O'Donoghue T (2002) Time discounting and time preference: a critical review. J Econ Lit 40(2):351–401

Gescheider GA (1988) Psychophysical scaling. Annu Rev Psychol 39(1):169–200

Gescheider GA (1997) Psychophysics: the fundamentals. Erlbaum, Mahwah

Han R, Takahashi T (2012) Psychophysics of time perception and valuation in temporal discounting of gain and loss. Physica A 391(24):6568–6576

Jaynes ET (1957) Information theory and statistical mechanics. Phys Rev 106(4):620–630

Jaynes ET (1968) Prior probabilities. IEEE Trans Syst Sci Cybern 4(3):171–190

Jaynes ET (2003) Probability theory: the logic of science. Cambridge University Press, Cambridge, United Kingdom

Killeen PR (2009) An additive-utility model of delay discounting. Psychol Rev 116(3):602–619

Kim BK, Zauberman G (2019) Psychological time and intertemporal preference. Curr Opin Psychol 26:90–93

Laibson D (1997) Golden eggs and hyperbolic discounting. Q J Econ 112(2):443–478

Luce RD, Suppes P (1965) Preference, utility, and subjective probability. In: Handbook of mathematical psychology, vol 3. Wiley, New York, United States, pp 249–410

McClure SM, Laibson DI, Loewenstein G, Cohen JD (2004) Separate neural systems value immediate and delayed monetary rewards. Science 306(5695):503–507

Samuelson PA (1937) A note on measurement of utility. Rev Econ Stud 4(2):155–161

Scharfenaker E, Foley DK (2017) Maximum entropy estimation of statistical equilibrium in economic quantal response models. Entropy 19(444):1–15

Scholten M, Read D (2006) Discounting by intervals: a generalized model of intertemporal choice. Manag Sci 52(9):1424–1436

Scholten M, Read D (2010) The psychology of intertemporal tradeoffs. Psychol Rev 117(3):925–944

Shannon CE (1948) A mathematical theory of communication. Bell Syst Tech J 27(3 & 4):379–423 & 623–656

Sims CA (2003) Implications of rational inattention. J Monet Econ 50(3):665–690

Takahashi T (2005) Loss of self-control in intertemporal choice may be attributable to logarithmic time-perception. Med Hypotheses 65(4):691–693

Takahashi T (2016) Loss of self-control in intertemporal choice may be attributable to logarithmic time-perception. In: Ikeda S, Kato HK, Ohtake F, Tsutsui Y (eds) Behavioral economics of preferences, choices, and happiness. Springer, Tokyo, Japan, pp 117–122

Takahashi T, Oono H, Radford MHB (2008) Psychophysics of time perception and intertemporal choice models. Physica A 387(8–9):2066–2074

Tuckman B, Serrat A (2011) Fixed income securities: tools for today's markets, 3rd edn. Wiley, Hoboken, New Jersey, United States

Urminsky O, Zauberman G (2015) The psychology of intertemporal preferences. In: Keren G, Wu G (eds) The Wiley Blackwell handbook of judgment and decision making, vol 1, chapter 5. Wiley, West Sussex, United Kingdom, pp 141–181

Weidlich W (2000) Sociodynamics: a systematic approach to mathematical modeling in the social sciences. Dover, Mineola

Weidlich W, Haag G (1983) Concepts and models of a quantitative sociology: the dynamics of interacting populations. Springer series in synergetics, vol 14. Springer, Berlin

Zauberman G, Kim BK, Malkoc SA, Bettman JR (2009) Discounting time and time discounting: Subjective time perception and intertemporal preferences. J Mark Res 46(4):543–556

The manufacturer's authorised representative in the EU is Springer Nature Customer Service Centre GmbH, Europaplatz 3, 69115 Heidelberg, Germany. If you have any concerns regarding our products, please contact ProductSafety@springernature.com

Printed and bound by CPI Group (UK) Ltd, Croydon, CR0 4YY

30/09/2026

02225559-0015